Free to Fight Again

RAF Escapes and Evasions
1940-45

ALAN W. COOPER

WILLIAM KIMBER

© Alan W. Cooper 1988

First published in 1988

British Library Cataloguing in Publication Data

Cooper, Alan W.
Free to fight again : RAF escapes and
evasions 1940-45
1. World War 2. Air operations by Great
Britain – Royal Air Force - Biographies.
I. Title
940.54′494′0924

ISBN 0-7183-0678-3

William Kimber & Co Ltd is part of the
Thorsons Publishing Group,
Wellingborough, Northamptonshire,
NN8 2RQ, England.

Photoset in North Wales by
Derek Doyle & Associates Mold, Clwyd
and Printed in Great Britain by
Redwood Burn Limited, Trowbridge, Wiltshire

1 3 5 7 9 10 8 6 4 2

FREE TO FIGHT AGAIN

Contents

Acknowledgements

My sincere thanks for the support and help given to me by the President, Chairman, committee and members of the RAF Escaping Society and in particular by the secretary, Elizabeth Harrison, whose support and encouragement were always at hand. My thanks also go to Susan Digges, for her great help with the typing involved; to Norman Franks for his help in the presentation of this book and all the staff of William Kimber.

To those who sent me their escape or evasion stories, and find they are not included in this book, my apologies. It was not possible to use all the material I was sent, but my thanks, nevertheless, for your help and support.

The escape and evasion accounts in this book are based on the personal accounts and official records of members of the Royal Air Forces Escaping Society. They are the stories of men who were shot down or force landed in enemy territory, in the Second World War, and were then helped to escape or evade capture by many gallant inhabitants of occupied countries, who faced death if they were betrayed. They were then known, and still are today, by a simple name: helpers. The stories in this book are theirs, as well as those of the airmen themselves. They are only a selection of the many that could have been chosen. The fact that many have had to be omitted for reasons of space is no reflection on the nature or quality of their evasion or escape adventures.

A.W.C.

Introduction

Escape and evasion have had a long and honourable record in Britain. Tales of such adventures fill the history books. Bonnie Prince Charlie, Charles II, and Winston Churchill himself are among the many famous people forced to flee for their lives. Yet recognition of the need for official help for escapers and evaders in times of war came only belatedly. During the First World War a small department of the War Office was set up, not so much to aid escapers as to make best use of the special knowledge that POWs acquired. It achieved little but the precedent had been established. When war once again seemed likely in late 1938, J.C.F. Holland, an enthusiast in irregular warfare who later masterminded the Commandos, established a small department, MI(R), for studying such guerilla warfare. Simultaneously A.R. Rawlinson, who had worked in the earlier first war organisation, began to explore the possibilities of giving aid to would-be escapers and evaders. The two projects combined under Major (later Brigadier) Norman Crockatt, who remained head of the new MI9 throughout the war.

The department was established over the winter of 1938/9 with an office in the Metropole Hotel in Northumberland Avenue. At first it had a double function: to interrogate enemy prisoners and to organise the escapes of, and collect information from, British POWs. The first of these functions became channelled into a department of its own, leaving MI9 with world-wide responsibilities for escape and evasions. It had five sub-sections: training, the planning of escape and evasions, codes, tools and interrogation. At first the emphasis was on escape from captivity, but after Dunkirk evasion came to assume equal importance.

It was official policy that it was the duty of all officers and

9

men to attempt to escape from captivity or to evade it. At best they would be free to fight again, and as Airey Neave says in his *Saturday at MI9* (Hodder and Stoughton, 1969) 'the return of trained soldiers and airmen to continue to the fight became a notable contribution to the Allied effort in war, and a source of anxiety to the Germans.' If the attempt to escape or evade failed, at least it would have meant that German troops or guards would have been pinned down to search or control the disturbance, thus also contributing to the war effort.

Many POWs were not temperamentally or physically cut out for escape or evasion; some became relatively passive 'parcels' – the name given by helpers to their charges – being passed down established evasion lines to freedom; but for many, such as those in this book and many others, being on the run called for calm courage, for independent and quick-witted thinking, for unselfishness and stamina. For the helpers, the penalty was death or deportation with a concentration camp at the end of it; if they were betrayed or discovered. Not many returned. The stories in this book are a tribute to them, as much as to the airmen themselves.

M.R.D. Foot and J.M. Langley in their *MI9: Escape and Evasion 1939-1945* quote a figure of 26,260 for the total number of British and Dominion evaders and escapers from all war theatres, of which 2865 were Air Force. For the Western Europe war theatres alone the figures are a total of 3631 of which 2138 were Air Force. Of these, as will be seen in the following pages, many returned to the fight and achieved great things: Bob Horsley, who went on to the Dambusting Squadron, Les Baveystock who went on to sink two U-boats, Wing Commander Embry who continued his distinguished career.

MI9 had some remarkable people working for it. There were, among others, Brigadier Crockatt himself, who had been awarded the DSO and MC in the first war; Jimmy Langley who escaped from captivity after Dunkirk despite the loss of an arm, and who made his way to the south of France with the help of an underground organisation, and was repatriated by the Vichy Government as unfit for military service; and Airey Neave who escaped from Colditz and made a spectacular return home via Switzerland and Marseille to the United Kingdom, there to employ his knowledge of escape and evasion for others at MI9 for the rest of the war, where his code name was Saturday.

The need for escape and evasion contacts became evident after Dunkirk when 2,000 servicemen were left wandering in the French countryside, and 50,000 became POWs. Things began to happen both sides of the Channel. In England, MI6, wary of the new subversive organisation SOE which mushroomed into existence with Churchill's strong backing 'to set Europe ablaze', offered its own help to the infant MI9 to set up an evasion line and contacts in occupied France. Colonel Dansey, the deputy director of MI6, arranged for a young Englishman, who spoke fluent Spanish, and knew the Pyrenees well, Donald Darling, and who had only just escaped from Bordeaux to go to neutral Lisbon and establish communications with occupied Europe. 'Concurrently with lines for intelligence from France, I was to endeavour to set going an escape line into Spain for those members of the BEF who had evaded capture by the enemy after Dunkirk and who were beginning to congregate in the south of France, at Marseille. I was to offer guides a fixed fee per head, per man delivered at our consulate at Barcelona or elsewhere.' Thus Sunday, as Darling was code-named recalled his mission in his memoirs *Secret Sunday* (William Kimber 1975). He reported first to a personage he only knew as '4Z', then to Langley and to Neave. From Lisbon, he was sent on to Gibraltar where he remained till 1944, receiving and interrogating evaders and escapers, and organising their return to England.

On the other side of the Channel from MI9, an equally important happening was taking place for the future of escape and evasion. Captain Ian Garrow of the Highland Division evaded capture after the Division's stand at St Valéry-en-Caux and made his way south. He was a tall distinctive Scotsman, not ideal build for subversive activities in hostile territory. But he reached Marseille where in common with other British servicemen he was interned by the Vichy Government in the Fort de St Jean at Marseille, free during the day but obliged to report for roll call. He used his time well, for he saw the need of a system of safe houses if servicemen were to be returned to Britain. His first safe house was that of the Scots pastor, Donald Caskie, who having preached against the Nazis from Paris, had made his way to Marseille and gained permission to reopen the Seamen's Mission, quite legally giving shelter to seamen and civilians, and secretly sheltering any British serviceman who made his way there. From the system Garrow established grew the Pat O'Leary line, one of the two most famous of all escape routes.

In Britain, the importance of preparing aircrew for the possibility that they might have to escape or evade was realised and regular lectures were given, often by former evaders. The emphasis was put on the need for immediate action: to get as far from the aircraft as possible (not always in practice the best solution), and in the case of capture to make the attempt to escape as soon as possible. Instruction was given on clothing, food, where to go, how to go, and in codes. Above all, the importance of retaining identity discs at the very least in order to prove their status was emphasised. Any doubt and they risked being shot as spies. Aircrew were issued with escape kits. After much experimentation on the part of MI9 it was found possible to print silk maps; Clayton Hutton, the idiosyncratic intelligence officer in MI9, one of Crockatt's earliest recruits, had a gift for such things. Besides the maps, he organised the design of compasses so tiny they could be disguised as buttons or collar studs or sewn into belts; later he organised the magnetising of pencils and razor blades which prisoners would be allowed to retain and which would act as compasses. Flying boots were turned into 'escape' boots, concealing a knife with the help of which the owner could convert the flying boots into ordinary walking shoes and a warm waistcoat! But the aid to evasion which became standard equipment was the escape box containing essentials for survival, benzedrine tablets, milk tablets, razor etc. It was so small that it would fit into a pocket, and was intended to give means of survival for 48 hours. Aircrew were also provided with currency of the countries they were flying over, and one of Hutton's silk maps.

As the war progressed, evasion and escape from North West Europe became more organised and despite betrayals of the lines and other tragedies, large numbers of Servicemen found their way back, either independently or under the auspices of MI9 London. The situation further afield was organised differently.

MI9 in the Middle East, run from Egypt, was under Colonel Dudley Clarke, who having served under Wavell in World War I, was summoned by him from his desk in England where he worked under Holland, to organise deception in the Middle East. From Cairo Clarke ran a fascinating and idiosyncratic organisation called A Force, of which the escape and evasion tasks of MI9 were only one part. The other role was deception, both strategic, misleading the enemy over times and places of forthcoming battle plans, and tactical with camouflage and dummy tanks etc under Major Jasper Maskelyne of the famous magic family. Escape and evasion were under the control of Lt Colonel Tony Simonds who ran a web of evasion lines across the Aegean.

In the Far East, the picture of escape and evasion was vastly different owing to the Japanese attitude to POWs. The escape of one prisoner could mean the death of his companions. The deterrents were great, and the chances of escape limited; the numbers escaping were correspondingly few. Foot and Langley quote: a total of 3346 out of which 3130 were Indians, and only 57 were RAF.

MI9 ran a base in New Delhi, set up in late 1941 under Lt Colonel Ridgway, and in Kwangtung, in Hong Kong, the British Army Aid Group worked for three years on rescue and intelligence, under Lt Colonel Sir Leslie Ride. He had himself escaped from captivity after the fall of Hong Kong, and, gaining the respect and co-operation of the Chinese for whom his mission carried out welfare work, he not only organised the escapes of such few prisoners who had the will to escape but brought out valuable civilians, from occupied Hong Kong, including all the dockyard workers to that the work of Hong Kong as a port was hindered.

The approach of the D-Day landings in Normandy brought

new problems for MI9. In the ensuing chaos after, it was hoped, the successful landings, MI9 realised that moving groups of evaders across France would be well nigh impossible. Airey Neave therefore proposed that a camp should be set up in the forests of northern France where evaders could be sheltered. It was an ambitious plan but it worked, with organisers being dropped in to set the plan going. Fréteval near Cloyes was chosen, partly because it had an active resistance movement. After D-Day, Airey Neave was in charge of the mission to evacuate the camp. Langley was given the task of collecting the POWs from German POW camps. But Arnhem, in September, brought its own problems with yet more escaping personnel.

In the autumn of 1944 Donald Darling was sent to Paris to set up a bureau for recommending awards to those French civilians who had actively assisted evasions – no easy task in the climate of those times, when everyone was a 'Résistant. de Quarante Quatre'.

In 1945 with the collapse of Germany, came the sad procession of survivors of the concentration camps – back to try to pick up the ruins of their former lives. Included in this were the helpers and organiser of the lines who had survived their ordeals. Looking after them was another task for Donald Darling and MI9. Finally in 1946 MI9 closed down the Paris Awards Bureau and then those at Brussels and the Hague.

'It seemed,' recalled Donald Darling, 'as if the close knit world of evasion must disintegrate, its elements scattered far and wide.' That it did not, is a tribute to one society – The Royal Air Forces Escaping Society, whose story will be found at the end of this book.

A.W. Cooper
London, 1988

The Royal Air Forces
Escaping Society

In 1981 a memorial plaque sculpted by the RAFES Secretary, Elizabeth Harrison, was unveiled in the crypt of St Clement Danes on 21 June. It was dedicated to the countless brave men and women of enemy-occupied countries who during the Second World War, without thought of danger to themselves, helped aircrew of the RAF and Dominion air forces to escape or evade and return to this country to continue the struggle for freedom.

The RAFES was established after the war with the aim of maintaining contact with the thousands of patriots who gave that help, and to assist the families of those that suffered death or other privations as a result of the aid they gave. The Association has brought helped and helpers together once again, and enshrines in tangible form the gratitude felt for their saviours by the evaders, a gratitude that will live in their hearts for ever. The stories of over 70 such men follow.

I

France

Two names dominate the story of evasion in World War II: Pat O'Leary and Andrée (now Comtesse) de Jongh, both Belgian by birth. The Pat O'Leary line was based in Marseille and operated within France, Andrée de Jongh of the Postman, later renamed the Comète line, ran a line from Belgium to the Pyrenees. Both were betrayed, both organisers sent to concentration camps, and by a miracle – and their own resourcefulness – survived and are alive today. Both lines continued, though not in the same form, after their organisers' arrest and operated until the Liberation.

Pat O'Leary was the operational name of Lt-Commander A.M. Guérisse, a doctor of medicine in the Belgian army. He had escaped to England, volunteered for SOE and was assigned the Q ship HMS *Fidelity* for sabotage on the coast of the south of France. Ian Garrow found him interned at Nimes after he had been left behind in error during an operation, rescued him and managed to get permission for him to remain in Marseille to organise evasion work. The line he took over and ran after Garrow was arrested in the autumn of 1941 stretched from the north of France to Marseille, and 'parcels' were taken off by sea or sent over the Pyrenees. He organised a chain of safe houses, including the flat of Louis Nouveau in Marseilles and that of the Greek doctor Rodocanachi, in which he had his headquarters. In 1943 he was betrayed and sent to a concentration camp. His work, however, continued though not in the same form.

Almost the only survivor of the line was a redoubtable elderly lady, who had run a safe house in Toulouse, Françoise Dissart. She continued to hide airmen in her home and send them through to the frontier until the end of the war. 'She was almost exactly as I had imagined her to be – a rough-voiced, tough dame with a strong midi accent, dressed in a black camisole and smoking constantly through a wooden cigarette holder. She pretended to be a crosspatch, but underneath was the kindest of women.' Thus Donald Darling relates in *Secret Sunday*. Other lines operated in France though not for so long or on such a large scale. There was the Marie-Claire line, run by the outspoken and determined Mary Lindell, Comtesse de Milleville. On the Gestapo's list, she was dropped back into France in 1942, where she was detailed to help the 'Cockleshell Heroes', those that survived after the commando raid on St Nazaire. She got them back to England; and thereafter ran a line from Ruffec near Angouleme, sending evaders through to Donald Darling in Gibraltar.

The organiser of the Marie-Odile line, was the Vicomtesse de St Venant, Alice Laroche, who sent evaders through to Gibraltar. She organised her line with the help of Gaullist gendarmes, who escorted her evaders in the underground and through ticket barriers using official passes. Sadly she too was betrayed in 1944 and sent to Ravensbrück where she died.

In Brittany Val Williams a former helper on the O'Leary line and Raymond Labrosse were dropped in to organise sea evasions. Something went wrong however with the evacuation arrangements, and Williams had to take his 90-odd evaders down to the Pyrenees instead. He was arrested with a small party, but managed to escape. Lebrosse, seeing the danger to himself joined up with Georges Broussine (code-named Burgundy) and reached Gibraltar with his help. Labrosse came back in to occupied France on a more successful attempt to organise sea evacuations from Brittany, together with another French Canadian, Dumais. Meanwhile Burgundy organised a line to Spain down which several hundred men were sent, 135 in 1943 alone.

There were other smaller lines operating as well. Donald Darling notes a total of nine in March 1943.

One of the saddest aspects of evasions and escapes from France is that all the dangers experienced and risks taken during their time in France, were often not at an end when the airmen crossed into so-called neutral territory. In Switzerland, they merely faced internment, and with luck and the unofficial help of the British authorities there, could often be helped back to Britain. Spain was another matter, as will be apparent in the pages that follow.

1   One of the First but not the Last

At 4 p.m. on 27 May 1940 as the Battle of France raged Wing Commander Basil Embry received instructions that his 107 Squadron, was to provide two sections of six aircraft each to attack the German mechanised units in the St Omer district. The evacuation of the fighting troops from Dunkirk had begun that day, and it was of paramount importance to delay the German advance. Embry had already had a distinguished operational career before the war, serving in Iraq, India, the Mohmand operations and Waziristan where he was awarded the first of his four DSOs.

His second world war career was to be equally distinguished, but on 27 May the chances of this seemed extremely slim.

When they arrived over the target area flying at about 6,000 feet, they were met by a hail of anti-aircraft fire. Embry's aircraft was hit four times and he was slightly wounded in the left leg, while he was on the run-up to the target. Nevertheless he managed to release his bombs. Just as he was turning away from the target, however, the aircraft was again hit and severely damaged. The elevator became inoperable and the rudder was only partially effective. He desperately tried to regain control by juggling with the engine controls, but was unsuccessful and the aeroplane slowly went out of control.

Immediately Embry gave instructions over the intercom to the crew to uncover the escape hatches and prepare to bale out. But from Corporal Lang, the air gunner, there was no reply and Embry presumed he had been killed by the AA fire. The aeroplane was now descending in an uncontrollable spiral, and Embry ordered his observer, Pilot Officer Tom Whiting, to abandon the aircraft. This he did, and Embry went to check on Corporal Lang, whom he found dead in the gun turret. Embry then baled out himself. By the time he had pulled the rip-cord, he had seen his aircraft hit the ground and burst into flames. Over an hour later the flames were still visible.

He saw to his horror that he was falling amongst motorised units that appeared to be German. By tugging at the support cords he managed to spill his parachute and landed in a field about 300 yards from the main road along which the Germans were advancing. Throwing off his flying kit, he rushed to a nearby hedge to hide. Within about two minutes a German motor cyclist appeared. He passed by, but Embry realised there was insufficient cover to conceal him for very long. He was making his way towards some high grass or crops, some 300 yards away, when suddenly he caught sight of Pilot Officer Whiting. They were still 75 yards apart, however, when once again Embry heard a motor cycle approaching. They both dropped to the ground, but Embry's position was pointed out by a French civilian. He found himself covered by two Germans, one with a machine gun, who treated him well but handed him over to some mechanised Prussian Infantry. As Embry recorded on his return:

'They were rather an unpleasant crowd, but there was present a German air force officer who spoke good English and seemed well disposed towards the RAF. He informed me that they had been heavily bombed by the RAF that afternoon and had suffered some casualties. He told me that the Prussian captain considered I should give him the German salute. I replied that as I held senior rank it was he who should salute me. The subject was not referred to again.'

Two officers then took Embry by car to the local German Air Force Headquarters. After about fifteen minutes the car was stopped, and he was told to get out as the German Army commander-in-chief wished to speak to him. This turned out to be none other than General Guderian who was in command of the Panzers. The C-in-C, who was on his way to German Air Force Headquarters, decided to take Embry with him. There he was handed over to a young officer by the name of McKeen, 'who told me that he had relations in Scotland. He spoke good English and seemed quite certain that German troops would soon be in England. He asked me how much damage had been done to London by German bombers. I asked him why he should think London had been bombed and he replied that he had got his information from the Official German Confidential Communiqués. He would not believe me when I told him that neither London nor any other town in England had been bombed. He then asked me if I intended to escape. I replied by asking him if he would try to escape if he were a prisoner. He replied by advising me not to try that night, as I was in one of the best guarded places in France and that I would be shot within a few seconds.'

The guard-house where Embry was then taken, was a stable. Next morning he was taken away by two military policemen, to Frevent, where the majority of the prisoners taken at Calais were confined in the football stadium. The officers were kept in the grandstand! In all there were about 4,000 prisoners, British, French, Dutch and Belgian.

At 1.15 p.m. they were formed up in drenching rain. The British officers were placed at the back of the column and carefully guarded. The behaviour of the guards was disgraceful as the prisoners had not been given any water or food for at least three days, and the other ranks were left in the soaking rain without any protection and generally herded around like cattle.

Just before sunset they arrived in a very wet condition at the large village of Hucqueliers, where they remained for the night. The officers were housed in the church and made as comfortable as possible by the good services of the local priest, who arranged for straw to be brought for them to sleep on and for villagers to bring them in cooked potatoes, the only food they were to receive.

Next morning they were on the march by 6.45 a.m. Embry decided that the time had come. As the 'rules' demanded, he informed the Senior Army Officer present that he intended to escape should the opportunity occur. Knowing they were marching towards the Somme, he decided to wait until after mid-day before making the attempt. He had observed that whenever they were passing through wooded country or along winding roads the guards became more vigilant, and so he decided to wait until about a mile and a half before reaching the next wooded area, in the hope that the guards would assume prisoners were unlikely to make a dash for it in open country.

At 1.15 p.m. they were marching along a road at the side of which was a bank covered with high grass sloping down about ten foot to a ditch. Then they passed a signpost to a village by the name of Embry. Taking this as good omen, he decided that this was it. The officers behind him bunched up and gave him the signal when the guards were not looking in his direction.

'As soon as they said go, I dived down the bank into the ditch and lay there until the column had passed,' he reported later. 'When I was in the ditch I saw that my position was in view of the road about three-quarters of a mile ahead and so I decided to move as soon as possible. To do this I had to cross some rising ground within full view of the road. I had just started to move when a French woman who was milking a cow signalled me to drop. As I did so some German motor patrols passed; when they were out out of sight she gave me an all clear signal, but she signalled me twice more to take cover before I reached a thick bramble hedge. I managed with difficulty to force my way into it but to my great discomfort found myself in about eight inches of muddy water; as I was already wet to the skin and the hedge provided such excellent cover I decided to remain there until dark.'

At 11.15 p.m. he decided to move and walking to the south-east came across a small farm. But as he approached it a dog barked loudly and woke up the old peasant farmer who lived there. He had struck lucky. Having identified himself he was welcomed with open arms – literally! His clothes were dried and his wound tended, and he was provided with a bed with clean white sheets. He was also provided with a double barrelled shotgun in case the Germans came! The village of Contes, half a mile away, was already occupied and the farm house had already been searched on three occasions. Embry decided next day it would therefore be prudent to leave the house itself and hide in the adjoining wood. It was just as well he did so. That morning, the house was again searched and Germans fired random bursts from machine guns into the woods.

At 10.30 in the evening Embry began his journey to freedom, once again making for the Somme. But by evening he was back where he started. The two roads and railway he needed to cross were busy with traffic. The same thing happened the next day, and on this occasion he was fired on although he successfully escaped. The next day he decided he would have to discard his uniform and walk openly by day, but by nightfall he had not managed to obtain any civilian clothes. It was back to square one, and his original hiding place. The next morning, 2 June: 'I found an old coat on a scarecrow in a field, which I put on in place of my tunic, and the old peasant farmer gave me a pair of trousers and a cap. Having completed my disguise I set off quite openly at 13.30 hours and by evening reached a position near Tollent.' The 'scarecrow' did not entirely escape notice, however. He was spoken to twice by German soldiers. The first occasion he answered in French, and the second he said he was a Belgian refugee, for he realised the German officer spoke far better French than he did.

The next few days he advanced slowly. The battle for France was still raging around him and he was delayed not only by German patrols but by French shelling and British night bombers. The latter's operations lit up the countryside with their reconnaissance flares so that night was turned into day, making his progress by night impossible.

By 9 June he was suffering from lack of food and a septic wound. He ran into a German patrol to whom he again trotted out the story that he was a Belgian refugee. They insisted he was an English soldier and struck him on the back with a rifle butt. He was put under guard in a farmhouse and told if he proved to be English he would be shot. There was clearly no point in hanging around. He asked the sentry for a drink, and as he handed him the cup he hit him on the chin. 'I slipped out of the room and took cover under a manure heap in the farm yard until dark.'

By dawn on the 11th he was at Daronier, and took refuge in a farm. His wound was increasingly painful, and he had to steel himself for some do-it-yourself surgery, extracting a small piece of metal from the wound. The result made his leg so sore, he had to remain all night at the farm.

The next day he ran into two men whom he was convinced were British soldiers in disguise. 'I slipped out of the house to confirm my belief and warn them that there were German patrols in the village. I had not gone more than 30 yards, however, when I ran into a patrol, and all three of us were taken to the German HQ in the village for interrogation.' The two men in actual fact were Frenchmen, not British soldiers. He realised that the German officer spoke Flemish, so instead of claiming to be a Belgian, he spoke to them in Gaelic. This flummoxed them, so Embry drew a map of England and Ireland, and told them he was Southern Irish and had escaped from the English police after being arrested about some bomb outrages in London. 'One of them told me to speak Gaelic so I replied by speaking very indifferent Urdu, which seemed to convince them my story was correct.'

They were all freed but ordered to go in a north-easterly direction. Embry decided to make for the coast and try to find a small boat. Being out of touch with the war's progress he was unaware of which parts the Germans had occupied already. Luckily some people brought him up to date on this and he decided to make for the Paris area instead, where he thought the Allies would be making a stand. He managed to find an evacuated garage and cycle repair shop, and put together a bicycle out of odd pieces. It took three hours, and he set off only to be stopped by a German soldier who demanded the bike. Once again he had to start walking, despite his bad leg.

When he reached Paris he was advised to make for

Bordeaux. The southern part of France was still unoccupied although France had now surrendered, and huge numbers of British and other refugees were flocking to the south for passage to Britain. He set out by bicycle on 21 June and was near Tours by nightfall. After one more clash with the Germans, he managed to obtain through some French officers, identity papers and a pass to travel free on all French railways. He immediately took a train to Toulouse and on the train he met a Lance Bombardier Bird, who had been captured on 5 June and escaped on the 9th. They decided to travel together. When they arrived in Toulouse they heard there was a ship leaving Marseille for England the following day, but arrived as the ship was leaving harbour. The only course of action was to go further south still and they made their way to Port Vendres, almost on the Spanish border. Once again, no ships.

Perpignan was the next stop where they hoped to hire or steal a boat for Gibraltar. Eventually, as he recalls in his memoirs, he reached Gibraltar with the help of the British Consulate at Barcelona and stayed until 27 July. Bird was held up in Madrid but HMS *Vidette* brought Embry back to Plymouth on 2 August.

After his return to England Wing Commander Embry had a price tag put on his head of 70,000 Reichmarks by the Germans. On 4 August 1940 he was awarded a second bar to his DSO, recommended by Charles Portal, C-in-C of Bomber Command.

In 1945, by now an Air Vice Marshal and commanding number 2 Group, Bomber Command, he was recommended for a third bar to his DSO. He had in all flown on 120 operations. Some of these operations in 1944-45 included attacks on Gestapo Headquarters at Aarhus, Copenhagen and Odense in which he flew under an assumed name and rank – Flying Officer Smith! Like so many of the evaders, as soon as the war was over, he got in touch with his helpers, including Paul, the first farmer who had helped him, who, with his wife, came to visit Embry in England.

2.   Out of the Frying Pan

One example of the fact that the danger was not yet over when evaders crossed the Spanish frontier is that of Donald Phillips. He had been in the Air Force for four years, having joined from school. In 1941, he was awarded the Military Medal, a rare award for the RAF, and the first for escaping from capture after being shot down. He had joined 150 Squadron as a gunner from 52 Bomber Squadron shortly before the war. His rank then, and up to the time of being shot down, was LAC, for the minimum rank of sergeant was not brought into service until the latter part of 1940.

His squadron had been posted to France on 2 September 1939 as part of the Expeditionary Force, and prior to the operation in which he was shot down and evaded capture, his aircraft had been forced down twice on previous occasions. On 13 June 1940, while stationed at Haussay, having already been out on a night raid, they came back hoping to get some rest, but it was not to be, as they were again called out to bomb troop concentrations on the Seine.

He was flying as wireless operator in his usual aircraft, a Fairey Battle, the aircraft which, with the Bristol Blenheim, had been thrown into the attempt to halt the German advance across France since the outset of the Blitzkrieg on 10 May. The Fairey Battle was no match for the Messerschmitt Bf109. On this night he was with his usual crew, Pilot Officer Gulley and Sergeant Berry. 'After locating our target,' he reported on his return, 'we split up from the other two aircraft in the formation to bomb and after dive-bombing the troops, started on our way back to base. I saw about 30 aircraft circling near Vernon-sur-Seine, and drew the crew's attention to them, but we thought they were probably Hurricanes.'

They soon found out their mistake – 'About 30 seconds later five of them broke away and came after us, and we saw the crosses on them. [They were 109's.] They started diving on our tail in line astern attacks while I kept up a continuous fire with the rear gun while Sergeant Berry handed me full pans of ammunition ... One of the 109's came in to finish us off and fired at us with his cannon, and hit the main plane and blew away the camera hatch. He apparently thought we were out of action but came in to about 30 yards' range and turned off. This gave me a point blank view of the 109's belly and I gave it a long burst. The machine caught fire, turned over and dived into the ground. Meanwhile we were already on fire at the petrol tanks and were almost hitting the ground. [Pilot Officer Gulley] seemed to be trying to be levelling out, but couldn't and we crashed into a field and bounced into another one. [Sergeant Berry] and myself were temporarily unconscious, and when we came round the whole of the aircraft was on fire. We got out and tried to get to the pilot, but couldn't as the aircraft was burning too much.'

They decided to make for some nearby houses for assistance, as they both wounded, but as they started to run across the field they were surrounded by Germans with machine guns. A doctor came, and they were taken to Vernon Hospital in an ambulance, where they stayed for a night, and were treated well by the German staff. Phillips was questioned by a Gestapo officer for about ten minutes, but he eventually gave up and went away. He lost touch with Sergeant Berry and later learned that he had been moved to a hospital in Amiens. He had burns to face, hands and eyes, though his sight did return after seven days.

After another hospital stay, Phillips' next staging post was a prison camp at Doullens. Here prisoners spent most of their time transporting flour in sacks from goods trains to storage houses and on two or three occasions transporting heavy 1,000-lb bombs. The conditions were very bad and guards very strict, mostly being young Nazi thugs; their food consisted of soup twice a day. The camp was an old fort on a hill and had been a pre-war prison for women. The cells were like cages, only 8 foot by 6 foot; in this area six men were kept. Phillips and a Private J. Witton of the King's Own Royal Rifles collected material for rope out of bushes and other places, and Phillips decided to make an escape attempt. He had had enough of captivity. From a soldier who had given up thoughts of escaping, having been recaptured on his first attempt, he got a civilian jacket which he hid under his tunic. From another he got a compass. Private Witton decided to accompany Phillips and he already had civilian clothing, having previously escaped from another camp.

'At 8.30 p.m. on 28 July, having tied our pieces of rope together, we attached one end to a tree and slid down a 60 foot wall at the back of the prison, which because of its height was not guarded. The rope broke half way so we had to drop the last 30 feet into muddy ground. Then we discarded our tunics, hid in a nearby wood till dark, and started walking south-east, the nearest point of the frontier.'

After that they walked by day and accumulated more clothes from French farmers and peasants working in the fields. They managed quite well for food, often being given something to eat and drink at the farm houses. On the advice of the French farmers they travelled by way of the fields and carried a pitchfork or hoe over their shoulders at all times. They swam the Rivers Somme and Marne, for the bridges were well guarded and Phillips took Witton's clothes as well because he was not a strong swimmer. They crossed the River Oise by boat – a risky venture because a fellow passenger was a German soldier. Luckily he did not speak French very well. They reached the frontier of unoccupied France at Chalon-sur-Saône on 14 August.

The frontier guards here were spaced at intervals along the road; and the frontier itself was the River Saône. Dodging between the guards, they concealed themselves in amongst a herd of cows and with sticks drove them towards the river. Still using them as cover they swam across into unoccupied France.

At Sennecey-le-Grand they reported to the military authorities who provided railway tickets to Lyon. Here they were promptly locked up, for though unoccupied, the south was controlled by the hostile Vichy-French. After one more move they landed up in Grenoble in the Alps where they stayed in a barracks. Here they were allowed out from 6 p.m. They became friendly with a pro-British Frenchman, who promised to help them escape in his car. 'So on Saturday 13 September, we got away from the barracks fairly easily and got out of town.'

The Frenchman picked them up on the Grenoble-Lyon Road and took them to Lyon and put them on the train for Perpignan, together with a Captain Stuart-Menteth who had joined them.

At midnight the following night, they reached Perpignan and an hour later set off to walk across country to the frontier. They rested, waiting for the night time before making the attempt to cross. When they reached the frontier at about midnight the following day they were challenged by two guards – 'so we dived into the woods as they were firing their automatics at us. Captain Stuart-Menteth dived into a vineyard and we did not see him again. Witton and I dashed into a wood on the opposite side of the road and then made our way over the mountains. We wandered around in the mountains for two days without food and eventually arrived at a Spanish farm where we were given food and shelter for the night.' They were exhausted and in tatters.

Soon after leaving this farm they were stopped by Spanish guards who asked them for papers. Of course they did not have any, so they were taken to the headquarters in a small village and once more they found themselves in prison – at Figueras. They were only allowed to leave the room about three times a day for about five minutes and were packed into a small stone room together. They left there under guard, packed into cattle trucks, for the next prison at Cervera, north-west of Barcelona, where they were at least given palliasses and a blanket. After six days they moved again, this time to the north, to the concentration camp at Miranda del Ebro, near Burgos. They were taken straight to the barbers where all their hair was cut off. Phillips and Witton spent three weeks here while the British Embassy secured their release, and then arrived at Gibraltar on 14 November 1940. The SS *Aquilla* brought them back to Liverpool on 4 December 1940.

3.   Escape from Vichy

One of the first men to be shot down and later to escape from Vichy France, was Sergeant Robert Lonsdale, an observer of 107 Squadron. On 10 July 1940 his aircraft, a Bristol Blenheim, was hit and set on fire and came down near Airaines, on the Somme, near Amiens. It was his fourth operation.

The pilot was captured but Lonsdale, with the gunner, B. George, managed to evade capture. They obtained civilian clothes and walked to Tully. At this stage of the war there were many servicemen still on the run after Dunkirk, and there they joined up with three Royal Artillery other ranks and continued to Oisemont. Here he was picked up by the Germans – 'they probably noticed my service boots,' Lonsdale said on debriefing. They took him for questioning and a search. Five days later, while being transported in a lorry, he jumped out and escaped. He crossed the Seine and the Loire and reached the demarcation line at Chabris on 11 August.

'During my walk through France,' Lonsdale recalls, 'I slept under hedges or in barns, when I could find them, but on only two occasions spent longer than one night in any one place. Consequently, I did not get to know any of my helpers very well, but they were all very brave and generous.

'After crossing the River Cher into the unoccupied zone, I went on to Valençay and Châteauroux where I met some British soldiers who said they were being taken to the south coast to be picked up by the Navy and taken back to the UK: There were about a dozen others and we were escorted on the train to Toulouse and then on to a camp at Agde, where there were another 15 or so British soldiers. This would be about 15 August. More soldiers joined us as the weeks went by but there was no sign of any efforts at repatriation. About the middle of October we were transferred to the Fort St Jean at Marseille.'

The portals of the Fort St Jean, which was the Vichy Government 'lodging house' for the countless escapers and evaders after Dunkirk, who had made their way south, bore the encouraging legend: 'You have asked for death. I will give it to you.' After January 1941 servicemen were lodged in St

Hippolyte at Nîmes, or La Turbie above Monte Carlo.

Lonsdale had arrived at an early stage. The escape line and network of safe houses in Marseille soon to be initiated by Captain Ian Garrow (himself an evader from Dunkirk,) and later to become the Pat O'Leary line, were not yet organised. However, just in operation by this time was the Seamen's Mission at 46 rue de Forbin, Marseille, run by the Reverend Donald Caskie. Up to the fall of Paris he had been Presbyterian Minister of the Scottish Church in Paris, and had left the city on the journey south on 11 June. A vehement preacher against Nazism he continued the battle in Marseille in a more practical way. He took over the abandoned Seamen's Mission, ostensibly for the aid of seamen and British civilians, but covertly to house vast numbers of servicemen escaping or evading the Germans. Run as a virtual club house it was an oasis with bolt holes and hidden panels hiding the uniformed men from the almost daily police raids. It became one of the cornerstones of the Marseille escape network.

Lonsdale was able to visit the mission and the Reverend Caskie and: 'it was through him and the Church of Scotland that the first news that I was alive reached my family. Without money, however, it was difficult to get any distance away from the city to avoid capture.'

By this time Donald Darling, the MI9 agent Sunday, was established in Lisbon charged with the task of organising escape lines and contacts in occupied France, and news reached him of the activities of Ian Garrow by now in Marseille and busy organising a network of safe houses and couriers. Darling set about making contact with Garrow and supplying him with funds for his work, to aid servicemen like Lonsdale. One of Lonsdale's companions, Gordon Instone, who later wrote about his adventures in his book *Freedom The Spur*, managed to obtain the necessary funds, 'and on 26th December six of us boarded the train at Marseille to Narbonne and Perpignan.'

They crossed the Pyrenees into Spain, but were soon picked up by the Guardia Civil and marched to Figueras. On 5 January they were transferred to Cervera via Barcelona where they stayed until 21 January. They were then taken to the notorious Miranda del Ebro. Eventually they reached Gibraltar on 11 April 1941.

On 13 March 1942, somewhat belatedly, Bob Lonsdale was awarded the Military Medal for his efforts in escaping. He was recommended for the DSO in 1944 for the 49 sorties he had flown, 45 since his return to the UK. However this was rejected in favour of a lower award, the DFC. Ironically the rejection was by Air Vice Marshal Embry, whose path had preceded his through France only a month before him in 1940.

4.   The President's Story

Flying Officer Lewis Hodges, captain of a Hampden, of 49 Squadron was detailed, on 4 September 1940, to attack Stettin, which he did successfully; it was on the way back that things started to go wrong. Course was set for Mildenhall; after an hour he asked the wireless operator for a fix, but was told that the set was unserviceable. The night was very dark and there were no lights to be seen.

Hodges decided to make a forced landing as soon as there was enough light to make it possible. At about 6.15 a.m. he saw an aerodrome which he thought must be St Merryn, near Padstow in Cornwall, but as he prepared to make a landing they were engaged by light flak from the ground defences. He made a beeline for the coast and climbed as fast as he could but just at that moment the fuel gave out and the engines failed. They were at about 2,000 feet at the time and Hodges gave the order to bale out. By the time the crew were out he was down to 1,000 feet and decided to make a forced landing in a field. This was fortunate, for the air gunner, Sergeant Wyatt, who had not heard the order to bale out as his intercom plug had come out, was still in the aircraft.

Together they burned all the documents in the aircraft, but as Hodges later told Helen Long, author of *Safe Houses Are*

Dangerous, it proved much more difficult than it sounds to set light to an aircraft. With no petrol left, a box of matches was somewhat inadequate to carry out the destruction of the aircraft as they were instructed to do by the squadron in such circumstances. They then set off in a south-easterly direction towards Spain having landed in Brittany, at Brieuc.

They 'kept in the fields the whole time,' he told MI9 after his return. 'We got civilian clothes in a farm on 12 September 1940, and later on in another farm we exchanged our service boots for ordinary boots. These, however, were not very good. In the farms we used to get maps of the particular department, from the backs of calendars, showing all the lanes and thus avoiding the main roads. Once, when we were without a map and going along a main road, we were stopped by French gendarmes who asked for our papers. We proved our identity by showing our tunics, which we had kept, and they let us go and gave us a new map.' On the 26th they crossed the demarcation line at Chauvigny.

Villagers took them to a château owned by a Frenchwoman married to an Englishman. She gave them a complete set of clothes, shoes and a little money, and they were sent on via Toulouse to Luchon, where they were told they would be safe. As they entered the town, however, they were stopped by two gendarmes who at first swallowed their story that they were Belgian refugees from Toulouse who had lost their papers. Unfortunately they had second thoughts, caught up with them and arrested them. They were put in a concentration camp in the château of Ile Jourdain, where there were 30 English other ranks and three officers, including Captain Ian Garrow. On 18 October 1940 they were sent to Fort St Jean at Marseille, from which Garrow set about building up his network of safe houses during his time outside the prison. Hodges had plans of his own:

'I decided to get a boat to Casablanca, and stowed away on a French cargo ship. I found four Poles, two Czechs and two British soldiers on board. At Oran we were slung off the ship and put into prison and after two days we were sent back to Marseille.' There Hodges was treated like a civilian and brought up on a charge of stowing away on a ship without a ticket. He was put in prison awaiting formal trial, for two months. The French officer in charge at St Jean got in touch with the General Staff in Marseille on his behalf, and he was let out on parole pending the trial.

At the end of January 1941 he was taken in handcuffs to St Hippolyte du Fort. The lawyer he had employed at Marseille told him his trial would be within the week. Then he heard that there was no chance of this trial coming up until after the war! Hodges had no intention of waiting that long. He gave Garrow, as Senior British Officer, his parole to surrender to the authorities, and turned his attention to means of escape. 'There was a man in the camp called Linklater [2nd Lieutenant], whom I had known at school. He spoke French perfectly and on being captured after the armistice pretended to be a Frenchman. ...He and I forged passes, giving ourselves five days' leave. With these we got railway tickets at a reduced price to Perpignan.' Linklater, Hodges went on to say, had done a good deal of work at the Fort in forging papers and getting men across the frontier.

They got a train to Perpignan and then a taxi to Laroque des Albères and walked over the mountains into Spain. But, as was to become a familiar story, the worst of their troubles were still to come. As they looked down into neutral Spain: 'The only visible signs of habitation were an old Spanish castle with four towers situated in a heavily wooded valley far below us, and in the distance a small cluster of white buildings which we assumed to be the nearest village to the frontier ...

'By this time we had decided on our plan. It was important not to get caught by the police as we knew that a period of internment would follow. We intended to walk as far as we could before nightfall and then hide up. The next day we were to continue in the direction of Barcelona where we knew there was a British Consul-General. We had maps, a compass, a little Spanish money, and food for about two days, and as cigarettes were very scarce in Spain we had brought with us as many French cigarettes as we could carry, to use as bribes.

'By evening we had reached the foot of the mountains.

Although the country was still rough and broken we could see cultivated vineyards only a short distance ahead, and we thought that the little village which we had seen from the mountain top must be close at hand. We were now following a rough mountain track where the going was much easier, and we were just considering where we were to spend the night when we heard a dog bark, and we were suddenly confronted by two ominous-looking officials wearing tattered green uniforms and carrying shot guns and pistols. Conversation with these individuals proved most tiresome, but we eventually gathered that they were customs officials and we were promptly arrested and escorted to their headquarters at the village of Cantillops, about a mile away.'

After interrogation they were sent to Figueras. Here: 'We were put into a small cell where we found two Belgians who were in the same predicament as ourselves. We were only kept in the cell a very short time, and were soon moved off to the Castello which was a military barracks. Here we were locked in a small stone room where we found some more Belgians and several Poles.

'In the evening some British troops arrived – lads whom we knew very well and who had escaped from the same concentration camp in France – making a total of fourteen people. Overcrowding was now very bad, and sanitary arrangements non-existent, and we had to sleep as best we could on the stone floor. The food was quite inadequate, and consisted mainly of soup twice daily and a little bread made with maize. This sudden change in the attitude of the Spaniards and the gloom of the Castello created despondency amongst us all, and we were a little apprehensive as to our future.'

Eventually they managed to contact the consulate and were told they would have to go to the prison at Cervera and stay for a few days, then go on to the concentration camp at Miranda del Ebro. Once there they would come under the British Embassy in Madrid, who would arrange for their release.

'Cervera was run by the Military authorities for the purpose of punishing refugees and prisoners of war who had crossed the frontier into Spain illegally. The prison staff consisted of a Spanish Army Lieutenant, quite an amiable individual and quite harmless, a sergeant who was completely inhuman and a civilian who ran a canteen at an enormous profit.

'This prison was indeed a dungeon. The building was a small and ancient one, and a high wall enclosed a courtyard about thirty yards long and ten yards wide. Access to the cells was gained by descending a short flight of stone steps which led into a long narrow passage; this passage was pitch dark, and on one side were the entrances to five cells, the doors of which were secured by massive iron bolts and locks. Each cell had a small barred window looking out onto the courtyard, and as the cells were partially underground the windows were almost level with the ground outside. Straw bedding, alive with lice, was strewn across the floor, and sanitary arrangements were of the most primitive nature. This was our first impression of a Spanish prison.'

But worse was to come. The journey to Miranda was in a cattle truck. 'For the next two days we endured the most unpleasant journey I have ever experienced,' he recalled. 'At the station fifty of us were locked into a cattle truck and we started on our long journey. By evening on the first day we reached Saragossa where we had to change trains, and after two hours wait in a goods siding we were locked into another cattle truck. By this time it was dark, and I cannot remember what time the train left Saragossa as I fell asleep through bodily fatigue and only awoke far into the night when the train came to a sudden standstill. I had no idea how far we had gone, but we seemed to spend the rest of the night either stationary or moving backwards.'

Finally they reached Miranda del Ebro, the most famous concentration camp in Spain – though famous for all the wrong things. All their hair was removed and it seemed very much like a POW camp in many ways, all run on military lines. The Spanish guards had rubber hoses to deal with anyone who put a foot wrong. At different periods men were being released in batches and Hodges suddenly found himself Senior British Officer: 'a somewhat dubious privilege,' he said later. He had to liaise with the military attaché in Madrid, letting him know about new arrivals and generally keeping things on an even keel. On 4 June – 'a day I shall always remember' – came the news that they were to be released after five weeks in Miranda. The Military Attaché came by car, picked up Hodges and another officer and took them to Madrid. At last they were in the Embassy and able to have a bath, a real English meal and to sleep in a comfortable bed. Hodges left Gibraltar, by air on 13 June 1941, and arrived at RAF Mountbatten on the 14th.

Two months earlier, his air gunner, Sergeant Wyatt, who had escaped from St Jean on 26 December 1940, had also arrived back in England. On his return to the UK, Hodges was recommended for the Military Cross, but he and Wyatt in fact only received a Mention in Despatches. However, Flying Officer Lewis Hodges, known as Bob by his friends, went on to have a distinguished career rising to Air Chief Marshal Sir Lewis Hodges and retiring from the RAF as Deputy C-in-C Allied Air Forces Central Europe. He is now, and has been since 1978, the President of the RAF Escaping Society.

5.   'Get Him Back'

Flight Lieutenant Frederick William Higginson, known to everyone as 'Taffy', was a member of 56 Squadron. He had flown in France and during the Battle of Britain, winning the DFM, and was an exceptional pilot having been credited with shooting down 13 German aircraft. However on 17 June 1941 his luck appeared to have run out. He was hit while on fighter escort to a bombing operation on Lille, though he was never sure by what, for there were no enemy aircraft about or flak. Whatever it was hit the aircraft on the port side and behind the cockpit. His left boot was torn off and his trousers ripped, while the control column of his Hurricane was broken off at the base. He took to his parachute and landed in a wood near Fauquembergues.

Coming out of the wood, he walked slap into two Germans who were looking for him; they promptly clapped him in the side car of their motorbike combination. On route, the Germans foolishly took more interest in a Messerschmitt Me109 flying overhead than in their prisoner, and Taffy was able to turn the handlebars hard and tip the lot upside down. The Germans were knocked unconscious but comparatively unharmed and Taffy was able to get away. Taffy recalls, 'I managed to get to Lille on 21 June, only four days after coming down.'

A member of the local Resistance, M. Dideret, took him to Abbeville from Fauquembergues to see the French Roman Catholic padre the Abbé Carpentier, a lynchpin of the evasion line run from Marseille. The Abbé Carpentier provided false identity papers for evaders and escapers in the Lille area, and agreed to do so for Taffy. Next day Taffy was handed over to a Paul Cole who sheltered him in his flat for eight days while the papers were prepared by the Abbé. (When a later evader, Flight Lieutenant George Barclay, stayed there he was surprised to find a photo of Taffy on the mantelpiece!) On the 29th he went back to collect the papers, and accompanied by Paul, went without difficulty to Paris where: 'I stayed in a hotel which was in fact a brothel.'

As he related on his return to England: 'On 1 July we took a train to Tours and then on to St Martin-le-Beau. Here we missed a pre-arranged contact with a girl at the post office; we therefore walked along the river until we saw a lady with a boat. She towed us across and we walked on to a main road. Very soon we were met by two German soldiers (an officer and a sergeant). When questioned Paul said, "He is an idiot (*un fou*) looking for work." We were asked for identity cards. Paul produced cards and argued volubly. The German sergeant then tackled me. I showed my card and the officer said, "It's a good card, now open your valise." It so happened that my valise was full of chocolate that had melted in the heat and spread itself over the contents. This was enough for the German officer. Paul then opened his valise which contained both special papers and a revolver which he managed to conceal in some dirty laundry. The soldiers never spotted these articles and said, "*Allez*". Throughout this episode I was impressed by Paul's ingenuity.'

They crossed the demarcation line safely, and reached Marseille where Paul's role was accomplished, after Taffy was left at a safe house. Taffy felt himself — and still does — enormously in Paul Cole's debt, as did the other evaders whom he brought down the line at this time. However Paul Cole, far from being a hero, has since been named one of the worst traitors of the war. He claimed to be an escaper from Dunkirk, Captain Harold Cole. Harold was his real name, Paul his code-name. However, the gallant sergeant — the captain was a self-promotion — had in fact absconded with the mess funds before the battle began. Quite when he turned double agent for the Germans is not quite clear, but it cannot have been long after Higginson's journey down the line. Among the first of his many victims was the Abbé Carpentier, who was imprisoned and executed.

The safe house where Taffy stayed in Marseille was that of Dr Georges and Fanny Rodocanachi. The Greek doctor and his wife had offered their home to Ian Garrow as soon as he realised the need for vast numbers of British servicemen to get back to fight again. In time the Rodocanachi flat became the headquarters of the Pat O'Leary line. One of Dr Rodocanachi's official duties was to serve on the Repatriation Medical Board for the Vichy Government, and he managed to get British servicemen repatriated on faked medical evidence. Eventually he was betrayed and sent to a concentration camp where he died. Fanny Rodocanachi escaped the same fate and after the war received on his behalf the posthumous Certificate of Commendation for Brave Conduct for his outstanding services to the Allies during the war. Fanny received the OBE.

As Helen Long recounts in her biography of the Rodocanachis, who were her aunt and uncle, Taffy stayed there during a crisis point for the line. One of his companions there was the recently arrived Pat O'Leary who was awaiting news from London as to whether he could remain to build up the evasion lines with the help of MI9. Then the vital message came over the radio from London – *Adolphe* (Pat's codename) *doit rester*.

Taffy recalls in Helen Long's book the way the Rodocanachis kept up appearances; the table was beautifully decorated, and Fanny was escorted to dinner on Taffy's arm – but dinner consisted of one plate of food between all of them, because of the food shortages and rationing.

On 4 July Taffy left by train with three companions for Perpignan, where he was handed over to a Catalan guide. The intention was to stay at the Hôtel Regina for ten days, but by the 16th nothing had happened, and Taffy decided to go it alone. On the way to the station, however, he ran into Corporal Mason, an Australian, whom he had met at Dr Rodocanachi's. He took Taffy back to the Hôtel de La Loge and they urged the guide to take some action. They were then taken to Banyuls-sur-Mer but were stopped by French gendarmes who took them to a police station to check their papers. They were very suspicious, but he might have got away with it, had he not hit one of the gendarmes! He promptly found himself in prison for six months for having false papers.

'I was taken to Port Vendres prison where the conditions were bad and then to Perpignan, where they were worse. I actually lost 15 kilos.' After a week or two in prison at Montpelier, he ended up in St Hippolyte in October and stayed there until March 1942 when he was told he would be freed. 'However, having got to Perpignan on 5 March we were promptly taken back as a reprisal for the raid on the Renault factory at Billancourt.' On the 17th they were moved again to Fort de La Revère, above Monte Carlo, and here they stayed, planning various methods of escape. Higginson adopted the pseudonym of Captain Bennett since it would have been a propaganda coup for the Germans had his real name been known. 'It was always better to pretend to be an army officer,' Taffy comments. 'The value of RAF officers was always rated much higher.'

London were equally anxious to get him out and back to England, as he was an exceptional pilot. O'Leary managed to get information about the Fort and found that the main sewer pipe came out on to the bank of a small stream through the foot of the hill at La Turbie above Monte Carlo, where the fort stood. Through Father Myrda, a Polish priest who visited the prison, and Val Williams, the White Russian emigré who later organised escapes by sea from Brittany for MI9, O'Leary made contact with Taffy, who was the senior officer. A hacksaw blade was smuggled in and he was told to select four others to get out with him.

Taffy recalls: 'In August 1942, with Flight Lieutenant Barnett, a New Zealander, Flying Officer Hawkins, Sergeants Derrick Nabarro and Pat Hickton known as "Hicky", we decided to try out a plan which was a little risky but worth a try. On the night we planned to go, (6th August 1942) a concert was arranged to cover the noise of our leaving. We had made rope out of string from Red Cross parcels, each of us had an old pullover and on our hands we had converted khaki caps to act as gloves.' In their room was a coal chute which led down to a kitchen, although the door was locked, barred and wired. Sergeant Melville Dalphond, however, had made a key.*

'We levered back the opening of the coal chute which was lined with barbed wire, we dropped down past this and then discarded our old pullovers. We then broke three bars across the window and let ourselves down into the moat, a drop of 25 feet using the rope we had made and saving rope burns by having our hands covered with our makeshift gloves. From there we made our way to the stinking sewer room and I and another chap crawled along the sewer tunnel to locate the exit. When we did, we found it would take some moving and broke the hacksaw blade trying. Then Derrick Nabarro came down and with his oversize feet he managed to kick the iron grill away and we fell out and down the hill amongst the sewerage.

'By now the alarm had been sounded. The lights came on and we ran like hell towards Monte Carlo. Val had promised to meet us outside with two other guides, Tony Friend, an Australian Inspector of Police, and Jean Nitelet, a former Belgian fighter pilot who had only one eye.† But somehow we

---

* He later got back to the UK, in October 1942, and was awarded the DFM.

† He had been an evader himself, reached England via the Pat O'Leary line and was dropped by Lysander back in France with a radio set.

missed them. They had been caught by the guards chasing us and had their names taken.'

They found they were in Cap d'Ail and waited until morning. Taffy had lost his ID card in the escape, and so it was decided to send Flying Officer Hawkins, who had a good ID card, into Monte Carlo in order to make contact. He went to the rendezvous that had been agreed should things not go according to plan. This was the unlikely venue of a Scotch Tea House run by Miss Eva Trenchard, who had been in the South of France since 1924. She was given the King's Commendation at the end of the war, for the help she gave to evaders. Here Hawkins met Pat O'Leary who arranged for them to hide away in an empty flat, which belonged to a hairdresser. As the hairdresser was in London, he was not aware that his flat was a safe house.

The food was first class; it was provided by a Monsieur and Madame Guiton (who later became hairdresser to Princess Grace of Monaco). They took advantage of their helpers' professions – Miss Trenchard served them with teas and Monsieur Guiton cropped Taffy's hair so that he would look more like the priest he was to be disguised as for the journey. Father Myrda provided a cassock, and travelled with them to Marseille.

In Marseille they stayed at another safe house which has since become famous – the flat owned by Louis and Renée Nouveau on the waterfront. A cultured, middle aged businessman Nouveau, with his wife, was very pro-British, and being outspoken never hid the fact even when his flat was used to shelter hundreds of evaders. It was he who made arrangements with London at the beginning of organised evasion for the urgent supply of funds for Ian Garrow, under his business cover. In February 1943 he was betrayed by the traitor Roger le Neveu, as Pat was to be a month later. On Nouveau's arrest, Renée was immediately sent by Pat to England to escape the same fate. Louis Nouveau was sent to Buchenwald like Dr Rodocanachi but unlike him was fortunate enough to survive.

On 17 September Taffy and Hawkins left for Canet-Plage, a

beach area used by hundreds in the summer. They were picked up on the 21st by a former Polish trawler the *Tarana*, which had been converted in Britain to a 'Q Ship', with concealed compartments, and was manned by a British crew. She regularly made the Gibraltar-South of France run on her secret missions, sending her dinghy ashore to pick up her 'parcels', as the evaders were known. Donald Darling relates in his book *Secret Sunday* how the crew drew lots, so many volunteers were there for the dangerous task of rowing the dinghy. The *Tarana* used to leave Gibraltar at dusk, completely repaint to become an anonymous merchant ship, and paint again once more into naval grey before re-entering Gibraltar.

Taffy stayed on the *Tarana* until the 24th when, off the Balearic Islands, they were picked up by the destroyer HMS *Minna* and taken to Gibraltar, arriving on the 26th. 'Many people on the *Tarana* had been sick all the way. On board, as well as us, were some 200 Polish refugees bound for the UK.' Taffy was then flown to the UK, arriving on the 30th.

'Taffy' Higginson was to reach the rank of wing commander, and be awarded the OBE, DFC, AFC and DFM.

6.   They Almost Shot Him

On 21 August 1941, Flight Lieutenant Denis Crowley-Milling DFC, later Air Marshal Sir Denis Crowley-Milling KCB,CBE, DSO,DFC, took off on his second operation of the day in command of B Flight of 610 Squadron, as part of a Spitfire escort to 24 Short Stirling bombers whose mission was to bomb the steel works at Lille.

It was on the return journey that the trouble started for Flight Lieutenant Crowley-Milling. He recalls: 'In a running fight with a number of Me109's ... I was hit behind the engine, damaging the Coolant system.' He made a forced landing with wheels-up in a field some miles south-west of St Omer. 'I

destroyed everything of importance,' he reported on his
return, having borrowed a box of matches from a young farm
worker. Like Hodges before him, though, he had trouble
setting fire to the aircraft. 'Even with the parachute dipped in
the fuel tank, I failed to do so,' he recalls. The farmer warned
him that German soldiers were not far away. He quickly made
for the Desvres Road, and took off his overalls and tunic. Two
German army lorries passed him but took no notice. At
nightfall he approached a nearby farmhouse and was
welcomed by the farmer, his wife and his son, who gave him
food, and a bed for the night.

The next morning he was taken by bicycle, by the farmer, to
his friend's house at Hucqueliers, where he was fitted out with
civilian clothes, which he wore over his uniform! They then
cycled on to Renty, where Norbert Fillerin and his wife ran a
safe house. 'Unknown to me, they thought I was a German
posing as a British pilot,' Crowley-Milling recalls, 'and had
almost decided to shoot me. However, when I realised
Monsieur Fillerin was questioning me about the destruction of
the IFF, I must have finally convinced them that I was British.
From then on I was in their hands.' Norbert Fillerin and his
wife Marguerite sheltered a large number of evaders.

'For about a week I lived with the Fillerin family, dodging the
German patrols.' Here he had his photograph taken for an
identity card. Then on 27 August, 'Monsieur Dideret, a
shoemaker from St Omer, collected me in a car from the
Fillerin farm at Renty, I stayed the night in his flat in St Omer.'
Here he met Jean Nitelet, the Belgian pilot who had suffered
an eye wound and was at that time unfit to travel, but who was
later to become invaluable in Marseille as radio operator for
O'Leary. 'Dideret took me by train to Lille, taking me to the
back of a butcher's shop where I met Paul Cole for the first
time. He took me to a flat where he was living with a
Frenchman's wife (the man was being held by the Germans).
Here I met up with a Czech sergeant pilot. After a few days
Cole took us by train to Paris via Abbeville, where the famous
Abbé Carpentier provided us with the necessary passes and
changed our identity cards. On route, at Béthune, I believe, we

were joined in our carriage by a number of British soldiers left behind by the French capitulation. They went as far as Abbeville where they were given passes to leave the Zone Interdite. As there were only four passes available, our guide had to make four journeys to get the party across the Somme, but the German sentries did not notice this.'

The Paris brothel known to Paul Cole now comes into the story again, for Crowley-Milling's party also lodged there, before leaving on the return journey to Marseille at daybreak. On the journey they were joined by Roland Lepers, a young lively Belgian who was an invaluable courier on the Pat O'Leary line, and was one of the first to become troubled by Paul Cole's suspicious behaviour, reporting it to Pat O'Leary.

The party took a train to Tours, then changed onto a slow local train. Finding the train full of German troops they promptly got out at the first stop. They waited for the next train, and eventually arrived safely at Marseille. Crowley-Milling and his companion spent the night in the Rodocanachi flat in 21 Rue Roux de Brignoles. Here Crowley-Milling discovered that he had been an apprentice at Rolls Royce in 1937 with their son Kostia!

Roland Lepers then took them, on the next day, to Narbonne and Perpignan, where they met the rest of the party and crossed the Pyrenees on foot to Figueras. From the time that he had been shot down it had taken a mere 16 days. However, as was so often the case, their difficulties were not over. Caught by the Spanish Civil Guard, Crowley-Milling spent time in various prisons, ending up in the concentration camp at Miranda del Ebro, where he contracted typhoid. After a month he was removed to hospital, and then repatriated by way of Madrid and Gibraltar and flew home in a Short Sunderland, arriving at Plymouth on 2 December. Corporal Wilkinson returned home on 4 January.

Norbert Fillerin was arrested early in 1943, but undeterred Marguerite continued the work. In December 1943 she too was arrested. The work *still* continued, however, for it was carried on with the help of neighbours, by their teen-aged children, Genevieve, Monique and Gabriel. After the war their parents returned from concentration camps shadows of their former selves. One of their early visitors after the war was Denis Crowley-Milling.

For the rest of the war Crowley-Milling continued flying from the UK, and then in the Far East and was awarded a DSO and a DFC and Bar. On 20 November, 1973, and now an air marshal he was knighted by Her Majesty Queen Elizabeth. He also became chairman of the RAF Benevolent Fund, at the same time as his old CO, Douglas Bader, was the Fund's President.

7.   Bale-Out From 150 Feet

Roy Wilkinson (Royce Clifford Wilkinson) had a rapid rise in rank as the German Blitzkrieg started, when flying Hurricanes with 3 Squadron. In May 1940 he was told by the Acting CO that he was now a flight commander. 'But you have two flight lieutenants and I am only a sergeant,' Wilkinson pointed out, startled. 'I know, but to hell with all the rules; you are the top scorer and the most experienced,' was the reply. [He had been awarded the DFM and Bar]. 'In fact I shall probably, when we are in the air, let you lead the squadron.'

In the squadron returns Wilkinson was listed as OC A Flight as a sergeant pilot, but the CO was told it was 'not on'. His answer was: 'I can and I have. I asked you to make him a flight lieutenant two weeks ago!'

'He stuck to his guns,' Wilkinson recalls, 'and I was made a flight lieutenant, back-dated to 15 May. When we got a new CO, he went on leave and left me as Acting CO: all in the space of one month, from sergeant to CO.'

Roy later flew with 121 'Eagle' Squadron. In January he was posted to 174 Squadron as CO, flying Hurricanes. On May 10 he left Manston at 1550 hrs to take part in a fighter sweep on Abbeville airfield. As he recalls:

'I was attacking Abbeville airfield (an Me109 base) when I was hit smack in the engine by a 40mm Bofors shell. I was at 'O' ft in the middle of the drome, but managed to pull up, over the aerodrome boundary and bale out at about 150 ft or so over the Bois de Crécy. My chute opened just as I hit the trees, caught in the branches, and lowered me gently to the ground. (Some people are born lucky!) The aircraft crashed about 100 yards away.

'I dumped my Mae West under a bush and made off into the wood, and hid in a ditch, with some broken branches over me. The Huns arrived about five minutes later, heading to the crash, which was burning fiercely. They didn't see me, so I stayed hidden until dusk. I went through the wood and saw the Huns searching the farm and farmhouse. I waited until dark, then went to the farm. I told them who I was and they invited me in.'

He was given food and then set off for Paris which he reached a day or two later.

'I had a shave in a barber's shop, which was very funny, as two Hun officers came in and wanted me to get out of the chair to give them priority; as my French was limited to schoolboy French, without thinking I replied in Arabic (the only other foreign words I could think of). One Hun then said to the other, "*il est fou*" at which I laughed, it seemed so funny and then they decided I really was mad, sat down and awaited their turn. I am sure the barber guessed there was something fishy, as he finished my shave, edged me out of the shop and didn't charge for the shave.

'I wandered round Paris, called in one or two bars, discreetly trying to get help. In the third bar, *le patron* gave me two metro tickets, told me to go away and come back at six o'clock, which I did. When I returned, he told me in a mixture of broken English he had no 'contacts' but if I went to Chagny I would probably get help there. I went to the Gare de Lyon and bought a ticket to Chagny (84 francs) and found the train would leave about 8 a.m. the next day.

'I found a scruffy hotel near the station (forbidden to German soldiers) probably a brothel; however I told the

Madame I wanted a room for the night and that I was an RAF pilot escaping. She gave me a room on the top floor, gave me a cheese roll and some wine, without coupons, and would not take any money.

'I went straight to the station in the morning to catch the train, and found that only two rear coaches were for civilians, all the rest were full of German troops, going on leave!! Every time it stopped at a station the troops got out and invaded the station restaurant. When we arrived at Chagny, the same thing happened, so I just got off the train as well, walked out of the station, and the German guard ignored me, probably thinking I had already been checked out. I couldn't find anyone to help me, but saw outside a café, a map of the area, so decided to head south, climb the barbed wire (demarcation line) and head for Macon, to try and catch a train to Marseille. At a small village near the demarcation line I was given some bread, eggs and milk and set off for the last mile, accompanied by all the village children (like the Pied Piper). Two of the children went forward and a few minutes later came back and managed to make me understand that the motorcycle patrol had just gone past, and would not be back for 20 minutes. I slung some sacks on the barbed wire and managed to climb over, into Vichy France …

'In the morning I carried on into the village of Marcilly-le-Buxy. I saw a man working in his garden and asked him the way to Geryon (the next village to Macon). He asked me if I was German. I said, no, RAF pilot.

'He took me to the café-cum-hotel, and the patron turned out to be the mayor of the village. [M. Peraudin] His daughter, who spoke some English, gave me a good meal, and laughingly explained that the man I had contacted was the local gendarme who had tried to tell me that I was now in Vichy France, and not to trust the gendarmes but it was OK in this village, as they were all de Gaullists.

'About an hour later a Mme Duhamel turned up with Abel Hénon, and a Belgian Abbé whom she was helping to escape. She had been in the French Deuxième Bureau, and had many contacts. The mayor took us all in his car to the Hôtel Terminus in Macon. Whilst I was there, two Frenchmen turned up, Captain Hambert and another. They questioned me for about half an hour about aircraft etc, and then decided I was genuine and not an *agent provocateur*.

'I then asked them who they were. "We are French Secret Service, we are now working for the Germans; but we work for you, you understand?" They then fixed me up with some false papers as Léon Boyer, as we would need a carte d'identité to board the train. We stayed the night in the hotel, after a good party.'

A week or two later he was taken to Lyon to the American Consul, George Whittinghill. 'Whilst I was there, Virginia Hall (*La Petite Souris*) arrived and managed to get two 1st class tickets on the night train to Marseille for herself and for me.' Virginia Hall was an American married to a Frenchman, and we shall meet her in several of the stories that follow.

On arrival in Marseille, Roy was taken to Louis Nouveau's flat, and there met Pat O'Leary. From there he was taken over the Pyrenees into Spain and eventually to Gibraltar where he stayed for about six days; he then managed to hitch a lift back to RAF Mountbatten in a Sunderland Flying Boat returning from a South Atlantic patrol.

Mme Duhamel was later caught and spent two years in Ravensbrück, but survived. In 1966, when she was visiting Roy she had a brain haemorrhage resulting from her experiences in Ravensbrück and died. She is now buried in Maidstone, Kent. Mme Duhamel was the godmother to Roy's daughter, Wendy.

Louis Nouveau, a merchant banker, was awarded the George Medal, after the war and his wife Renée the MBE. It was in his flat that Airey Neave and many other evaders were sheltered, a meticulous – and well hidden – record being kept by Madame Nouveau. For a short period he operated from Paris, in charge of bringing parties to the south and during this period he set up contacts with a resistance group in Brittany which was to prove invaluable after the virtual collapse of the Pat O'Leary line. Louis Nouveau was arrested in February 1943 while bringing a party of British across the Demarcation Line and sent to Buchenwald.

George Whittinghill provided funds to no less than 4,000 British and Allied subjects, and was awarded the OBE. One of those he helped was Jimmy Langley, later on the MI9 staff.

George's fiancée was Maud Georgina Harris, the daughter of the eldest brother of Sir Arthur Harris, the C-in-C of Bomber Command. In October 1942 she finally got out of Vichy France just before the whole of France was taken over by the Germans. George went on to Monterey in Mexico. When she arrived in London Georgina worked at the Foreign Office but later married George and was able to join him. They now live in Paris.

Roy Wilkinson finished the war as a wing commander, having commanded No 1 Squadron in 1942-1943, and was awarded the OBE for his evasion to add to his DFM and Bar. He is officially credited with having shot down some nine enemy aircraft. From 1947 to 1968 he spent all his holidays in France staying with many of his helpers and friends. He made a point of travelling some 2,400 miles to find and thank them all.

8.   Escape from Brittany

In February 1943, 35 Squadron were based at Graveley in Huntingdonshire and a part of the Pathfinder Force. 35 Squadron in fact, had been the first Pathfinder squadron when the Pathfinder Force was formed in 1942. In 35 Squadron, as in many other squadrons, were many Canadians. One was Flying Officer Gordon Carter, a navigator in the crew of Flying Officer James Thomas, known as 'Tommy' to his crew. When Gordon Carter was shot down, it more than changed his whole life. Gordon Carter recalls: 'We took off in Halifax TL-B at 18.20 hours on 13 February 1943, to mark and bomb the U-Boat base at Lorient. (We must have crossed the north coast of Brittany, on our way south, just about where I now live.) In addition to it being the 13th of the month, it was my

13th 'Op' and I carried escape kit No 13, a number of which I have since taken a good view! My log-book records that we dropped four green Target Indicators [TI's] and three 1,000-pounders on the aiming point, when, and over which, we were hit by heavy flak.'

Thomas gave the order to bale out, and then as Gordon recalls: 'I virtually landed in the arms of a young lad whose immediate words to me were "*Tu es mon frère*". We were in a ploughed field and he collected my 'chute and led me to a nearby stone farmhouse. (I returned shortly after the war and recovered a piece of my chute, which had been hidden in a haystack. I also returned [after the war] with my four children and as many grand-children, only to find the farmhouse in ruins and the erstwhile inhabitants long-since moved away or dead. We were shown around by a neighbour, who was ten when I fell from the sky and who remembered the whole episode.)

'The young man who took me in was called Lapous, which means "bird" in Breton. ...' The hamlet in which the farmhouse was located is called Kerlescoat which means the 'Hamlet by the Wood' in Breton, and is some 12 kms south-west of Carhaix, on the (now) D82. (In those days it was little more than a dirt lane; now it is quite a wide tarred road.)

'In addition to the young Lapous' parents and a wizened old grand-mother by the hearth (as always in old Breton houses), many neighbours looked in, to shake hands, to bring a bottle of cider or of wine, to bolster their spirits at the sight of *les Anglais*. For by then, our mid-upper gunner, Napoleon "Nap" Barry, RCAF, had also been recovered from a field a little further away and was now among us.

'We slept together in the *lit clos*, a traditional Breton cupboard-like bed, with sliding doors. We were awoken before dawn, given some civilian clothes, a shopping bag and some bread, and seen on our way before the German garrison in Carhaix showed up. They were scouring the countryside for the crew of the 'plane that had crashed near Loudeac a few kilometres to the north-west of Kerlescoat. I should add here that the canal *de Nantes à Brest* flows between these two localities and that all the other members of the crew fell in a stick on the far side of the canal. They met with different fates and the only one I ever saw again was Tommy, in 1984!

'So Nap and I set out in the half light, heading generally south-east, towards remote Spain! As night was about to fall, we picked out an isolated farmhouse near a bridge over a stream, the Pont Rouge and tried our luck. More by chance than anything, we introduced ourselves as Canadian airmen (though English, I too was RCAF); the reaction (in French) was: "You're welcome. You wouldn't have been had you been English"! (Shades of the shelling of the French fleet at Mers-el-Kebir …).

'We were taken in by a family who fed us and put us up for the night, the girl even washing our feet in a basin by the hearth. Very early next morning, the man of the house accompanied us, pushing his bike. He left us at the bus stop. The bus was already packed with people and crowds were pushing and shoving to get in, mostly country women in their coiffes – Breton head-wear. Nap and I managed to squeeze our way to the rear door and I dared all, shouting to the driver who was trying to close it that we were *des aviateurs Anglais*. That was good enough for him. He got us on board somehow. The bus was headed for Ponting, due east, where, a man on the bus who had overheard me told us, we should look up Pierre Valy at the Grand Café …

'Valy told us that Tommy and one or two others had been recovered by the Resistance and were on their way. During our stay at the Grande Café we met a chap who called himself Guy Dubreuil and whose real name was/is Guy Lefant. Guy Dubreuil was a case of reality being truer than fiction. He was an agent working for London, organising the reception of arms drops. His (accurate) theory was the thicker you laid it on, the less chance you had of being caught. He went round in an Austin Reed shirt, called his dog RAF, carried a ferret around in a cage called Hitler which sat on a million francs worth of banknotes (dropped by the RAF), slapped "V-1918" licence plates on his motorbike, had reversible Pétain/de Gaulle framed photographs at home – which then was a rented country house on the outskirts of St Meen-le-Grand. He bluffed his way through thick and thin, when helping the Gestapo hunt the parachutist who had been seen coming down the night before, none other than ... himself. He passed himself off as a big-time black marketeer, who were known to be up to all sorts of tricks.

'Nap and I went along with Dubreuil on his outings, lugging suitcases of Sten Guns and ammo on our bikes, always but always at the time of day when there were the most Germans about. He had us with him when his W/Op transmitted to London from the bedroom of a couple of elderly ladies in Ploermel, to which he travelled by train, when the RAF hadn't shot-up the engine. It was in Ploermel that Nap and I reported to the Mairie (the Town Hall) that we were bombed-out victims of the raids on Lorient (*sinistrés* is the French term) and claimed ration cards and clothing coupons. We also had ID cards issued to us. I chose Georges Charleroi as my *nom de guerre*, to keep my initials.

'Guy Dubreuil arranged for us to be picked up by a Royal Navy submarine off the north-west coast of Brittany. He sent his "pathfinder cyclist" to check the spot and to report conditions in the *Verboten* Coastal Zone. Meanwhile, Nap and I had picked up a tall USAAF Texan who was nicknamed "Petit Pierre", whom I had been asked to authenticate by the Pontiery Police Chief, a M Loch, who was an active member of the Resistance. Indeed I was told that if I – and no one else – considered him to be genuine, fair enough. If I was in any doubt, he would be shot there and then. As it turned out he came from the USAAF airfield not far from Graveley, where I had recently lunched (spaghetti and meat-balls) and I was able to pin him down on local details.

'Dubreuil, Petit Pierre, Nap and I duly set off for a cove due north of Sibiril which is 7-8 kms due west of St Pot-de Leon (itself NW of Morlaix). We travelled by taxi to the boundary of the Finisterre department, some 35 kms east of Morlaix. We lunched in a country inn near the Ploujean Luftwaffe base, the only 'civilians' in a crowd of Luftwaffe officers (Dubreuil's theory at work again). We hoped to God that none would notice our bulging breast pockets in which we had tucked our revolvers. (In retrospect, we should have been smarter to do without ...) As it was, the taxi owner had a fit when he later found bullets which one of us had spilled onto the back seat of his cab!

'So we walked the 35 odd kms to Morlaix, where we caught a local train to St Pol-de-Léon. As we left this train and headed for the station exit, French and German police, checking passengers' *Ausweise* (passes) which travellers were expected to carry in the forbidden coastal zone, turned to Petit Pierre for his. We were just in time to intercede in French – which P.P. did not speak – and explain that we were on our way to the *Ausweis* issuing office, before P.P. panicked and gave the whole show away! As it was we were issued *Ausweise* without any difficulty and lunched on *bigornots*, ie winkles, in a local cafe.

'The very first evening the pre-agreed BBC message came over the clandestine air, "*La plume de ma tante est rouge*". We borrowed bikes and set out at dusk for our rendezvous. The cove had been described in the wireless exchange between Ploermel and London as having a low cliff on which grew alder trees and a large rock in the middle. Night soon fell and our troubles started.

'Nearing Sibiril we were stopped by a German Army sentry posted outside a house in which German officers were having a boisterous shindig. This was touch and go, for a shout by the guard and we had had it. But Dubreuil was at his extravagant best and in a stream of French, English (!) and German, had the sentry bemoaning the fate of the German armies at Stalingrad ... We made off and skirting some German positions in the countryside, finally reached the beach. We huddled by the rock and waited. In due course we saw a single flash at sea, the submarine's signal. But to our despair nothing happened and a couple of hours later we grudgingly made our way back, unhindered, to St Pol-de-Léon. (I found out at MI9, and later for myself, that there were twin coves a couple of hundred yards apart and deduced that the submarine's dinghy had put it at the other one!)

'We were by now more than Dubreuil could cope with. He

therefore turned us over to the monks at the Trappist monastery at Timadeuc, near Rohan, in central Brittany. The tradition whereby the monastery acted as a refuge for men for fourteen days with no questions asked was then still observed by the Germans. (They later raided the place and deported the Fathers, Father Gwenael, "White Angel" in Breton, dying in the camps.)

'The three of us spent an extraordinary week in the monastery where the vow of absolute silence prevailed. Only the Father Hostelier could speak to us. By day we strolled in his gardens; at night, in our austere cells, we listened to the droning prayers of the monks. Meals were good, though, including the home-made liqueur of Mirabelle plums.'

A few days later a young man called Georges Jouanjean came to collect them. He was a member of the Brittany resistance group with which Louis Nouveau of the O'Leary line had established contact before his arrest in that same February, and which was to organise successful sea evacuations for the next year. 'We thereupon,' recalls Carter, 'took the night train to Paris. We made for Jouanjean's ("Geo" to us by then) contact address, to which he had earlier delivered Tommy Thomas. We sat in a café while Geo checked that the way was clear. He reappeared in great haste for he had found the door to the flat sealed by the Gestapo. Had we shown up a couple of days earlier we would have walked into the trap …

'There was no way out of our predicament so we returned to Brittany by the following night's train. Geo took us to Carhaix where we split up, Nap staying with Mme Marchais and Petit Pierre with Mme Correc, a dentist. …

'I stayed with Geo's aunt, Mme Rouillard, and grandfather, Edouard Rouillard. Shortly thereafter, Geo decided to entrust me to his elder sister Lucette Cougard who lived in Soursin. In order to make our bike ride from Carhaix to Soursin less conspicuous, he asked his younger sister Jannine to accompany us. This she did and was impressed by the fact – as she still is today (I married her in 1945) – that I cycled at her speed and repaired her chain while her brother was racing on ahead.

'Jannine and I spent a happy fortnight or so in Soursin,

where my neighbour was the Austrian Commanding Officer (whom I greeted every morning when we opened our shutters, our respective bedrooms being across the street from one another). We went for walks; went to the local movie, attended soccer matches, and so on. ... (Lucette's husband, Raymond, was awarded the King's Medal for Courage, for the numerous airmen he and his wife had sheltered before and after me. Lucette still lives in Carhaix but Raymond has since died.)

'Geo and Raymond asked me one day whether I would go along with a scheme to hi-jack a new German MTB going out on trials in the next day or two from the western harbour of Douarnenez. Preposterous though it sounded, I said yes, for I had to grab any opportunity to relieve my helpers of my presence and get back home. There was no time, however, to involve my two colleagues in Carhaix.

'We left the next day for Douarnenez, having as a rendezvous point the railway station, located in the twin town of Tréboul. We were to contact someone there who would answer to the password "Napoleon". For the first couple of hours no one showed up. In desperation, I put to a man who had been lingering some distance away: "Êtes-vous Napoleon?" He was! The reason why it had taken so long to make contact was that they were expected to arrive in a car belonging to a Resistance associate, Job le Bec, but which had turned out to be unavailable.

'We were led to a flat in Douarnenez where Claude Hernandez hid us, as well as a number of evading Frenchmen, until nightfall. After dark we single-filed at long intervals down to a shed on the quayside at Tréboul harbour, where we met yet other escapees and were briefed. Each one of us – we nineteen – chipped in 10,000 francs (not much at the time) to cover costs, principally diesel fuel ... for by then we had learned that we were to escape in a derelict fishing boat, a far cry from the MTB! As I had no money a local priest, the Abbé Cariou put up the money for me. (I reimbursed him after the war).

'The odyssey of the *Dak'h Mad* ("Hang-on" or "Persevere" in Breton,) is one of the epics of the war and has been oft recounted in books (I have three of them at home) and newspaper articles. In brief this is what happened.

'As the German sentries on the quay moved away, we dropped down onto the harbour floor (the tide was out), ran for the *Dak'h Mad* and disappeared below deck. Absolute silence was impressed. After a long and somewhat anxious night, our 21-year-old "Master", a local fisherman called Lili Marec, came openly on board, started the engine up and we headed out on the tide for the spot where all boats were checked out by the German military customs, the "Gast", presumably initials or an acronym.

'Since the first day of the German occupation every vessel leaving Tréboul or Douarnenez had been boarded by the Gast during its check. We had to be cleared without being boarded, for there were a dozen and a half of us in the hold. Marec therefore idled the boat to within a few feet of the Gast dock, but too far for a jump on board. He explained that he was off to collect some fuel across the bay and be right back. The Germans yelled back to heave to alongside. At that crucial moment, Henandez and an accomplice breezed into the Gast office and started a rumpus of their own. One pretended to be an electrician who had repairs to carry out. The other bitched about having had something of his stolen. It was enough of a commotion for the Customs men to drop their guard and to shout us off with a *Raus* (get going). We did, rounding Mistan Island and making for the still distant open sea.

'A map of Brittany will show that Douarnenez is at the head of a deep bay. We had a long chug out to the sea, sails straining to help the engine along, and headed due west to get as far from the German MTB's and destroyers in Brest as possible. We were probably saved from interception (our failure to return had by now been reported) by the worst storm at sea which Marec and the many sailors (Xavier Trellu was a famous yachtsman) and fishermen on board had ever experienced. I somehow struggled out of the mixture of vomit, diesel fuel and sea-water sloshing all over us in the hold and joined Marec at the tiller, hanging on for dear life.

'The next day we headed north, yours truly navigating by "astro", ie educated guesses as to our position in relation to the sun, at night, the stars. We ran up a French flag with a Cross of

Lorraine tarred on it, (our names were later embroidered on it and it is now in the National Resistance Museum in Bordeaux).' After losing direction in fog, 'we spotted a small lumpy island in the distant haze which I guessed might be St Michael's Mount. We chanced it and soon saw cliffs on the horizon. Then appeared a fishing boat, heading for us. English? Irish? French? We stood by to either welcome it or do it in. It turned out to be a Cornish crabber from Cadgwith! We had made it ….

'Lili Marec lives still near Douarnenez. We are often in touch. One of the "crew", Marcel Guillion, recently retired as a Concorde captain, has a house in Ploubazlanec, a mile or so from where I live. Xavier Trello, now in his 90's, is still alive. Those who helped us on shore in Douarnenez are all dead, including the Gast Customs men, who were shot for letting us through.

'The BBC message announcing our safe arrival was *Sainte Anne a bien fait les choses*: "Saint Anne took care of things nicely." For we sailed in sight of "her" chapel at Ste Anne La Palud, a couple of miles up the coast from Douarnenez. My four kids, three girls and a boy, all have Anne as a middle name and today, a coincidence no doubt, Jannine and I live in a village whose patron saint is St Anne. Last but not least, my small boat, moored in a cove at the foot of our lane is none other than the *Dak'h Mad II*.'

One year later, while back flying with 35 Squadron, Gordon Carter was again shot down on a raid to Leipzig. On this occasion he was taken prisoner after some while, and ended up as a POW in Stalag III until being liberated on 2 May 1945.

'I returned to the UK on 9 May and then returned to France to find Jannine on the 19th. We were married on 9 June 1945. She was given away by her brother Geo Jouanjean.'

Being shot down on the Lorient raid really did change his life. He found help, friendship and love. Although he took his new wife to Canada in 1945, they later returned to Jannine's native Brittany where they now live.

9.   Sole Survivor

'The other day Winston showed me a thrilling account of a RAF pilot crashing with his 'plane in the maquis of Haute Savoie.'

Thus begins a memo from Clementine Churchill, written from 10 Downing Street. The pilot in question was Squadron Leader Frank Griffiths, AFC, who at the time was with 138 (Special Duties Squadron) at Tempsford. By then he had completed 23 operations with Bomber Command and 22 with Fighter Command. At his debriefing he reported:

'We crashed at the village of Meithet about 0115 hours (15 August 1943). All the others except Sergeant Maiden, who was thrown out of the aircraft, were killed at their crash stations ....'

'I was knocked unconscious, having had my right arm broken and my left shoulder blade fractured, as well as head injuries. After about ten minutes I got out of the aircraft in a semi-conscious state and started to walk from the fire. Italian soldiers got hold of me, took off my Mae West and parachute harness, and began to march me to a lorry at the top end of the village. We had just begun to walk when a petrol tank exploded in the burning aircraft. The two Italians shouted something about bombs and ran away. I walked off and got into a field where I hid in a ditch.

'There were a number of explosions, and bullets were flying about. It was probably at this time that Maiden was shot. I crawled out of the ditch and began walking up the road. I had got out behind a crowd of people who were watching the burning aircraft and did not see me. I walked up the road towards Epagny. After I had gone a short distance a Frenchman on a bicycle passed me going towards the fire. He immediately swung round and caught up with me, asking if I were English. He took me to his house at the top of Meithet. I collapsed before I reached the house, and he carried me the remainder of the way on his bicycle. His mother attended to my injuries, and half an hour later I was put in touch with an organisation which arranged my journey to Switzerland.'

As he recounts in his excellent memoirs *Winged Hours*, after his injuries were given rough first aid and he was given civilian clothes, Frank Griffiths was taken to Ma Braque a restaurant on the main road, where he met the local Maquis and a local doctor gave some more expert attention to his wounds. Here Griffiths stayed, dividing his time between Ma Braque and the mountains during the daytime to avoid the local Gestapo, who were apt to drop into the bar all too often. His presence was hardly secret, however, owing to a constant and somewhat unnerving stream of visitors. He was given the sad news that all his crew had died in the crash save one, and he had been shot while being recaptured. He too was now dead.

The next step towards his destination, Switzerland, was to move to a small hamlet called Les Goths, near the town of Cruseilles.

His hostess was Mme Mimi Pallud, who explained her visitor to her neighbours as a relative in her care from the lunatic asylum at Lyon. To explain the fact that his face and arms were covered in bandages, she told them that he had been attacked by another patient. No one appeared anxious to talk to him!

Three days later he was introduced to a girl of about 22. The time had come to make the attempt to reach Switzerland. A man courting a girl would not attract as much attention as a man on his own. They were driven near to the crossing point in an old Citroen car propelled by a gazogène wood burning apparatus, and made the crossing just before sundown. As he told MI9 on his return:

'We crossed the field without incident and had walked about half a kilometre down a lane when a command of "Halt" rang out. We halted. The Swiss challenging us was so cunningly concealed that we didn't even know where the challenge had come from. A pause ensued and Annette with the usual feminine attitude towards men and their commands started to walk forward again. I grabbed her arm and tried to explain that it was asking for trouble to start forward again once you had been halted. Eventually the mystery voice appeared coming from behind a tree. He seemed quite prepared to let us have it and brandished a bayonet at our throats. His mood changed when he saw that Annette was a woman and that I was in no fit state for making any trouble. He told us to go to the guard-house further along the road and report. Much to my surprise he didn't accompany us and I was able to uncock my Colt and put it on "Safe" before we went in. I thought the Swiss might take a poor view of it if they found that it was all set for firing when I was on Swiss territory.

'An enormous man in a correspondingly large car eventually came to fetch us and drove us into Geneva to the Hotel Bristol where rooms were already prepared for us. He seemed to be a man of some importance in Switzerland. We were challenged five times between the frontier and Geneva and despite the fact that he had a couple of fishy-looking customers in the back of the car without any identity papers, the journey was without incident. We arrived at the Hotel Bristol at midnight, just six days to the hour (Swiss) after I crashed near Annecy.

'Next morning at 9 o'clock I was eating a breakfast of white rolls, strawberry jam and coffee with Annette in her room when two men came in. One was a Swiss of the Intelligence Service, and he was so typically English I could guess who it was right away. It was Victor Farrell. I had arrived. The only thing that worried me was being caught in such a compromising situation by another Englishman. What on earth was I doing with a wife and child in England, having breakfast in the bedroom of a luscious blonde in Geneva. C'est la Guerre!'

In Switzerland, Griffiths was subjected to a comfortable internment in the Hotel Bristol owing to his injuries and for medical attention. Victor, nominally the Passport Control Officer, but in practice MI9's agent in Geneva, began work on plans to get the 48 aircrew at present interned in Switzerland, back to England. But they were coming to nothing, and as Frank related in *Winged Hours* (William Kimber, 1981):

'If I liked I could be interned with other aircrew, now at Arosa. I knew that it was my duty to get back to England if possible and to carry on with the war, but there was another reason which far transcended the call to duty and that was the strongest force in man; the desire to get back to a certain woman ... and she was in England.'

The only practical way out of Switzerland was: back into

occupied France, there to meet an arranged pick-up aircraft from England. Griffiths and his companions Joe and Freddie were to catch the train to Paris from Annemasse, just across the border. Unfortunately they chose the wrong day to arrive. There was an alert on and they missed their contacts. Luckily they were helped on their way to a safe house, that of Madame Roche. Here Frank and his companions were hidden but in the unrest in the town their last opportunity for reaching Paris in time for the pick-up vanished.

Now Griffiths was to meet one of the great characters in the story of French evasion – Françoise Dissart who ran a safe house at Toulouse, and had come to Annemasse as courier, for Frank and his companions. Françoise was no Annette. She was nearly 70, with a face like a horse, and was no gentle personality. She cross-questioned Frank intensely, doubting his bona fides, while her henchman was ready to deal with him the moment he put a foot wrong. Fortunately his identity was confirmed with London, and the rail journey to Toulouse began. Françoise's aim was never to escape notice, but to go out of her way to draw attention to herself, diverting the limelight from her charges. Eccentric as she was, this was always successful, and they arrived at her villa in Toulouse safely. Here she lived in untidy homeliness, with Thérèse, who was half-Irish. The other permanent resident of the house was Françoise's cat, Mifouf, as eccentric as her owner. Here Frank met another evader, Joe Manos, a young American air gunner, whom Frank got on well with, but who did not believe in the need for too much discretion. Listening to UK broadcasts and teasing the cat were two of his peccadiloes. Françoise survived the betrayal of the Pat O'Leary line and continued her work to the end of the war. She later received the George Medal.

Frank and Joe spent much of their time training for their journey across the Pyrenees. Frank was still not completely well, and if they were to make Spain successfully fitness was essential. On 27 October, the next stage of their journey began: to Narbonne and then to Perpignan. At Perpignan they met a new contact, a Catalan named 'Antoine'. His real name was Marcel and he came from Marseille. He told them to meet him on a bench in the local park at 4 p.m., when he would lead them to a farm in the mountains owned by his uncle. As he sat on this bench, Frank noticed, scratched on the back '*Per Ardua ad Astra*'*. Evidently he was not the first RAF evader to pass by. Antoine and his uncle took Frank and Joe through the mountains of the Pyrenees, to meet Paul, their new guide, who would take them over the frontier. The last part of the journey they were led by Manuel who, by his looks, was a relation of Paul's.

Once successfully over the frontier they were left on their own at a farm between Boadella and Pont-de-Molins. As Frank related to MI9 later:

'After about three hours at the farm, Manos and I walked into Figueras in time to catch the morning train to Gerona. We got our tickets without difficulty, but as we were getting into the train we were both arrested by the Civil Political Police, who wore a grey uniform and grey caps with red bands and fascist badges. They took us to Police HQ in Figueras.' Thereafter Frank had just as great an ordeal as many others had experienced, and did not arrive at Gibraltar until the end of November.

On 2 January 1944, Squadron Leader Frank Griffiths was recommended for the DFC by the Station Commander of RAF Tempsford, and it was endorsed by Air Chief Marshal Sir Arthur Harris on 7 January. Françoise Dissart GM died in 1957. In Toulouse there is a full size statue in her memory.

10. Merlin's Magic Carpet

At 5 p.m. on 16 August 1943, Sergeant Harold Merlin, known to his friends as 'Bob', took off from Lydd in his Typhoon fighter-bomber to attack the Luftwaffe fighter base at Abbeville.

* A few years ago the Secretary of the RAF Escaping Society, Elizabeth Harrison, tried to trace this bench through the Mayor, but his reply was that all the benches had been changed but only recently. Her idea was to trace the bench and that if possible it be acquired for the RAF Museum at Hendon. Unfortunately it proved impossible to trace the marked bench.

Before the war he had been a journalist. Now he was a sergeant pilot in 175 Squadron, part of 2nd TAF which had just been formed. During his attack he was hit by flak, and crash-landed in a field in the vicinity of a small town of Auxi-le-Château, which was about 25kms NE of Abbeville. The time was 5.30 p.m. His No 1, Flying Officer Tommy Hall (an Australian) saw him crash, but did not know whether he had survived as the Typhoon exploded.

'After regaining consciousness I escaped from the crash and hid in a wood. I was bruised and with a head wound which was not serious but which bled a lot. After nightfall I proceeded to walk eastwards and came finally to a hill, just beyond Doullens, at about daybreak. I dragged myself to the top of it and took cover. I had walked cross-country over a distance of some 20kms as the crow flies – I was no crow however, and must have walked considerably more than that. There had been countless fenced-off fields, I remember, and every time I had to pass under the wire my head wound would open again and bleed.

'Doullens had a Wehrmacht garrison and as it happened on that day units of it took to field exercises on the hill where I was hiding. They set machine-guns; one of them only a few yards away from me, and it quite deafened me when they fired it. During a break in the exercise one of the soldiers dropped his trousers and relieved himself in front of the bush where I had concealed myself.

'At dusk, and after the Germans had packed up and left, I set out again. Parched with thirst I waylaid a child who was carrying a can of milk back from the fields. My sudden appearance must have frightened him, and I could not have been looking at my best, because he screamed, dropped the milk, and ran. I was not able to save much of the milk to drink. By the time I reached the small village of Lucheux much later that night I was quite spent. I had been stumbling and staggering about, and collapsing to the ground every so often, from sheer exhaustion. I found a barn, entered it, and promptly passed out in the hay. I went to the owner's house the next morning and I was given food. Later, the local Resistance was contacted and a man was sent to me. We disposed of my

battledress and I was given farm-worker's clothing which was
far too small for me – I am 6'2'', and I exchanged my flying
boots for shoes about three sizes too tight – I wore 11's. When I
visited the farmer some 25 years later – he's died since – he still
had my boots which he had incautiously kept as a souvenir and
he showed them to me.

'I cycled to Frévent with my Resistance escort and met there
the local man in charge, a dentist by the name of Hetroit ....

'Being bilingual in French I was asked by the Resistance to
help them and I agreed to do so. One Jo Becker, living at
Auxi-le-Château, was a civilian sub-contractor to the German
NSKK who at that time were starting the construction of the
then top-secret V1 ramps with which the whole of the province
of Picardie was soon to bristle. Becker, a native of Lorraine and
a fluent German speaker and whom the Germans held in
complete trust, had by the very nature of his work access to all
the V1 sites being built in the Auxi district and beyond, also to
other military installations, airfields, etc. Since he also engaged
in wholesale black-marketing, he was in close touch with a great
many Germans, some of whom were very senior.

'The cover for me which Jo Becker and I decided upon was
for me to be supposedly employed as his driver. In
consequence and for the next two months almost, I was able to
drive with him all over the Pas-de-Calais and the Somme and to
take note, of course, of everything I saw everywhere we visited
– the secret V1 sites especially. At the time, I was lodging with
Becker at Mme Lanciot's in Auxi-le-Château, next to the
doctor, Georges Hibon, who got to know me well and know
what I was really doing. I used to sit up at night and record,
with map references or on Michelin map tracings, the German
installations I had visited during the day. I got quite used to the
noise of German soldiery carousing in the cafe next door, and
to the frequent sound of jackboots thumping the pavement
outside my window.

'In another cafe Becker deliberately introduced me one
evening to the NCO in charge of the flak battery that had hit
my Typhoon – Jo Becker used often to do things like that. He
did, however, introduce me as his driver, not as the pilot in

question! The German was admittedly rather drunk and buying everybody rounds in celebration of some medal – or was it promotion he had just received for his exploit in shooting me down.

'Apart from visiting V1 sites and other German establishments, there was other work that Becker and I frequently engaged in. Using his unlimited petrol supply and his special Curfew and the Restricted Zones passes, we used to visit RAF and USAAF aircrew in hiding, taking to them food, clothing and whatever else they and their hosts needed. Sometimes we would move them to other safe-houses, or to assembly points for their onward journeys ....

'By late October 1943 I felt my cover was wearing dangerously thin and that my continued presence at Mme Lanciot's was not fair to her and to others whom I knew in the town. Also, there were signs the Germans were beginning to suspect me, and anyway I had collected enough intelligence by then and the priority now was to get it urgently into official British hands. Since I was not in contact with any of our accredited agents with radio sets, and was reluctant to seek access to them, I decided to make for Switzerland and our Embassy there.

'Putting the first leg of my journey to good use, I travelled by train to Paris as escort to a group of five or six RAF and USAF evaders, none of whom spoke French. I had rather good false papers: my identity card, that named me Pierre Lenois, of Abbeville interior decorator; and a *Carte d'Invalidité, de 50% ou plus*, that gave me the right to travel at 75% reduced fare, but more importantly often discouraged further enquiries by Germans at identity checks. As for my intelligence reports, the papers had proved quite bulky, so I had stuck them end to end and rolled them up into a tight scroll which I carried hidden inside a hollowed out loaf of French bread. Upon arrival at Gare du Nord in Paris, I handed over my *convoi* of aircrew to the woman member of the *filière* [escape line] who had been assigned to meet us – she had no trouble spotting us. We parted company and I went my way.

'I spent some time in Paris, probably a couple of weeks,

looking up contacts who had been given to me at Auxi and for ways and means to get to Switzerland. I was lodging in a *maison de passe* – an unofficial brothel, near Place Denfert Rochereau. It was run by a friendly and helpful Corsican, named Toronelli. His establishment was frequented by other Corsicans, most of whom were pimps and cut-throats. I became quite friendly with them, especially with one who was known as Toni and who gave me some money.

'At last with the name of a Maquis contact in Annecy, I caught a train and got there without noteworthy incidents. The man came to me in the small Annecy hotel where I spent the night, and confirmed what I already knew: that the season was now too advanced – we were in mid November – for a mountain crossing into Switzerland, because all the passes were snowed under. He could, however, provide a guide for me to St Julien, a small town on the Geneva border, where there was the possibility of a contact. So we caught the bus the next morning, the guide, who turned out to be a child of 12, and I. We arrived at St Julien at dusk: there were police and German troops everywhere – the Unoccupied Zone of France no longer existed then. After some trouble at a road block and identity check, I told the child to leave me. A few close shaves later I was lucky enough finally to meet a farmer who owned a potato plot on the other side of the border fence …

'Early then on that last morning, wearing a labourer's smock to cover my town suit, I was driven in a cart, together with the other half dozen farm-workers, through the gate in the fence which had been opened for us by the German sentry after our pass had been examined ….

'After jumping off the cart on the Swiss side, for a while I dug potatoes with the others, but soon, helped by the mist, I started to drift away. I was picked up by the Swiss border patrol, who, it seems, had had their binoculars on us from the start.' With some difficulty he managed to see the British Air Attaché, who was Air Commodore West.* 'I handed over my French loaf to him,' Merlin recalls. 'When taken out and unrolled, my scroll

* Air Commodore Freddie West VC,MC, who had won his decorations during WW1.

stretched right across his office floor, and his was a largish office. AC West dubbed the scroll and the information it contained "the Merlin Magic Carpet".

'Pending confirmation of my identity the Embassy handed me over to the Swiss authorities, probably advising them to put me temporarily on ice, so the Swiss promptly jailed me for illegally entering the country .... When at last I was released into the Embassy's custody, I was lodged in a rather shabby residential hotel to which I was confined, except for authorized visits to the Embassy. A few RAF evaders and a couple of Red Army escapees lodged at the same hotel and were under the same movement restrictions. I was asked by Air Commodore West whether I was prepared to return to France and undertake some aircraft spotting for RAF Intelligence, and I said I was. As a result, I was to spend several days in the Embassy strong-room studying and memorizing the latest order of battle at the Luftwaffe airfields in the north of France. I was to visit these airfields – a round dozen of them, and report changes. However, just when my briefing was over and my mind bulging with the information I had stored, my mission was called off by London, to AC West's regret, I must say.

'So I was then packed off to the ski resort of Arosa, where, our Embassy kept two chalets of escapees and evaders, almost all aircrew. There, subject to police internee restrictions and under our own hierarchically imposed military disipline, we all ski'd by numbers. Just after Christmas, Air Commodore West came up to visit us. Having asked to see me, he told me in confidence that he had a Christmas present for me which he was sure I would appreciate: the V1 sites which I had reported on my "carpet" had just been successfully bombed by the RAF.

'By spring (1944) I was getting really bored with the ski-ing and the constrained though confortable idleness of our lives as internees, and I had read all the chalet library books .... I decided on a further escape, this time back to France, taking two fellow internees with me. Our escape was successful: we travelled by train to Porrentruy and walked across country and across the border to Audincourt. Our journey was not without its trials. Suffice it so say here that I safely delivered both my companions into the hands of the Resistance, near Audincourt and I was informed later in the war that they had been safely returned to the UK.'

Having seen to his companions' safety, Merlin travelled by train to Paris first class. During the journey the train was stopped and everyone was searched. All was well, however – Merlin returned to his previous lodgings where he had stayed back in November 1943. Here he stayed until 22 July when he hitch-hiked to Frévent, and then walked on to Sibiville where he contacted a member of the Resistance who sent him on to Berles where he stayed until 14 September.

During these weeks he became the leader of a Resistance group, and undertook a lot of mopping up and re-occupation operations after the Allies had swept through in their push to Belgium. He was driving, he recalls, a Wehrmacht Volkswagen that he had acquired from the retreating Germans. On the bonnet he had mounted a MG42 light machine gun on the lines of the British Bren gun, and had used this to dislodge some groups of Germans that had been left behind. Some were well armed and not all were demoralized, especially the SS troops.

His machine gunner was 'Tommy' Thompson, a Canadian aircrew who had been shot down in the district. They captured and marched off several hundred prisoners during the first two weeks in September.

On 14 September he drove to Vitry to locate his old squadron 175. He arrived in his German car with an Alsatian dog in the back, a former police trained dog which had formerly belonged to a German officer, whom they had had to execute. It was re-named Schnapps and later became the 175 mascot. (Sadly when Merlin left for the UK in 1945 the dog was left behind and poisoned by the Germans when the squadron was stationed in North Germany.)

'I was returned to the UK at the end of September 1944, about a fortnight after the liberation of the North of France. The RAF was displeased with me because I had been away for so long and "fooling about". Had the War Office not put in a good word for me I should probably have been officially reprimanded (for dereliction of duty?) ....

'On Christmas Day at noon, in the course of what became known as the Battle of the Bulge, I was shot down again while engaged in a squadron attack against German armour in the Ardennes. Unable to jump I consequently crashed with my aircraft, and I was miraculously lucky to survive. Though injured and fallen inside enemy-held territory, I was lucky again to be rescued by a US Army patrol. My belated Christmas dinner was hosted that evening by the American Divisional General at Eupen.'

11.   Sky Pilot

'Oh God, help me!' Flight Sergeant George Wood prayed as he tried to get out of his doomed Whirlwind aircraft of 263 Squadron, on 23 September 1943. The squadron had flown from Bolthead, Salcombe, just before mid-day, reaching the target at noon.

'I had been hit by flak just as I dropped my bombs on the airfield at Morlaix. Later 10 Group HQ reported that I was missing, believed killed as my aircraft had been seen to disintegrate after being hit. However, I managed to bale out and came down near the flak battery which had shot me down, but they were so occupied in trying to shoot the other Whirlwinds down it gave me the chance to get away.' Luckily the German gunner had orders not to leave his gun.

Having no time to bury his parachute, which in any event was entangled in a tree. George Wood made a run for it. He had thrown away his gloves and helmet, later hiding his Mae West under a pile of logs. Reaching the River Dossen, he could see what looked like a monastery on the far side and decided to try and cross in the darkness. Meanwhile, he climbed a fir tree for cover. Nearby he could see a Château, (Kerorin). Germans were everywhere, searching for him. They came very near to his hiding place but fortunately they looked in every direction but up! When darkness fell he attempted to cross to the monastery he'd seen, but sank up to his waist in mud so had to give up that idea. Returning towards Morlaix he made for the farm the Germans had already searched, on which the Château stood.

'I made my way to the farm at Ploujean and myself comfortable in a barn. In the morning an assistant gardener, André Cras, came in and found me and went and fetched the owner of the farm, M. Gueguen. He gave me dry clothes and made me a hideout in a haystack, and then brought me bread, fruit and wine.' On this day, George was handed a note by M. Gueguen which read: 'Wait for two days. Courage.'

'My whereabouts was reported by Albert Huet, a local bus driver and staunch Resistance man, to his leader, Captain Lucien Marzin of the Maquis. The following day, one of the bravest men I am ever likely to meet, arrived in his car, Dr Le Duc. After talking to me for a while he said he would return later, which he did, with a man known as 'Lulu'. At the Doctor's house I met Madame Le Duc and they took my photograph so I could be provided with false papers, the stamp for which Madame Le Duc had acquired when officials were looking the other way. I now became Pierre Floch, a student from Montpellier.

'I was then taken to the home of Captain Marzin at Villa Kerjoac. The household consisted of Mme Marzin, their son, daughter, grandfather and grandmother. The grandmother, Mme Boucherie, although bedridden, was invaluable as her bedroom looked out on to the front of the house and she was able to warn us of any approaching Germans. The plan was that I be got away by boat. Two boatbuilders, Ernest and Leon Sibiril, of Canterec, were planning to sail to England in one of their boats in a few days as one of the brothers had been condemned to death by the Germans. During the occupation they had built some ten boats and sent them to England. Each new boat being made in France had to be declared to the Germans but as each one the Sibirils finished was sailed, an old one was put in its place on the stocks and the Germans never spotted what was going on.

'I was taken to Lulu's house and spent three days there waiting for the launching which took place in the darkness of 31 October/1 November. It, in fact, fell off the ramp with a resounding crash but the noise of the sea seemed to drown the sound from the German sentry nearby. At about 1 a.m. on 1 November we set sail in the ship named *Requin* for England. She was about 24 feet long and had a sail and a motor. When we started it was quite calm but soon got rough and out of the 30 hour journey I spent 24 being sick. While I was being sick the two Sibirils calmly ate oysters! Near the Eddystone we were intercepted by a minesweeper and taken aboard.

'Before I had left France, I asked for a souvenir of the German Field Police whose job it was to try and catch me, so Dr Le Duc went down into the middle of Morlaix at night and with some difficulty tore from the wall a sign, about 2½ feet long, with the words "Feldgendarmerie" (Field Police) written upon it. This now resides in RAF Museum at Hendon. Mme Marzin would go into the local library and put in her bag all the books written in English, and then return them, without the library ever knowing. In my time with her I read all the books in English they had in the library.'

A message was sent to 263 Squadron on 1 November 1943, which read: 'Flight Sergeant Wood arrived in good health at Plymouth.' He was the first evader from 263 Squadron. Getting back somehow made up for the fact he had taken the CO's aircraft on this operation and had not brought it back!

'The Germans, when they found my borrowed aircraft named '*Lochinvar*', thought they were searching for a VIP as the aircraft had quite a few swastikas on the side which usually denotes an ace.'

Upon his return, a BBC radio message was sent for his helpers: 'The Pacific squalls have arrived' and later, for the benefit of the Marzin family, 'Have you got the beer for the postman?' Which had been a phrase George had learnt from a French phrase book while staying with the family.

In 1954 George Wood was ordained into the Church. Being saved when being hit on 23 September 1943 had a lot to do with this. He feels today he was saved for a purpose.

12.   Special Duties

When John Brough joined 138 Special Duties Squadron (the same squadron as Frank Griffiths) as a rear gunner in July 1943, he was 21. There were two Special Duties Squadrons, 138 and 161, working in conjunction with SOS and in great secrecy from Tempsford in Bedfordshire. Their role was carrying supplies to the Resistance in occupied countries and dropping and picking up agents there for resistance work. The squadrons first used Lysanders and Whitleys but by the time that Brough joined 138 Whitleys had been exchanged for Halifax bomber aircraft – modified by the removal of the mid-upper turret and with a trap door built in to the well of the aircraft.

The mission that John will never forget began at 7.20 p.m. on the night of 3 November 1943. They were bound for a drop somewhere in south-eastern France. They crossed the French coast at 6,000 feet and dropped to ground level to avoid enemy radar. As they approached the dropping zone, however, the weather deteriorated rapidly with low cloud and heavy rain. They made a number of runs, but could not locate the reception committee, so the pilot, Pilot Officer Hodges, decided to make one more run and then abort the mission. As he lined up for the run-in, however, there was a shudder, the aircraft stalled and crashed two miles from Marois in the department of the Ardèche. In the impact the rear turret and nose had broken away and John Brough was thrown clear.

'At this stage,' he recalls, 'I must have blacked out as the next thing I remember was coming to, lying on the side of a mountain. By a miracle I was unhurt. I scrambled down to the wreck of the aircraft which was about two or three hundred yards away down the hill. Pieces were scattered all the way down the mountain, but I was beaten back by the flames and the heat of the burning aircraft.'

The other members of the crew had all been killed in the crash. John blacked out once more, and when he came to again found he was lying in a stream, still on the mountain. There was nothing he could gain by remaining at the scene of the crash, so he made his way down the mountainside.

'At the bottom I spotted a French farmer, a M. Crozen, who took me into his cottage, where I met his wife and small child. My French was schoolboy style and he spoke no English but by sign language, which in these circumstances always seems to work, we communicated quite well.'

The farmer provided John with an unusual breakfast by RAF aircrew standards: bread and roasted walnuts. He then indicated that he should follow him to a small wood. Here he was to stay until dark, when the farmer would return. In the evening they returned to the cottage, where John was introduced to a lady – Mme Giraud – who said she could help him. She took him to her home in the village of Marcols-les-Eaux, and looked after him. Next day, she said, she would contact people to help him and that evening a Captain Faure and two of his men arrived by car.

They took him on to Valence, hurrying to arrive before curfew. The following day John was introduced to Mme Ayre, a Scot married to a Frenchman. She acted as interpreter, as the men wanted some questions answered. 'I told her that at this stage I could only divulge my name, rank and number.' The men were suspicious of John's bona fides as the Germans had found seven bodies in the aircraft, which was the normal crew for a Halifax. Where, they wanted to know, did John fit in, being the eighth? John was able to explain that on that night they had been carrying an extra man, Captain J.A. Estis of the USAAF, as second pilot. They radioed to London for confirmation and once this was received all was well. They told him that a pick-up flight was being organised to bring out two special passengers, and arrangements could be put in hand for him to accompany them.

'They got me civilian clothes,' he recalls, 'a blue sports jacket, grey flannel trousers, brown shoes and a black beret. The next day I was given a complete set of ID documents, travel vouchers and a ration book. I was taken around Valence to get used to having Germans around.'

Later John was taken by train to Lyon. It was an uneventful journey. His forged documents were checked at the barrier of the station at Lyon. They passed with flying colours. At the station he was met and taken by car to a Château near Lons-le-Saunier, run by three ladies, Mlles M. and E. Bergerot and Mlle Wurtz. He also met Raymond and Cecile Aubrac, and their three-year-old son Jean-Pierre. Raymond was the Resistance leader in the south of France. His wife was also in the Resistance, and carried out a daring rescue mission of over 70 Resistance fighters from prison, including her husband. She was Jewish which made this all the more dangerous.

The pick-up plan was put into action and a message was sent to London. The aircraft's arrival would be broadcast on the BBC French service. If the broadcast came on at 1.30, 7.30 and 9.30 then it meant that the aircraft was coming, if it was not broadcast three times, then it was not. On a few occasions it was broadcast once and even on one occasion twice, but not three times, and finally the plan was cancelled for the time being.

'I spent Christmas at the Château,' recalls John, 'but later went into the hills and spent some time with the Maquis. During this time I attended supply drops; it was strange seeing it from the ground and not in the air.'

On 4 February 1944, with John back at the Château, another pick-up plan was put into action, under the code name 'Bludgeon'. Unfortunately something went wrong with the instructions. When the pilot, Flight Lieutenant JR Affleck DFC, DFM, arrived there was no reception committee for him; it was elsewhere. Four days later it was once again set up, still under the code name 'Bludgeon', and on this occasion the message was received on three occasions, 1.30, 7.30 and 9.30, which meant the pick-up was on.

'About 10.30 p.m. we all made our way by car to the chosen field,' says John. 'Members of the Resistance, the local Gendarmerie and many helpers, arrived at the field and formed two lines holding pocket torches. In due course the aircraft arrived, a Hudson flown once again by Flight Lieutenant Affleck and he flashed down his signal, then made a circuit of the field. On his final approach, when a few hundred feet above the field, large landing lights were switched on, just long enough for Affleck to see the ground, then he was down.

He taxied the length of the field and turned and returned to the starting point, then swung the Hudson around ready for take-off. But the port wheel got stuck in boggy ground. Affleck revved for all he was worth but the aircraft was firmly embedded up to the axle. Horses and oxen were brought in, but their attempts to pull the aircraft out failed.'

The helpers then brought spades and dug a trench from the wheel of the aircraft, right out to the firmer ground. Meanwhile the aircraft's crew were burning anything that was secret, code books etc. They were working to a deadline, for Affleck had to leave the field by a set time in order to reach the French coast before the daylight. Fifteen minutes before zero hour they decided to make another attempt. The engines were started and the Hudson gradually eased itself out of the mud. The Aubracs, who were also coming to London with Brough, boarded the aircraft, Affleck revved the engines, and they set off down the field. Near the boundary mark in the field the aircraft hit a bump and bounced into the air at a speed of no more than 50 knots per hour, but with superb skill Affleck got the Hudson up, just skimming the trees as he did so. It was marvellous airmanship on his part.

The journey home was uneventful until they were about half an hour from the French coast when Mme Aubrac, who was nine months pregnant, became unwell. The pilot decided, as soon as they had crossed the coast, to radio ahead for an early landing at Tangmere, but later she recovered a little and they continued to Tempsford. When they arrived they were taken by bus to London, and here Brough left the Aubracs as he had to report to the Air Ministry. He wished them good luck; and they returned it.

'Later, years after the war,' John recalls, 'I found that my aircraft had hit a rock on the mountain and ploughed over the other side. The local people there have erected a plaque on the rock of Bourboulos in memory of the seven men in my crew who were killed. "During", the plaque reads, "an unknown mission in support of the Armies of Liberation, comrades of the French Resistance movement, for the life of France and the rebuilding of liberty." The bodies of the seven men were all buried in the local village cemetery at Marcols, but the body of Captain Estis was later exhumed and taken back to the USA. The other six, however, are still there and their graves tended by the locals. They are never without flowers.'

Cecile Aubrac had a baby girl after she left France. She had promised that if the baby was a boy she would name it Maquis, and if a girl Mitraillette, 'Little Machine Gun'. The baby was named Catherine Mitraillette Aubrac.

On 4 February 1944, the pilot of the Hudson, Flight Lieutenant John Robert Affleck, was recommended for the DSO. Included in his citation for this award was the 8 February mission.

13.   With the Maquis in the Snow

In July 1943, Pilot Officer Reg Lewis had just completed his tour of operations with 214 Squadron and had been recommended for the DFC. However, the completion of the tour meant the crew splitting up to go on various instructors' duties. In many ways these could be more dangerous than operations, since circuits and bumps with unknown qualities as pilots could be pretty dicey to say the least.

His pilot, Squadron Leader Thomas Cooke DFC AFC DFM, thought of a way to keep them together; to join one of the Special Duty Squadrons. They joined 138 Squadron at Tempsford, and after undergoing training in the art of dropping agents and supplies to the Resistance into enemy occupied territory, they started their new job in October. By November, Reg who was the navigator, had been promoted to flying officer and had been awarded the DFC that had been recommended in July.

That winter the weather was very bad, and by the time February arrived there was a back-log of agents waiting to be dropped. On 7 February 1944 the weather cleared a little and they were assigned to drop an Army captain on the outskirts of Marseille, a trip of 700 miles.

Reg was now 21 and so far Lady Luck had been with him and his crew. The Halifax II took off at 7.45, although the weather had deteriorated. There was a lot of cloud and they were not to see the ground again until they baled out. About an hour from the dropping area they developed engine trouble, then the starboard-inner engine suddenly caught fire. In the opinion of the flight engineer, Flying Officer Gornall, (who was on his 48th operation) it was caused by a cracked carburettor, as all the temperature and pressure gauges were normal. This was Reg's 41st operation and it 'certainly looked like being my last'. For Thomas Cooke it was his 63rd operation. They carried on but the plane then began to lose height since it was running on three engines and was rapidly icing up. The order was given to bale out.

Along with the wireless operator, bomb aimer and later the pilot, Reg left via the rear hatch. He came down in deep snow, while the aircraft crashed in the St Rambert d'Albon area, south of Châteauneuf d'Isère. He could hear dogs barking and people moving about, so after hiding his parachute, he hurried off until he came upon a solitary house. It was now about 1.30 a.m. on 8 February. At first he decided to continue as the occupants would be asleep, but then he returned as he could not find another house in the area. After hammering on the door many times he saw eventually one of the upstairs shutters being opened. An elderly woman, Mme Marie Girardin, looked out. She was shocked to see a man in the middle of the night dressed in flying kit, but she soon came down accompanied by her 14-year-old daughter. 'With the help of drawings and schoolboy French I made understand that I was a British airman,' he later said at debriefing. They decided he should stay the night and in the morning they would try to get him help.

The next day he was given a suit belonging to Mme Gilberte Pellerin-Girardin's husband, who was away. Her mother, Mme Girardin, had gone to get help from the local Resistance. He was given a bicycle and taken to the village of St Marcel. There the chemist, M. Chancel, was a Resistance leader as well as pharmacist. In the back room of the chemist's shop he met three of his crew, Robert Beattie, James Reed and Pilot Officer Bell. M. Chancel put them in touch with the Maquis and also introduced them to Peter J. Ortiz, an American Marine Corps captain, who was an SOE agent. He had his Marine Corps uniform with him and used to walk round in occupied France wearing it. When he was promoted to major his new insignia was dropped by air to him. He was to arrange their journey to Spain later.

They joined the Maquis in a small cabin in the snow-bound hills, and stayed for about three weeks. Then they were forced to leave when one of the young members of the Maquis became the worse for drink and boasted of the guests they had hidden in the hills. Later he was dealt with! Peter Ortiz took them to stay with a Mme Sambuc. There they remained for some three weeks in one room. Here Jacqueline Kern who was 22 and another niece, Ines, visited them as they were learning English. They were also couriers for the Resistance. Eventually they were taken to Valence, given railway tickets and told to travel to Carcassonne, a fairly large French town at the foot of the Pyrenees Mountains.

The train sped through the night with the four of them occupying different corners of the carriage, while pretending they did not know one another. By day break they stopped at Narbonne near the Mediterranean coast, and to their horror a detachment of German soldiers embarked. Some of them got into Reg's compartment and began to chat with the passengers, but luckily for the evaders did not try to engage them in conversation. This was easily their worst moment so far.

On arrival at Carcassonne they made their way to an address they had been given. They were fed and allowed to sleep till nightfall, then given a loaf of bread, a hunk of meat and a flask of wine and driven nearer the mountains. Then Reg recalls, 'We began to climb up steep and never ending slippery snow covered hills and then across the Pyrenees.' One of their guides was Antonio Guardia Socada. The peaks of the tallest mountains in the Pyrenees are 10,000 feet high, and all the time they had to be on the alert for German troops guarding the Spanish Frontier.

At last there came the point where they were told they were in Spain. It was a moment of great joy. All their effort in getting so far seemed now worth while. After a further day they reached a Spanish farm. From there they were taken by lorry to Barcelona, by car to Madrid, then on to Gibraltar, where they arrived on 11 April. From there they flew to Lyneham on the 12th. The other three members of the crew, including Squadron Leader Cooke, arrived at Gibraltar on 4 May and Whitchurch on the 5th. Reg discovered later, that the night after they came down a Hudson of 138 Squadron had come in to pick up another evader, Sergeant John Brough, and could have lifted them out also, if they had known. This would have meant they could have been back at Tempsford within hours of going missing. Instead it took some two months.

'In 1972,' Reg recalls, 'I re-visited France. I was determined to find the first house at which I had knocked, and the people who had helped me.' The lady who had looked out of her shuttered window was no longer there. Mme Girardin was, however, still living in the area, now 77 years old and in good health. In one farmhouse a family showed a set of overalls of the type worn by the agents he had dropped on missions. This pair belonged to François Cammaerts who was one of the chief Resistance leaders in the south of France. It was he they had tried to drop on 7 February 1944. No wonder his being delivered there was vital.

Along with Jacqueline Kern, Reg visited Mme Sambuc, also now 77, still very alert but very fragile, Jacqueline herself had not had an easy life, having contracted TB and been in hospital for some while. She was now working as a secretary in Nice, and it was here that Reg spent a week with her. The chemist, M. Chancel, had died in 1952. His widow proudly showed Reg a photograph of him being presented with the King's Medal for Courage, and also his Tedder Certificate, for all aspects of resistance work and evasion.

But the Chancels' story was a tragic one. On 15 June 1944 the Germans, having learned of his connection with the Resistance, had come to arrest him. He, of course, had gone, but in reprisal they took his 13-year-old daughter and raped her, but then set her free. Not content with that they returned, took her, once again abused her. On this occasion she succumbed to their terrible treatment and died.

14.   The Last to Cross

The first crossing of the Pyrenees by the Comète line was on 17 October 1941, when the first three men, Privates Jim Cromar, Bob Conville, and Alan Cogan were taken over by Andrée de Jongh. (The first man from the RAF had been Jack Newton, whom we shall meet later.) After Andrée de Jongh's arrest, the line continued under the Baron Jean Greindl and then Baron Jean-François Nothomb, and the last five men were taken over on 4 June 1944. Three were USAAF and two RAF, Pilot Officer Len Barnes and Sergeant Ron Emeny.

Pilot Officer Barnes' Lancaster, ND530 of 630 Squadron, had been shot down by a Me110 night fighter on the night of 15 March 1944, west of Reims on the return run from bombing Stuttgart. Five of the crew baled out, the others died. Barnes was the only one to survive and evade successfully. As he later reported to MI9 on his return:

'I landed in a field about four miles north-east of Dravegny. I buried my parachute, Mae West, harness and the tops of my flying boots, and started to walk south-west by my compass. A mile further on I saw a parachute hanging in a tree. I dragged it clear and buried it, but I forgot to look for the name on the 'chute.

'A short while later I reached Dravegny and walked through the town. I found some water and drank it, but I did not stop to fill my bottle, as a dog started to bark and I thought I had better get away at once. I continued across the fields to Cohan which I reached about 0530 hours (16Mar). In the distance I saw a farmer leading his horses towards a farm. I waited until he had gone into the house, when I entered a barn and hid under the hay.

'At 1030 hours, when I thought there was no one about, I came out of my hiding place and took out my maps. I was looking at them when a man appeared and, as he had seen me, I declared myself to him and asked for help. He brought me food and drink and allowed me to bathe my eye, which I had hurt as I baled out. Two more men appeared and showed me my position on the map. I returned to the barn, and at 1500 hours a young girl, who could speak English, came to see me. She questioned me closely and examined my kit. She left shortly afterwards, saying that she would send a friend to see me that evening. That evening a man came for me, and from this point my journey was arranged for me.'

It sounds simple put that way. It was not.

The man who came for him turned out to be an ex-French Army captain. He kitted Barnes out with the de rigueur beret and an overcoat and fortified by sips from his companion's bottle of whisky, he accompanied the captain to what was to become his home for the next ten days. The farm belonged to Pierre Martin and he was marooned here, with what seemed like an endless diet of red wine. He was taken to see the remains of his Lancaster P-Peter, and his emotions can be imagined as he saw the shattered plane. The two gunners had been buried, Pierre told him, at a local cemetery. The reason he was being kept so close to the site of the crash was that it was hoped that the Germans would by now be spreading their search area further afield. Unfortunately they began to retrace their steps, and Barnes' position became precarious. It was time to move.

His next stop, after a narrow squeak with a German patrol, was in the nearby village of Fère-en-Tardenois, in the home of a member of the Maquis, the French sabotage and Resistance organisation. He stayed with the Coigne family for nearly six weeks. His presence inadvertently became known to the neighbours, but no harm was done.

While he was there, the Maquis became involved in a shoot-out with the Germans when the RAF flew over to drop supplies to the Maquis. Because of the tense situation Barnes was taken to a large house nearby where another evader, Bill Jacks, was already hiding. He was there a week, after one night sleeping in the woods with only wild pigs for company. Then disguised as a butcher, Barnes was moved on to Paris, together with Jacks.

Here they were moved from house to house, and then separated. Len's new safe house had a very special owner. '*La Petite Souris*' Virginia Hall, wife of Philippe D'Albert Lake, whom we met earlier and shall meet again in connection with Operation Sherwood.

The usual rigorous interrogation to avoid plants followed, and Barnes met another evader who lived but two minutes from his own home in the East End – Ron 'Curly' Emeny. They discovered that Comète was looking after some 20 Allied airmen in Paris, waiting to 'post' them on. It was decided that five would leave for Spain the next day: Len and Ron; and three USAAF airmen, Lt-Colonel Thomas 'Speedy' Hubbard, Major Donald Willis and Second Lt Jack Cornett. Their journey, though not without its dangers, was successful and as they crossed the border a Spanish farmer brought them good news. It was 6 June and the Allies had invaded Normandy.

But even in Spain they were not safe. They were lodged in a farmhouse but discovered that they were uncomfortably close to the Spanish border still. The children of the house had been ordered by their mother not to tell the airmen where they were, which Barnes found puzzling. Very puzzling. He was determined to move on, for he had a feeling that everything was not as it should be. He was right! The five airmen left without their guides, ignoring their frantic shouts to return. They found out later that the guides had been intending to hand them back to the Germans. The reward? A sack of corn for each betrayed pilot! Later Don Willis wrote in his diary: 'We had been saved by the "impetuous Englishman" who wanted to keep on the move.'

15.   'My House is Your House'

Flying Officer Bill Alliston hit the ground hard. His doomed 10 Squadron Halifax bomber had been attacked by a night fighter on the night of 10 April 1944 knocking out and setting fire to the starboard engines. A shell had burst in his mid-upper turret tearing half his flying helmet away while the straps were pulled around his throat choking him, but he managed to pull it back onto his head, relieving the pressure on his throat. He remembers:

'I climbed out of my turret and staggered towards the nose of the aircraft. I could see the starboard wing on fire and the pilot fighting with the controls to enable us all to get out, although he himself had little chance. I was in fact the fifth man to bale out; the only two left in the aircraft were the pilot, Flight Lieutenant Barnes DFC, and the flight engineer Sergeant Matthews. I learned later that Barnes and Matthews were killed in the crash; the remainder got out okay. Two were POWs. Sergeant Howell, the rear gunner, got out but was later found to be dead. The other two plus myself were on the run. We were on this occasion carrying an extra man as a second pilot.

'When I hit the ground for some reason I had my tongue out and bit it hard and it soon began to swell up like a balloon. I felt I was finished and just lay there waiting to die. I thought my back was broken, but suddenly my chute, which was still spread out along the field I had landed in, began to pull me along the ground. I collected my thoughts and began to haul it in. We had been told to bury our chutes in our escape lectures and they made it seem like a piece of cake, but when opened the chute was like a bell tent. I had hurt my right leg which was stiff and swollen and my left eye was closed but I began to crawl on all fours across the field and across a lane and into another field, and so on until I had crossed some four fields in all. I was making for a fire I could see ahead, which must be our crashed aircraft.

'While I was resting in a wood a figure came towards me. It turned out to be our navigator, Flying Officer Maurice Steel, whom we called 'Junior' as he was only 21 whereas I was 32. As he reached me, the bombs in the aircraft went off with a terrific bang. We had, in fact, come down about three miles apart, but strangely, within a couple of hours, we had found each other. In coming out of the aircraft I had lost my left boot and sock, so I made a makeshift boot out of strips from my Mae West and, because of this our subsequent progress was slow.

'In the area of Berzy-le-Sec, where we had come down, we came across a house and knocked on the door, and were greeted by a man, his wife and three daughters. They were a little suspicious, not surprising, as they were already sheltering our wireless operator, Flight Lieutenant Johnny Collar, who was in the barn at the back of the farm house. We were given coffee and the lady of the house, on seeing my damaged eye, got some warm water and ripped a piece of material off her nightdress and began to bathe it. She also did the same with my leg, in which I had a piece of shrapnel. She made the wound bleed which, later I was told by a doctor had helped a great deal. When I fell asleep the lady cradled my head.

'Johnny Collar then came in. He was the Signals Leader on 10 Squadron and had been blown out of the nose of the aircraft when it blew up. He said that we should be on our way, as the family could not possibly feed all three of us for any length of time. And so we set off hoping to get to Paris.

'That night we hid in a copse and when I awoke all I could see was what I thought was a pair of jackboots, but then I saw it was a man in civilian clothes. He was holding the hand of a small child. I put out my hand to him which he took. I then said in sign language, 'Don't tell that we are here.' He replied in sign language to say he wouldn't. He then said, 'Polonais, Polonais', telling us he was a Pole. However, Johnny did not seem to trust him, so I warned the man that if he talked we would cut his throat, and ran my finger across my throat. He understood I think, and I then gave him some money which he did not want to take but I insisted. He said he would be back at 6 p.m. True to his word, he did come back with coffee in a flask, cake, bread, some Salami sausage and six boiled eggs. Also he had with him a pair of lady's Wellington boots with a heel, I managed but only just to get them on. They were skin tight on me, but better than nothing at all.

'That night we slept in a Dutch barn. At 6 a.m. we awoke and saw a man walking along so we called him. He came over, and asked "*Aviateurs anglais?*" We said yes and he kissed us on both cheeks, then said he would help us.

'The area we were in was Armentières. He said he would lock us in a hut and bring someone to see us. Junior was not keen on being locked up so I asked the man if he would swear to come back and not give us away? He said he would, going down on his knees to endorse his promise. Then Johnny said to Junior, who spoke French, "Tell him we trust him." He then threw his arms around me and said how pleased he was to be trusted by English officers. We were then locked in the hut and off he went. When the door opened later there stood à tall man, named Labrevois, with his son Bernard. Taking us in his lorry, lying on the floor covered with sacks. Labrevois took us to his home. In her kitchen we met Madame Labrevois who was a very tall lady. She flung her arms about us and said, "War! To think that tonight three wives or three mothers mourn three husbands or sons". She then took hold of her young son and said, "I hope it is over before he is old enough to have to take part".

'She then began to wash my face and then a meal was prepared for us by her daughter, Michelaine. They had a radio in the farm which of course was illegal. It was in a cupboard and after eating we suddenly heard "Bom, bom, bom, boom" (Beethoven's Fifth Symphony) (three dots, one dash, morse code for V – V for Victory) coming over the air and then the BBC news in French and then in English: "This is London calling". To hear this warmed me greatly, I did not feel so far from home and safety at that moment.

'On the fifth day a doctor was sent for to take a look at me, but as the Germans kept a strict check on the movements of doctors a plan was arranged that the little boy, François, would go in the street with a bandage on his head and say he had fallen down, and that a doctor was coming to see him. When he arrived he came straight up to see us. He managed to get my left eye open with oil in a teaspoon, warmed over a match and used another matchstick to roll my eyelid back and get it open, before cleaning me up. Apparently a piece of jagged metal had hit my eye and closed it. He then said a good job had been done on my leg. My tongue, would soon go down and he gave me some oil to bathe it with.

'We were then moved to a disused farm house as it was getting a little dangerous in the area where we were staying. We stayed for ten days. It was a lonely place. We could just about look out of one small window upstairs and took it in turn to keep watch. We coveted our watch periods at this window and would get very upset if one of the others pinched more than his allotted time ....

'Then a vet came to see us. He took us in a lorry to Soissons to meet a man whose bravery cannot remain untold, Maurice Dupré. We lived in a shelter at the bottom of his garden for no less than five weeks, and then we were taken on a food relief lorry to Paris. Johnny Collar stayed on to help the Maquis with a radio that was playing up, but while he was waiting to get to Paris the family he was with were arrested. He, however, escaped through a window and hid in a wood.

'In Paris we were taken to a block of flats by a group of medical students who had formed their own Resistance group. They told us we would be taken by ambulance to a hospital where we'd meet other Resistance people. So, Junior and I were put on stretchers, covered with blankets, and the ambulance hurtled through Paris at great speed to the hospital. Here, after the usual cross-examination, he was told "Flying Officer Alliston, we will do everything we can do to help you".

'A girl of about 18, named Mimi who was a nurse, then said she would take us on the Metro to her flat. The Metro was full of Germans and it was a frightening experience. Her flat was very grand and I asked her how she had such a lovely flat at her age, she said, "I was married today. Today is my wedding day", then her husband came in, Yves Allain. He spoke good English and welcomed us there. So there was I, playing gooseberry on their wedding day and honeymoon. I told him this and he said, "Sir, my house is your house". That very night, his wedding night, he was going out to help, with others using torches, to guide a Lysander or Hudson in, carrying an agent.

'We were then taken in the usual manner to the South of France and then over the Pyrenees by a Basque guide Robert Piton. Suddenly he turned round and announced, "You are now in Spain". Later we were arrested by the Guardia Civil and taken to prison. I was taken to hospital with a fever and spent seven days recovering. From here we were taken in an Embassy car, a Humber Snipe, accompanied by Captain Creswell (code name Monday) to the Embassy in Madrid, where we met Sir Samuel Hoare, the Ambassador.

'From here it was onto Gibraltar, as many before and after, would go and then on to the UK. In London we were interrogated and then sent to Blackpool to a re-habilitation centre to put on weight and generally become normal again. I spent the next three months there, and then came my survivor's leave.

'Two days after we had left, Maurice Dupré in whose garden we'd lived, was arrested. Johnny Collar was there at the time but escaped. Maurice ended up in Dachau where he was tortured and later died of typhus. Not one word did he utter in all that time of whom he had worked with or whom he helped. The true sign of a great and brave man. In the meantime John Collar reached Paris and was there when French troops liberated the City on 21 August 1944.'

In December 1944 Bill was recommended for the DFC; the award was chiefly for his successful evasion, the full story of which was in the recommendation for this award. Post-war, Bill became a very active member of the Escaping Society and in 1973 its Chairman, and served in this capacity until 1975. In 1980 very suddenly, and at the age of 68, Bill died. He was an avid member of the RAFES Speakers' Panel.

16.   Operation Sherwood

With the planned forthcoming invasion of France, MI9 were faced with a number of additional problems. Hitherto, evaders and evasion lines had been almost entirely dependent on the rail network to convey 'parcels' through occupied France to the Spanish frontier, or to the Brittany escape point. Now, with a concentrated bombing campaign directed at lines of communication, in order to hinder German troop movements and supplies, it was clear that other arrangements had to be made for sheltering escapees and evaders until, it was hoped, Allied advancing forces could liberate them.

The plan concocted by MI9 was called 'Operation Sherwood', for, like Robin Hood and his Merrie Men, evaders were to be hidden deep in a forest. This was the forest of Fréteval, between Châteaudun and Vendôme, south-east of Paris and east of Orléans. Another such camp was set up in Brittany near Rennes, and evaders from Brussels were to be sheltered in the Ardennes. MI9's main organiser for 'Sherwood' was the Belgian Baron, Jean de Blommaert. As Airey Neave, the MI9 organiser related, 'in *Saturday at MI9* his task was not easy, for he had not only to recruit support from villages nearby to Fréteval, on whom he would depend for supplies, but to persuade the organisers and helpers of the evasion lines still running, notably Comète and Shelburne (Brittany) that they should co-operate with the scheme, rather than continue to use their existing networks.' Another problem was to persuade the local Resistance that there should be no sabotage work near the forest in order not to draw German attention to it. The site had been planned with a view to avoiding its being in the line of any retreating forces.

In April, de Blommaert was parachuted back into France to begin his task. Also parachuted into France was Squadron Leader Lucien Boussa, a Belgian serving in the RAF,* to organise the camp locally. He was accompanied by his radio operator François Toussaint.

'On June 6th, the day of the invasion,' Airey Neave relates in *Saturday at MI9*, 'Allied airmen were moved into the forest and the camp began.' However, some of the first inhabitants had been waiting in the area for some weeks. One of them was

---

* Boussa shot down two German aircraft during the invasion of his country in 1940. Joining the RAF in England he shot down a further 5 enemy aircraft by the end of 1943, flying with 350 (Belgian) Sqdn, on Spitfires.

Sergeant Charles Foster Weir, from Midlothian. He was a mid-upper gunner in a Stirling of 218 Squadron who took off from Woolfox Lodge on a bombing mission to Beaumont on 1 May 1944. The Stirling was attacked by two Focke-Wulf 190's and the tail unit set on fire. The Australian pilot, Flying Officer Noel Eliot, ordered, 'Abandon aircraft,' and Weir baled out near La Borde. His parachute became entangled in the trees and it took him about an hour to get himself free. After hiding the parachute, he started to walk north. He walked for several hours before sheltering in a barn. The first Frenchman he saw did not answer his request for help, but later a boy from the house, took him inside. From there on he was in the hands of the Resistance, and became one of the early inmates of the Fréteval camp. In his memoirs Weir recalls his arrival at Fréteval:

'I was glad when after creeping along without making it too obvious we approached a large, dark, ominous looking forest. Without any preamble we entered it and plunged along a faint but clearly discernible track. We hadn't gone far when several men materialised from behind trees and bushes and greeted us. There were a few hurried whispered introductions and as we were led deeper into the forest our guide departed whence he'd come.

'About fifty yards farther on still following the narrow path we entered a small clearing. On one side of it stood a weird and wonderful contraption which proved to be a charcoal burning portable grate while, on the other side, there was some sort of shelter formed by draping a tarpaulin sheet over two or three strong crosspoles affixed to suitable trees. The sides had been pegged to the forest floor so I supposed it could rightly be called a tent, and this proved to be our new home.

'As it was quite late in the afternoon when we got there and the thick canopy of the leaves shut out even more of the light we were invited to inspect our new abode and while this was taking place a coarse canvas sack was given to each of us with the instructions to fill it from a pile of straw we could see there. When this was done we were handed a blanket each and allocated a place in the shelter where we could lay out our mattresses.

'We were awake early. The routine of the camp appeared to be regulated to conform with the day and night. That is, we arose when daylight broke and we went to bed not long after it was dark. There was an excellent reason for this, of course. There were several paths through the forest although only two or three were used to any great extent. One had to keep to those paths too, there were very few places where one could take an independent line and not to be torn and scratched by a thick, almost impenetrable profusion of bramble or wild rose bushes. We learned this early on. After breakfast that first morning, fried eggs with bread washed down with a passable coffee, we were taken to the spring ....'

The problem of organisation in the camp grew greater as the numbers increased. It eventually grew to a grand total of 152 men. The main problem was food. A former gendarme with the code name André, whose real name was M. Omer Jubault, had already obtained the help of a miller, M. Ciron, to provide flour to the bakers, and organised meat, milk, butter and eggs from farms situated within a 30 kilometre radius of the camp. After some twelve days about fifteen tents were already up and cooks organised, the cooking being done with charcoal, so as to eliminate any tell-tale smoke.

Each day the tents were recovered with fresh branches to avoid the camp being detected from the air. Once a week a barber, M. Barillet, came to cut hair where necessary, and this, as Weir recalls, proved a great morale booster. What to do with their time proved a problem. Look-out positions had to be manned on a three watch system of two hours on and four hours off. But Weir recalls his first watch graphically:

'In the cathedral stillness of the night every little sound appeared to be magnified a hundred fold. As none of us had had a very restful sleep the previous night, it was decided to institute a three watch system of two hours on watch and four hours off. My watch, as I recall it began at midnight and although my pilot spent some of it awake to keep me company those two hours dragged. If nothing else it gave me a wonderful insight into nature at its rawest. Because of the thickness of the undergrowth the forest abounded with life and most of it, or so it seemed to me, came alive at night. I didn't have to prick my ears to follow the unseen drama taking place close by. First I would hear a slight movement as some predator eased softly in search of prey. Occasionally I would hear the frantic flurry as some intended victim sensing the nearness of the hunter would scramble away to a safer place. Once or twice the victim wasn't so lucky as evidenced by the squeals of the latter when the predator got to it. There isn't a sound more harrowing to the ears than the scream of a rabbit when the stoat gets to it. If nothing else it eased the tension and lessened the strain of constant listening. If the animals couldn't conduct their life and death struggle for survival in absolute silence there was little chance of a human being approaching us without us having ample warning. I was glad when that night watch was over.'

As the numbers of men began to increase, strained relations resulted, as Charles Weir recalls:

'It was about this time we had the election. Yes, an election in the heart of enemy-occupied territory. From what I understood at the time the French were a little unhappy at the internal organisation of the camp. Further, I don't think they, or their masters back in London had envisaged quite so many of us being collected and taken to the forest. It was becoming unwieldly too, a logistical nightmare for those who had to supply and feed us. On top of that there was some dissent within the camp. I don't suppose this was unforeseen. Crammed together, a large group of men especially from two different armed services, where a certain rivalry was known to exist, and all the ingredients of trouble are there. Curiously enough, although there was a huge preponderance of Americans amongst our members it wasn't from that source the trouble emanated. While there had been some bickering between the two factions and on one occasion, blows, they got on reasonably well with each other. It was antagonism created by one or two of the RAF members which created the discord. They seemed to feel that their seniority in rank as well as their length of stay in the forest gave them privileges not accorded to the rest of us. I hadn't any views on the subject but there were many who had and it was decided that a change of leadership was needed. What they wanted was a man, not necessarily an officer, whom the majority respected and were willing to acknowledge as the final arbiter within the framework laid down by the Resistance. I expected an American to be elected because they had an overall majority in the camp so I was surprised and pleased when an Australian, my own pilot, was elected almost unopposed. He wasn't a particularly forceful man but he had a way about him which defied non-cooperation; the "right man for the job" as one of the Americans put it. At least he commanded by the wishes of the vast majority and not through some minor clique.'

After some while, it was decided to create a second camp, those who wished to remain where they were, could do so, or those who wished to move on were escorted away to form the new camp. By this time there were 25 tents, and the new camp was to be ten kilometres away, at a place called Richeray. Jean de Blommaert took command of it, and with him went Sergeant Gordon Hand, who had been an air gunner with 432 Squadron and had been shot down by a fighter on 9 May 1944. He recalls that the number two camp was a much better site than camp number one, with a slope down to a small stream – a great asset. They cut down some small trees to make tables of about ten foot long with seats attached. A cook house was formed, along with a platform in the stream which facilitated washing for personnel, and a boon for cleaning and storage of the meat which was brought in. Most meals were of beans and bread, and a hard boiled egg. This luxury was for those suffering from the need 'to visit the latrine too often!', as Hand puts it.

MI9 was now organising parachute drops, and Hand recalls one Halifax dropping containers with boots, booze, bug powder, bombs for the local partisans, small suitcases of money, and printed invasion money. This was in case of emergency after the invasion had taken place, if something went awry with the liberation plans. Sometimes there was an alert. Although the Germans did not come into the forest, they would machine gun the paths as a matter of course. During their time in camp

a Golf Club was started and tournaments organised, the balls
and clubs fashioned out of wood. Hospital tents were erected
where the ill and wounded could be cared for, by airmen with
some idea of hospital work. A Dr Teyssier came regularly to
give treatment, and to have serious cases evacuated to a secret
hospital, run by a widow, Mme Despres. On one occasion one
of the helpers who was escorting five airmen, Madame Virginia
d' Albert Lake, (Virginia Hall, whom we met earlier) who was
an American by birth and with her husband Philippe belonged
to the famous Comète network, was intercepted by German
Police. The evading airmen managed to escape and arrived at
the camp successfully. Madame Lake whose accent betrayed
her origins was arrested, but not before swallowing a
compromising document showing the local Maquis the route
to follow and situation of camp number one. After many
concentration camps she ended up at Ravensbrück, where she
nearly died of starvation. Fortunately she survived the war.

Once her arrest became known the camp was alerted and the
airmen got ready to flee to pre-arranged meeting places. In the
home of the forester M. Hallouin which was near camp number
one, his wife prepared a big fire in the chimney place which
she was going to light if the Germans arrived, to act as a signal
indicating danger.

Thoughts of escape, without waiting for liberation, eventually entered their minds. Weir decided against it, but two
Americans decided to go, taking two bicycles from a nearby
village. Their escape caused a furore, not only because of the
theft of the bicycles, a valuable commodity, from people who
were helping them, but because if they were captured they
endangered the whole camp. But liberation was not far off as
Charles Weir recalls:

'We had been expecting rescue for some days before it finally
came. From our position in the forest we saw many signs that
our stay in the forest was coming to an end, but the fates
conspired to tantalise us. Often during the day we could hear
the sounds of distant gunfire but it was the night that excited us
most for we could not only hear it more clearly, but on
occasions see the gunflashes lighting up the sky to the west. The

temptation to desert the forest and go to meet them was almost overwhelming but we resisted it. Commonsense dictated that it would be foolish to risk capture at this stage when all we had to do was wait a few more days and our position would be overrun by the Allied armies.

'That those few days might be a few more than any of us believed was brought home to us when one of the lookout positions reported the passage of a squadron of German tanks moving westward along the narrow road to the south of the forest .... We could imagine what might easily happen if the Germans chose to defend the forest to the westwards of us ....'

In MI9, Airey Neave was detailed to organise and lead the liberation of the camps. From Le Mans he tried to organise transport and liaise with the Americans, who were planning an advance perilously close to the forest. He had the luck to run into an SAS Squadron whose help he enlisted for the liberation. But they were dependent on US transport, and the American authorities adamantly refused to loan the required lorries. Thus the liberation was delayed and, dispirited and angered, some evaders broke cover and celebrated with local girls. The risks of a backlash from the Germans were great, but in the event, Charles Weir recalls:

'The arrival of our rescuers was something of an anti-climax, at least it was to me. I was in the camp at the time. I recall the people manning the post to the north of us running in excitedly to demand we come and watch the fireworks. We did. When I arrived at the post I was greeted with a dull thud. I glanced in the direction of the pointed fingers and there, in the distance, in the direction of where we knew an airfield lay, a huge cloud of smoke was climbing rapidly into the clear blue sky. Like everybody else I scanned the sky eagerly for a sight of the aeroplanes which were inflicting the damage but we didn't see a solitary one ....

'I think it was the following day the Americans arrived. It was a peculiar convoy they brought with them too. Several jeeps, trucks and rather decrepit buses. With their usual aplomb they entered the camp and immediately began distributing from a pile of cartons they'd brought with them. I found myself clutching a box of K rations and a whole carton of Chesterfields. It was almost overwhelming. For weeks and weeks I had rolled cigarettes, when I could get them, from the butts of other cigarettes, now here I was with a whole carton of cigarettes. It was almost too good to be true, so I smoked a couple, one after the other, while I still had the chance. As one of my friends remarked, rather wryly I thought but appropriately as he enjoyed his cigarette too, "Thank God it was the Americans who arrived to get us. If that had been the British it would have been one cigarette between two!" I think it is fair to say his words accurately summed up what happened during the few days afterwards.'

When they were handed over to their own troops at Bayeux, they were treated with some indifference. They insisted on delousing them, much to their indignation since they had been able to keep themselves clean while in the forest. Despite, by now, obviously having enormous stocks of equipment, all they could manage to issue them with was an Army battledress, a pair of army pattern boots, RAF gaiters, an RAF shirt without collar and of course an RAF cap. Charles Weir recalls with some feeling:

'Our dress set us up for nicely for the Military Police, when they turned us loose for the evening! Before the evening was over I think we must have met half the Military Police in Bayeux.'

Each year at Fréteval, there is a ceremony attended by the men and women of the Resistance, who gather outside the village hall at Villebout for a short march to the little village church. They hold a service and afterwards they go to the forest. To commemorate the camp in the forest they have erected a monument almost exactly at the spot where the inmates had a lookout point. There, floral tributes are laid in memory of those who stayed there and later returned to operations, only to give their lives later in air battles over Germany.

An association was formed by the camp's founder, Captain Jean de Blommaert, for all the men who had been in Fréteval forest between 9 June – 13 August 1944, when the camp was liberated by the American 3rd Army.

17.   'I Never Saw a Thing'

On the night of 3 May 1944, 17 Lancasters of 460 Squadron set off from RAF Binbrook to attack Mailly-le-Camp, in France, a large camp known to be used by the Germans for the training and reinforcement of front line Panzer units. In one of the Lancasters was 19-year-old rear gunner Sergeant Bryan Morgan, who had been in the RAF for just under two years. They had reached the area of Châlons-sur-Marne, and Bryan was watching for the approach of an enemy 'plane, or, worse still, a stream of tracer which would mean they were being attacked. The pilot's voice broke through his concentration: 'Twelve minutes to the target, extra sharp watch, rear gunner!' Bryan recalls:

'We were hit amidships; I never saw a thing. Somebody, I'll never know who, screamed through the intercom – "We're on fire." I turned my head and peered through the small observation window – whoever had said that wasn't kidding! At the first glance I realised nothing could save the aircraft. The interior was a mass of flames. I searched frantically for my parachute. As suddenly as it came the panic left me, I smiled, realising it was no longer a useless piece of extra baggage, but a life-saver.'

According to the book you have to ask the pilot's permission to bale out but in the circumstances Bryan decided to forget it. He opened the turret doors and lifted his feet high above the gun's control column so as not to catch his feet after leaving the aircraft.

'At this instant of "glorious" parting, the aircraft disintegrated. One wing tore past my head like a flaming rocket. I was spinning like a top and at the same time losing all sense of direction.' He recalls saying to himself, 'Pull yourself together, open the white umbrella, there's a good boy!' 'I pulled the handle and waited – a jerk and I was the right way up. I looked down; what was that long silver streak in the grey darkness there? As it came nearer, it became a river, then a bridge was somewhere beneath me, my feet touched the road and I had visions of doing somersaults, instead the impact was

less than that of jumping off a doorstep. With horror I saw that
the road was the bridge!' It was then that he heard the thud of
marching feet. He turned and saw six men marching away
some 50 yards to his right, men with helmets well down over
their ears – Germans!

He tried frantically to recall the lectures he'd half-dozed
through on how to evade. He could only remember that
bridges should be avoided. 'There seemed to be one way out,'
he recalled – 'over the side and into the river. Although my
family from far back all seemed to join the Navy, I hated the
water. Fear welled up inside me and made me feel momentarily
sick. First I must get rid of the parachute, and there appeared
to be only one way to accomplish this, so gathering it up in my
arms I dropped it over the bridge hoping that the weight of the
harness would sink it …. The sight of that swirling water didn't
encourage me but there being no alternative I reached up and
climbed on the low parapet surrounding the bridge and with a
quick look in both directions closed my eyes and jumped, feet
first, into the water.'

He went down like a stone, and as he surfaced again, was hit
on the back of the neck by the bow of a moored barge. Soaking
wet, he made his way ashore. 'Then without any warning, the
moon disappeared and it began to rain hard. The rain made
me feel safer. There was a grey anonymity in the rain. In the
sunshine you felt people were looking at you. They had time to
look and you stood out clearly, in the rain they were busy
keeping dry and they didn't look at you so directly.'

Three hundred yards ahead he saw a large farmhouse.
When he got to the door he heard French voices within. This
encouraged him to knock on the door. It flew open and there
stood a very large man. In pidgin French Bryan managed to tell
him who he was. 'His vast hand came out and gripped me by
the shoulder and pulled me into the kitchen – the large oaken
door was slammed shut and bolted. Immediately, as if by a
given signal the room was filled by five more men who had
been hidden from view as I stood in the doorway.

'The big man came and patted me all over (obviously they
had American films in France too) then said in good English,

"You will be quite safe here provided we are satisfied that you are what you say you are. We are the Maquis." He then left the room to get his daughter Jacqueline (later to be murdered in a most unpleasant way by the local Gestapo, when caught carrying messages to and from the local Maquis HQ which for two years had been situated above a café and next door to the Gestapo HQ), a delightful young Amazon of some eighteen summers – a true daughter of her father, but much better proportioned. Jackie then supplied me with some old clothes into which I changed instantly. It wasn't until then that I realised how soaked I really was.' Bryan's clothes seemed to weigh a ton – those of us who have been exposed to rain and gone home and changed in front of a warm fire well realize what a morale booster it is to be warm and dry again.

'Jackie who couldn't speak a word of English (not that it mattered in her case!) but could cook like a dream, made a magnificent omelette as only the French can!'

The farm belonged to M. Raymond Champenois, who had been wounded in WW1. The big man's name was Pierre. He asked Bryan if he would stay a little while as they were going to join their group of about 30 strong.

'Next morning we set out in two Citroens for the forest – I found a large scale Michelin map in the car and noticed they would be passing through two villages to arrive at their destination. As German patrols were not unknown, even in the villages – I wondered how they would maange. I soon found out!'

They stopped short of the village and one of the men walked in. His job was to ask the villagers if any Germans were about and if not he returned to the car. The first village was clear, so when the man returned they made Bryan sit in the middle of the back seat, flanked by two men with Sten-guns. The windows were wound down, and the front passenger sat with a revolver in one hand and the Maquis flag in the other – this he held out of the window. Then into the village, with horns blaring and tyres squealing to a halt in the square, then out everyone jumped, guns flashing, and stood guard at each corner of the car. The villagers loved this open show of defiance and came running out of their houses shouting 'The Maquis' at the top of their voices.

'I was introduced as 'the English Courier' which was a general excuse for having my hand pumped and face embraced by anything from two hundred to three hundred villagers. The champagne (all stamped 'for the victorious German Army') flowed and I personally ended the day considerably the worse for wear! This way it took five days to cover 31 miles but as Pierre said 'as long as we arrive in the end.'

Bryan's next safe house was in la Chaussée-sur-Marne, owned by André Etchegoimbery. Here he met his bomb aimer, Len Williams, again and they stayed until 23 May, when they were passed on to a farm at Le Fresne-sur-Moivre. They were hidden in a barn across the road from the farm, and were fed by Hélène, the daughter of the Jeanson family.

They were told that in the next village their navigator, Flight Sergeant Orbin, was being hidden, but they never did meet up with him, although Len met him later in Paris.

They stayed until 30 August, and as Bryan recalls: 'Some of the time we lived in the woods where one member of the group was very good at trapping rabbits. The group also included a Russian who had escaped from a work-party in Eastern Germany and walked right across to France.

'I became ill and was now down to 7 stone. Every gland in my body was swollen and I was having difficulty walking, and before I became too ill I left the group to try and obtain medical help. However, I became so weak that I had to give up my quest and went to another farm, where these good people looked after me. After about two weeks there, I could hear the sound of gunfire and my helper told me that the Germans were retreating. On the following day she rushed into the bedroom in the middle of the morning indicating that she had seen American tanks in the village. I asked her if she could find a vehicle with a Red Cross on the side and about an hour later there was a sound of heavy boots in the kitchen, the door opened and in came two American GIs. I hardly felt the hands of the kindly US Army Medic who lifted me on to a stretcher, then on to the back of his Jeep, and so to the Field Hospital and

England. I remained in an American hospital for six weeks having also contracted severe dermatitis and scabies.'

Len Williams arrived in the UK on 6 September, having made his way with the US forces to Paris. Four of the crew had died in the aircraft when it crashed and are buried at Châlons-sur-Marne.

The Jeanson family still live in Le Fresne and are now great grandparents in their 80's, Bryan visited them in 1983 for their 60th wedding anniversary.

The efforts that Raymond Champenois made in WW2, on top of his WW1 wounds, made it necessary later for his legs to be amputated. He was placed on the grants list of the RAF Escaping Society and provided with a wheelchair to enable him to get about his farm.

Of the force sent out to Mailly on 3 May 1944, 49 did not return, and five of these aircraft were from 460 Squadron.

18.   D-Day Evasion

On 6 June 1944, the day well known as D-Day, Flight Lieutenant Gordon Thring was detailed as part of the spearhead for the invasion. In Stirling 'E' for Easy and one of the eighteen aircraft of 620 Squadron, they were to tow gliders of the 6th Airborne Division to the Caen area to reinforce troops dropped the previous night. His air gunner was Flying Office Gerry McMahon who had already completed one tour of bomber operations with 97 Squadron, and had been awarded the DFM. He was the ideal man to have in the rear of the aircraft.

The evening before they had dropped a full complement of paratroopers safely on target, and despite being hit by flak landed at RAF Fairford at 1.45 a.m. on the 6th. Now at 7.30 they were off again. Gerry relates the story of that mission:

'Although we had originally set off leading our squadron, in what appeared to be a clear sky, as we arrived at our rendezvous on time, we soon became a little cog in a very big wheel, and the surrounding air, both forwards, side and back, was just a solid mass of aircraft and gliders. On crossing the English Channel, the sight in the air appeared to be reflected in the sea in that, as far as the eye could see, the English Channel was packed with shipping of all sizes – all heading in the same direction. As we approached the French Coast, we witnessed several lines of heavy naval ships bombarding the French Coast ….

'We released our glider in the dropping zone and headed for the wood at low level. Regrettably, this gun position saw us coming and hit us first. The first thing to blow was the petrol tank on the port wing, which blew the wing up and the aircraft onto its back. As rear gunner, my first indication that there was something wrong was when my ammunition came up out of the chutes and hit me in the face. Because of the 'G' pressure, we were in a position to do absolutely nothing.

'However, my skipper, had given up trying to fly the aircraft through normal elevators, etc., and had his feet up on the dashboard, pulling back on the stick in the fond hope that we would pull out of the dive. It was then that one of the miracles of war happened, in that the aircraft came over off its back, and we made a beautiful belly landing in a ploughed field that would have done justice to any pilot under normal circumstances. The skipper was awarded the DFC for this piece of flying.

'The whole crew left the aircraft completely uninjured, and we were able to run some twenty-five yards into a wheat field before the remainder of the aircraft exploded and was burning furiously. Within minutes, the aircraft was surrounded by German troops, and, from the gist of their shouts, we realised that they thought we were still in the aircraft. We stayed in this position in the wheat field until about 11.00 a.m. As all the Germans had then left the scene, we had a crew conference as to what action we should now take. The position being, of course, that we had an invasion going on some miles behind us and odd pockets of paratroopers would be on either side of us.

All we knew of our flight position was after we had been hit, we had about-turned and headed back over enemy territory but, from where we were, it was impossible to accurately pinpoint our position.

'It was then decided to wait until dusk and, just as the light was falling, along came two figures which, at first glance, appeared to be wearing American helmets. One of the crew, in his excitement, even though the men were whistling "Lili Marlene", cried, "The Americans are with us", and leapt out to greet them. I think it was sheer reaction that made us stand up and, by this time, the two so-called Americans had leapt off their bicycles and were covering us with machine guns. Never has one felt so small. We were then marched to a nearby German Army Camp, where we were locked in a room, still wearing our guns, to await the arrival of the German officer. He very quickly put a stop to the nonsense, and we were immediately disarmed of all visible arms.

'As I was the only member of the crew wearing a decoration, they presumed I was the captain and I was called forward to meet the Army captain. He proudly announced that he was educated in England and that he would interrogate me in English, but he must first search me. As his hands were about to search, starting under my armpits, I reached into my battledress and withdrew my escape kit in its plastic container and wallet of foreign money, and handed them to him quite openly. He said, "What are these?" and I said that the escape kit was my ration for three days, and that the wallet of money contained personal papers to be opened only by the Gestapo, to which he replied "*Ja, Ja*. I understand", and handed them back to me. I put them back into my battledress top and was horrified to hear the clunk as the escape hit my hidden revolver. However, by this time I was already stepping backwards, and the German captain did not appear to hear. He seemed satisfied with his search, so I continued to walk backwards and Flight Lieutenant Thring stepped up as next in line to be searched. Each member of the crew adopted the same patter as I did, and we were all left complete with our escape kits and money.

Then during the night the Germans marched them off as they had been ordered to retreat nearer to Caen. Gerry McMahon was one of the unfortunate men picked out to carry a 16-stone wounded German soldier. He did not appreciate the honour.

'One of the German soldiers eventually found a stretcher which enabled us to use four men to carry a corner a-piece. In our weary state, this man weighed the proverbial ton, and we resorted to a ruse whereby, every few yards, one of us took it in turns to shout "Halt", which not only stopped us, but brought the whole company to a halt as well. Each time, the captain had to return to our position to find out why the company had halted. En route we also watched, against the night sky, large fires in some town or other which was being bombed. The general consensus of German opinion throughout the company was that we should be tied up and left to burn with it.

'However, after a while, we managed to find a motorcycle by the side of the road, which had been abandoned petrol-less, so we sat the wounded soldier on this and pushed it to the top of the hill. On reaching the top, and seeing that there was a steep decline on the other side, we accidentally let go of the motorcycle and the soldier disappeared into the dark. He was later found in a ditch at the bottom of the hill, and his language was not appreciative of the help we had given him. The German captain then decided that it would be safer for him to look after his own wounded, and we did not see the wounded man again after this.

'We marched all night and, as dawn approached, we arrived at a château which had obviously been for some considerable time used as a German headquarters. Listening to the conversation, on arrival, we understood that all staff officers of the headquarters had withdrawn and now this was to be a fighting garrison. We were shown into a barn and a guard was placed on the door.'

Over the next 24 hours McMahon discovered that the hayloft doors gave access into the grounds, and had a hoist and pully. That night he decided on escape.

'I gently eased the wooden hay loft doors open, and noted

with pleasure that there were no sentries in sight at this end of the barn. Also, there appeared to be just the right length of rope on the hoist and pulley for me to swing over the château wall, but I would have to take my chance on what was on the other side of the wall. I took hold of the hook and jumped for the wall, but, instead of completing the swing, I plunged violently straight downwards, ending up in a tangled mess at the base of the barn wall. After rubbing my various sore spots, I discovered that the reason was a simple one – the other end of the hoist rope had not been secured to the wall! I made a reconnaissance of the grounds and noted the positions of the German sentries after which I headed back to the barn and this time I secured the hoist rope to the wall and climbed back up the rope and through the hay loft doors. All of the crew were sound asleep, so I hid my revolver and ammunition back in the bales of hay and settled down. In the morning, I explained I had just done a reconnaissance of the grounds and had decided against escaping. By this time, there was a considerable amount of activity outside and, on two occasions, the Germans entered the barn to count that we were all still present.

'During the day, the château suffered numerous rocket attacks by hedge-hopping Typhoon fighters, and was gradually reduced from its three storeys in height to a load of ground rubble, and the morale of the German troops was equally low. Talk between the soldiers indicated that they believed they were surrounded, but they no longer had RT communication and, apart from the captain, no-one to advise them as to what state the war was in.

'Early the next morning, Typhoon fighters again started to carry out rocket attacks, and the German soldiers moved out into a slit trench, dug in the grounds, and asked us to leave the barn for our own safety. I collected my gun and ammunition and hid them again in my battledress, and we then joined the Germans in the trenches. This was indeed most fortuitous because, exactly three minutes later, the barn was struck by two rockets and went up in a flash of fire and smoke. There was some talk amongst the Germans about sentries being killed during the night on the opposite château wall to that from whence the invasion was coming, and they were convinced they were surrounded.

'During this afternoon, the German army captain sent for me and for the skipper. We found the captain in a room in the basement of the château, admiring his stubbled face in a mirror and, as we entered he turned round, obviously embarrassed, and said, "Me no English gentleman". He then uttered the most amazing things, saying, "I wish to surrender to you, myself and 40 men." This came completely out of the blue, as far as we were concerned because, although we had caused the rumours, we had no idea how far behind enemy lines we were. However, we decided to take a chance and said to the Captain that we would only accept his surrender if he surrendered in the proper military fashion and marched with the men fully armed, to give themselves up.

'This was how a queer little party of armed Germans, and ourselves, set off from the château, in the general direction of the coast. I also insisted that no matter what happened en route, there was to be a strict discipline and no talking within the ranks. This was also fortuitous in that on the march another 21 fully armed Germans joined us, thinking that we were going to reinforce the German front. These 21 were hand-picked snipers who had been left behind to cause havoc during the Allied advance. We marched for over three miles and were suddenly surrounded by Canadian soldiers. We shouted that the Germans were our prisoners and were coming in to surrender. After seeing them safely into a Prisoner of War cage, the Army Captain gave me a receipt for one German officer and 61 other ranks.'

Gerry and his crew had been shot down, imprisoned, escaped and returned to the United Kingdom in just four days.

On 14 June 1944, Flight Lieutenant Thring, a Canadian, was recommended for an immediate DFC.

19. The Fatted Calf

It was on an operation to bomb a rail junction at Vierzon in the Loire area of France, to prevent reinforcements and supplies reaching the Germans after D-Day, that the evasion story of Sergeant Ernest Harrop began.

At that time he was a wireless operator, serving with number 100 Squadron at Grimsby, flying Lancasters. The night of 20/21 June was a night-fighter's paradise, for the moon was bright and the stars were shining vividly! On such a night they would be an easy target for night fighters and would need that extra bit of luck to survive. They did not get it.

As they approached the target, the pilot, Pilot Officer Kay, who always liked to have an extra pair of eyes on the look out, asked Harrop to go into the astro dome. It was just after this that they were hit. There were two loud explosions and flames started to appear. Harrop grabbed the fire extinguisher, and then realised that the flames were coming from the area where he kept his parachute. As it seemed likely he was going to need it in the near future, he grabbed the 'chute pack and then set about the flames once again. He caught sight of the navigator leaving and assuming he was about to bale out, left the extinguisher and hurried forward, clipping on his parachute as he went. When he got to the front everyone had gone, so he took hold of his parachute handle and he too dived out of the front hatch. It was lucky that he did so then, for the aircraft crashed only a mile from where he landed.

'Looking down,' he recalls, 'I noticed what appeared to be a river and as I thought I was in the vicinity of the river Loire, I decided to pull on my cords, and close the 'chute so I would hit terra-ferma before I drifted any further.

'Carefully gathering my 'chute to leave no traces and removing my Mae West after taking out my torch, I hid them very securely in the bushes and proceeded from the area as soon as possible, in case I had been spotted on my descent.'

Using the North Star as a guide Ernest Harrop had begun to make his way across country when he heard voices. Whether they were French or German he could not be sure, so he hid behind a hedge and decided to stay there until morning. After a while, as the shock of baling out had begun to wear off, he felt a pain in his right side which seemed to be getting worse. In case it immobilised him, he decided to make a move immediately, and came to a single storey building.

He gave a 'V' knock on the door, and a girl's voice called out in French to which I replied, 'Mm'selle, RAF'; she called out again and I repeated myself. Whereupon the door opened and I was confronted by a man in his shirt, his wife and two daughters aged 16 years and 11 years. They were M. and Mme Giraud and their daughters Janine and Ginette.

'Although they had heard the aircraft overhead and the crash, they were very suspicious as they knew the Germans had many ways of infiltrating into the Resistance. Anyhow, they decided to invite me inside where I took out my language card, and asked if the enemy was around, and they said not in the immediate vicinity. I then asked them where I was, and he pointed to a large map of Europe on the wall about 5 feet x 5 feet and after a quick deduction I estimated my position about 240 miles on the wrong side of our lines. It was a village called Vouzon, about half way between our target and SSE of Orléans.

'Having convinced them of my identity, and told them of my pain, I was given the eldest daughter's bed, while the four of them slept together.'

Next morning the local Resistance leader, Henri Renaud de la Faverie, brought a doctor who examined Ernest, and to his relief, told him he was all right apart from some bruised ribs.

The next four days he spent in a dug-out in the woods, while the search for him was on, Henri bringing him coffee and in the evenings the Giraud family brought him food. His only other company was the squirrels, and the constant sound of German motor cycles roaring up and down the lanes. On the fifth day he was taken back to the house and given workman's overalls.

'While I had been in the forest,' he recalls, 'they had made a small hole in the wall of the room where I was to spend the next few weeks (in the daughter's bedroom). On the other side of the wall was conveniently placed a horse trough, in front of which were four rows of red roof tiles; right across the barn and up to the roof, which had been there for years. (As if someone had expected me going there.) They had got some new timber which they nailed together with a piece down each side and one along the top, under which was stretched a wire, enabling the girl to hang her garments on, this was to conceal the hole; and was made to lift up on two hooks, and if there were any Germans or strangers around I was to climb inside – which only happened on a few occasions.

'On my return to the house they gave me a charred cigarette case and part of a human scalp to identify. It was only then that I knew our mid-upper had failed to bale out.

'I was introduced to a baker who lived about four miles away, on the other side of the forest and every Tuesday he brought me a little white bread, which I can assure you was very much appreciated. On the sixth week he invited M. Giraud and myself to a meal at his house, to which we went on the two cycles, setting off as it was going dusk, four miles through the forest, and of course, without lights. For our main course they had killed a calf (unknown to the Germans) and it was the first time I had ever eaten veal, and it was delicious. It was a full French meal with the usual selection of wines to wash it down, and by the time we had got to the coffee and liqueurs I was half way under the table. In spite of the feast, I managed to ride back in safety, and arrived at about 3 a.m. much to the pleasure of the family, who had feared we may have been picked up.

'The Resistance asked me if I was prepared to take up arms with them. Of course I did not need asking twice, providing I was allowed to wear my uniform to which they agreed. On the Thursday morning of my seventh week, I was introduced to the members of our party, eight in all, and we went to a secluded spot for a trial shoot, using the Sten gun, Bren gun and the Lee Enfields, which had been dropped by RAF aircraft.'

Unfortunately Ernest was then struck down with acute appendicitis. The doctor told him they would try to get me through German lines to the Americans who had fought their way to Orléans the day before. Arriving at Orléans all the bridges had been demolished so they had to get me across the river to the American army.

'That was where I parted from my French friends, and after having to prove my identity I was taken several miles before we arrived at a suitable field hospital able to perform the operation, which had ruptured and gangrene had set in.'

The Americans flew Ernest back to England on 23 August where pneumonia and pleurisy was diagnosed. It was seven weeks before he was fit again. Even then he could not go home until he had been sent to London, on 10 October, for his MI9 interrogation.

In 1985 Ernest re-visited the grave of Johnny Sharpley, the mid-upper. He had been hastily buried by the Germans, but the local people had exhumed his body and re-buried it in the local churchyard. When he left the cemetery he was met by a teacher and his pupils who asked him the full story of that night in June 1944. It turned out that each year on 1 July they went to the grave to pay homage and place flowers on John's grave.

He also went with Hubert, the son of one of his helpers, to visit the tomb of his father who had died some years ago. The reason? As Ernest says:

'I owe to these people the last 43 years of my life, and I shall never forget them.'

20.   Dined Like a King

There is an element of humour in every situation. In the case of Pilot Officer Russell Gradwell of 9 Squadron it occurred while his Lancaster was being attacked by a fighter on 8 July 1944.

'In this silent, tense, situation I heard someone laugh and could not believe my own ears. A few moments later I heard it again. I asked, "Who in the hell's laughing?" as I couldn't see much to laugh at. The mid-upper gunner, Bill Best, replied, "It's me, Skip, Bill, he's hit my hydraulic lines on one side and

I'm going round and round out of control. Not to worry, I'm giving him a burst every time I go by!"

They were on their way to attack a flying boat dump at Creil, when they were attacked just before crossing the coast. The fighter vanished eventually, and they assumed they had shot it down. Although the aircraft had been hit many times, it was still able to carry on, and none of the crew was injured. But the delay cost them dearly. They were 15 minutes late over the target, by which time they had it to themselves. They also had the 'undivided attention', as Gradwell put it later, of the German ground defences.

As soon as Atch Atkinson gave the call, bombs gone, Gradwell set course for home. But they were already on fire, and 'I realised that, with the effect of the oxygen in the air that we were flying through at some 200 miles an hour, the flame was acting like an oxy-acetylene blow torch and was cutting its way through the wing.' He had no alternative but to give the order to bale out.

Gradwell was last to leave, and was knocked unconscious, only coming to on the descent, with no recollection of how the parachute opened.

After trying to get his bearings by the stars, he decided to move north-west to get as near as possible to the British lines, for this was a month after D-Day. Making a detour round a village, he decided to hide overnight so that the hunt for him would with luck, have been called off.

'It was July and the weather was warm and the night a fine one so I lay down in the grain, well hidden, and feeling more secure than at any time since I landed. I must have fallen asleep, because the next thing I knew was that it was daylight. As I lay there, I watched a squadron of Typhoons go overhead. (The thought crossed my mind, if only I could get up there they would give me a lift home.) After watching them for a few minutes, I decided to sort out my escape gear and, as I sat there, I realised that it was going to be a long trying day and, as the sky was clear, it was going to be very hot too. A few minutes later I heard and saw a cutting machine drawn by two horses approaching. When it was some 30 yards from me, it stopped and two men began to go around the machine with oil cans. As I looked closer in the daylight, I realised that I had gone into the centre of the field but that, down through the centre of the field, was a footpath dividing the field into two. The two men and the cutter were obviously about to start cutting on my side of the field. I thought, therefore, that the best course of action to take was to approach them while they were stationary.

'In my best schoolboy French accent, I called, "Hey, Messieurs." At this they both looked up and came around the machine to join me. Again, in my best schoolboy French, I tried to explain who I was, which, sadly, meant nothing at all to them. I then pointed to the RAF letters in the centre of my wings and, when they realised that this meant Royal Air Force, which they said over and over to each other in their French accents, they then became very excited. They rattled off in French, both speaking at the same time and arms waving. I could understand none of this gabble but I kept hearing *cacher*, *cacher*, which means to hide. At this moment a young couple came down the path and joined us and then the four of them became excited and again spoke very quickly in French. Again I picked up the word *cacher, cacher* ....

'I was eventually escorted into the farmhouse, Belle Assise ... The farmer's name was M. Carron. I was taken straight into the kitchen by the farmer and his wife and was asked if I was hungry. Whilst I was very hungry I remembered that we had always been told how short food was on the continent and only to accept food if one was desperate. Therefore I said, "*Non, Madame.*" To which she replied, "*Ça ne fait rien,*" and disappeared down some cellar steps to reappear a minute or two later with the biggest piece of steak I had ever seen. She got out her frying pan, into which she placed about half a pound of butter and then the steak. A bottle of wine was produced as was a loaf of white bread and another large pat of butter. I dined like a king. When I had finished the steak she then produced a large bowl of fresh strawberries and a pint of fresh cream. The meal was rounded off with a cup of ersatz coffee.'

A little later two Frenchmen arrived who asked him for the names of his crew. He learnt that sadly, his wireless operator,

Sergeant Price had been killed when his parachute failed to open but that the second pilot, Flight Lieutenant Oldacre, was safely in the hands of the Resistance. The next day Gradwell was reunited with Atch Atkinson and over the next few days they were kitted out as Frenchmen.

'We were moved on from Belle Assise because I felt that Mme Carron was putting herself and her family at risk by introducing us as English evaders to all and sundry who happened to call at the farm looking for food and I was concerned for their safety. It would be better if we were moved on.

'M. Maigret called for us about one o'clock one afternoon in a two-wheeled covered waggon and we felt like the early pioneers must have felt going out into the unknown.

'We travelled through Beauvais and Arnoy and finished up in Villier St Bartholomé at about 4 p.m. To avoid any suspicion, the waggon pulled into the farmyard belonging to a M. Noel and we were taken into the house. I later discovered that M. Noel was head of the underground movement in the village and kept in radio contact with Britain every day in spite of the fact that, at one time, he had 40 Germans billeted in his barn.

'M. Maigret went off with the wagon and we were introduced to a couple named Marcel and Germaine Dubois, who were to take over the next stage. Marcel worked on the land at one of the local farms and Germaine was a part-time seamstress. After about half an hour we left M. Noel's farm and were taken by Marcel and Germaine to their house. We were to stay with them for the next six weeks. About this time, Les Sutton, the rear gunner, Bill Best, the mid-upper gunner, Pete Arnold, the navigator, and Tommy Linch, the engineer, were all brought to the same village and concealed all together at the house of a Mme Blanchard.

'As we had to lie low and keep to the house and garden, we passed our time firstly by chopping logs for them for the winter and then, Marcel borrowed an apple crusher and press and they used to bring cartloads of cider apples to the house for us to turn them into cider with this equipment. The only time that we left the house was on a Sunday, when, with Marcel, just after the end of the curfew at 6 a.m., we would leave the house and go up into the woods to collect mushrooms and snails to eat. We used to return at about 10 a.m., when everyone was at Mass and the village was quiet.

'This we did on several Sundays without event, until one Sunday on our way to the woods, we were just crossing the main street in the village when a vehicle came down the road. This meant that we had to wait to cross the road. Atch Atkinson foolishly stepped back into the shadows whereupon the vehicle stopped very quickly and out jumped three Germans, all armed. I think they suspected an ambush because of Atch's action and they called us to them and told us that we were out during curfew hours. We denied this and an argument ensued. By this time, thanks to the patience of Germaine, my French was quite good – in any case as good as the French of most Germans I hoped. Atch did not speak any French but knew exactly what the argument was about and this prompted him to show his watch. Unfortunately, being a Canadian, he had a Builliver watch, which had the name in large letters half way around the face. Fortunately, the Germans didn't see this and I think, having seen by the watch that it was 10 to 15 minutes past six, were satisfied that our story that we were farm labourers going to milk the cows at a nearby farm, was true. The warrant officer told us to go, which we did as quickly and as nonchalantly as we could.

'We continued on our way up to the woods and got our supply of snails and mushrooms and, with our makeshift bags, made out of the shirts off our backs, full of snails and mushrooms, we started back to the village.' Between them and the village however, was a string of parked German vehicles, and they had to run the gauntlet, as casually as they could.

'We all arrived home a bit shaken and I came to the conclusion that the Sunday morning walks were getting a little dangerous and we would not go again.

'But the battle was getting closer, and by the next day was only a mile or so away. Once more then we prepared to move. Then the church bells began to ring. The British had arrived.

'Every villager was out in his garden overjoyed that the

British were there and Marcel and Germaine were so proud to be able to say that "The British", in the form of Atch and myself, had been with them for six weeks! To celebrate this, each villager in turn would dig up from its hiding place in the garden, a treasured bottle of wine or spirit and produce glasses to drink a toast. The news preceded us along the route and the glasses and bottles were out ready and waiting for us to get there. By the time that we reached Atch [who had been taken to the village to ensure they really were British tanks], we were rather merry.'

The next day they were taken to a château owned by a Mme Ravel and once more dined in style.

'Mme Ravel gave us a meal to remember with all the correct wines and trimmings and finishing with a cup of real coffee, for which she had paid the equivalent of £35 for half a kilo. After this sumptuous lunch, we said our goodbyes and went out and hitched a lift in an army vehicle which took us down to Vernon. The brigadier that we were taken to took us across the pontoon bridge at Vernon in a half track vehicle so that we could sit on the top and see the wonderful feat performed by the Royal Engineers in building this bridge under fire from the other bank.'

They were liberated at Bayeux, put back in uniform and by the beginning of September were back in London – to army rations!

21.   A High Price to Pay

It was 18 July 1944 when Albert De Bruin, who despite his name is British, was sitting in his lonely mid-upper turret of a Lancaster bomber of 630 Squadron bound for Caen, in Normandy. They were about to assist the advancing British Second Army by bombing fortified villages ahead of them. At about 2 a.m., near Revigny, as his Lancaster was about to make a bomb-run a sudden burst of flame came from the port outer engine. They had seen no fighters, so assumed they had been hit by flak. Albert called the pilot and told him of their problem, which was acknowledged, but their problems were just beginning. Albert recalls:

'I was searching the sky for any fighters, starting at 12 o'clock and working my way around the sky clockwise.' As he did so, the starboard engine caught fire and he called on the intercom, 'Hello, skipper, starboard outer alight.' In the same calm manner came the reply, 'Roger, standby.' They flew on now with both engines alight and with still a full bomb load.

'I remembered the 23rd Psalm,' recalls Albert, 'and said a prayer, thinking that was the end.' Suddenly the skipper, Gordon Maxwell, said: 'Attention crew, attention crew, abandon aircraft, I repeat abandon aircraft.' Albert went to the rear part of the fuselage and clipped on his 'chute, and with the rear gunner and wireless operator close behind him opened the door on the starboard side. To his horror he saw smoke and flames streaming back from the engines. He sat on the step and counted to 20 as they were at 17,000 feet at the time. Finally he jumped into space and all became quiet except for the comforting rustle of silk and the sound of gunfire and bombs in the distance.

'As I came down in the moonlight,' he says, 'I saw a silver strip below which was the River Marne. I manipulated my 'chute to make sure I landed on the side of it rather than in it and a strong smell of vegetation came up. Then I landed.'

His first thought was to get out of the area as quickly as he could. As daylight broke, he saw a farmhouse in the distance and decided to ask for food and water. He did not stay very long, however, and when he was out of sight, he changed direction – just in case. Quite suddenly, a boy stepped out in front of him. He had an arm band on reading FFI (Free French of the Interior). He pointed a revolver at Albert's head and ordered him to walk ahead. After a short while he was met by a small group, the leader of which turned out to be a Russian; his aide was a British Army sergeant. They asked him for proof of identity and Albert produced his ID discs which he carried round his neck. They then gave him the frustrating news that had he turned up one night earlier, they could have flown him home by Lysander.

In the forest he came across a large farmhouse built like a fort, with walls on all sides and high wooden doors at the entrance. He kept this under observation for 48 hours and on 22 July decided to approach it, sheath knife at the ready. An old man was chopping wood near the entrance but he did not see the knife Albert was carrying. He said, 'I am RAF. Do you have water?' The farmer merely nodded towards the house from which two men appeared, one M. Gillete and the other M. Bernier. They asked his name, rank and number and where he was born. By the time he was taken into the house a message had been transmitted back to the UK, asking if there was such a person. The reply had come back, 'yes'.

The reason for their caution was natural for the Gestapo had been planting bogus aircrew, and any local people who had offered help were shot. The next person he met was English-speaking, M. Schmit, the local baker who had been a chef in a London hotel and had lived in Chelsea for many years. He arrived on a bike and began to question Albert about London. Did he know Chelsea? Who were the Chelsea Pensioners? What colour were their uniforms and hats? Did he know the streets in London, the hotels? On and on it went.

'Then out of the blue: would I like a 295 (Leave pass)? I said, "Yes right now." Then I was asked what colour it was and where did I get one? He then said to the farmer, "He is okay; He's RAF".' Having proved Albert's identity beyond doubt, they produced a bottle of wine to celebrate and they toasted each other.

One day the Resistance left a dead stag on the door step. He recalls, 'I helped to cut it up, and then we burnt the carcass.' It made a fine meal with a glass of wine. On 3 August, however, he was told the Germans were in the area in great numbers and he was taken to a home in the village of Robert-Espagne. A gendarme came to collect him but told him not to speak to him on the way. He was to walk behind him, and was given a coat to cover up his battledress, and a rake to carry in the normal style of a local farmer.

'We set off and passed a German guard on route. He looked at me, then looked away and did not notice I was shivering with fear!'

In the garden of a house he met a M. Evrard, secretary to the mayor, who greeted him: 'Bonjour, monsieur. You are another of my sons.'

He was introduced to Mme Evrard, and they did indeed treat him like a son. Each day he became used to seeing Germans walk past the window.

'One day came a message that another of my crew was at the farmhouse so I was taken back to meet him. When I arrived I was amazed to see British 'Tommies' in uniform in the orchard eating apples. They said they were on their way to Belgium to carry out a sabotage mission. At the farm I met our rear gunner, Sergeant Leary. He was going to try and get to the border. We parted company and I made my way back to the village.'

The next day the leader of the local Resistance offered him a sten gun and suggested he join in a shoot-up of the Germans. He decided it was better to keep a low profile however and was taken back to M. Evrard by the gendarme, later he heard that the farm he had been in had been raided and all the men had been shot. The Evrards' turn was not long in coming:

'As we sat down to eat, rifle butts crashed on the door. "The Germans are here!" shouted Evrard. The gendarme and I were taken into the bedroom where a trap door in the floor was opened and down we went into a cellar. In the meantime the Germans had been stalled to give us time to hide.

'We heard shouts and feet running around above, then Mme Evrard's voice through an iron grill; "Leave quickly, the house is on fire". The house by now was ablaze. As we stepped out of the trap door once again, I had decided to cut my own throat if I had been trapped rather than burn to death, but I got out so God was with me. In the garden I climbed over a wall – just in time, as an SS trooper threw a grenade into the house. I made my way into the woods and hid watching the village burn and hearing voices as the Germans looted all they could and piled it up in a big heap then danced around it like Indians around a totem pole.'

When daybreak came he cautiously ventured back into the village and enquired about Mme Evrard. From a woman coming out of the ruins of her house he learned she had been taken into care at the local school house.

'The Germans were coming back, she said, so I left and went back into the woods. While in the woods I saw Germans marching a line of men along and then minutes later the rattle of machine-gun fire. The men had been put to death. There, but for the grace of God, could have been I ... I felt sick inside.'

Later he heard heavy gun fire and in the distance saw a jeep. Suddenly in a puff of smoke it had gone – a direct hit by a German shell. Any moment he expected a German tank to appear but none did. Then a man came running into the woods shouting Albert's name. Terrified, Albert grabbed him and said, 'You will give me away!' The man told him the Americans were in the village and wanted to see him. 'I said in reply, "If this is a trap you will die first," and showed him my knife. But he was telling the truth. There through the trees were three US vehicles, one a jeep with an officer. He shook my hand and said, "I am bloody glad to see you, we have been waiting for you." '

They were a recce unit. 'He told me 57 men had been shot, including M. Evrard. The price of my evasion had been very high ....

'Four of my crew, including the pilot Gordon Maxwell, were killed. I found out later that after I had left the aircraft it had been attacked by a fighter and exploded after crashing. The bodies were collected by the local people and buried.' Albert heard no more from Sergeant Leary, and the records do not show either that he became a POW or that he successfully evaded and returned to the UK.

On 24 May 1986 Albert De Bruin visited Revigny again for a memorial service. He was met by the mayor of Robert-Espagne, and taken to meet Mme Bernier again, and her son Robert. He visited the cemetery at Viller-le-Sac and laid a wreath on the graves of his fellow crew members and then on to that of

Monsieur Evrard, then to meet members of the village. He also laid a wreath on the graves of the Resistance men shot by the SS troops. Mme Evrard had since died, but he met some of her relatives. He told the mayor, 'My body may be in England, but my heart is with the people of Robert-Espagne, with whom I share this great tragedy.'

22.   They Did it Twice

To conclude the French section of this book are three stories with one thing in common: each of the pilots evaded or escaped successfully, not once but twice!

First, there is Sergeant John Mott. He was the pilot of a Whitley bomber of 78 Squadron, which took off from Dishforth to bomb the dockyard at Lorient. The aircraft was hit and caught fire, and Mott baled out, landing on the north-west edge of Lanvollon. The rest of the crew also baled out successfully, all but one being caught and immediately made POW's. The exception was Sergeant MacMillan, the rear gunner.

John Mott managed to find a hiding place straight away in Lanvallon, and from there on had a series of helpers. On 6 January 1941, a M. Hevin took him to M.and Mme Delavigne in Nantes, Brittany, where he stayed until 26 September 1941. M. Hevin was later arrested by the Germans and was shot on 22 October. Mott stayed in Nantes, and changed safe house five times while his helpers sought a means of escape for him. In the middle of August his rear gunner, Sergeant MacMillan, turned up, and he went to stay with Mme Flavet. On 22 September the Flavet family and MacMillan were arrested.

Mme Delavigne recalls, 'The leader of the organisation, Claude Lamirault, was to ensure the escape of the two airmen. Unfortunately the Flavet family and MacMillan were arrested. Having been informed immediately and not knowing the leader's address, we decided to do all we could to save Mott. We had recourse to a so-called Pole, in reality a Hungarian Jew, with whom we were slightly acquainted, in connection with passing letters into the Unoccupied Zone. He refused at first, but after the financial side had been arranged, he agreed, and on the night of 26 September, Sergeant Mott and 'Rips', as this agent was called, left 6 Boulevard Admiral Courbet, on bicycles, the airman having my nephew's cycle. They travelled by the express to Bordeaux, and then went to the house of a Pole called Selk, living in St Sulpice des Pommiers, by Sauveterre de Guyene (Gironde). It was Selk who got the pilot across the line of demarcation. Rips was to rejoin him and facilitate his entry into Spain.'

On 4 October, Mott reached Toulouse, and as he recalls: 'On the 12th I crossed over the frontier of Spain. Once there I kept walking, to the British Consul who passed me on to the Embassy in Madrid. On 14 November 1941, I arrived in Gibraltar and left in a Sunderland flying boat on 13 December, arriving at Pembroke Dock on the 14th.'

On 5 March 1942, the Delavigne family were arrested. The Hungarian Jew was a double agent. M. Delavigne was taken to a civil prison at Nantes and Madame to a German Military prison at Ryes des Rochette. They were later transferred to a prison in Bordeaux, together with their nephew Maurice Cybulski. They realised after their interrogation that someone had talked. Maurice died later in April 1943, having caught a chill while in his cell. The Delavignes were released in July, but it had been a near thing. Next time they were not quite so lucky. They continued their work sheltering evaders; then, as Madame Delavigne related:

'On 25 January 1944, at 12.30 p.m. the Gestapo again arrested us. We were taken to Place du Maréchal Foch, and immediately interrogated. The interrogation turned on my trip to Poitiers. I refused to reply and in consequence was kept for 16 hours with fetters on my ankles and shackles behind my back in the cellar of the building in which the German Police had their headquarters. I then made up a long story, without giving any names, and did everything I could to get my husband cleared.

'I was interrogated on two further occasions, both enlivened by a soujourn in the cellars. On the second occasion I was there nearly 30 hours and heard the screams of the unlucky Frenchmen who were being tortured there.

'I still refused to give the names and details Dr Rupert, [the head of the local Gestapo] demanded. After having slapped my face several times, he said, (I give his exact words) "In Germany we respect women", (he was telling me!), "but I shall treat you as a man, and I shall put it out of your power to do us harm; you're going into a concentration camp until the cessation of hostilities." I can give no account of the interrogation of my husband, as I never saw him again. Through friends in the prison gang, I know that he left Compiègne on 25 March, and in company with other deported people travelled to Mauthausen. He was kept there in quarantine and then sent to Camp No.1 at Gouzen where he died of exhaustion in January 1945.

'As for myself, I was sent from Nantes to Romainville. Then to Aix-la-Chapelle, Düsseldorf, Hannover, Hamburg and finally to Ravensbrück, where I arrived on 21 March 1944. On 3 March 1945, I was one of a group of prisoners sent to Mauthausen. On 22 April, we were liberated by the International Red Cross.

'When we left for Germany, Dr Rupert informed my mother, who was 82 and blind, that she would have to get out of her house within 48 hours, and that he himself would occupy the apartment as a reprisal for our having worked against Germany.'

During her first term of imprisonment at Bordeaux, Mme Delavigne was encouraged to remember people she denied knowing, by being held barefoot on an electric stove, with the result that she was unable to walk for some time after her release. Despite this, she revealed nothing to the Germans. When she was released she weighed only four and a half stone instead of her normal ten stone.

John Mott's story did not end with his successful evasion to England. On 28 May 1942, now a flight lieutenant with 161 Special Duties Squadron, his Lysander failed to take off after landing at Châteauroux. Mott was captured, and after spending time in several prisons in France was sent to Gavi Campo No.5 in Italy. There he remained until the Italian armistice in September 1943. The prisoners were sent to Austria by the Germans, by train, providing possible avenues of escape. Mott's was by cutting a hole above the buffer of the truck. He and other officers dropped off in turn. He injured his head on leaving the train, but still managed to get away. On 30 September, he teamed up with another officer POW, and together they travelled to Tarcento. Joining up with some Partisans they were taken to Ziri in Yugoslavia.

During his time in Italy, Mott recalls 'While staying at one place, we were given a bath. This turned out to be in a bath tub in the kitchen, with all the family in there at the same time! We got into the tub with our underpants on, but the three daughters of the family saw this and pulled them off. When we went to bed there was only one bed, so we slept at one end and the three girls at the other.'

In Ziri, he met Flight Lieutenant Carmichael, who had been captured in North Africa in November 1941, and had made two unsuccessful attempts to escape in 1942. He too had leapt from the train and successfully evaded recapture. They now had to make their way back to Italy, as the Partisans had been attacked by the Germans, and the POW's had to break away from them. They did so in pairs, Mott teaming up with Carmichael. They travelled together to Calla, where they stayed until 3 December 1943, when the weather improved.

In February 1944, they stayed with a Contessa Cancellucia, and before this, with Signora Lucia Tea and a Czech named Polak, who was escaping from a political prison and was renting a house in Italy.

Given false identity cards, they and a lance corporal went to Valvasone, whence an Italian officer took them by train to Bologna. Direct to the coast, they borrowed money to buy a boat, but when after a week nothing more was heard of the Italian who had promised to obtain one for them, they divided the money with other escapers in the vicinity and went to Fermo. En route they were given a further sum of money and there they met two more officers and two other ranks, who had also borrowed money with the same objective. A hull was obtained and, having fitted it out and collected three more escapers, they embarked on the good ship *Pitch and Toss* on 17 March 1944. A RAF RDF Station was reached at Ponte Della Penna, on 19 March 1944.

In August 1944, John Mott was recommended for the MC, but was later awarded the MBE.

23.   Stormy Landing

The second of the evaders to have a repeat performance was Flight Lieutenant Bob Milton of 220 Squadron, Coastal Command, who on a patrol off Brest on 31 March 1941, ran into an electrical storm and had to make a forced landing, in his Hudson, at Maille, near Poitiers. Neither he nor the other three members of his crew, Sergeant Houghton, the second pilot, Sergeant Burridge, the wireless operator, nor Sergeant Griffiths was injured. They detonated the IFF, buried the secret papers and maps, but, as usual, they could not destroy the aircraft. Then, as he related later to MI9:- 'We kept together and with the help of French civilians, who paid for our railway tickets, made our way via Limoges to Marseille. Here we were arrested at the railway station as we had no papers. We were sent to St Hippolyte near Nîmes for internment, on 13 April 1941.'

Milton, however, was determined not to sit out the war in prison: 'In July 1941 I attempted to escape with Lieutenant Hewit by sawing through the bars of a window, but we were recaptured immediately by the guards. On 7 October 1941, accompanied by Lieutenant Parkinson, I escaped again but was recaptured at Nimes on 17 November 1941.'

In March 1942 he was sent to Fort de la Revère, Nice, where Taffy Higginson was already installed. In September 1942 the officers were separated from the men and sent to Lyon, and thence, about the beginning of October, to Chambarand.

'On the evening of 16 November 1942 I again escaped with Lieutenant Hewit. We had secured the co-operation of a French lieutenant and a French sergeant. From them we obtained the badges and stripes necessary to convert our clothes into passable imitations of French uniforms. Accompanied by the sergeant, we walked past the guard and out of the camp, where we were met by the lieutenant who took us to a house nearby.

'Here we got civilian clothes, forged identity cards and false demobilisation papers. We stayed in the house for a few days when our host then arranged for us to be taken to the railway station of St Marcellin in the Commandant's own car, driven by his army chauffeur. We caught a through train to Marseille, arriving there on 22 November 1942. After some little time we met a British officer, Captain Cooper, and made contact with an organisation which arranged our subsequent journey for us. On 29 December 1942 I arrived at Madrid. On 15 January 1943 I arrived at Gibraltar.'

That was not the end of Milton's adventures in occupied territory, however. On 11 June 1944 five days after D-Day, and now with 65 Squadron which was part of the 2nd TAF, his Mustang fighter was shot down by an Me109 and was forced to bale out. As he later related to MI9:

'I landed in the Orne River in the southern outskirts of Caen, and there I disposed of my parachute and Mae West. The escape aids and tins of food that I had in my pockets, I hid about my person, and then I took out my revolver, cocked it and waited to see how many Germans were coming after me. A minute later about 20 to 30 Germans came running up on foot, so I threw my revolver, knife, and ammunition belt into the river and was taken prisoner.

'All of them crowded around and started yelling at me, one of them in broken English, "What kind of plane?" When I did not answer, he started bashing me around, and his comrades followed suit. Meanwhile the others looted my pockets and took everything that I had, including my identity discs, but they missed my watch.

'Then they took me off to an SS Headquarters where they were not too bad and stuck a bandage around my head and gave me cigarettes. They did not start to question me at once. In fact an SS Captain told me in perfect English that he knew that I would not give him more than my name, rank and number. He let me sit down and smoke, and then went away and left me alone in his office. Ten minutes later he returned and gave me over to the custody of the Feldgendarmerie.'

They took him away and put him in a solitary cell where they stripped and searched him again, taking his shirt and leather gauntlets, but missing his watch once more. 'After waiting another hour and a half, I receivied a call from one of the members of the Légion de Volontaires Français Contre le Bolshevisme. He was a Frenchman in German uniform, and particularly obnoxious. He had come with a couple of Luftwaffe NCO's to question me about certain technicalities of my aircraft, and when I refused to answer, the NCO's started bashing me around the head. This continued about a half hour until I passed out, and when I woke up, they took me off to a nearby schoolhouse, which had been converted into a prison and was run by the SS serving with the Feldgendarmerie.

There he found a group of over twenty servicemen, some of them injured quite badly. The Germans however denied them medical aid and food until he answered questions, which he refused to do. After dark an NCO guard brought a French doctor to dress the wounds.

'Next morning the Frenchman who had brought us food before, arranged with the French Red Cross to provide lunch for all the prisoners. However, before the lunch arrived, all twenty-five of us were assembled and marched off down the road to the south. After a day's marching they joined a column of 350 Canadian prisoners.

'During the march, two Canadian officers escaped, and the Germans threatened to shoot ten out of twelve officers that remained if anyone else tried to get away. One of the Canadian men who could speak German overheard a discussion as to whether they should shoot us then and there just for good measure. That night local French people fed the column and the next morning a French priest gave us some bread and hot coffee, after which the column started off again. They made me ride on the bumper of a truck and act as an aircraft spotter, and this I did all the way to Rennes. We arrived at Rennes on 15 June and there were put into prison, in an old French barracks at the Camp de la Marne, on the outskirts of the town.

'On 6th July they marched us down to the local goods yard and put us in cattle trucks – 40 men or 25 officers to a truck. They gave us a loaf of German bread each and told us that it would have to last us for three days. We started off that night towards Redon, as that was the only line open, and as soon as the train started, we four started to cut our way through the front of the truck with a penknife and hacksaws from Escape Kits. We had to stop sawing whenever the train stopped, which was quite frequently, as we made too much noise. The German guards were all together in two different cars, and each time that the train stopped, they would jump out and station themselves at intervals on either side of the train.

'At about 0600, 7 July, we arrived at Redon where they left us in the marshalling yards to fry in the sun all day. An American Medical Officer, Captain Ernest N. Gruenburg, was allowed to leave the truck and attend to the men who were passing out from heat exhaustion, and he was kept busy!

'Then at about 2300, we set off for Nantes via Savenay. As the engine had now been switched to the other end of the train, and as our car was now going in the opposite direction, we thought that it would be unsafe to try to jump from our old hole and considered starting a new one. However, we discovered a rotten board on the inside of the car near the right hand door, and using the bench as a lever, we managed to pull one plank out of the side of the truck and open the latch on the outside of the door, after removing the mass of wire which held it in place. We waited an hour or so for a suitable opportunity to jump out, during which time the train stopped once, and we managed to put the latch and the wire back in place before the guard came to inspect it. Finally we decided to take a chance, and when the train slowed down to about 15 mph, we opened the door wide, and I jumped first. As soon as we hit the ground, we lay flat on our faces and rolled in as close to the wheels as we could, in order to avoid being seen and machine gunned by the guards on the trucks behind us. No one saw us, and the train continued on its way, taking with it the other members of our car who were going to jump out at three minutes intervals.

'Once clear of the train we got out our compasses and struck out to the north-east from the vicinity of St Etienne de Mont Luc, planning to get out of the coastal zone and eventually make for our lines. We walked across country every night, lying up in woods near farms in the daytime, until we reached the forest of Teillay, where we decided to await the American advance. Here we built ourselves a house and remained a fortnight, being fed and cared for by two charcoal burners.

'On 6 August we contacted the advance reconnaissance patrol of the 8th Infantry Division, were taken to the headquarters of the VIII Corps, and then to the Third Army PWE at Avranches, where we were received by the Third Army representatives of IS9.'

On 12 August 1944, Bob Milton was recommended for the DSO but was later awarded the MC.

24.   'Back in Two Months'

'Back in two months.' This was the message the last of our three 'double evaders', sent from his Spitfire after he had force-landed in the Pas de Calais on 25 January 1944. It was based on experience, for it was precisely two months since he had returned to England after his last mission.

On the first occasion, Flying Officer Henry Furniss-Roe (Bill, as he is always known) of 66 Squadron had crash-landed his Spitfire in Normandy on 22 August 1943. Bill recounts that his Spitfire was part of a bomber escort when it was attacked by enemy fighters. He shot one down and was then himself shot

down near Evreux and crash-landed the aircraft. He saw
Germans coming up the road to look for him so he ran close to
a hedge and into a wood to hide until dark. After dark he
found a small cottage in a wood. The door was opened by a
man to whom he explained who he was and he invited him in.
There was only one room with several children in it and one
woman. He was given some potato soup and Calvados. It was
his first experience of this fire water, and it caused much
merriment when he coughed and spluttered after drinking it.
He was told they were not in the Resistance but they knew
someone who was. They told him of their great fear of
Germans finding him there, so he was given some food and a
bottle of wine and taken into woods again by the man who
showed him a thick clump of bushes and he told him to stay
there until the following night when he would return for him.

Bill was cautious, however, and decided, after he had left to
move to another clump of bushes about 50 yards away. He slept
fitfully during a surprisingly cold night, and was awoken by the
sounds of people crashing about. He saw two woodcutters
working, then later several Germans in line abreast obviously
looking for him. Fortunately they passed by and did not see
him. The woodcutters left at midday and he was alone with
millions, it seemed, of very hungry flies. About dusk his helper
returned with another man and they both had bicycles. As he
could not see anyone else around, he revealed himself, and was
greeted enthusiastically. He was introduced to the other man
and told he was to follow him on a cycle, about 50 metres
behind him, to his house, as he was in the Resistance. If he was
stopped for any reason Bill was to ride on past and not say
anything. He was given an old mac to wear, and they set off.
They had 6 kilometres to go and passed several groups of
German soldiers who luckily did not take any notice of them.

He was sheltered in a cellar for a few days while identity
cards were provided – as a deaf mute – and he was taken to
Paris by train. They arrived at Paris without problems. Bill
followed his courier some 20 yards behind. After some time
he saw him go into a bar and beckon from the doorway. Bill
went in, and met the owner, Mme Fabre, who was very stout

and about sixty. She was a volatile, French woman and smothered Bill with hugs and kisses. He was introduced to her son Georges, who was about 25, slim, with dark, slicked-back hair, and to Bill's surprise, he was also introduced to everybody else in the bar, including an Englishwoman married to a Frenchman. He was horrified at this casualness but was assured by the Englishwoman that Clichy (where they were) was always a very tough area and out of bounds to German troops – even the police walked about in fours. He was given a tremendous welcoming party during which he made the acquaintance of his first hole in the ground loo!

He stayed there altogether about a month, during which he was taken all over Paris by Georges, just like a tourist – Georges took great delight in taking photos of Bill beside German soldiers! At weekends he accompanied Madame and Georges to their country cottage about 30 miles from Paris on the train. Georges worked at the Renault factory and seemed to spend most of his time in sabotage. While he was there, Bill had his 20th birthday, which was celebrated in the bar by a party of about 50 people and a quite incredible number of presents.

The next step was to get him over the Pyrenees. He arrived safely at Perpignan and walked out of the station to a small house. Here he was handed over to a small hunchbacked woman, who looked about 70. The Australian and he were given a super dinner with lashings of wine and brandy, Bill recalls. They stayed the night and the next day.

The following evening they were put into the back of an old wood burning lorry and driven about 30 miles where they were dropped in a field. To their surprise there were about 20 people there – mostly Dutch and French who wanted to escape from occupied Europe. They were introduced to the three Spanish guides who were to guide them across the Pyrenees. They were warned it would be hard going and very cold – 'It was!!' Bill recalls. 'We had to go over the highest parts to keep away from German patrols – food was provided and shelter in huts. My most memorable meal was a delightful soup – tasty and hot – until I went back for more and saw the meat content was a pair of sheeps lungs with lights attached, but I still enjoyed the second bowlful. It was incredibly cold – several had very bad frostbite and were left to make do as well as they could. I slipped on an ice patch into a very thorny bush which made my legs bleed badly – which soon became infected.' He managed to make it to Spain – only to find himself clapped in prison at Pamplona.

'My legs were very bad by this time and I could hardly walk. Nobody seemed to know how I could contact the British Consul and nobody seemed very interested. One guard was very covetous of my Omega watch so I managed, with help from the Spanish prisoners, to tell him I would give him the case of the watch now if he would contact the British Consul for me and the works when he came to see me. Two days later the British Consul came out and I parted with the rest of the watch. It took about another week for the consul to get the charge of entering Spain illegally against me waived and to get my release. I was then taken to a nursing home where I spent about three weeks whilst my legs healed. I was then put into an hotel in Pamplona where I stayed for about two weeks.

'After this time, about 30 of us, who I had not met before, were taken by coach to Madrid and via a very drunken day at Williams and Humbert Bodega at Xerez to Gibraltar. We spent about a week on the rock being kitted out and medically examined then flown back to UK in a Catalina which took 22 hours!! After interrogation I was sent on a month's leave and then back to my squadron.'

But not for long!

On 25th Janaury 1944 he was in occupied France, for the second time around: again he was flying a Spitfire as bomber escort, and was forced to crash-land. Instantly he was surrounded by Germans from the local flak battery, and taken at gun point to the battery and locked in a wooden hut. After a while he was given food and water and interrogated by an English-speaking German officer. He refused to give anything more than number, rank and name. The German was very pleasant and did not put any pressure on him. Bill was told he would be taken to POW camp the next day. He was left alone and on inspecting the hut he noticed the window frame was rotten. He waited until all was quiet, then picked away at the rotten frame with a knife left from his meal and managed to remove the whole frame. He stepped out into complete darkness. He began walking, then he heard a lorry. He watched and saw it was stopping at huts to collect refuse. Carefully he went towards it and saw it was driven by a Frenchman with one helper. He waited until their backs were turned, then went under the lorry. When the lorry started up he found a convenient ledge for his feet and hung on. After two or three more stops, they drove out of the camp with Bill underneath. After about 200 yards they stopped at a crossroads where he dropped off and they went on without him. It was about 4 a.m. so he went into a field and found a good hiding place for the next day.

'After dawn,' he recalls, 'I did not hear or see anybody until about 11 a.m. when much to my surprise a Frenchman came straight up to me and asked if I was English. There was no point in arguing so I said yes. He told me he was delighted as they had been looking for me since yesterday, after the crash. He put two fingers in his mouth, whistled, and a cart with two horses came galloping up the road. When it reached us I was pushed into the load of hay and we ambled gently along. I was taken to a house and put into a cellar with an American, Colonel Leon Blythe, who had been there for a couple of weeks.' The cellar was jointly owned by the Fillerin family, and their neighbours, with whom Crowley-Milling had stayed earlier, M. and Mme Vincent-Ansel. Madame Fillerin had recently been arrested, and the children were now carrying on the work.

'We spent about a week there awaiting identity cards and civilian clothes, after which we were put on a train for Paris. During this journey a German soldier got into our carriage and said, *Guten Morgen*. To my horror Leon answered him saying "Good Morning" – whether the German thought he was speaking bad German or whatever I don't know – but no further conversation ensued. At Paris a guide took us to a very expensive flat in the exclusive Bois de Bologne area, where Leon and I stayed in the attic for about two weeks. During this time and the subsequent four weeks we were in a hotel, I was engaged in interviewing personnel who claimed to be British but about whom the Resistance were worried might be German infiltrators into the Resistance network. The hotel was incredible. There must have been some 100 Allied personnel there. We then went by train to the south and some 40 of us walked across the Pyrenees to Andorra.' This time Bill's reception was very different as the end of the war was in sight. On arrival in Andorra they were taken to a nice hotel by somebody from the British Embassy in Madrid; then after two or three days sightseeing they were taken by coach to Madrid, 'then usual drunken spree at Williams and Humbert and then down to Gibraltar and flight home.'

As before, Bill had managed to get a message through to his father and mother, first from Barcelona, and then on 25 March from Madrid. While here he was interviewed by the British Ambassador, Sir Samuel Hoare. Bill arrived at Greenock on 10 April. His two months was not far off the mark. When he arrived in the UK he spent a little while working with MI9, alongside Lieutenant-Colonel Jimmy Langley, where he was told he had been recommended for the MC. The recommendation was in fact, for the MBE, dated 17 July 1944, and signed by the AOC of Number 84 Group, Air Vice Marshal Brown, but in the end it did not go through.

II

Belgium

The evasion line that was to become known as Comète or Comet began in Belgium in 1940 when the 24-year-old Andrée de Jongh began helping British invaders, at first unknown to her family. In 1941 she arrived in Bilbao with a party of evaders and, with some difficulty due to her youth and sex, persuaded Monday, the MI9 agent in Madrid, Sir Michael Creswell, and MI9 in London to give her the funds to set up a line from Belgium through to the Pyrenees. It was an enormous undertaking, but so impressed were they with her that they agreed. The line remained under Belgian control, however, till 1943, though funded by MI9. In 1941 Andrée was forced to leave Brussels and her father Frédéric, headmaster of a school at Schaerbeek, ran the Belgian end of the operation. Donald Darling recalls: 'Apart from her bravery and devotion to the Allied cause she was a superb organiser and a leader; her associates always obeyed her implicitly. It was as if she had been born to this kind of clandestine and very dangerous work, for she had an extraordinary flair for it, as well as the physique and will power.'

The Gestapo suspected her activities almost from the beginning, and her father too left Brussels for good for Paris in April 1942. Three of the Brussels organisers were arrested a few days later, and though the Comète line continued from Paris it seemed as if the Brussels end was doomed. However a phoenix arose in the shape of the Baron Jean Greindl, a 36-year-old helper on the line who worked under the code name Nemo. He continued the work and one of his early successes was the Manser crew whose story is told in this book.

The line operated through a system of couriers taking parties of evaders by rail. One of the earliest guides was Andreé Dumont, otherwise known as Nadine or Dédée whom the Germans mistook and arrested for Andrée de Jongh whose nickname was also Dédée. Other girls took her place. Peggy van Lier, for instance, later to marry James Langley, and Nadine's older sister Michou, who became a principal in running the line in 1943 and 1944.

Andrée de Jongh rented a safe house near Paris for her evaders, and put in charge of it a young French girl Elvire Morelle. Elvire had broken her leg on an earlier crossing of the Pyrenees and had been taken down the mountains in great pain on a mule quickly found by their chief guide Florentino. She later resumed courier duties, but on a trip to Brussels in November 1942 was arrested together with other helpers on the line.

Raymonde and René Coache ran another safe house on the Comète line, at Asnières, near Paris. In the south of France, Comète's organiser was Madame Elvire de Greef, 'Tante Go' as she was known. She ran a safe house near Biarritz at Anglet, and through her husband who worked at the German Kommandantur, she was able to obtain blank identity cards and other useful perquisites.

Andrée de Jongh accompanied parties over the mountains herself, as will be seen. Florentino Goicoechea, the chief guide was a Basque, by profession a smuggler, who before the war had taken part in the Spanish Civil War and fled from Franco to live in France; he was awarded a George Medal for his invaluable help. Another key helper was an Englishman, who lived with the de Greefs under the name Albert Jonion. His real name was Johnson and Airey Neave relates that he was responsible for the return of 122 men in two years. On the border, Francia Usandizaga, a Basque farmer's wife, sheltered evaders before their crossing. She however was arrested and died in Ravensbrück.

In 1943 disaster hit the Comète line when Andrée de Jongh was arrested in January and in Belgium Greindl suffered the same fate shortly after. Yet the line survived. A young courier, Jean François Nothomb, code named Franco, took over from Dédée. Though at the same time as Dédée many of her helpers were also arrested, the de Greefs escaped and by February the line was operating again under Nothomb and Johnson. The last evader was taken over the Pyrenees on 4 June 1944, as has been related in the preceding chapter. Nothomb however was betrayed early in 1944, but like Dédée, whose position in the line the Germans never realised, he survived the war.

In 1986 Dédée, now Comtesse de Jongh, recalled those days: 'We lost all kinds of liberty and freedom. Our own laws counted for nothing – there was only one law, the German law, and that could change each day. The death penalty was always there, written on posters in cities and villages for helping any former allies. You could be searched at any time – they could do what they wanted and steal what they wanted. German soldiers were parading in the streets, arresting and killing people in front of you and ill treating others for nothing at all. The Germans had offered a million Belgian francs to anyone who would denounce my father.'

Another key worker for the resistance in Brussels was an attractive Belgian woman, Anne Brusselmans, and it was she who played a major role in the first evader's story included in this chapter.

At the end of the chapter an evasion story from Belgium's neighbour Luxembourg is included.

1.   First in 'Tante Go's' Book

Radio communications for occupied nations was vital if links were to be maintained with the outside world. On the fall of Brussels, Anne Brusselmans was approached by pastor Shintz to translate the news from the BBC in London into French. These news bulletins were then distributed amongst safe friends. Anne Brusselmans recalls: 'I was then asked to help British soldiers stranded in Belgium (after Dunkirk) by giving them civilian clothing and money to help them on their own way of escape. Then came the first British air raids on Germany in 1940/41 and as planes were shot down we started to have airmen on the run, and I was asked if I would keep them in my home until they could be got away. This, I said, I was prepared to do, so Major Gierse, a retired Belgian Army Officer, came to see me. His job was to find billets for these men.'

Anne continued to shelter evaders and organise their escape until Brussels was liberated in September 1944.

'It was a team job and each of us a cog of a wheel. Without them all nothing could have been accomplished, from the farmer who fetched the men in the dark, to the guides who took them across the border; the doctors who helped the wounded, and the hairdressers who made them look their best. It was wonderful adventure, that is if you were not caught. Each one of us knew the price we might have to pay and yet the job was done.'

One airmen helped by Anne was Sergeant Jack Newton of 12 Squadron. His aircraft force-landed at Borgerhout airfield in August 1941 having developed engine trouble on the way back to base. The Germans at the time were under cover in shelters, as bombers unable to reach Antwerp by their deadline were jettisoning their bombs on the airfield. That gave Newton and his crew 20 minutes to destroy the aircraft and escape.

With two other members of his crew, the pilot, Flight Lieutenant Langoise DFC and Sergeant Copley, the wireless operator, he made his way to Liège and then Brussels arriving there on 14 August 1941 but they were then split up. Newton went to one address, and the other two another. Newton did not see the other two again, but found out later that they were caught and became POWs. Newton remained in Brussels in a safe house owned by Mme du Porque. Here he met Sergeants Larry Burk RAAF, a Pole, Janek Budwunski, and Albert (Al) Day RCAF who had been shot down with 77 Squadron on 7 August. Their story was not short of interest. Opposite the house lived 'two ladies of ill-repute,' Newton recalls, 'who were visited frequently by German officers in staff cars. In return for their services they were given large boxes of food, the bulk of which was distributed up and down the street of which a fair share went to us. It was a case, for the Germans, of biting the hand that feeds you.'

Before he left Belgium, Newton stayed in two other safe houses. One, in Waterloo belonged to M. and Mme Evrard. 'The bedroom I slept in at Mme Evrard's had been used by two Germans who rode a motor bike and sidecar, on which they carried a machine gun. Each night they took the gun off and left it in the bedroom with the oil dripping on the bedroom carpet. They soon left as her little terrier dog barked at them all night. When I slept there he was happy to get into bed with me and sleep. Who says animals are not a good judge of character! M. Evrard was a keen gardener and named a climbing plant "Mary Newton", after my wife.'

The second safe house was run by Mlle Becquet. 'When I was with Mlle Becquet I had a terrible raging toothache. She had been teaching me a little Spanish and so I was passed off, to the dentist, as her Spanish nephew. She supplied some silver coins which were melted down and used to fill three of my back teeth, and they lasted until 1981 when I started to use dentures. Her brother was a monk, and looked like Friar Tuck with his build. Under his woollen cassock he had a Sam Browne belt with a holster in which he carried a .45 revolver. In two large pockets he had cigarettes, whisky and bully beef.

'Mlle Becquet used to read Belgian books to me in English so as to improve her knowledge of the English language. She came upon the prayer – "You will be delivered from the hand of the enemy". She cut it out and told me to keep it; I did and still have it today.'

Newton met Pilot Officer Howard Carroll at Brussels railway station en route to Paris and the south. Newton had taken the place of Al Day who was ill with pneumonia. There was also a Belgian in the party, Gérard Vasquez. 'At a station on the Franco-Belgian border we met Andrée de Jongh (of the Comète line) who was to escort us all the way into Spain. She took us on trains all the way to a farm near St Jean de Luz, at Anglet.' Here Newton met Mme Elvire de Greef, Comète's organiser in the south of France. With her son Frédéric and daughter Janine she had been sheltering evaders since June, and Janine acted as a Comète courier between Paris and the Pyrenees. In all Elvire de Greef helped between three and four hundred airmen, and kept a diary of her work in which Newton was the first RAF airman to record his name.

'When we set out from here to cross the river Bidassoa, we ran into problems,' as Andrée de Jongh recalls: 'Owing to the conditions, violent rains, the water was too high and violent to cross, so we were obliged to go back to the farm near Hendaye but in the mountains. We had only one idea in mind, to lie down and sleep, and this is what we did on the only bed, happily a large one, and we lay like sardines in a tin.'

Jack Newton recalls: 'We were fully clothed and the married men slept next to Dédée and the single ones on the outside.'

When they set off again, they crossed safely into Spain. The Belgian, Gérard, left them then to go via Lisbon, planning he told them, to join the Belgian Forces in the UK. 'He said he would let my wife know,' remembers Newton, 'and my parents, and so I signed my name in his diary. This he showed my wife when he reached England but I did not catch up with him again until 1982. I stayed with him in Brussels on that occasion and he once again showed me the diary and a box of medals. He had been, in fact, an SOE agent and had been parachuted into Belgium.

'Meanwhile, when we reached Bilbao, Dédée stayed with us for some three days. We were the first airmen to have crossed this way. [Hitherto evaders had been Army personnel.] I remember the day when we were crossing from France over the mountains to Spain, and I turned and spat, saying "Dirty Boche". I was pulled up by Dédée who said, "I don't mind you saying Dirty Boche, but you have spat on my beloved country." To make amends for what I had done I got down on my knees and kissed the ground.'

After the war Anne Brusselmans, sometimes called 'The Belgian Pimpernel', was awarded the MBE for helping some 176 airmen and in 1959 she was the subject of *This Is Your Life* on British Television. In 1986 the President of the USA, Ronald Reagan, granted her permanant citizenship in the US to live with her daughter. He chose to notify her of this in person, by telephoning her. 'I never shook facing the Gestapo, but I did talking to President Reagan,' she afterwards commented. She was decorated by the USA, Poland, England and her own country Belgium.

2.   Maximum Effort

It was the end of May 1942 and a make or break period for Bomber Command and its new Commander-In-Chief Sir Arthur Harris. Determined to prove the effectiveness of his policy of bombing German industrial cities, he laid on a massive force of bombers numbering 1,046 to attack Cologne. The date was 30/31 May 1942 and it was the RAF's first 1,000 Bomber Raid.

At Skellingthorpe, the base of 50 Squadron, it promised to be a warm day, but somehow there was a feeling that something big was in the wind. It's a feeling that most people during the war, who lived on a bomber station, could always sense. At breakfast there were already rumours of a 'maximum effort' that night. 'Just my luck,' thought Pilot Officer Robert Horsley, as he had just teamed up with a new crew and had only three more operations to complete his first tour. It was, however, to prove a most remarkable crew. The operation did not augur well for them, as Horsley relates:

'I checked in with my new skipper [Pilot Officer Leslie Manser] and learned that we were detailed to fly over to Coningsby and pick up a Manchester aircraft and, on the return trip, we were to carry out a Night Flying Test (NFT). We collected the Manchester, "ZN-D". Inspection of the fuselage told the tale of many flak encounters – it had patches all over the place. The mid-upper turret had been removed and, in general, it looked completely worn out. The NFT was duly completed and we touched down at Skellingthorpe; although the equipment worked, Les Manser complained of poor climbing ability. The general conclusion reached was that the "lucky" crew who were to use that aircraft on ops that night would really have their work cut out. In fact, I commented to Manser that I didn't rate their chances of returning very highly. He laughed and said, "Don't worry Bob, we'll most probably be that crew." ' Sure enough, when the crew list was posted for ops that night, the crew of ZN-D was:

Captain, Pilot Officer Leslie Manser; Co.Pilot, Sergeant Leslie Baveystock; navigator, Pilot Officer Richard Barnes; wireless Op, Pilot Officer Robert Horsley; 2nd Wireless Op, Sergeant Stanley King; front gunner: Sergeant Alan Mills; rear gunner: Sergeant Ben Naylor.

'They were all freshmen with the exception of Barnes and myself,' says Bob. 'They were also all much older except Manser who was only a few days younger than I. (I had only just turned 21).'

The second pilot of 7301 ZN-D was Sergeant Leslie Baveystock. He had recently joined 50 Squadron and had been trained on Hampdens and had only five operations in his log book. At the time of the Cologne raid he had the magnificent total sum in his log book of fifty minutes' dual, and one solo circuit of ten minutes.

Bav as he was known, usually spent the evenings in his billet writing home to his wife Bette. With great difficulty Bav had persuaded his flight commander to give him the weekend off to meet Bette, and arranged to meet her in Lincoln on the Saturday. It was not to be:

'I wandered over to the admin building,' he recalls, 'and was surprised to see a large excited crowd around the notice board. I went over to hear one fellow say, "Seventeen crews on Ops! Christ, we haven't got that many planes, what are we going on? Bloody bicycles?" Elbowing my way up to the board I scanned the long list of names of crews going on ops that night. Somehow I knew that in spite of my 48 hour pass I would be on it. Sure enough, I was, and I had been crewed with yet another crew with whom I had never been before .... The skipper seemed to be very young, and was tall and good-looking, and my guess was that he had come straight out of college before joining the RAF. He seemed a very friendly sort of fellow.'

Bette Baveystock was naturally disappointed at the loss of her weekend, but was cheered up by Les. As she recalled later: 'I did feel the RAF were a bit mean to mess up a perfectly good weekend for us.'

'At the briefing,' Bav remembers, 'there was great excitement when it was revealed that the target was Cologne, and there would be over 1,000 bombers on the target. The mess hall hummed with excitement – that awesome figure of over 1,000 aircraft over the target at one time had yet to sink into our brains. It was too fantastic for words.

'There I met up with Manser's NCO crew and did my best to join in with them. I particularly liked our rear gunner whose name was Sergeant Mills. He was a most happy and friendly individual and it was apparent that all the crew liked him in the same way as I did. Our front gunner was a Scotsman, also a sergeant whose name was Naylor. A very solid unshakeable type though perhaps having some of the attributes of the Scots in appearing slightly dour. The other NCO in addition to myself was Sergeant Stanley King. He was second wireless operator on the crew and normally would have manned the mid-upper gun turret.

'I met the rest of the crew at the flight office when we got into the transport to take us out to the aircraft. In addition to Manser there was our navigator, Pilot Officer Barnes. In fact he wore pilot's wings and had been trained as a pilot, but for some reason I never fully understood had become Manser's navigator. The last member of the crew was also a pilot officer whose job was wireless op/gunner. He was a brand new officer having had his commission only a few weeks, and he was young, boyish, and extremely handsome. With his officer's hat set at a jaunty angle he looked to be the epitome of what every young boy would fancy himself to be; this was Bob Horsley.'

At 9 p.m. it started to get dark and the crew of L7301, set out in the crew coach to the aircraft. Bob Horsley turned to his friend Johnnie Tytherleigh (who was later to be killed with 617 Squadron on the Dams Raid) and said, 'I won't be back tonight, Johnnie, but I expect to hit base again before the end of the year.' He laughed and said, 'See you at de-briefing in the morning.' At first all went well. They reached and bombed the target successfully.

'Then, as if the last command had been a signal for the Germans,' Bob recalls, 'the searchlights coned us and the flak burst all around our aircraft and there were sounds of flak striking us. Manser immediately dived the aircraft to port and downwards to the roof tops to get us out of trouble. As we approached the roof-tops, the searchlights were switched off and the flak ceased. Manser levelled the aircraft and brought it under control. The rear gunner [Naylor] reported that he had been hit by the flak and, I reported some smoke coming out of the port air vent, a few moments later the port engine burst into flames. Manser quickly feathered the propeller and extinguished the fire. He asked the navigator for a course to the nearest master diversion airfield, Manston, and ordered the crew to jettison everything possible. The tail of the aircraft had been so badly damaged that it made flight on one engine difficult; it appeared that the elevators had been damaged and it made pitch control very bad.'

The rear gunner, Naylor, had been wounded and Horsley went back, despite the smoke in the aircraft to give him first aid. Meanwhile, Baveystock, Barnes and Mills were jettisoning everything possible to try to lighten the load. 'I had only just finished dressing Naylor's wounds and I was about to help with the jettisoning,' Bob writes, 'when Manser, in a very calm voice, almost as if it was a practice crew-drill, said, "*Put on parachutes*" – I acknowledged and handed Naylor his 'chute and told King and the others to clip on their 'chutes. Then Manser said: "I can't hold this aircraft any longer – good luck jump, jump, jump." At that, I ordered Naylor and King out, but – it seemed as if they couldn't believe me – they insisted that I go first. The rear door had been jettisioned, and although the crew drill was to dive through the opening, the low set of the tail plane, to my mind made this risky, so I sat on the step and rolled out. There was no counting to ten that night, as we were so low, and, as soon as I saw the tail plane pass over my head, I pulled the rip-cord. There was a sudden jerk as the canopy opened and slowed my fall. "Ankles together and knees slightly bent," I ordered myself. In a matter of seconds I hit the ground – splash – I had landed in some very wet marshy ground. A few seconds later I heard the aircraft crash.'

Bob Horsley believed he was still in Germany, though in actual fact he had come down east of Tongerloo, in Belgium. It was 2 a.m. in the morning. On reaching some woods he settled down to hide for the rest of the night, but as it begun to rain very heavily he turned back. Dawn was just beginning to break and he still had not found a suitable hiding place when suddenly around the corner came a young lady riding a bicycle. 'Here I was, in full view – dressed in RAF battledress. It was no use running, as I am sure she would have raised the alarm, so as she passed I gave a smart Nazi salute and said, "*Heil Hitler*". She looked startled and sped on her way.' Bob made off towards some woods and shortly came upon a signpost pointing to Bree. In the woods he consulted his silk escape map. By tracing a rough track from Cologne to Manston, he eventually found it. He could not believe his luck as it was just inside the Dutch/Belgian border on the Belgian side.

'The sky was becoming overcast and threatening rain,' he remembers. 'When I had checked the signpost I had noticed a small house on the outskirts of a village. It was still pretty early and there had been no sign of life, so I thought I would hide near the house and watch for activity and see if I could make some contact. It was just after five o'clock when an old lady came out into the backyard and started feeding the chickens. She went back into the house and then I made my move. I went up to the door and knocked. She opened the door and I pointed to my uniform and said, "*Je suis* Royal Air Force, RAF". As soon as I said RAF her face lit up and she took me inside. Gave me some black-bread and a glass of milk. She spoke quietly and said, "*Mon fils – il est le gendarme – il dort – s'il vous plait, silence.*" I had no sooner finished eating, when her sleepy son, the gendarme appeared, still clad in his nightshirt. I asked him the way to the coast and he confirmed my position on my map, but he warned me to keep off the main road as German cars were continually passing up and down. He was going to give me some civilian clothes to hide my uniform, but, as his mother appeared to be scared, he changed his mind.'

In the meantime Bav too, also wet through, was unsure
which country he was in. Unlike Horsley he had no escape pack
and apart from a knife which he had tucked into his flying boot
before he left, his one possession was a soggy handkerchief.
After a short while, trying to follow a course west by the stars,
he came into a clearing lit brightly by the moon: 'As I did so I
suddenly became that there was a man standing some thirty or
forty yards away from me on the opposite side of the clearing.
We both seemed to spot each other at the same moment and
immediately froze. His figure was not obscured by the shadows
from the surrounding trees and he appeared to be in a dark
grey uniform and I felt sure I had encountered a German
soldier. I could not see well enough to know if he was armed
and thought it unwise to run in case he was. So I just stood quite
still and left the first move to him. I felt so unprotected that I
slowly slid my hand down my side and took my knife from my
flying boot. The blade was still open and its rough handle soon
nestled snugly in my hand. The other man made no move and
through the passing of time could only be measured in seconds
our period of inactivity seemed like an age.

'Then the man made a slight movement and called out in
English, "Who's there?" "It's me, Les Baveystock," I stupidly
replied. He ran, or rather hobbled, towards me, and with utter
relief I realised it was one of our crew. As we drew together I
saw it was Stanley King, our second wireless operator.
Overjoyed at finding a friend instead of an enemy, we clasped
each other in our arms and danced around in the moonlight,
like a couple of demented pixies. The utter relief after our
moments of terror in the plane, and the subsequent jump was
terrific, and for some moments we babbled away to each other
with complete disregard for our present predicament. Then
just as suddenly our position dawned on us and we quietened
down and looked around ....

'We quickly took to the shadows and once more I set off
towards the west. I helped Stan as best as I could but our
progress was so painfully slow. I explained to him how I
intended to escape to Gibraltar and that well before dawn we
must find a cornfield and hide up for the day. My chief concern

was on account of my saturated clothing and my plan was to strip off as soon as the sun came up and try and get myself dry. We would have to lie doggo all day without food or water, and then, if not discovered, to push on when nightfall arose, and get further away from the crashed plane before seeking help.'

This they did, until driving rain brought on cramps and 'I knew it would be quite impossible to lie there all through the day. So I called out to King and told him I would have to find shelter. My actual words to him were, "I might as well die in a prison camp as lie here and die of pneumonia." And anyway I was pretty sure that we were in Holland.'

They made their way into a large farmyard, where they were confronted by a lady of about thirty years. She was of course astonished to see them standing there, but then saw the wings on their battledress and said, 'R.A.F.' and showed them into a little out-building. The farm was owned by the Nijsken family, in Bree. The family consisted of elderly parents, two brothers and a sister.

Back in Lincoln, Bette Baveystock heard the sound of engines returning, with relief. As she related: 'I got up soon after 7 a.m., got all prettied up for breakfast and my date. He didn't show up for breakfast – he must have been delayed. I listened to the news; 44 missing in the biggest raid so far. After breakfast I wandered upstairs again. He couldn't be long now. Then I came down in case he was waiting downstairs for me – still no Bav. By 11 a.m. or so I couldn't keep away from the phone any longer. I rang and asked where he was. The officer I spoke to left the phone to enquire and then came back and said in a very measured tone: "There's no news for you yet, Mrs Baveystock". It was left to a Padre to break the news that afternoon.'

In the meantime Bob Horsley, at 8 a.m., left the house he had been staying at and took a slightly different route than the gendarme had shown him, just in case he had changed his mind and told the Germans. He entered a barn and was confronted by an old lady who made it quite clear that he was not welcome, emphasizing this by taking a swing at him with her broomstick. He took the hint.

His next contact was more helpful and took him by bike 'down a lane by the side of a large house. We got off the bike and went into the back garden and he hid me in the shrubs and said he would go and get the lady. A few minutes later, a very charming lady of about mid-thirties and her young 14-year-old daughter were introduced to me; Madame Groenen and Mariette. They both spoke perfect English and she explained that her husband was the local doctor of Tongerloo. I was overjoyed when she told me that Mills and Naylor were hidden in her house and she had arranged for them to be moved that night; unfortunately, it was only possible for two to go onwards that night, due to lack of escorts. Her husband had also forbidden her to help any more escapers [he was working for British intelligence and wanted to keep a low profile] and so I would not be able to enter her home, however, if I would care to sleep in the barn, she would arrange for me to move on the next night. Her daughter took me to the barn and I found comfort amongst the straw. Mariette went off to get me some food and after about twenty minutes returned with some sandwiches and a glass of milk.

'I awoke at cock-crow, and looking at my watch it was only about 4.45 a.m., I felt very cold and cramped. I arose and walked about inside the barn to generate my circulation. I sneaked outside and in the shrubbery attended to my nature-call. At about six o'clock Mariette arrived with more sandwiches and the good news that Mills and Naylor were safely on their way. The bad news was that they had heard that the Germans were searching the area and that I should go away and hide in the local copse and, all being well I should return at 5 p.m., when her mother would introduce me to an escort to take me on to my next contact point. She took me out of the barn and across a field to a small copse where I was instructed to hide.'

After a narrow escape from a German search party he was taken to his next rendezvous: 'My guide was Jean Bruels, a young man of about 28 years of age. He preceded me on his bicycle by about ten yards. We rode through the minor roads and lanes, only once covering a stretch of main road just a few

hundred metres for our destination. We had covered about
four miles when we turned off the road through a farm gate,
down a track into a farmyard. We dismounted, and left our
bikes by the side of a haystack and he cautioned me to be
careful because if the servants saw me they might tell the
Germans. He led me to the back of the farmhouse, through a
back door into a cobbled hallway; under the stairs was a
doorway, I was ushered through; there crouched in the dim
interior, in the candle-light I found Les Baveystock and Stan
King. There was a very excited but silent reunion. We were fed
again on black bread, sausages and coffee, all of which tasted
delicious. We were then briefed that we would be moving on
again that same night, immediately after dark as we had a long
way to travel before dawn; they wanted us out of the area as
quickly as possible.'

Baveystock and King meanwhile had been sheltered by the
hospitable Nijskens family. Bav was determined to get back to
Bette and started making plans to reach Gibraltar. King's ankle,
injured in his drop, was not up to the journey, and they decided
to separate. Before this plan could be put into operation,
however, news arrived about the aircraft. Manser had been
killed, one crew member had been captured, one was in hiding
(Horsley) and two were on their way to Liège (Mills and
Naylor). Arrangements were in hand to pick both Bav and
King up the following evening.

As Bav relates: 'At this good news both King and I were
overjoyed, and utterly amazed at the way that the local people
had so quickly got the complete story. But now we must stay
where we were because the men had work to do, which I guess
would be milking their cows and feeding stock. So King and I
settled ourselves, still amazed at the good fortune that had
befallen us.'

Liège was their first destination. They set off on bikes to pick
up a train to Tongres, Horsley looking after King, and Bav with
their guide, Gertrude Bruels. Bob Horsley takes up the story:
'Soon the train was packed to capacity and we chugged onwards
towards Tongres. I kept my eyes on Gertrude who was further
up the coach, standing with Les. Time seemed to drag, the sky

grew lighter as we passed through village after village. Soon another young man joined Gertrude, they chatted for a while, then with a smile and a nod at me from the young man, he sidled up to me and joined Stan and me, he shook my hand and greeted me in Flemish. Then at the first opportunity he whispered that we were to follow him when he got off the train. Shortly after that the train pulled into the main square of Tongres. There were German soldiers everywhere, but, fortunately, lots of other people crowded the streets. We duly dismounted with our new-found friend. Gertrude had gone off with Les. (I never saw Gertrude again, in May 1943 she was arrested by the Gestapo and she died in Ravensbrück Concentration Camp).'

They went on to Liège and Bob recalls: 'There to be met by two dear old ladies. We were told that we would be staying there for a few days until they could contact London for instructions; it was even suggested that they may even send an aircraft over to pick us up. I thought that this was indeed too good to be true, to risk an aircraft to pick up a pilot officer and two sergeants!! Later, Les joined us and we were treated like Royalty. The owner of the house was the Préfecteur of Police of Sector VII in Liège; we only met him for a short time, just after our arrival. He was a tall, quietly-spoken gentleman; he did so much to help the Allies and was later shot by the Gestapo.'

From there Horsley went with Bav to Brussels. Here their safe house was the Evrards'. Bob again: 'We entered, there to be greeted by M. and Mme Evrard and their beautiful sixteen-year-old daughter Gisèle. I just couldn't take my eyes off this pretty young girl, with her long brown hair and her deep brown eyes.

'Shortly after my arrival, Les Baveystock came in with his guide, a young man called Pierre Vansteenbeck. The apartment was underneath one of the government buildings which had been taken over by the Germans and was being used as the German Ministry of Information; the whole block was situated opposite the Palais de Justice. The apartment was very large and modern, with four bedrooms, a large lounge, and well furnished. M. and Mme Evrard, kept me playing bridge, morning afternoon and night; in retrospect, very wisely, thus diverting my attention from their pretty daughter. The second night of our stay, it was announced that we would visit their friends for a party. At about 7 p.m. we left the apartment and half-way up a flight of stairs in the building above, we passed through a small door into the archives; there were stacks and stacks of files; not German I was assured by M. Evrard. Eventually we left through another small door and up two flights of stairs we entered another apartment. There we were greeted by M. and Mme Vansteenbeck, their son Pierre and Stan King, Ben Naylor, and Alan Mills; this was certainly a great reunion. Ben's wounds had healed beautifully, he had a bright new scar over the bridge of his nose; otherwise he said that he was none the worse for wear. We spent a delightful evening together; plenty of good food and good wine. It was truly a happy evening. (M. Vansteenbeck was shot, in the same archives, by the Gestapo and left to bleed to death, in spite of pleas from his family to be allowed to attend to his wounds. That was in May 1943.)'

Bav now takes up the story: 'Bob and I were told that we would be off on the next step of our journey that evening to Paris. M. Evrard told us that our guide would be a pretty little girl named Dédée. She was the daughter of one of their leaders and very courageous. The other three members of the crew would have to stay a little longer with the Vansteenbecks as it would not do to move too many of us at one time. We were sorry they would not be coming with us but eager to get away on the journey home. Mme Evrard busied herself some spare underwear and a spare shirt that I had been given and later went into the market to get food so as to give us a good meal before we set out. I can remember Bob and I sitting around a table while Gisèle helped prepare the vegetables and we chatted to her. My spare shirt etc were packed into a little green leathercloth case that had belonged to Gisèle, and then at about 5.15 p.m. there was a knock at the door of the flat and M. Evrard welcomed in our guide. We were introduced to her and I marvelled at her youthful appearance. For she was completely different to Gisèle, being much smaller and even more demure in appearance. She stood talking to the Evrards clad in a long black wool jersey cloak which had an attached hood turned back over her shoulders. I stood and watched her as she talked, marvelling at the youth and innocence of this almost fragile little girl who was about to risk her life in escorting us over the border into France. And a feeling of gratitude welled up in me which I had a difficulty in controlling. For although she did not have the same magnificent bloom of youthful beauty as Gisele, she nevertheless had a certain indefinable air and a look of the Madonna in her eyes that aroused the strongest feelings of protective instinct in me. I was to be with her for only some fourteen hours, and most of those in complete darkness. But I carried a picture of her in my memory standing in her black cloak, till the war was over and nearly three years had passed.'

The girl's name was 'Dédée' Dumont, also known as Nadine. She remembers: 'We had to spend the whole night in the train arriving in Paris at 6 a.m. The clothes the boys wore fitted quite well, although Bob's was a little short. Their suits were cut in a beautiful grey material which during the war was scarce. Our other companions in the compartment looked very modest in contrast. The people in the compartment tried to make conversation with us so the boys pretended they were asleep. They seemed to think the boys were police in civilian clothes. I soon reassured them we were not, and to my surprise they got up on the seat and started to unscrew the tiles from the roof and into the roof was stowed sacks of flour which they were going to sell on the black market in Paris. They were very professional to the extent they dulled the bright marks that the screwdrivers had made on the heads of the brass screws.'

At about 1 a.m. the train arrived at the Belgian/French border where everybody had to get out of the train, for customs and passport control. Suddenly Bob Horsley remembered he had some of his escape kit in his pocket. He sidled up to some crates nearby and emptied his pockets, hiding behind the crates as he did so.

They followed Nadine through the customs check and passport control. She did all the talking, then led them back to the train. By now all their seats had gone and so they sat on their cases in the corridor taking turns to have Dédée on their laps. 'Here I was,' recalled Bob, 'sitting uncomfortably in the dark with this pretty little Belgian girl on my lap, her arm around my shoulder while I cuddled her close in the only way possible under the circumstances that we found ourselves in. My right hand lay across her lap as there was just no room for it to go elsewhere. So, quietly I whispered to her, "*Pardonez-moi, Mademoiselle*". She turned and whispered, "*Pourquoi?*" For the very life I could not remember the meaning of this simple word and this she must have realised, for she said, "Why?" I shrugged my shoulders and replied, "*J'ai une femme et une petite fille.*" I could not see her face but the sound in her voice told me that she was smiling when she replied, "It does not matter." '

Their destination was Paris. Bob Horsley recalls of the journey: 'Throughout this journey and on subsequent occasions, Les and I communicated with each other in Morse Code. The first occasion was a sudden pressure on my left arm; I quickly recognised a long squeeze for a dash and a short squeeze for a dot. Subsequently, messages were continually passing between us. So, it was in dawn's light that I received the message – 'Paris – Eiffel Tower ahead on the port bow'. I glanced out of the window and there was this marvellous sight of the Eiffel Tower. At last Paris. It was 10 June 1942.

'The train duly pulled into the Gare du Nord. Instructions were to follow Dédée but not to talk to her. Without incident we followed her out of the station and across the road and into a café. Dédée went over to a table where there were four or five people sitting, and beckoned us to join them. We were introduced to Andrée de Jongh, the head of the Comète Line escape route. Andrée was to take over and see us safely to Spain.

'We ate a very hearty breakfast, which to me seemed like a banquet. In spite of rationing the French seemed to eat enormous amounts of food. When I saw Les finish his meal and place his knife and fork English style, vertically, I recalled the escape lectures, so I nudged him, placed mine French style, horizontally, he corrected his fault; a fault that could have been fatal.'

Nadine was arrested in August 1942, together with her parents. The Germans were under the impression that because of her nickname, Dédée, she was Andrée de Jongh. She was kept in prison for 12 months, being interrogated daily, and finally sent to Ravensbrück and Mauthausen. She survived her long ordeal and returned to Belgium in 1945. Her mother was released, but her father was burnt alive by the retreating Germans. In 1945, Andrée Dumont or Nadine which was her code name, was awarded the King's Medal for Courage in the Cause of Freedom, while her sister Michou was awarded the George Medal. She recalls of this particular journey: 'I was pleased to deliver my packages.'

Les Baveystock continues the story: 'But now Bob and I were following this new Dédée, down into the Metro itself. She obtained the tickets for the three of us and we stood silently waiting for the next train which soon appeared. We followed inside but sat down some few seats away from her. To my amusement and to Bob's we found ourselves directly opposite two Luftwaffe girls who looked very smart and attractive indeed in their grey uniforms and forage caps worn jauntily over their blonde heads. They took no notice of me but were obviously interested in Bob. For, as I have said earlier, he was young and good looking with a fresh boyish complexion and hair as fair as either of the two girls, who now eyed him with approval. For among typical French people in our compartment he stood out like a sore thumb and must have convinced them that he too was a German. I looked around at Bob and was half amused and half annoyed to see that he was doing his best to get off with them. I could not but see the funny side of it, but was scared stiff in case they tried to get into conversation with him. I do not think that Dédée de Jongh had seen what had been going on, and I am sure that at the time Bob did not realise how stupid he was to risk larking about in this way. However it did not last very long as a couple of stations further along the line Dédée rose from her seat and we followed her from the train, after the exchange of more smiles between Bob and our Luftwaffe blondes.

'Emerging from the station we found ourselves in the

suburbs of the City, but exactly where we were I had no idea. A short walk and we were taken to some flats where a girlfriend of Dédée's lived on the first floor, I think the building was 10 Rue Dudinot near the Rue de Babylone. This girl was a little older than Dédée, and even to this day I do not know her name. We all had breakfast together and then the girls left us alone for the day. They took our identity cards and papers and told us we could write or read but on no account to leave the flat or open the door to anyone. Then having shown us the bathroom and provided us with a razor they departed, telling us that they must now procure new Identities for us etc.

'Bob and I had a good clean-up and then stretched ourselves out on a couple of beds. But of course sleep would not come as we were still too excited with all that was happening to us. So we just lazed around and chatted all day. At about five o'clock that evening Dédée returned with a tall good-looking girl whose name I afterwards found out to be Elvire Morelle. She walked with a slight limp which I took to be some sort of deformity from childhood. But years later I was to find that this was not the case. She had fallen earlier in the year while crossing the Pyrenees with a party of escapers, and had broken her leg. She had been left in the cold and snow while help was sought and later had been carried out on the back of their guide. But by the time proper attention had been given to her, things had not gone right, with the result she now had this pronounced limp. But once again a far worse fate lay ahead of her in the months and years ahead. Thank God we do not know the future.'

Once again they set off for the Metro they were taken to a smart restaurant. There, as Bav recounts: 'We were told that shortly we would go to the railway station to catch our train to the south. There we would meet two more men about our age who were going to come with us. One of them is a Belgian boy, she explained, and we know all about him and he is genuine. But the other man is an airman whom we do not trust. He seems to know nothing about the Royal Air Force and has been unable to answer many of our questions. We think he may be a German who is passing off his lack of knowledge by saying he is a Canadian and only arrived in England a few days before the raid in which he was shot down. Another reason to suspect him was that no other members of his crew had been found close to where he had landed by parachute. And so Dédée and her friends now faced a terrible decision. Should they take him on the last final lap of the escape line and risk him exposing them to the Gestapo. Or should they liquidate him? So, continued Dédée, we have arranged to have him brought to the railway station where you must question him yourselves and decide whether he is genuine or not.

'I turned to one of the men in our group, and asked, "What will you do if we think he is a traitor?" He shrugged and replied, "We will need to dispose of him." "But how?" I questioned. Casually he replied, "We will suggest that before we board the train we should all use the toilet. Then when he is occupied we will have to shoot him."

'I marvelled at his coolness, little knowing that in a few months time, two Germans masquerading as Americans serving with the RAF, would infiltrate the escape organisation and later cause the arrest of many people in Brussels. So, armed with this knowledge, and feeling very uneasy at the decision Bob and I might soon have to make, we left the restaurant and walked together to the railway station. Here we met our "doubtful" airman.' Fortunately, Bob was able to vouch for him since they had both been at the same OTU and the Canadian Harold de Mone was able to name to Bob's satisfaction, the prettiest WAAF in the sergeants' mess. 'And I for one,' recalls Bob, 'breathed a heartfelt sigh of relief that it had not been our job to give the "Thumbs Down".

'We settled ourselves into our compartment which I was delighted to find was a first class one and I sat in one corner opposite Dédée and relaxed. And now I was able to really take stock of this quite remarkable girl. I judged her age to be about twenty-four and she was an extremely alert and vital person. Her movements were quick and definite as were her thoughts and repartee. For now she spoke almost entirely in English which fortunately the young Belgian lad with us could also understand. She seemed to be always smiling and brimful of enthusiasm and I was not surprised to learn later that she was full of energy and vitality.'

Bob takes up the story: 'At about six in the morning on 11 June 1942, the train pulled into Bayonne station; Les and I were instructed to stay put and Andrée left with Hal and Jean. After about ten minutes the train pulled out of Bayonne station, there was no sign of Andrée. We immediately suspected the worst, therefore we alerted ourselves in case we had to make a speedy exit; at least we knew we were not far from Spain. However, our fears were soon allayed when Andrée entered with two other ladies; the elder was code-named 'Tante Go' and the other was her daughter Janine. 'Tante Go' told me that they were checking papers very carefully at St Jean de Luz and, it would be very unwise for me to have to pass through the checkpoint. They had arranged another method for me to leave the station; again they pointed out that I looked too much like a German and the German checker may think I was a German deserter; how I hated my Germanic looks. The plan was outlined as follows: I should get off the train and I should go straight into the *Pissoir* on the platform, then exit by the back door, walk across the marshalling yards to a gate, where I would see a man with an Alsatian dog. I should follow him and he would lead me to my hiding place.

'Now, I had never been inside a French *Pissoir* and in my mind it was like any other English Gentlemen's toilet, imagine my horror when I later discovered that the wall was just above waist high and one urinated whilst saying "hallo" to the rest of the world.

'The train pulled into St Jean de Luz station, the last stop before the Spanish frontier. Suddenly I was on my own again. I dismounted from the coach, confusion, reigned supreme; due mainly to the raucous behaviour of the Spanish soldiers. This to my mind was a great help and would divert attention from myself. I walked casually through the crowd and found my *pissoire* and entered it; the shock of lack of privacy was quickly dispelled. I urinated, fastened my fly, and casually sauntered out of the back exit, in full view of the passing crowds. I saw the exit in the distance and wandered over the tracks, constantly expecting to hear a shout of alarm from behind me; if that occurred I would have broken all long distance records across those tracks. I acknowledged a hearty *Bonjour* from one of the workers. I spied my man and his dog at the gate and was soon out of the danger zone, following my leader. I settled down to follow my man, who seemed in no particular hurry, having to stop every few moments to let his pet have a sniff at some delightful scent and cock his leg to leave his visiting card.

'The alleys and streets were almost deserted and after about ten minutes, my guide stopped, gave me a slight nod and vanished inside a doorway. A few moments later I followed him, he was waiting just inside and took me up two flight of stairs to his flat. We entered, he closed the door, shook my hand and gave me a hug. He could not speak any English and spoke only the local Basque dialect. He quickly produced some coffee, cheese and black bread and we ate whilst we waited for the others to arrive.

'About half-an-hour passed before Les and Andrée arrived. They were delighted that everything had gone so well; they had indeed been concerned about me. Their passage through the checkpoint had gone off without a hitch. Andrée told us that Hal and Jean were cycling from Bayonne and should be in St Jean de Luz later that evening. However, she had to make arrangements for our journey over the Pyrenees so we could expect to be there for a few days.

'The apartment was very neat and clean; it appeared that the man lived alone and would be looking after us; he was chief-cook-and-bottlewasher, and, he made some first class paella. We had numerous visitors; evidently the word was out that I was an air force officer; the local Resistance all called to pay their respects. The chief of a Resistance group brought a map with him and carefully marked the locations of all the German coastal batteries, their calibre, location of the bomb dumps, etc. from St Jean de Luz to just north of Bayonne. By the time he had finished he had given me a very thorough briefing. He then rolled up the map ad ceremoniously presented it to me, saying, "God save King George and good luck".

'After he had gone, I decided that such valuable information had to be taken with me. Les had not been in the briefing, so I didn't need to worry him about it. Anyway, I had already rid myself of all my uniform so, if I was caught going over the Pyrenees and ended up in the hands of the Germans I would most likely be shot as a spy anyhow, so what was there to lose?

'On 14 June 1942, three days after our arrival in St Jean de Luz, Andrée de Jongh reappeared; she had evidently been over the Pyrenees and arranged our reception. It was now time for us to move on. That evening Les, Hal and I escorted by Andrée and another man set off to walk to Urrugne, which was a small hamlet in the foothills of the Pyrenees. We walked through the lanes and the fields, without incident. It was a lovely June evening, mildly warm and oh, so quiet. There was a happy carefree atmosphere as we walked along, Andrée, ever cheerful and chattering. Eventually we arrived at the home of Françoise Usandizaga. We rested up as we waited for it to get dark. We were briefed by Andrée that we had a 22-mile walk ahead of us, through the mountains, where it rained every night of the year. We were to be guided through by a Basque called Florentino: we were instructed that, if we met anyone, we had to say we were Belgians escaping from the Germans. This information was especially for any Spaniards we were likely to meet that night.'

Bav describes Florentino: 'A huge man who had been watching from the window when we first arrived, came over to the table and shook hands with us. His name was Florentino. Bob and I sat at the table and were soon joined by a grinning Hal de Mone and his young Belgian friend. We were given a bowl of milk and some sort of cheese to eat and we sat somewhat bewildered by our surroundings, while we listened to Dédée conversing animatedly with Florentino. We could not understand what passed between them but it was obvious that a strong bond existed between them. For he was indeed an extraordinary man. Probably about five foot eleven in height, he was as broad as an ox, with huge hands and powerful shoulders. His face was tanned by the wind and sun and had a rugged splendour about it. His nose and mouth had the quiet strength of a man who lives very close to nature, and with his black beret perched flatly on his head he looked the very picture of a true Basque. I understood now why Dédée had looked at my nose and face when deciding that it be safe for me to go through the barrier on our arrival at the station of St Jean de Luz, for in many ways I resembled him. Though I was a very pale shadow compared to Florentino, who would have made two of me without any bother.

'It was time to move out. We made our farewells and gave undying thanks. We then, in single file, followed Florentino into the darkness. Although we had been told to keep quiet, Andrée kept up a continuous patter of whispered chatter. The night got blacker, the clouds thickened. Otherwise the silence was punctuated by the occasional croak of a frog and an occasional resounding explosion from Florentino's gut; Andrée giggled and said, "It isn't me, but just follow the smell." The cheap red wine which Florentino drank certainly, when mixed with goats cheese played havoc with his inside.

'Every now and then, Florentino halted, listened and changed direction. The cloud was heavy and full of that rain which Andrée had predicted. On and on we trudged, higher and higher into the mountains. Soon the drizzle started shortly to be followed by a steady rain. "Good," I thought, at least we should not be worried by any tracker dogs.

'After about four hours we came to a river. Andrée told us this was the border and we had to be careful. Florentino told us to hide in some shrubbery near the banks; he then went off to scout for a safe crossing and the location of patrols. We waited quietly, in a few minutes I could smell cigarettes, then we heard the patrol; two or three guards walked along the path between our hiding place and the river, it was so dark we could only hear them. We waited patiently for Florentino's return, it seemed like an age, but in fact was only a matter of a few minutes. We had been warned not to rush across the river which was only waist deep at that time of the year; we had to wade slowly in order to keep the noise level down.

'Florentino returned and the order was given to move off, again a word of caution not to rush, take it slowly. With hearts beating fast and adrenalin flowing we slowly followed

Florentino, in single file through the icy water which truly came up to our waists, a few minutes later we were all safely across. Now came another tricky part. We were at the base of a very steep incline which had to be climbed, in the pitch darkness, as quietly as possible. It rose almost 200 feet upward. Slowly we followed our leader, not a word was uttered. We no longer felt the cold of the water nor from our soaking wet clothes,the climb kept us warm, finally, after about twenty minutes we reached the top. There was no time to rest, we still had a long way to go; silence was still the key note. Although we were now inside Spain, the Spanish were always on the look-out for smugglers and could be quite trigger-happy.'

Once in Spain they were taken to San Sebastian and the British Consulate, and then on to the Embassy at Madrid. Bav describes his emotions: 'Bob and Hal and I had a brief interview with the British Consul.* He told us we must speak to no one concerning our experiences since first baling out, until we met a man in Gibraltar named Donald Darling. This man and only this man must hear our story. Our next step would be to go to Madrid where we would be taken care of in the Embassy. It was now the afternoon of 13 June, exactly two weeks since the day I said farewell to Bette in Skellingthorpe. Just two weeks apart from a few hours. Yet it almost seemed a lifetime away. I somehow didn't even feel that I was the same man. For here I was sitting in a strange room in a strange house … with only Bob's familiar face to remind me who I was. And even Bob had not known a fortnight ago. But most of all was the knowledge that I was now in Spain.'

At this time Bette had in fact got a message that Bav was safe. Her aunt ran a boarding house and one of her guests was a Polish officer working at MI9, altough of course she did not know this. In conversation one day she told him about her niece's husband being missing. On his return to London he looked up recent messages which had come in concerning RAF personnel, and saw that Les was in Liège and with the underground. For the next weeks he kept a watch on his

* Probably Sir Michael Creswell, MI9's agent, Monday.

progress and when he knew he was in the Embassy at Madrid he rang Bette with a very brief message. 'The name and number of the person you are interested in is alive and well.'

On 27 June the crew of 'ZN-D' were all re-united, except of course for Les Manser and Pilot Officer Barnes, who was a POW. After splitting up from Bav and Bob Horsley in Brussels, Naylor, King and Mills went to the safe house run by M. Vansteenbeck, head of the Service 'Luc'. There they remained till 17 June while Naylor's wounds were tended and identity cards were obtained. They then began their journey to the Pyrenees via Paris where, as Naylor and Mills reported on their return: 'The father of Dédée took us to his flat and [we] met two Poles serving in the RAF ...' There the party split up again. Sergeant King and a Pole were taken to Asnières, where they were sheltered by a Mrs Thomas (French) who had a grocer's shop. They stayed there till the evening of 22 June. 'We (Sgts Naylor and Mills) were taken to a house in a suburb ... owned by a Captain Violette, a wood fibre merchant who had been an interpreter in the French Army. He was a new member of the organisation and we were the first he had sheltered.'

On 22 June they met Sergeant Mills again and left for St Jean de Luz with Dédée and Elvire Morelle, and reached Spain on the 25th. After their reunion with Bav and Bob, they were taken to Gibraltar, where they were met by Donald Darling. Bob Horsley recounts the debriefing: 'The rest of the day was spent being debriefed by Donald. The main emphasis was to impress upon us not to tell anyone the names or addresses of where we had stayed on our journey home. In fact, that night, he had a bit of a party for us and invited a number of army officers along; I remember a tall Black Watch officer trying to quiz Naylor about his escape and, Naylor not being very tactful, told him in no mean terms to 'get stuffed'. I believe Donald Darling got quite a kick out of Naylor's candid approach. The next day we were kitted out with new battledress and basic essentials. I moved into the officers' mess, met the CO who, within a few hours had me playing water-polo for the RAF officers that same afternoon.'

Even when they left for Britain on 6 July, their responsibilities were not over. As Bob recalls: 'After about six days basking in the Gibraltar sun, orders came through for us to board the troopship *Narkunda*, bound for Gourock, Scotland. Before leaving, Donald Darling saw me and asked me to keep close to a so called Belgian 'Priest' who was on the boat, I was instructed to stick as close as possible and try to make sure he never had any communication with any of the escapers. I was informed by Donald, that the priest was in fact a German agent and they wanted him to get safely to England and for him to make his contacts; once these connections were established the MI5 boys could pick up the whole ring. (About six months later they 'bagged' about 20 spy contacts).

'Late in the afternoon our ship set sail, we had an escort of two destroyers and headed almost due west at full speed. I established contact with my Belgian "priest" and found to my great delight that he played Bridge, so we formed a formidable partnership for the rest of the voyage.

'At dawn the next day our destroyer escort had gone, we were on our own cruising at about 22 knots, still heading westerly. The journey to Gourock was without incident, and on 12 July 1942 we were safely tied up in Gourock; my escort duties to the "priest" had ended.'

The five of the crew were safely back in England. The cost as recorded by Bob Horsley, was great: 1. Flying Officer Leslie Manser killed in action and awarded a posthumous Victoria Cross; 2. Flying Officer Richard Barnes DFC injured and Prisoner of War; 3. Doctor Groehen imprisoned but released by advancing troops; 4. Madame Groehen imprisoned but later released through lack of evidence; 5. Gertrude Bruels arrested by the Gestapo. Died in the gas chamber at Ravensbrück; 6. Préfecteur of Police Sector 7, Liège, shot by the Germans; 7. Armand Leviticus died in Concentration Camp; 8. M. Vansteenbeck shot by the Gestapo, November 1942, his wife ended up in a concentration camp; 9. M., Mme and Mlle Evrard arrested November 1942, ended up in a concentration camp; M. Evrard died shortly after being released at the end of the war; 10. Mlle Dédée Dumont arrested August 1942, imprisoned for 12 months before being sent to a concentration camp; her father was burnt alive by the Germans; 11. Andrée de Jongh arrested June 1943 and sent to a concentration camp which she survived; 12. Florentino arrested after being machine gunned in the legs; was snatched out of the hospital by the French underground; 13. Françoise Usandizaga arrested and died in Ravensbrück.

On the credit side Horsley himself received the DFC, and since his christian name was incorrect on the citation, the mix up allowed him to return to operations, with Bomber Command. He joined 617 Squadron, the famous Dam Buster squadron – Les Baveystock received the DFM, and transferred to Coastal Command, where he had an outstanding career. He sank two German submarines, was commissioned and was awarded the DSO and two DFC's for the submarines and sinking enemy merchant shipping.

Hal de Mone received an immediate DFM, and was taken off operations, since he had been helped by a major escape line – perhaps as Bav says, his tour had been 'An all time record for its brevity.' He had been shot down on his first operation.

As soon as Bav was back he wrote to the CO of 50 Squadron praising Manser's action; 'it is to Pilot Officer Manser's coolness and courage that the rest of the crew owe their lives.' Two weeks later the announcement of the VC came through. In the 1960's Les Manser's VC was presented to 50 Squadron at Waddington, by his brother Cyril Manser. Five of his crew were present at the handing over. Frédéric de Jongh did not survive imprisonment after betrayal, but Dédée, his daughter, was presented with the George Medal at Buckingham Palace in 1946; her mother came with her on this visit. The Air Ministry presented her with a clock in the shape of a bomber cockpit, at the time, she said, 'When you thank me, you thank my friends, many of whom are dead.' She had returned from Mauthausen on 7 May 1945, having been a prisoner for over two years. She made the trip over the Pyrenees some 30 times. After the war she went to Africa to work with lepers and was created a countess by the King of the Belgians in 1986.

Florentino, her faithful guide on many of her trips was

returning from one sortie to Spain in the summer of 1943, when he was seen by a German patrol and shot at. He was hit in the leg in three places but managed to roll down the mountain side and hide the papers he was carrying. They arrested him as a smuggler and not as a guide assisting evaders. He was taken to a hospital run by nuns. The Resistance were determined to get him out – Tante-Go, Madame de Greef, remembers: 'I was able to visit the hospital several times thanks to a friend, the doctor had not as yet put his leg in plaster. To delay any action by the Gestapo, we were able to get an entry pass to copy and had one made out as coming from the Hendaye Gestapo. He was told by a friend that we were coming for him.'

'The next day an ambulance drove up to the courtyard, my husband, M. de Greef was acting as a Gestapo agent, and was shouting orders in German. The two stretcher bearers were Resistance men and the driver was the Mairie d'Anglet Concierge. Florentino was soon put on the stretcher and amidst a lot of shouting in German was taken out to the ambulance and away. He was hidden in a small house at the back of a yard whose entry was a garage watched by the Germans. They were not there at the time, having been enticed by an offer of a drink while the ambulance drove in. The Gestapo from Bayonne turned up later but were satisfied that the Hendaye Gestapo had taken over responsibility. Florentino at last had his leg set properly, but he always had one leg shorter than the other. My husband had played his part well as he was well known in the area, but nobody realised it was him.'

Florentino died in 1980 and is buried in Ciboure Cemetery near Bayonne. In 1987 the RAFES had a large plaque put on his grave. After the war he was awarded the King's Medal for Courage In the Cause of Justice. When it was put in front of the King for his approval they described him as an importer/exporter, a tactful way of describing his smuggling activities.

3.   The Village Priest

On 16 April 1943, Lancaster W4366-R of 12 Squadron was hit by flak over Pilsen and on the return flight fire broke out. Sergeant Tom Hutton, wireless operator and air gunner, the rear gunner Sergeant Rudkin and the bombardier Sergeant McKay, heard an order to bale out, which they obeyed. However there had been some confusion about the order due to the intercom and in fact the aircraft was brought successfully back to base. But for the three who baled out, their return took somewhat longer. Sergeant McKay fractured his hip and was captured. Rudkin and Hutton began the long trek home again.

As Hutton relates: 'I was fortunate to land uninjured on the top of a tree and was eventually met by our rear-gunner. You can imagine our relief at landing safely and our concern at finding ourselves in enemy territory. We believed we were on German soil but hoped that with a bit of luck we might be in France.

'We had barely congratulated each other on a narrow escape when we heard dogs barking and felt sure that a German patrol was already on our heels. It was a moonlight night and about 03.45 hours. We decided that the best action was to get as far away as possible from the spot where we landed, before dawn.

'To fox the bloodhounds we imagined to be on our trail, we jumped into a stream and followed it for a considerable distance. It was bitterly cold and, hearing no further baying, we decided to leave the stream and secure a hiding place before dawn.

'The excitement was beginning to tell and seeing an isolated house, we were sorely tempted to knock and hope for the best. Realising that we might be in Germany, better judgement prevailed and we pressed on, eventually reaching a main road. It seemed to be a good idea to lie behind the hedge in the ditch, in the expectation of someone passing by and overhearing their conversation – thus giving us some indication of the country we were in. Some cyclists passed speaking French; we sighed with relief and thought "Thank God – we are not in Germany."

The first person they met, a cyclist, advised them to keep to the fields and then 'we eventually contacted a farmer who spoke fluent English, having spent 18 years in Canada. It took a long time to convince him that we were actually members of the RAF, and not Germans masquerading in the hope of contacting patriots, but when he finally decided to accept us we knew we were sure of able assistance and our spirits consequently rose. He stated that, as most of the villagers had seen us and knew we had contacted him, the Germans would pay him a visit that night for questioning. He said that because of this he was sorry he could not take us to his home. However, he led us to a wood and told us to remain under cover and that he would return later. At nine o'clock that night he picked us up and led us to within 100 yards of his home. He gave us some blackbread, greasy potatoes and ersatz coffee. Although we had not eaten since leaving England and we had no appetite – probably because of the food and the excitement.' The following night he took them to a pre-arranged spot to meet another patriot by the name of La Fontaine. Their first helper was Eugene Josephs, a staunch Resistance worker, together with his daughter. After the war Hutton met Josephs again, now the receiver of many awards for his work.

La Fontaine took them to the village of Musson, where the village priest sheltered them. Father Georges Goffinet was an outstanding character. Hutton relates: 'The village priest of Musson was aged about 35 years, with a most charming manner which belied his great strength of character, his determination and fierce loyal patriotism. He greeted us with a warm, friendly smile and a firm handshake. Although he did not speak English he could sing one or two songs in the language. He entertained us to "Horsey, Horsey, don't you stop" on the piano and sang the words with a delightful accent.

'Venetian blinds covered the two large windows fronting his house. A huge letter 'V' was superimposed on each blind – 'V' for victory. The Germans clearly did not recognise this gesture of defiance; they probably thought it was a decorative motif if they considered it at all.

'One day Father Goffinet returned from a visit to Liège with an automatic pistol he had obtained there. He declared, meaningfully, that he was looking forward to using it. During his visit to the town he observed German troops waiting outside a cinema with large lorries. He realised that they were waiting to apprehend young men and women as they left the cinema. They were to be despatched to forced labour camps in Germany. Father Goffinet entered the cinema and warned the manager that the Germans were waiting outside. A message was flashed on the screen, and the young folk left by a rear exit.

'We were the first airmen whom Father Goffinet helped. Thereafter he helped many British and Allied aircrew along the escape line. Eventually he became suspect and seeing "the red light" he decided to accompany the next batch of evaders to England. A German priest contacted him as he was preparing to leave on his final trip, and begged him to be allowed to join the party. The German declared he was anti-Nazi and wished to flee to England. As he was a fellow priest Father Goffinet trusted him and agreed to accept him for the journey. When the party arrived at St Jean de Luz, the German priest, if indeed he was one, betrayed him. Father Goffinet was arrested, as were many of the helpers throughout the escape route. Father Goffinet was tortured and imprisoned in Buchenwald Concentration Camp.

'One day the inmates were herded into the main compound and informed that the Americans were twenty-four hours away and that on their arrival they would be liberated. They cheered, but their joy was short-lived; the guards opened fire from the watch towers with their machine guns and mowed them down. Father Goffinet died in the arms of an American soldier the following day. On 10 July 1945, the day my second daughter was born, I received the news I have just mentioned about Father Goffinet's fate. My wife and I decided that we must name the baby Goffinet in memory of my gallant friend and helper. In July 1955 I took Goffinet to Belgium; she spent her tenth birthday at Father Goffinet's convent, where the good sisters made a great fuss of her. She saw Father Goffinet's name heading the list on the village War Memorial and also that the village square was named Goffinet Place. My daughter is justly proud of her name.

'We arrived at Sprimont railway station in the evening to be met by Joseph Brasseur and Arthur Defosse. Joseph Brasseur was the proprietor of the village garage; Arthur Defosse was the village postman. We were conducted to the Brasseur home. Joseph was very involved in underground activities, including stealing food coupons from the local town hall to provide food for the many young people hiding in the woods and elsewhere to avoid arrest and deportation to forced labour camps in Germany.

'On our third day at Sprimont, Joseph Brasseur arrived home very agitated. We had heard that he was 'suspect' and he expected a visit from the Germans. He announced that we would have to leave the house immediately. We were taken to the home of Arthur Defosse and his wife Zenerine. Hortense Brasseur visited the Defosse family daily with food and cigarettes for us. We were well fed, no doubt from the black market sources. The Brasseurs declared that we had to make a long strenuous journey to reach England and so they intended to build up our strength.

'We were made very welcome in the Defosse home, as indeed we were wherever we stayed. They had two little girls – Adele aged four years and Marie aged six. The children were warned not to mention to anyone, that two airmen were staying at their home. They never did! Arthur's income did not permit feeding two extra young men with healthy appetites, but as stated above, the Brasseurs provided the food. Entrance to the cellar was through a trap door in the garage which was used as a workshop. The trap door was concealed by wood shavings scattered around a work bench. Should patriots occupy the cellar when a strange or hostile visitor sought admittance to the house, a push button situated at the back of the front door was pushed by the heel of the foot and this operated a red light in the cellar, warning all to keep quiet. He survived the war and received many decorations for his Resistance activities. His wife Zenerine was a very enthusiastic supporter of all his anti-Boche actions.

'I moved to Wattrelos on 1 June 1943, staying overnight in Brussels. Rudkin was to follow later. Henri and his wife

Cerealia, welcomed me most warmly when I arrived at their home in the Rue de la Paix. Their home contained two bedrooms – one large, the other small. Normally they occupied the larger of the two, and their young daughter Rosealine had the smaller one. However, they insisted, that I must use their room, and accordingly, they moved into Rosealine's.

'Henri was a small, insignificant-looking man, but he had a large and generous heart and was quite fearless but somewhat foolhardy; for example – one night when he and I were returning home after a convivial evening in a café owned by a member of the Underground, Henri, for no apparent reason, produced an automatic pistol out of his pocket and fired a shot across the canal on our right. It was a stupid and dangerous action; curfew had started half an hour earlier and we could have been in trouble for that alone. Fortunately, there were no German patrols in the vicinity or I might not be writing these notes. He had taken too much drink!

'Henri was employed in the local Town Hall and he used his position to further the progress of the Resistance movement whenever he could. In order to fool the Germans he wore a Field Marshal Pétain lapel badge to indicate that he was a collaborator. Henri derived pleasure in taking me to cafes in the evenings to introduce me to trusted friends. They would come to our table one by one and luck was with us – we were never stopped for our papers.

'Cerealia kept a hand grenade in an empty flower pot under the downstairs front window, where the path leading to the front door could be seen. She declared to me that should the Boche come up the drive to the house she would destroy them with the grenade – a very courageous lady and as dedicated to the destruction of the hated enemy as her husband.

'One night when Henri and I came home from visiting a café, Cerealia informed me that Captain Michel had called and advised that I was to leave at 0800 hours next day. Next morning I left with the captain and he took me to his headquarters in Lille where I was joined by Rudkin, a Canadian Flight Sergeant named Ford, and a Dutch civilian who was wanted by the Gestapo for operating an Underground Press.

We soon left for the railway station where Captain Michel handed us over to our guide, who was to conduct us to St Jean de Luz, via Paris. The guide's name was Pierre and he had a limp. I did not learn anything more about him.

'We left the train at the village next to St Jean de Luz and walked singly at a distance of 100 yards, following our guide who led us to a house in the town. This part was particulary dangerous as there were literally thousands of Boche in the vicinity; St Jean de Luz being a very heavily defended town. However, we got through; a night's rest and preparations were made by our friend Pierre for a Basque guide to lead us over the Pyrenees. These arrangements including bribing a German guard who could not have known that he was closing his eyes to the escape of RAF aircrew.

'That night we crossed the Pyrenees and were taken to a farm where we rested all day. The journey over the Pyrenees took 12 hours and one was almost tempted, several times, to give in. Our close confinement, particularly during the six weeks in Sprimont, made itself felt; one needed to be physically fit.'

Having reached the British Embassy and then Gibraltar, Hutton and Rudkin arrived at Liverpool on 24 July.

Afterwards, he heard that one helper, M. van Despye, had been arrested and tortured. He never fully recovered from his treatment and died in 1959. His daughter Rosealine came to stay with Tom Hutton when she was 14, but, sadly, died in a drowning accident a few years later.

4.   'Father' Weare

It was 26 April 1944 when Brinley Weare walked out of the briefing room in his lucky suede flying boots. He had so far flown to Germany on twelve occasions and the operation tonight to Essen was to be his thirteenth. As well as it being the thirteenth, they had to fly a new Halifax aircraft, HX326N, as their own aircraft was being serviced. The target was Essen, which to most aircrew was known to a tough one.

'It was uncanny,' he recalls. 'None of the crew spoke; we were absolutely silent from the briefing to the aircraft. The wireless operator owed somebody some money and went straight away and paid up. I was nineteen years old. Only two years before I had been working in the Co-op at Watford and here I was, about to climb into a four-engined bomber, and fly right into the heart of the German defences.'

On their way home, they were hit by flak in the nose, and were attacked by two fighters at the same time. The starboard wing was set on fire, and Weare, the flight engineer, cut the engines. The skipper, Flight Lieutenant Allen, gave the order to bale out. The bomb aimer and navigator had both been killed, and as Brinley believes, the two gunners also. They were at 23,000 feet, with the Halifax lurching all over the sky. He selected his parachute and crawled into the pitch darkness of the shattered nose. There he found the body of the navigator lying across the escape hatch. He tried to lift him up to get the escape hatch open, but of course he was a dead weight, and Brinley collapsed from lack of oxygen. 'I felt warm and comfortable just like when you drop off to sleep. Just then the aircraft went into a dive, then a spin, then it blew up!' The cold sub-zero air brought him back to consciousness. As he was falling he jerked at the rip cord but nothing happened. In desperation he clawed at the parachute pack on his chest. Looking up, he saw with great relief the awning open out. 'My body jerked then slowed down, but my lucky flying boots did not – they kept going! When I hit the ground I just ran, ran, and ran in my stockinged feet. Eventually I collapsed in a small wood.'

When he woke again it was about 7 a.m. He was very cold and his head seemed to belong to somebody else. He looked down at his leg, and could see a piece of shrapnel sticking out of it. 'And so I began smoking the twenty cigarettes that I had with me, during which time I carved the shrapnel out of my leg with my knife. I bound up my leg and started walking again, and for the next three weeks I slept during the day, under trees and bushes, and travelled by night.' One day he came to a long strip of concrete which he took to be the start of a road, but it turned out to be a runway, and in Belgium. It was a German airfield, as he was soon to find out, for the door of one of the huts opened and out came a German, luckily he was not seen. He then entered a small wood and came face to face with two men.

'We were as surprised as each other, but luckily they were members of the Resistance and took me to a farmhouse. Here, there was a little old woman, her two sons and a daughter. The girl insisted on bathing my feet but it took me about ten minutes to get my socks off. I was given a couple of eggs and a small piece of bacon, which after living on raw potatoes was a banquet indeed. The problem now was how to get me away. The two men were from the White Brigade as the Belgian Resistance was called. They found me a civilian suit and a pair of clogs and we walked along the railway line to the nearest town which was Tienen. There were Germans in the main street when we arrived at a café full of troops drinking beer. I strolled through them not knowing quite what was going on.'

He hid in this cafe for three days, when a smartly dressed man arrived, who asked Brinley all sorts of questions. Not knowing who he was, he only gave his name, rank and number. The next day he returned with another man, and Brinley was once again interrogated. By now, the Germans were so near, that every day was adding to Brinley's tension. That evening they took him to another house in Tienen, where he stayed with a butcher and his wife. This house was situated just across the road from Gestapo Headquarters!

The problem now was how to get him away. This they solved in a novel fashion. 'Then they turned up one day carrying a coffin, took off the lid and told me to get in. Being only nineteen and not really wanting to be transported in a coffin for a while yet, I said, "No fear, I am not getting in there." They said, "Yes, yes, you must it's the only way, we have worked it out." So reluctantly I got in and the lid was replaced with just enough of a gap for me to breathe. Nevertheless it was very dark and not at all pleasant. They took me out to a hearse and drove me to a chapel, where I got out, and its original occupant was put back and buried!

'Here I met someone whom I would remember all my life, a priest, Father Pieter Palmaerts. He gave me a spare cassock and collar etc. What I did not know at the time, but later found out was that while I was being taken to the chapel in the hearse a squad of German soldiers were marching in the opposite direction towards us. They had stopped and made a passage for the hearse and presented arms to the coffin. What would have happened if they had insisted on escorting us to the graveside is anyone's guess. Maybe I would have been buried alive at the tender age of nineteen.'

Brinley was given a bicycle and with Father Palmaerts, cycled through the middle of Tienen, but he did not make a very convincing priest. For one thing he was riding on the wrong side of the road, and for another he was whistling. They attracted the attention of a German who was controlling the traffic, but the Father made out to him that Brinley was heading for a cycle track on the left hand side of the road. This somewhat bizarre journey led him to the village of Glabbeek, where he was sheltered by the village schoolmistress, Emma Beuyninckx, and her nephew Karel.

'If the Germans were around I crawled through a trap door under the floor boards, my only companion being a huge spider. My hair was dyed blonde and I was given false papers. During the day I was the never seen son, Constance Van Lack; during the night I worked with the underground, but that is a story I wish to keep under my borrowed cassock.'

One souvenir Brinley Weare still has from those days is a Nazi officer's silk handkerchief. All he will say about that is that the officer did not need it anymore.

If they ever needed money they 'borrowed' it from Post Offices, where the Germans issued ration cards. The collaborators, known as the Black Brigade, got a little more than their share, but they balanced the scales. After a while Brinley was told that an aircraft was coming to pick him up, and got ready to leave. Somehow the Germans got wind of it however, and began searching the villages. 'They found me in the garden, but my Flemish was now good enough to deceive them to such an extent that I helped them look for me!' But in the next village where a Canadian was hiding, things did not go so well. Germans stormed the house, and when the Canadian made a dash for it, they caught and killed him.

Brinley stayed here for five more months until the British Army arrived in the village on 14 September 1944. A German list of people's names was found and showed 100 people in the village were under sentence of death. The name of Emma Beuyninckx was at the top.

Brinley was sent to Brussels where he was interviewed, then sent home to England. 'When I walked into my parents' home in Watford they looked at me as if they were seeing a ghost as they believed I was dead.'

Father Palmaerts died on 22 March 1986. To the time of his death, he had on his bedside table the photograph of Brinley Weare, dressed as a priest.

5.　Tante Betty and Uncle Jean

On a simple headstone in Schoonselhof, Belgium is the name of a man who had come 15,000 miles to fight a war. He was Pilot Officer John Lawrie, from New Zealand, who had been a pilot with 514 Squadron. On 12 August 1944, he had taken off with his crew in Lancaster LM 180 – 'G for George' to attack Russelsheim. In his crew was Sergeant Tom Young, the flight engineer, on his twelfth operation. The mixture of nationalities and the age of the crew was typical of the men of Bomber Command. In this crew were a New Zealander, a Scot (Tom), two Englishmen and three Australians. Their ages ranged between 19 and 21.

At 10.30 p.m. they got the green light from the control tower and took off. It was John Lawrie's 13th operation and the remainder of the crew's 12th. They reached the target successfully and bombed it and had reached the south-central

Belgian border when they were attacked by a Ju88 night
fighter. It all happened so quickly. The rear gunner saw tracer
and then the fighter itself. He gave the evasion call to Lawrie
and opened fire himself, but the Lanc had been hit on both
mainplanes and the starboard inner engine was hit, and it later
began to give off sparks and then intermittent flames. It was
feathered successfully but the crew, in the meantime had been
told to put on parachutes. Being the flight engineer the loss of
fuel from the damaged engine was of great concern to Tom
Young. His gauges told him the grim story. Even if they stayed
up they probably wouldn't make it.

'We had great faith in John Lawrie,' recalls Tom Young. 'He
had some 521 flying hours in his log book. His life's ambition
was to fly, so we felt we were in the best hands. But of course we
needed a slice of luck at this moment, as it was the pilot's 13th
op' and the date was 13 August. So we did not have a lot going
for us, when both port engines cut out. We were down to less
than 1,000 feet when the order to bale out came. I handed
Lawrie his parachute and then baled out. We were at 700 feet
when I left the aircraft and the wing was ablaze.'

In a village 17 km south of Ghent, a young man was staring out
of his bedroom window. He saw the aircraft on fire, and then
crash. The next day it got around that a 'plane had crashed two
villages away at Balegem. Many people had turned up to look at
it, and also word had got round that parachutes had been
found between Scheldewindeke and Balegem. The young man
was Eric De Surgeloose who, twelve hours later, came face to
face with Tom Young. He had heard that an airman was
wandering about and he and his father Tony went out to look
for him, taking with them civilian clothes and food, keen to find
the airman which turned out to be Tom.

As Tom himself relates: 'A mile or so up the canal I was
caught up by a young man about my own age. He had cycled,
and only just in time because I had intended taking to the fields
and forsaking the towpath.

'In halting English he had identified himself as Tony from
Gavere and required me to prove my identity, which I did. He

advised me to hide in the adjacent field. I was tired and fell asleep in the field, under the warm sun. On awakening sometime later, I saw a group of young men and an attractive girl apparently searching the area.

'After again providing proof that I was a member of the RAF aircrew, they explained their wish to help and that it would be necessary to remain in the field another day, whilst arrangements were being made for my transfer to a safe house elsewhere. Too much was already known in the village and they had their share of collaborators. Later in the afternoon, the girl, Arlette, would return alone with a change of jacket and trousers (to enable me to get out of RAF uniform) and a little food and drink. It was thought that a boy and girl would attract less attention in an area which was quiet and a popular Sunday afternoon walk for the locals. The leader of this group was Eric de Surgeloose and the other men were Tony, Sylvan de Smet and Fernand Poirot.

'Instructions were given to me to walk up the canal towards Ghent (some 15 miles) setting off at 6 a.m. prompt the following morning. Everything being OK, I would at some stage be caught up by Eric and the password "Churchill" exchanged between us, and later a third party at a large bridge on the outskirts of Ghent. I had no problem getting off in the morning, since I had been kept awake half the night suffering from mosquito bites and a little from nerves. Eric caught up with me by cycle and in addition to the password gave me a sandwich, cognac and beer to sustain me.

'I must have walked more quickly than estimated since I found no one waiting in the vicinity of the bridge. After resting awhile I had a walk about and saw Eric some distance away, I therefore returned to my former position by the bridge and sat down to await the next move. It was not long in coming, the third party approached me and greeted me by saying, "Shut up, and follow at a distance." I cannot now remember his name, and he died a year or two after the war. He took me along a route which was through backstreets in a poor area of the city, and at one stage we travelled by tramcar. He bought the tickets and we sat at opposite ends of the car. I remember that several

German troopers also boarded the tramcar and my heart missed a beat, but no checks were carried out.'

He was sheltered for a few hours by an old lady and 'The other lady arrived then: and was introduced as "Tante Betty". She was middle-aged and could well be described as middle class, a very strong character and brave. She told me about herself and her family after quickly satisfying herself that I was a genuine British RAF officer. Her husband was "Uncle Jean" and she had two young daughters, Madeleine and Gilberte, but she had a temporary extension to her family with the addition of a Belgian Army Captain, Henri Mees of Ghent, who was wanted by the Germans for espionage, also a Jewish lady, Flore Italiander and her daughter of some four years of age, Cirla. Flore's relatives, including her husband, had been taken by the Gestapo and were never seen again. Flore did have a sister left to her, but she was in London. Tante Betty had warned her family that I would be going home with her, and if anyone thought the danger would be too much they would have to make other arrangements for their accomodation. None did, and I was glad of it.

'Having exchanged formalities we said goodbye to the lady of my first refuge and we walked through the city, passing the soldiers on guard at the many canal bridges. She had declared that if we were stopped at all I would be known as her gardener. Unknown to Tante Betty her husband had followed her, not withstanding he was a man in retirement and not in the best of health. His purpose was to satisfy himself that I was whom I was supposed to be and his recognition was more or less immediate. (Good job none of the Germans took a closer look at me.) We arrived at my new home (of six weeks) without incident, and was very warmly welcomed by all.'

In September 1944, Ghent was liberated. When Eric de Surgeloose arrived in the town he was told that a lady nearby had come out into the street with a British airman whom she had hidden. It turned out to be Tom Young.

In 1971, Tom was able to find out what happened to his pilot from Nestor Heyden, who lived in the area of the scene of the crash. He had found what was left of the gallant John Lawrie and placed the remains in a box, and buried them in a flower bed. Nestor related:

'Only after the war when the British were enquiring about anyone who had crashed or been killed in the area, did I point out where I had hidden the box: this was exhumed and put into a coffin and taken away to be given a Christian funeral and then buried where it lies today.'

The radio operator, Sergeant Durland, had broken his ankle on landing and was taken prisoner by the Germans. Later he escaped while the convoy he was in was being attacked by British fighters, and was the first of the crew to get back to the UK. The remainder were, like Tom Young, in hiding. Sergeant Chester-Masters, the rear gunner, was in hiding in Brussels as was Sergeant Carter, the bomb aimer, and they reappeared when the city was liberated in September 1944.

6.   The Train

In September 1944, Flying Officer Stuart Leslie of 429 (RCAF) Squadron, found himself in a civilian Gestapo prison in St Gilles in Brussels. Before this he had been in a military prison in Brussels, where, since he would only tell them his name, rank and serial number, the German Luftwaffe officer who interrogated him, told him he would be treated as a spy and transferred to the Gestapo prison at St Gilles. He had been picked up wearing civilian clothes, and with forged identity papers. His adventures had begun five months earlier.

After his Halifax III left Leeming at 10 p.m. on 1 May, the aircraft was hit by flak as it left the target area, which obviously damaged the controls. Stuart Leslie gave the order to bale out, as he could no longer hold her, but suddenly the aircraft exploded and he was blown out. He landed within 200 yards of the aircraft, and discovered later that all the other crew members had been killed. Leaving his parachute where it was, entangled in a fence, he immediately ran to the nearest field and hid for the night. His left eye was closed by congealed blood, and one leg was a mass of bruises. In the morning he discovered he had landed at Oudenaarde, in Belgium. He began to walk towards France, and after two days and nights of hiding managed to contact farmers, who in turn brought two girls who could speak English. Alice and Elizabeth Van Vassenhove were from Brussels, and were on their Easter holidays. He was given a bed and even a pair of pyjamas, and even more importantly a steaming hot bath which did wonders for his aching body. 'I shall never forget the experience when I got into a clean bed that night,' he recalls.

He stayed there until 25 May, when he received a message from Brussels to say that they were ready for him. Alice in the meantime had gone to Brussels and acquired an ID card for him. Alice and Stuart Leslie set off on bikes for Brussels.

There he was handed over to another guide, and stayed in several different places until the end of June when he was taken by car to a château, about fifteen miles from the city of Namur. The next day two Americans and an RAF flight lieutenant arrived to join him. On 6 July, they set off by lorry towards the Belgian Ardennes, but at the village of Spontin, they were stopped at a German control point. During a search, one of the Americans spoke in English and the game was up. They were prisoners. Stuart Leslie recalls:- 'The time in St Gilles was anything but pleasant. Extreme overcrowding, lousy beyond description, food – very little – terrible to the extreme, and the visits to Avenue Louise – the Gestapo Headquarters – threats etc., not the greatest of excursions beyond the walls and iron gates of the prison. The long time in solitary confinement – a filthy broom closet – had its effect too, so when we were evacuated from the prison to the train by lorry – with our only food being a Belgian Red Cross food box, tinned horsemeat and hardtack, weak sugar candies – a new facet of life was upon us.'

The train passengers were the 15,000 male and female civilians who were being held by the Germans at St Gilles prison. On the night of 1 September, without the knowledge of the station master and in great secrecy, 32 wagons were assembled. The sub-station master, Michel Pettit, who was a member of the Special Brigade, was present at the station and his attention and fears were alerted to these wagons. The last train that went through with 900 people on it, bound for a concentration camp, did not return. At 6 a.m. it became evident that the Germans were evacuating the prison, but even before they had left by lorry, an order was given to the railway workers to hinder the movement of the train from the depot. Fully armed SS men were in charge of the evacuation, but the prisoners were not going to give in without a fight, and although in the end men and women were subdued by the use of rifle butts and clubs, the departure of the prisoners was delayed, and also brought notice to what was happening. As the lorries were being taken through the streets to the station, messages were being thrown out, telling people, to warn their parents, 'Help us, stop the train'. Instead of force, the railway workers decided to use the rule book.

The train chosen by the Germans was a type 33, and sabotaged by pulling the oilpipes away from their mountings, so the Germans had to choose another train. This was type 1202. By now it was 12 noon and the Germans were getting very impatient, but as the engineer, George, did not start until 12 o'clock, they had to wait for him. But as soon as he arrived, by arrangement he said he felt sick and went home again, hence more delay. Another engineer, Van de Vacin, was told to take his place and he did everything in slow motion to waste time. He then pretended he had fallen off the train and sprained his ankle. It was now 2 p.m., and the Germans were getting very hot under the collar and demanding another enginner be found. At 3.30 p.m., the train had still not left.

'When they finally moved off, there were three German guards behind the driver, Louis Verheggen, and the fireman Leon Pochet. They drove into a cul-de-sac and then into the station, where the signals were changed to red. This was despite the Germans demanding the train be taken to Antwerp. In each wagon at this time were 85-100 people, but they were told by the workers, "Don't worry, this train won't cross the border." '

They finally left at 5.55 p.m., but only at a snail's pace, all along the line the signals were against them, despite the Germans urging them to go through when the signals were against them. Then the engine broke down and another had to be sent for. Engine number 109 arrived, but then Verheggen, the engine driver, disappeared and the German officer was so furious with the three guards who were supposed to be looking after him, that he hit them. Suddenly, like magic, all the guards had vanished.

Stuart Leslie remembers: 'Our spirits were uplifted considerably when we were able to break open one of the locked side doors of the car, and escape plans formulated. Even then many wanted to just stay put, but after dark, prior to abandonment of the train – Royce MacGillroy, a USAAF sergeant gunner, and I dropped out of the car and ran for the darkest part of the marshalling yard. We made it although our imaginations must have been working overtime as we thought we could hear firing of shots, shouts of soldiers, dogs, literally everything trying to catch us again. We spent the night in a factory type building near the railway yards – we must have slept through sheer exhaustion and poor physical condition – and waited for the next day to dawn.' There were moments of humour in what had been a very serious and dangerous time. After the train had been released people were seen running down the road carrying on their backs carcases of pigs taken from the slaughter houses. Then the senior German officer in charge of the train, a tall man, was last seen cycling away down the road on a child's bike.

'Tired, grubby, hungry and thirsty,' Stuart remembers: 'we ventured up into the streets proper, looked to women waiting in a line up at a baker's shop in hopes of buying bread. We were warned that there were still many Germans around, but that the Allies were coming – Soon, everyone hoped. We were to be in on the liberation of the city. We were apprehended by a chap – a Belgian, formerly of the Merchant Marine on the New York run – and provided with a razor, cold water and towel in his small flat, to allow us to be a little more presentable for the liberation celebrations.

'The flags of Belgium and Britain, even a Stars and Stripes, appeared from windows, and throngs of people spilled onto the streets and walked towards the city centre and the incoming Allied troops. The first such that we encountered were the British Buffs (Tank Regiment), who were intent on following the retreating Germans, but were being kissed and hugged and literally dragged from their tanks by the Belgian women. What a sight! The first support troops we encountered, a British 2nd Army jeep – corporal driver, major British army plus a USAAF colonel-advised us to get to the Hôtel Métropole and someone would soon be there to provide for us. We were some of the first to arrive there.

In September each year as many people as possible who were on the train gather for a reunion in Brussels, one of which, although in a wheelchair now and 87 years of age, is the train driver Louis Verheggen.

*

Lastly, a remarkable tale of evasion from Belgium's neighbour, Luxembourg.

Six Got Home

Sergeant Robert Parkinson volunteered for the RAF on 24 April 1940. He wanted to be not a pilot or navigator but an air gunner; nothing else would do. It took two years but, in 1942, he made it and was sent for gunnery training.

At OTU he crewed up with Warrant Officer Bob Cant, pilot, Sergeant Syd Horton, wireless operator, Sergeant George Thomas, navigator and Sergeant Denis Teare, bomb aimer. At that time they were on Wellingtons. When they arrived at their squadron, No.103, they were joined by Sergeant W. Milburn, mid-upper gunner and Flight Sergeant E. Dickson, flight engineer.

'When we began operations, they were all the same – bloody dangerous!', says Parkinson wryly. 'Our last operation as a crew was on 5/6 September 1943 to Mannheim.' They took off from

Elsham Wold in good weather at about 2030 hours. They were about half an hour from the target when they lost the port inner engine and began to lose height and airspeed. Parkinson heard the bomb aimer say, 'Bombs gone', and they set off for home. The starboard inner was now playing up however, so they were flying on the two outer engines. The warning came to prepare to bale out. Parkinson turned his turret to the normal position, opened the doors and clipped his parachute to his chest harness.

'Then another engine went,' he recalls, 'and we were flying on the starboard outer engine only. Bob finally gave the order 'bale out, bale out'. By this time the one and only engine was on its last legs. I left by swinging the turret to one side and rolling out backwards. Bob had kept the aircraft straight and level which was a miracle in the circumstances.' Meanwhile Bob Cant had been given his parachute. He clipped it on his chest and made for the front hatch. As he tried to get out of the hatch however, his 'chute got caught round his helmet cords, so he had to climb back in and untangle the cords, then bale out.

Bob Parkinson in the meantime was floating down in a world of his own. 'It was so quiet and peaceful, I felt very relaxed. I hit the ground with a thump and rolled over a couple of times. I had landed in a field near a road. I pulled in my 'chute and took off my flying gear. Then I saw another 'chute coming down about 100 yards away so I began to sing a song we always sang when we crossed the English coast on our way back home – "Salome". It acted as a password on this occasion.' A figure ran towards him – it was Syd Horton, the wireless operator. His first words were, 'Give me a fag, Bob.' They cut pieces out of their parachutes and put them round their necks as scarves, then headed south west hoping to make Paris. They had landed in Luxembourg. On debriefing they said:

'After walking for about two hours we heard someone shout and ducked into the hedge. Two German guards approached, found us, and took us to a house which appeared to be a sort of guardroom. We had not removed our tunics or chevrons. A German corporal who spoke quite good English took particulars from us (rank, name and number). He then spoke on a telephone. He called out an escort of two men, youths of about 17 or 18 years of age. We had to follow these; they were very casual and kept their rifles slung; we walked for about 10 minutes.' Parkinson asked them if they could smoke and they gave permission, so they asked them for a light. Parkinson hit out at one of the guards, and Horton knocked the other one over. There was very little scuffling. 'We pushed them into the ditch, which was very swampy and ran for the woods. We do not know whether we had merely knocked them unconscious or whether they were more seriously injured.' They cautiously continued their journey to Paris.

'After a time we saw a party of Frenchmen working under a supervisor in civilian clothes. We also saw a French lad walking with a horse and cart, and we beckoned to him to approach us, which he did. We had by this time reached Rupt-St Mihiel, and removed our chevrons, but were still in battledress and flying boots. By means of signs the French lad indicated to us that a motor bicycle nearby belonged to the supervisor of the working party, who would give us away, and that it would be wise to lie low until he had gone. When we heard the motor bicycle start up we stayed where we were for a time.' A young couple appeared after a while and took them to a house where they were given civilian clothes and fed.

The two airmen then joined a train at Bar-le-Duc and reached Paris on 10 September. From their debriefing statement: 'We walked out of the station with no difficulty and thought we would make for the suburbs, as we had been told to do at our lectures. We walked through Paris all day, somewhat lost, and at about 1800 hours we saw a Roman Catholic priest whom we approached. We have no idea in what part of Paris we were, except that were near a very large race-course. The priest took us to a sort of school and fetched a priest who could speak English, and who inspected our identity discs, etc. to make sure we were British. From this point on, our journey was arranged for us.'

In Paris they were horrified to see men, women and children being urged along by rifle butts and fists, and dressed only in sacks, en route for forced labour in Germany. Parkinson never forgot the sight. During their stay in Paris they were passed from houses to house. In one an old lady, and a man showed them into a room with two double beds. They slept and spent the next three days there, being able to eat well and have a good wash.

'We were then moved on,' recalls Bob. 'A woman of about 30 took us to a house where there were three men drinking. We were given a drink and I did not remember anything until the next morning when I awoke in bed. They told us we would be collected, and that night another lady came and took us to her house. She did not have a lot of food but we did get a cup of tea, also a packet of 20 cigarettes, they were Lucky Strike. When I offered her one she said, "No, for Bob and Syd." I nearly cried. That day she took us on the Metro back into Paris as we had been living on the outskirts. We were passed on to two teenage girls, but just at that time an air raid came and we had to go in an air raid shelter. In it was a Luftwaffe officer with his girl friend. We were in the hands of these very brave girls, and we learned that they were only two left of a group of 18 – the others had been arrested, tortured or shot. They wanted to buy us a drink in a bar, but we declined on the account of the danger they were already in.'

They were then put on a train to St Hilaire. The train was full of German troops, but they were not discovered, were taken by van to Douarnenez Bay in Brittany, and put on a small fishing boat. The skipper was an old sea-faring man, and going below deck they found many Frenchmen who were going to the UK to join the Free French Forces. However, they were stopped on the way out when Germans boarded the ship for inspection, and they could all hear the jackboots on the deck above them. Fortunately the Germans did not come below.

They took a dog leg course to avoid U-Boats, and 'we spotted an aircraft,' Parkinson recalls, 'which came in low and flipped its wings. The pilot then started to circle us. It was a Spitfire, and when we saw what it was we began to shout and sing and wave anything we could lay our hands on, with the sheer joy of getting home and having made it. The Spitfire was replaced by a naval motor torpedo boat, which stayed with us until we got to

Falmouth. The reception we got from the Navy was out of this world.'

Both Bob Parkinson and Syd Horton were recommended for the Military Medal, but in the end only received a Mention in Despatches.

What, however, of the pilot, Bob Cant, whom both Parkinson and Horton had praised in their debriefing for his handling of the aircraft?

'For the first twenty hours,' he recalls, 'I stayed in a little hut, then crossed a canal. As I did so two Frenchmen approached, who had seen me come down. They took me to a house, and after two hours, in walked my mid-upper, Bill Milburn, who had come down about five miles away.' They heard next day, that the Germans were in the area looking for them, and later they were taken to another house, where they were given civilian clothes. No shoes could be found to fit Bob Cant so he stuck to his flying boots. Two boys on bikes then escorted them to Verdun, where they were taken to a Mme Poitieux. They stayed with her for ten days. Forged papers and ID cards were provided, and Cant became a Corsican who was deaf and dumb. Two ladies, Susan Jamin, the wife of a local dentist, and Mme Krieg, whose husband worked on the railway, were to take them on further. They then had a celebration party with cigars etc. One young girl scrounged some cigarettes from the Germans and gave them to Bob. Next day they left on the 5 a.m. train, destined for Belfort. At Belfort they saw, to their alarm, that the platform was packed with Germans waiting to board. They quickly avoided the main entrance, as it was being checked and escaped through a back door in the ticket office, which led outside where a pony and trap was waiting.

Finally they arrived at the Swiss frontier. As soon as they crossed of course, they were arrested and for many months they remained living in a hotel, as internees, leading a heavily restricted life, although they were allowed some skiing in the mountains. But they decided that the time had come to escape back into France. Here they were invited by the Resistance in one town to shoot two Gestapo agents that had been caught, but they declined. By the time that they reached Grenoble, it had been liberated by the Americans. Here Bob met Wynford Vaughan Thomas, the war correspondent. From this area they were flown out in a Dakota to Naples, Casablanca, Algiers and then to England, landing exactly one year after they had left to bomb Mannheim.

Sadly their helpers' fates were not so fortunate. Mme Krieg and her husband were later shot while helping evading airmen, while Mme Poitieux and her husband were arrested and ended up in concentration camps. Her husband died under torture; she survived the war, but only just.

Flight Sergeant Eric Dickson, the flight engineer and known as 'Dicky', also made it to Switzerland. 'Walked to Salmagne. Contact wished to hand me to Germans searching for another crew. Fought with same,' he laconically reported on his return. From Salmagne he was helped on his way to the frontier near Delle, and then over the frontier by a 'small organisation … Madame Krieg is the working agent, who actually transports people across frontier. All people are passed to Neufchâteau or Toul and then taken by Mme Krieg to a farm outside Belfort. News of transport of escaper is wired to the farm, and escaper is met at Belfort by pony and trap. The same night the escaper is taken to another farm where the local smugglers have their headquarters. Mme Krieg often accompanies the evaders over the Swiss frontier where she has contacts in villages and at Basle.'

The navigator in the crew, Sergeant George Thomas inevitably known as 'Tommy', was the unlucky one – the one who did not get back. Yet he reached the Pyrenees, but he ran into a German frontier patrol. He was taken to Toulouse and then the civil prison in Paris, named Fresnes. The Germans both threatened and tortured him, but he did not reveal anything; he was sent to Stalag IVB at Muhlberg, and then Kulwitz, where he was liberated on 17 April 1945, by the Americans. He had only one good lung when he came out of the Paris prison.

Sergeant Denis Teare, the bomb aimer, had come down in a tree.

'I carefully released my harness,' he recalls, 'and climbed down. When I reached the ground I still had, gripped in my shaking hand, the rip-cord handle. I had no idea where I was, and took stock of what I had on me and what to do next, but whatever else, I knew I was on the run: an evader from the enemy. I started to walk and kept walking. Of course everyone was asleep and the only sounds were dogs howling in the distance. They always seem to sense someone is around long before humans. I realised it would soon be light and I must get out of sight, to get some sleep. I settled down after washing my feet in a stream as they were now very sore and blistered from walking in my flying boots. However, I only slept for about three hours, but I felt a lot better and more relaxed than I was before.

'After walking some while I came to a railway line and a canal, and it was here that I encountered Pierrot and Pierre, who were guarding the bridge over the canal. The important bridges were guarded by the Germans and the less important ones by local Frenchmen conscripted to do the job. If the Germans found a guard absent from their post he was punished. When the Frenchmen realised who I was they danced around shaking my hands. Here was I, in front of them, a real *aviateur anglais*. It turned out Pierrot was mad on aeroplanes and at night would listen to our bombers going over. When Pierrot went away for a while Monsieur Pierre seemed uneasy but then produced a piece of black bread and a slice of bacon ....

'When Pierrot returned he took me to his home and when there, with some pleasure, he tried on my battledress uniform. Then a white-haired old lady arrived. She had a quaint French-American accent, and she was very tall. Despite being 70 years old she was also upright and erect. Her name was Mme Barbierri, and her husband had been in the French Army during the Great War, and been awarded the Croix de Guerre and Medaille Militaire.'

Denis told her he was hoping to get to Spain in civilian clothes, but she told him that this was impossible. He would be caught and shot in a few hours. He must always keep on his

RAF shirt and trousers so that if he was caught he would be treated under international law as a prisoner of war. It was clear that she doubted the Germans would honour this law.

His routine over the next few weeks was the same each day, and time dragged. Each evening he and Pierrot listened in hushed tones to the news from London. Then he was told that in a week's time an agent, who could speak English, was coming, bringing an ID card with his photograph on it. He would then be escorted to the coast, where he was to be picked up by a submarine. The thought of being in England in the next few days was marvellous news. Even English rations seemed preferable to the black bread he was living on at present. But the next day he learned to his sadness that some of the organisation who were to help him had been arrested ....

'The 22 December came, and with it my 22nd birthday. It was then that Mme Barbierri came to see me with the bad news, that twelve of the best Resistance men had been executed in Paris, and all communications were cut. I was then told to get out of the house. I collected my few belongings, including the Land Army badge my fiancée had given me on my last leave. I thanked the old lady for all her help and said I was sorry we should leave on such bad terms but she was in such a frenzy that I did not get a civil answer.

'As I came out, M. Barbierri, came along and was surprised to see me outside and begged me to come back. This I did and found the old lady's rage had gone as quickly as it came. She went away and made a pan of black coffee and even produced a bottle of whisky, but I decided I must leave the cottage within a few days, having been there for over three months.'

Denis next went to a cheese merchant who lived on the other side of the village, named M. Collin. He had helped two US airmen on their way to England. He said he would take him to see an English-speaking lady, and with her he could travel to the Spanish frontier as man and wife. I thanked him but he said nothing was too much for France and her allies. He carried a revolver and said that the Germans would never catch him alive. Later, however, he was captured by the Gestapo and taken to various concentration camps including Buchenwald.

He survived and was released by Allied troops in 1945. His crime was not in helping Allied airmen, but hiding Frenchmen from work conscription. If the Germans had known about Denis and others he had helped, he would have been shot.

That night Denis was introduced to an old friend of Pierrot's, M. Valiant, who had escaped from forced labour in Germany. He had been put to work in a railway engineering factory, and spent day after day standing in clogs in water. He soon realised that if he was going to survive he must escape, and this he did, and had now arrived back in his village. He came in on two sticks suffering from bronchitis and frost bite. Before he had left he had been a healthy, fit 19-year-old, who was the star footballer of the local team and hoped to become a professional. Now he could hardly catch his breath let alone a football!

In January 1944, Denis was taken by car to join a Resistance group. Sitting in the car was a short, broad-shouldered man wearing a leather coat and beret. His name was M. Clément and he told him in no mean terms that he hoped he wasn't a Gestapo agent in disguise. Until his identity had been proven, he was under suspicion and that if he were an agent he would soon be dealt with. He was given an ID card with the name Denis Thomas Lebenec, born in Carnac, Brittany, and a ration card and coupons. His age was given as 25, an age that, as yet, was not being conscripted for work in Germany. He was taken to Revigny by train and here he met a Louis Chenu, a carpenter, and his brother Jean, aged 18.

On 10 February 1944, he was taken to meet Mme Stref, whose husband was still in Germany as a prisoner. 'I then became part of the Maquis,' he recalls, 'and was issued with a rifle and twenty rounds of ammunition. My life now changed to a member of the Resistance and not an escaping airman. It was to be 12 months before I would arrive back in England.' During his time with the Maquis he became fluent in the French language and as good as any trained spy in the art of sabotage and resistance work, probably more than we shall ever know.

'When I did return home, I was sent to Blackpool to recover, and to put on some weight. This I did, but found my only problem was nightmares. I relived my time in France each night, but when I told the doctors about this I received little help. They did not seem to understand, and so I decided to write my whole story down and get it out of my system.'

This Denis did, and it was later that by using these notes he was to write his own book called *Evader*. Now he says:

'I owe my life to the loyalty, courage and kindness of the dozens of French people who risked death and torture to protect me. A debt of gratitude I will never ever forget.'

III

The Netherlands

At the outbreak of war MI6 laid the groundwork of an intelligence organisation in Belgium and Holland to supply information in the event of German occupation – not then thought to be a serious possibility. Two factors contributed to the undermining of their very considerable efforts: the first was the capture by the Germans early in 1940 of the head of MI6's operations; the second was the suddenness with which the occupation took place in May 1940. An even worse tragedy was to overtake undercover work in Holland when in 1942 the German Abwehr under Colonel Giskes took over the wireless sets of captured SOE agents and played them back to SOE HQ unsuspected and unchecked, with the result that over 50 agents were dropped straight into enemy hands. Even when two escaped and managed to find their way to England to tell the story they were not believed. The escape of these two men was organised by the Dutch Paris line, run by a Seventh Day Adventist John Weidner who helped many Jewish refugees and evaders to safety, either to Switzerland or down to Spain.

The Comète line in Belgium, anxious to establish a Dutch link, continually pressed MI9 for a Dutch organiser and in February 1943 a Dutch girl Trix Terwindt was parachuted in – sadly, to a German reception – one of the victims of Colonel Giskes' 'England Spiel'. She was one of the few that survived the war. In June of the same year Dick Kragt was more successful; although his wireless set and equipment were seized, he evaded and remained at large to do sterling work for evasion, sending over 100 evaders through to the Comète line by the time of Arnhem. Arnhem itself posed a huge problem as regards the

Air Chief Marshal Sir Basil Embry. (*RAFES*)   Robert Lonsdale. (*R. W. Lonsdale*)

Denis Crowley-Milling with Norbert Fillerin shortly after the war ended.

Left Pilot Officer Lewis Hodges at Upper Heyford, 1940. (*Sir Lewis Hodges*)

Snapshots from Taffy Higginson's album taken inside Fort de la Rèvere in 1942.
Below far left Flying Officer Bob Milton.
Below left Inside the wire. Higginson is in the centre of the group. (*via F. W. Higginson*)

Above right Georges Jouanjean. (*Gordon Carter*)

Right Gordon Carter's Halifax, a photograph taken by the Resistance. (*Gordon Carter*)

Below Wedding day for Gordon Carter and Janine, 1945. (*Gordon Carter*)

Above far left Wing Commander Frank Griffiths. (*Group Captain Frank Griffiths*)

Above left Bob Merlin with Jo Becker and Mrs Merlin after the war. (*Bob Merlin*)

Left Schnapps, Merlin's Alsatian. (*Chris Thomas*)

Top The Rev George Wood. (*Evening Argus, Brighton*)

Above right Sergeant Wood's aircraft. (*Rev G. Wood*)

Right Sergeant Wood and souvenir. (*Rev G. Wood*)

Above John Brough's crashed Halifax. (*J. Brough*)

Left Reg Lewis. (*R. L. Lewis*)

Below 28½ years later, Reg Lewis knocks again on the first door to which he went for help. (*Reg Lewis*)

Right Len Barnes. (*Len Barnes*)

Below From right to left: Bill Alliston, Maurice Steel of his crew, and helper Henri de Brossard. (*Michel Tabarant*)

Bottom left Virginia and Philippe d'Albert-Lake in 1984. (*Len Barnes*)

Bottom right Bill Alliston (in the middle) with Madame Dupré. (*Mrs Alliston*)

Left The camp de Richeray in the forêt de Fréteval. (*Gordon Hand*)

Below The camp de Richeray. (*Gordon Hand*)

Bottom A recent picture of Gordon Hand at the Fréteval memorial, with the gendarme, M. Omer Jubault. (*Gordon Hand*)

Right Bryan Morgan (*Bryan Morgan*)

Below Bryan Morgan with Elizabeth Harrison, secretary of the RAFES, in 1985. (*Alan W. Cooper*)

Bottom Gordon Thring and Gerry McMahon. (*Gerry McMahon*)

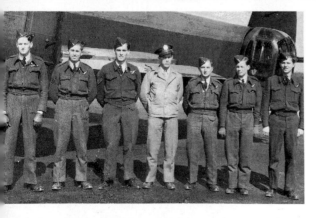

Left Henri Maigret on motor-bike. (*Russell Gradwell*)

Middle left The crew of Russell Gradwell's M-Mike JA690 in hiding. (*Russell Gradwell*)

Bottom far left Flight Lieutenant Ernest Harrop (third from right) and crew. (*E. Harrop*)

Bottom left Ernest Harrop (centre) with helpers. (*E. Harrop*)

Top Sergeant Albert De Bruin. (*Albert De Bruin*)

Above Albert De Bruin (third from left) with helpers. (*Albert De Bruin*)

Right Flight Lieutenant Bob Milton. (*Bob Milton*)

Above left Bill Furniss-Roe. (*Bill Furniss-Roe*)   **Above right** John Mott. (*John Mott*)

Below The fitted-out boat and crew in which Mott escaped from Italy. (*John Mott*)

Florentino. (*RAFES*)

The De Greef family; a photograph taken just after the war in their living-dining room where the family passed the war years. The modest furniture helped to fool the Germans. Frédéric is absent from the photograph, as he was in the army. (*Janine de Greef*)

Above left A wartime photograph of Dédée and her father Frédéric de Jongh. (*Comtesse de Jongh*)

Above Anne Brusselmans in 1986. (*Anne Brusselmans*)

Left Andrée de Jongh in Africa, 1980. (*Comtesse de Jongh*)

Above right Gisèle Evrard in 1942. (*Les Baveystock*)

Above far right Les Baveystock. (*Les Baveystock*)

Right Les Baveystock, Dédée Dumont, Gisèle and Bob Horsley today. (*Les Baveystock*)

Far right Dédée and Les Baveystock. (*Les Baveystock*)

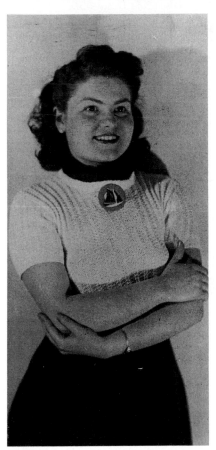

Above left 'Father' Brinley Weare. (*Brinley Weare*)

Above Stewart Leslie in 1943. (*Stewart Leslie*)

Above left Tom Young and crew. (*Tom Young*)

Left The Hon Angus MacLean PC. (*The Hon Angus MacLean*)

Right Bill Milburn, Bob Cant and Dickie Dickson on the run. (*Bob Parkinson*)

Below Left to right: Syd Horton, W/OP; Denys Teare, bomb aimer; Bob Cant, pilot; Bob Parkinson, rear A/G; Tommy Thomas, navigator; Bill Milburn, mid upper A/G; Dickie Dickson, engineer. (*Bob Parkinson*)

Bottom Reunion in the Isle of Man. Left to right: Thomas, Teare, Milburn, Parkinson and Cant. (*Bob Parkinson*)

Wally Simpson and Geoff Liggins on return. (*Wally Simpson*)

Wally Simpson's crashed aircraft. (*Wally Simpson*)

Frank Fuller in 1962 with Mr and Mrs Gérard Bloëm. (*Frank Fuller*)

Frank Fuller (second from right, back row) after joining up with Canadian troops. (*Frank Fuller*)

Above far left Warrant Officer Harry Simister. (*Harry Simister*)

Above left Frank Dell in 1945. (*Frank Dell*)

Far left Flight Lieutenant Harry Burton (left). (*Sir Harry Burton*)

Left Harry Simister, on first contact with Comète. (*Harry Simister*)

Above Bill Magrath in 1945. (*Bill Magrath*)

Above right D. V. Smith and crew. Standing (l to r): Vance, Smith, Parish (pilot), Lees, Marshall. Kneeling: Krulicki, Farley. (*D. V. Smith*)

Right Bill Magrath's crashed Blenheim. (*Bill Magrath*)

Far left Air Vice Marshal Donald Bennett. (*Mrs D. Bennett*)

Left Sergeant Harry Walmsley. (*Harry Walmsley*)

Below left Donald Bennett's crashed aircraft. (*Mrs D. Bennett via François Prins*)

Above right Axel Sonne in 1945. (*Harry Wilson*)

Right Wilson's shot-down crew. Standing (l to r): Sgt Wilson, Sgt Winkley, Sgt Bragg. Seated: Sgt Finch, Flight Sgt Loncon, Sgt Longhurst. (Flight Sgt Harris is absent). (*Harry Wilson*)

Below Harvey Firestone and helpers. Standing: Mowinkel Nilsen, Einar Evensen, George Deeth, Magnus Hauge. Seated: Harvey Firestone, Gordon Biddle. (*Harvey Firestone*)

T. W. Reynolds and crew 1945. (*T. W. Reynolds*)

Garrad-Cole's ID card. (*Garrad-Cole*)

Inside the POW camp at Sulmona, 1941. Garrad-Cole is on the extreme left. (*Garrad-Cole*)

Lt Hinton Brown walks home. (*Hinton Brown*)

Lt Hinton Brown on his return. (*Hinton Brown*)

Two of Bell's helpers, Fabio Gaiba and Signora Zamboni, in 1975. (*R. F. Bell*)

Lt R. F. Bell. (*R. F. Bell*)

Wing Commander Edward Howell. (*E. A. Howell*)

J. W. Macfarlane. (*J. W. Macfarlane*)

Squadron Leader George Houghton of the Late Arrivals Club interrogating Italian POWs in the Western Desert in 1941. (*Group Captain George Houghton*)

Drem. (*Terry Blatch*)

Terry Blatch at Lakopane in 1943. (*Terry Blatch*)

Arthur Newman with his father. (*Arthur Newman*)

Left Alan Day. (*Alan Day*)

Below Left to right: Sgt Turnbull, W/O Bradshaw, W/O Reid, Flight Sgt Goodbrand, Sgt Mason, Sgt Somers, Flight Sgt Taylor. (*Bill Goodbrand*)

Right Ray Sherk. (*Ray Sherk*)

Far right M. F. Mackintosh with the torch which was in his breast pocket. RAF hospital, Cairo, 1942. (*M. F. Mackintosh*)

Below right Escape by camel. (*M. F. Mackintosh*)

Below far right Yadem with Mackintosh and his wife. (*M. F. Mackintosh*)

Top left Pilot Officer T. Armstrong, Squadron Leader D. Frecker, and 'G'-George,
6 December 1942. (*T. Armstrong*)

Middle left Pilot Officer T. Armstrong (sitting) with (l to r) S/Ldr Frecker, Msud, Sheik Ali Ben
Athman, Sgt Clarke, Mohammed and the Armoured Car Crew 1st King's Dragoon Guards.
(*T. Armstrong*)

Bottom left Ken de Souza and crew. (*K. de Souza*)

Above left Flying Officer Ian Ralfe (pilot's seat). (*Ian Ralfe*)

Above right Eric Fisher on his wedding day. (*E. Fisher*)

Below 11 Squadron Catalina landing. (*Ian Ralfe*)

Above left Johnson on his return. (*R. Johnson*)

Above right Townsend and Foley at Base Camp, enemy territory, New Britain, 1944. (*Air Chief Marshal Bill Townsend*).

Below left Robert Johnson. (*Robert Johnson*)

Below right Bertie Brown (left). (*Bertie Brown*)

large numbers of evading servicemen which Airey Neave went out to solve. Operation Pegasus was launched to take evaders across the Rhine. The first crossing was successful, 138 reaching safety, but a repeat operation in November ended in disaster. After Neame's mission was complete he returned to England and Kragt continued to aid evaders, including Brigadier John Hackett, until the end of the war.

*

1.   In Safe Hands

In 1942 The Hon Angus MacLean, later Premier of Prince Edward Island in Canada, was a flight lieutenant in the Royal Canadian Air Force and flying Halifaxes with No.405 'Vancouver' Squadron from Pocklington in Yorkshire. On the night of 8/9 June, he was taking part in a 1,000 bomber raid on Essen when the aircraft came under heavy anti-aircraft fire. Whilst approaching the target at 18,000 feet a burst of flak caused the Halifax to flip on its back and start an involuntary spiral dive. Angus managed to regain control of the damaged aircraft at about 10,000 feet and continued the attack. On the return run, however, when roughly east of the Zuyder Zee they were attacked by an Me110 night-fighter. This attack resulted in the loss of both port engines and it was obvious that the already damaged aircraft would not get them home.

Angus was able to circle at about 2,000 feet to enable the crew to obey his 'bale out' command. However, when his turn came the Halifax immediately went into a dive and he had to return to the controls. He was able to set the machine to climb, but as he prepared to jump it started rolling, causing him to be caught in the hatch for a moment before he fell free.

'I myself,' he reported to MI9 on debriefing, 'landed about 0400 hours on 9 June about one and half kilometres south of Zaltbommel in Holland, a town to the north of Hertogenbosch on the railway between Utrecht and Amsterdam. The aircraft had been fairly low when I baled out and my parachute opened just in time. I landed flat and injured my back. The aircraft crashed 150 yards away in the next field. The aircraft was burning, and my first thought was to destroy my equipment in the fire, but I saw objects running around the fire, so I threw my parachute and mae west into an irrigation ditch and put clods of earth on top of them.'

Movement away from the crash area was his next concern and he started walking along a nearby canal until he could cross it by a road bridge. As he had lost a flying boot when he baled out, he found this difficult and looking for a place to rest he made his way to an orchard that he could see a short way away. The grass fields were wet with dew, and in order to hide the trail he was leaving, he rounded up some cows and drove them before him so that his footprints would not be visible. After crossing the field he milked one of the cows, drank the milk and then went to sleep under a hedge around the orchard. He woke at about noon, but, as there were workers in the field remained under cover until he had confirmed his position from his silk map.

As Angus stated in his debriefing report: 'About 1900 hours I saw two girls picking strawberries in a garden near me and went over and spoke to them. They were delighted when they realised I was a British airman. They showed me my position on the map, and their brother brought me a bottle of ersatz coffee. Their grandfather then arrived and wanted to take me with him. I was rather dubious, as he seemed to be talking angrily to the girls. One of them, who understood my broken German, assured me that he was merely cross with them for having talked to me too openly.'

He was told to stay in a nearby orchard until the next day, when they would return. No one came however, and he set off on his own. He was given hot milk and clothes by another farmer and 'I then set off towards the main road. My difficulty was to get out of the district in which I had come down and which was practically an island. I went to the village of Hedel ... and at the last house saw one man in the yard. I went in to speak to him but there were a number of people there and I was chased off. I said I was going to Zaltbommel, and once I had got clear of the village I hid in some bushes for about three hours, during which time three Germans passed separately on motorcycles. I thought they might have been searching for me, though perhaps they were only despatch riders. I then went on to an isolated signal box on the railway line. There was only one man in the box and I tried to explain to him that I wanted to jump a freight train and get off the island. I could not make him understand me clearly, and probably he thought I wanted to know whether passenger trains stopped there. I did, however, manage to gather that there were German guards on the railway bridge, there were none on the road bridge. I had just got back to the road when a freight train stopped at the signal box, but it was too late for me to try to get on it.

'I decided to chance the road bridge and walked back through Hedel. The ordinary road bridge had been blown up and there was a pontoon bridge across the river beside it. There was a long approach to this pontoon bridge, and I could not see whether or not the bridge was guarded. As I went along the approach I could see a large group of people and a Dutch policeman. Shuffling alongside a woman who was pushing a baby carriage, I went up to the group and found the centre section of the bridge was open to allow a boat to go through. The policeman was on the opposite side of the gap. When the bridge was closed we all trooped across, and the policeman did not stop anyone.' He managed to find shelter with an old woman and young man on a houseboat, and remained there from 10 June to 18 July.

After this period, and by now reasonably recovered from his injuries, he was restless to continue his journey. During his stay with the Pagie family on the houseboat they had made contact with the underground organisation, and preparations were rapidly put into action. As a consequence he soon found himself passing through Belgium and then into France. In a matter of weeks he had been into three occupied countries. Until his arrival in Paris, his identity had been taken for granted, but while staying with an engineer called Nevo, to whom he had given his Masonic ring for safekeeping, and who was a member of the Comète line, he was rigorously interrogated. He came up with the right answers, and thus soon after this he was introduced to a new guide, Frédéric, who led him to an apartment where there were two other airmen. A few days later they were taken to the large villa at St Maur, which was run as a safe house by Elvire Morelle. Their guide to the villa, which they found out later was the Paris headquarters of the Comète Line, was Dédée de Jongh whose father, Frédéric, known to them as 'Paul', was the leader of the Comète line in the Paris area.* It was at this time that Angus was given an Identity Card which had been stolen from the Commandant's office at Anglet near the Spanish frontier, with appropriate signatures forged by Dédée, a latent talent which she had developed.

They were then taken by train to the south, and then into the foothills of the Pyrenees, with Dédée in the lead. After they had crossed the river Bidassoa, which was running high and bitterly cold as a result of recent rains, Dédée gave each of them – Geoff Silva, Jim Whicher, Angus and James Goldie, who were respectively the 37th, 38th, 39th and 40th evaders to cross the Pyrenees with the Comète Line, a silver ring. The rings showed the seven Basque provinces and were made from English half-crowns!

They were eventually met by a car and taken to the British Embassy in Madrid. After about ten days, Angus was interviewed by the Air Attaché and informed that the Government had an arrangement whereby members of the Gibraltar garrison could visit Spain on leave. He was also told that a certain 'Captain Collie' of the Staffordshire Regiment was now absent-without-leave and the Spanish authorities had been notified. As a result of this conversation, 'Captain Collie', in the form of Angus Maclean, reported to the Spanish police the next day. He was given an armed guard, taken for a meal in a local restaurant, and taken by train to La Linea the same night. Following questioning by a Spanish official he was released into the 'custody' of the British Consul. Having successfully passed through the 'Snare Andalusian', which was one of the many methods used to get evaders away, he was interrogated by Donald Darling to prove his bona fides.

On his return to England by boat, he was questioned by Airey Neave. The reason for this additional interest from the authorities was the fact that he was the first evader to have spent some time in Holland. In September 1942 he was recommended for an immediate DFC, for his efforts in controlling the damaged Halifax and ensuring his crew's safety.

* He was arrested on 6 June 1943, and shot on 28 March 1944.

Whilst attending a Comète Line reunion in 1977, Angus found himself sitting next to a Mrs Nevo. She told him that some time after he had left the care of her son, her son had been arrested, and her husband had all the things her son had been given. Amongst these items was a ring, which had an unreadable name but a readable number. Angus told her that when he returned to Canada he would send her a copy of his service papers which would confirm his number. A few weeks later his ring was returned personally by Lucien Lamawieux, the Belgian Ambassador to Canada, 35 years after he had left it for safekeeping.

2.   Arnhem Evasion

On 20 September 1944 a letter was sent to Mrs Simpson from the commanding officer of 299 Squadron, Wing Commander Douglas Tiptree. This followed up the telegram which she had previously received advising her that her air gunner son, Sergeant Walter Simpson, was missing on air operations. On 19 September, two days after the Arnhem battle, known as Operation Market Garden, had begun, no communication had been established with 1st Airborne Division. The enemy opposition in that area was far greater than had been expected and the fortuitous arrival of a Panzer division, on rest, provided stiff opposition.

The air supply route to Arnhem on this day was changed to a southerly one, partly due to the weather and partly because it was hoped that the Germans would not be so well prepared for the change in direction. Take-off, however, was delayed until after mid-day because of continual bad weather.

For this operation 299 Squadron was to despatch 17 Stirlings. Finally, in the early afternoon, all seventeen aircraft took off on their support mission. In the rear turret of LJ868, letter 'R', flown by Flying Officer Geoff Liggins, was Sergeant Walter Simpson, known as Wally to his friends. They took off at 12.45

p.m. carrying 24 containers and panniers. At about 4 p.m., having successfully dropped their supplies into a wood north of the Rhine from a height of about 2,000 to 2,500ft, the aircraft was repeatedly hit by light and heavy flak and the port wing was set on fire. Flying Officer Liggins decided to crash-land the aircraft.

Wally Simpson left his rear turret to take up a crash position. After landing they finally came to rest, having first done a ground loop, on the southern bank of the Rhine about two miles south-west of Arnhem. They landed in the water meadows of the river behind the church at Oosterbeek with the turret just clearing the water's edge. On impact the aircraft had broken up and was burning fiercely, and only the two RASC despatchers, Lance Corporal Prior and Driver Braid, and Simpson escaped free of injury. Simpson helped the badly injured wireless operator, Warrant Officer W. Rudsdale, away from the burning aircraft then realised that the flight engineer, Sergeant D. Gaskin, and the bomb aimer, Flight Sergeant K. Crowther, were still trapped inside. He returned twice into the blazing wreckage to release and rescue them and on the last occasion got clear by only about 30 seconds before the petrol tanks finally blew up.

In the meantime the pilot, Geoff Liggins, and the navigator, Flight Sergeant F. Humphrey, were rescued by Prior and Braid. During this time some Dutch civilians arrived, among them a lady doctor and nurses. Liggins was in great pain and was given morphine by Braid. All this was being done under German sniper fire and 88mm cannon shells which were being aimed at the burning aircraft. The injured men were carried away on makeshift stretchers made from ladders and taken to the village of Driel, where they were tended by Mr Hendrick, a first aid man, and Cora and Reat Baltussen. Hendrick had a special pass issued by the Germans, which enabled him to carry out his duties and which meant he could tell the Germans that the wounded were in far too serious a condition to be moved, although in actual fact many of the dressings and bandages were merely 'window dressing'.

Meanwhile Prior, Braid and Simpson spent the night in the

open air, as Wally Simpson describes: 'We decided that we should now stay put where we were until it got light the next morning. We slept under the stars that night in what we stood up in, and I can say that lying down in a Dutch water meadow all night can get mighty cold in mid-September.

'During the night a patrol passed within a few metres of where we were lying. We saw their silhouettes against the sky. We froze, not daring to take in breath in case we should be heard.'

(It was not until many years later that Wally found out that this 'patrol' had in fact been friendly and had been searching for the crewmen.)

Just to the left of where the patrol had passed was a drainage tunnel about 60 centimetres square, which led to the riverbank and gave shelter from the weather as well as the bullets which seemed to be flying about during the day. This was to be the fugitives' home for the three days, their only food time coming from the 24-hour ration pack which Simpson had remembered to take from the aircraft's dinghy. It contained Horlicks tablets, sweets and chocolate which were shared out during the period of hiding. They had no water as they were unable to reach the river, due to the presence of the enemy.

While there they had a visit from a Dutch farmer from Driel who brought along someone who could speak some English, but he could tell them only that the British were expected on 23 September and that the crew should 'lie doggo'. He was understandably nervous, as were the villagers, for five people had been shot a few days previously for assisting evaders.

Simpson takes up the story: On the afternoon of 23rd we watched a drop by paratroops and later a patrol came along – they were Poles. On their way back from the patrol they picked us up and took us to their HQ in Driel. Here we were introduced to the Polish general and some British officers.'

On the Friday evening Simpson and the others were able to visit their comrades in the makeshift hospital and collect some of their personal belongings. They discovered that the bomb aimer, Flight Sergeant Crowther, had had to have the lower part of one leg amputated, due to gangrene having set in in a wound in the heel.

On the Saturday evening Simpson, Prior and Braid were taken by jeep from Driel, along the dyke road to Nijmegen. The night was spent in the back of a 30-cwt truck, covered in camouflage netting and parked amongst trees. The next day saw them on the move again, this time to Reichwald to join up with 30 Corps, under the command of General Horrocks. Here they spent two to three days and night under canvas and Simpson recalls: 'It was here that I wrote to my parents to say I was safe and well and trying to get home. I have that letter today in my scrapbook.'

From the forest they got on to a transport column which was to run the gauntlet through the two-mile corridor known as 'Hell's Highway'. In this they were fortunate for on the previous day only three trucks out of 27 had got through, the remainder having been shot up by the Germans. Their journey then took them to Belgium where they were interrogated at IS9 and given the luxury of a bath and a change of clothing. This was now 28 September and on that day a letter was received at Wally Simpson's home stating that he was missing. They arrived in England the following day.

On his return to England Geoff Liggins recounted the events of 19 September when Simpson had rescued the crew members from the burning aircraft and, on 3 October, Simpson was recommended for the CGM. When this recommendation reached Air Officer Commanding 38 Group, however, it was considered that the MM was more appropriate, and this was gazetted on 27 March 1945.

In 1957 a letter was sent to Cora Baltussen in Driel by the former bomb aimer, Sergeant K. Crowther, in reply to one she had sent about Mr de Groot, the leader of the party of Dutch men responsible for having sheltered the crew. Crowther had to tell Cora Baltussen the sad news that Geoff Liggins had been killed in a car crash in 1955, but repeated that the five men whom she and her compatriots had helped were deeply grateful and indeed were indebted for their lives to the actions of those brave villagers.

Today Wally Simpson is an active member of the St John's Ambulance Brigade and is a Serving Brother of the Order of St John.

3.   Ninety in Mass Evasion

Another aircraft shot down over Arnhem on 19 September was the Dakota flown by Pilot Officer Christie. The co-pilot was Frank Fuller. Frank recalls: 'I was there! Yes I was there all right – on the ground at Arnhem on that third day of the battle, when things were starting to get really hot. But I should not have been there – on the ground, I mean – you see I was an RAF pilot, not one of the airborne troops and I should have been on the way back to base in the Dakota aircraft, which was now a crashed wreck – also on the ground beside me.'

The starboard engine had been hit and then the port engine knocked out. Fortunately the aircraft did not catch fire as two Dakotas had done in the formation ahead of them; but they were very low – less than 1,000 feet up. Supply dropping from the type they were on had to be carried out at a low altitude and low speed – throttled right back, the nose down. They were halfway through their drop, when hit. In the circumstances and at a height of less than 1,000 feet they did the only thing possible which was to glide straight ahead and try to crash-land. Luck was with them. Despite Arnhem being situated in wooded countryside, they suddenly saw a clearing in a forest, and by clipping the trees and putting down full flaps, they were able to put her down on her belly. The aircraft slithered and bumped along towards the trees at the far end, and would have hit them but for a small railway embankment which had been built to haul ammunition trucks from a dump in the forest. They hit this at a fair speed, slithered over it and came to a halt, only a short distance from the trees. The force of the impact had thrown all the radio and radar instruments into the doorway through which the pilots walked back into the crew compartment, so this means of exit was out. However, on the starboard side of the cockpit the aircraft had split apart, so they were able to squeeze out and jump to the ground.

In the rear of the aircraft, the navigator, wireless operator, and four Army despatchers (usually from the RASC) whose job it was to see that the crates rolled out of the aircraft satisfactorily, were still alive, although two of the soldiers were badly hurt. A crate had fallen on them and they had been crushed. Christie and Fuller carried them out as there was still a danger of fire, and made them as comfortable as possible. As they were doing so a group of German soldiers came from the far side of the clearing and began firing, so they had to leave the soldiers and dash into the wood. As the injured men urgently needed medical attention, it was the best thing for them in the long term. The Germans perhaps assuming they had the complete crew, or that those who had got away were armed, fortunately did not pursue them into the wood, preferring to patrol the edge. There did not seem to be much of a problem, as their own paratroopers were only a few miles away at Arnhem. They knew the plan was for the main ground forces (30 Corps) to fight their way up to Arnhem, relieve the airborne troops, who should by then have control of the bridge over the Rhine, and then advance into northern Holland. But as history now shows, this did not work out as planned, and what had turned out as an offensive attack became a defensive rearguard action.

They soon found out the battle was too fierce and confused for them to head for Arnhem and after lying low for a day or two set out north, out of the battle zone with the idea of contacting the Resistance. As they moved through the woods during the day they saw odd groups of Germans and so decided to wait for nightfall before moving on. Frank takes up the story: 'Just as it was getting dark two Jerry soldiers came walking along the edge of the woods towards our concealed position. They were laughing and talking to one another; when immediately opposite, one handed his rifle to the other, walked into wood a little distance, and stopped about a yard or so from us; another couple of paces and he would have stood on us. We hardly dared to breathe – it was a toilet call and we were almost the Jerry's lavatory! The next few minutes seemed like hours and after the Germans had gone, we all swore we had heard each other's hearts beating.' Darkness came without further shocks and they continued on their way.

At dawn they hurried over a field, climbing a fence and

found themselves on a road, where a signpost told them they were near Hoenderloo, a small farming village, so they decided to call at the nearest farm. Everything turned out well and they were soon in the farmhouse drinking milk and eating some very welcome toast and eggs. The farmer was Gerard Bloem. Nobody on the farm could speak English, but one of the farmer's sons went off on his cycle and soon came back with an Underground worker, Jort Frans Smit, who was the school teacher and who could speak English.'

For the next two months they were moved from place to place by the Dutch people, living in barns, chicken huts and goat houses, but spending most of the time hidden in underground hiding places which had been dug for them in the sandy soil of a young pine plantation on a local estate. They often had to be moved from these hiding places when the Dutch game-keeper got news of the German officers' shooting sprees. On one occasion they spent the day in the attic of an woodman's unused house – on the very day the Germans chose it as a meeting place and were there all day beneath them. It meant keeping still and quiet for the whole day, and they were glad to get back to their hole in the forest that night.

Among their helpers at this time were Cornelius Van der Kooj at Hoog, Jan Oosterbroek, Mr Kerscherre, and Jon Obbink at Arnhem. The evading party increased to six when a paratroop major and glider pilot sergeant were brought in by the Resistance to share the 'digs'. The party now began to get a little restless, but were then told of the Pegasus plan which had been carefully worked out by the Dutch Resistance and MI9 over the past few weeks. There were by now hundreds of Allied personnel in hiding and the Resistance decided that a mass escape should be tried. The Resistance had reconnoitred the route from northern Holland down to the Rhine. They had checked the route chosen thoroughly, and the risk was worth taking. Dates had been fixed, and Allied forces, still on the southern bank of the Rhine would be sending amphibious craft across at a certain spot at a certain time. A supply of Sten guns had been dropped by the RAF especially for this show. One such mass crossing had already successfully taken place.

The first job was to gather together the whole party from a widespread area to one convenient spot, which the Resistance achieved without any trouble and in magnificent style. Fuller's party were actually packed tight into a motor van and taken to a particular farm. On three or four occasions the van was stopped and German voices were heard questioning the driver, but they seemed satisfied and the van went on. Later, in the dim light of a barn, Fuller noticed both British and American airmen and even Navy personnel. The senior Army officer in charge was a British colonel, and he organised the marching formation of the party with the Dutch guides. The fighting men, mostly paratroopers, had the Sten guns and were positioned in front, to the sides and at the rear of the column. There were about ninety men in all. Those who had lost their uniform or part of their uniform were fitted out with new ones, so as not to be shot as spies if captured. When the time came to move off they were to march for two nights and rest for two days and then on the third night they were due at the appointed spot on the Rhine.

Frank Fuller remembers: 'All went well until we were within forty-five minutes of our rendezvous, when we were challenged by a German sentry whose voice wavered as he stammered, "Halt, – who goes there?" The column halted and there was silence for a few seconds, then the sentry repeated his challenge and started firing. The whole area was soon alive with Germans, machine guns chattered and the escort of paratroopers returned the fire. The Germans were also firing flares to light up the place. The time had come to put an emergency plan into action, as Frank explains: 'We had made plans for such an eventuality; I would partner our navigator, the other pilot (Christie) would go with the wireless operator. We would split up and try to make our way to the appointed place on the Rhine.' Fuller and the navigator soon came to a main road running east and west, but it proved to be hopeless as there were hundreds of Germans around so they decided to head north. They had only gone a short distance when they were challenged by another sentry who, when they did not answer his challenge, once again began firing. Fuller shouted to the navigator to run and that was the last he saw of him until the end of the war, for he was later taken prisoner. Fuller ran as hard as he could. A dog was chasing him, but gradually the barking stopped, and he fell down completely exhausted, in a field of tall wet grass. As he lay there he saw the red Very lights coming up from the south bank of the Rhine. This was the signal that the amphibious craft was at the allotted spot to pick the evaders up. At that moment he felt very disappointed, but was so tired that nothing much mattered and he soon fell asleep.

When he awoke it was light, and he was soaked to the skin and so stiff that he could hardly stand up. It took him an hour to get himself walking again. He had no idea where he was and was not so successful this time in contacting friendly Dutch people and had several doors shut in his face, before being taken in at a small cottage in Utrecht by a Dutchman called A.J.W. Hilhorst. Here he was given food and drink and allowed to take his clothes off to dry them by the fire after the family had gone to bed. They were naturally very nervous because of the number of Germans around, and asked him to leave by dawn the next morning. This he did, but the Dutchman must have got word in the meantime to the local Resistance, for he was approached in the woods nearby and guided to a hiding place where several RAF chaps were already in residence. The guide's name was Van Eyden and this was at Amersfoort.

Two days later Christie, the pilot, was brought to the hiding place, but not the wireless operator, as he also had been taken prisoner. For the next five months until April 1945, just after the Allies crossed the Rhine into northern Holland, which was to be 'home' to Fuller and Christie. Of the ninety men in that fantastic attempted escape bid, over sixty were killed, wounded or taken prisoner. Fuller believes a few managed to reach the appointed spot on the Rhine, and the remainder succeeded in getting back into northern Holland to rejoin the Resistance.

IV

Germany

The famous escapes from POW camps in Germany are well documented. Some escapes were successful first time; some people went on making attempt after attempt, undaunted by failure; some escaped only to meet their death as in the notorious Great Escape from Stalag Luft III. It was a firmly held tenet that the quicker the attempt to escape was made the better, and the really determined had hardly entered the gates before they were checking round for various means of escape and contacting the escape committees which sprang up in the camps. Treatment after recapture varied from camp to camp, from periods of solitary confinement to being sent to other, less easy-going, camps or to concentration camps or death after the notorious Commando order had been given. At first escapers tended to make for Switzerland – Airey Neave did so for example, and was then faced with having to cross occupied France with an escape line. Sweden or South-East Europe became alternative destinations.

*

1.   Home Run

Flight Lieutenant Harold Burton was the first RAF officer successfully to escape from a German prisoner of war camp in World War 2. His imprisonment was the result of being shot down whilst taking part in a bombing mission with Number 149 Squadron from RAF Mildenhall.

At his debriefing Harry stated: 'I left Mildenhall about 2030 hours on the evening of Thursday, 6 September 1940, in a Wellington aircraft on a raid to burn the Black Forest. We did our job and, on the way back, did a reconnaissance of some lights on the ground, coming under fire from heavy flak. As far as I know we were not hit. About ten minutes after that the port engine started to show signs of heating up and, a little later, seized up altogether. After that we threw out everything to lighten the plane, sent out an SOS, which was received by our home station, and from then on lost height until I had to give the order to abandon the aircraft, which we all managed to do safely ... Before jumping we had all seen what we took to be the Belgian coast.

'After my crew (namely Pilot Officer G.M.R. Smith, Pilot Officer D.A. McFarlane, Sergeant Bailey, Sergeant Peacock and Sergeant Barnes) had baled out, I destroyed the Secret Wireless Identification Device and then left the aircraft, landing in a swamp, where I immediately hid my parachute.'

It was daylight before he emerged from the swamp, using a magnetised trouser button as a makeshift compass, and found himself at the Authier river. He saw a farmer driving some cows but did not approach him and waded into the river with the intention of following it to the sea. After walking for about two miles he hid in some reeds and rested and sunbathed in the warm sunshine for the day. At nightfall he started out again and passing through an orchard was able to obtain some apples, further on he supplemented these with some sugarbeet and corn. As dawn approached Harry hid once more and rested during the day preparing for the night's walk ahead. Somehow he had lost his compass so decided to keep to the river, but finding that there were so many guarded bridges and roads crossing it, thought it better to head across country.

As he reported: 'I lay down by a dyke and was awakened, though not observed, by a troop of German cavalry. I followed this dyke until I came to a clump of bushes, and there a German sentry stepped out. I had blackened the buttons of my uniform with mud and wore a scarf hanging over my wings so he did not realise who I was at first. He questioned me for a little time and then realising what I was, called out the remainder of the guard, who escorted me to Fort St Mahon (a few kilometres south of Berck on the opposite side of the bay of Authie). I was then taken before a German officer in St Mahon; he did not question me but turned a German sentry out of his bed for me to sleep in.'

After interrogation, he was moved to the civilian airport of Brussels and placed in a cell that was already occupied by his second pilot. He could also hear his navigator and wireless operator nearby. Not being sure of their surroundings they were very careful not to discuss any matters that might have been of help to their captors.

They had several moves and then on 16 September, a party of about 60 officers and men, including Harry and his crew, was sent to Stalag Luft I at Barth. During the journey several attempts at escape were made by others on the train but none was successful.

On arrival at Barth they were left in the compound and the searchlight turned on them. A headcount was taken and they were put into a reception hut and held there the next day while some French pilots were moved out of the main camp. The huts they took over were wired for microphones and they were warned by the Senior British Officer, Squadron Leader Stevenson, to keep a guard on loose talk. It was then that they discovered that the food they had been given for the journey had been intended to last them for three days! The other POWs in the camp came to their aid after being told of their predicament by a German officer.

On their second day at Barth, Harry and the other new arrivals were subjected to a very rudimentary search. His second pilot had managed to conceal a small compass in his left sock – the Germans only asked him to remove the right one! The food ration at Barth consisted of a cup of coffee for breakfast – soup for lunch – a fifth of a loaf of black bread and a cube of margarine for supper with a second cup of coffee – in no way compared with the Dulag Luft. Coupled with a strict but fair regime, this led to a hot-bed of escapism and Harry became the 'Officer Commanding Maps' for the escape committee. Several attempts were made but without success, the reward for failure being ten days' solitary confinement. Harry was prepared to take this in his stride when he was 'sent down' for complicity in a failed escape.

'On 18 May 1941,' Harry reported on arriving in Sweden, 'whilst engaged in making a tunnel, I was caught by a German guard and sentenced to five days' solitary confinement commencing on 22 May. Thinking that there might be some slight chance of escaping, I smuggled into the solitary cell a map covering part of the route I intended to follow, two bars of chocolate and a packet of raisins. The solitary confinement cell consisted of a small room in a wooden building, with one normal-sized barred window. The bars of the window were fixed by screw nails onto the outside wall and by stretching as far as possible out of the window I could loosen the screws. This I did on successive nights and by the morning of the 27 May I was ready to leave.

'On this night I got out into the compound and took out the screws in bars of the adjoining cell, the occupant being Pilot Officer Newman; he intended to follow me after an interval of one hour. From the cells I made my way to the main gates of the compound. The gates are double and made of barbed wire. A sentry outside patrols a beat of 100 yards, passing the gate every three minutes. There a light shines on the wire to the right of the gate and three searchlights sweep this area every ten to fifteen minutes. Lying in the shadows I scraped a trench under the gates and when the sentry was at the other end of his beat I ran fifty yards to the next barbed wire fence, which I climbed.'

The escape operation had taken Harry three and a half hours to complete and it was 2.30 a.m. when he actually cleared the camp. He made his way to the railway line and followed it in the direction of Stralsund for about five kilometres, when he hid and rested for the remainder of the day. Although his physical condition was good he was now beginning to tire from thirst and was soaking wet from the heavy rain that was falling. He found an empty beer bottle and was able to use this to pick up some water from a lake about three miles west of Stralsund. This set the pattern of his movements, sleeping during the day and walking at night, until he arrived at the outskirts of Sassnitz in the early hours of the 30 May.

He discovered the ferry for Sweden left at 1630 hours, and thought about ways and means of getting on board. 'The only possible way seemed to be by going on the trucks. Having studied them for some time I found out the trucks which were loaded and were going on the ferry, and while they were loading the trucks I went round to the other side and got in below a truck and hung on to the axle (it was an express mail van). At about 1615 hours the trucks were pulled on board and I sat on the deck under the truck.' He amused himself on the journey by removing all the address labels on the luggage belonging to Germans. 'When the ship reached Trellenborg I again hung on to the underside of the truck and was pulled off in the same manner. The journey took four hours. I landed at 2030 hours on the 31 May at Trellenborg. I gave myself up to the Swedish police who took me along to the Police Station. I spent five days there and was well treated. I then went to Stockholm.'

On 19 July 1941 the King approved the award of the Distinguished Service Order to Flight Lieutenant Harry Burton. This award was a direct response to his successful escape. He had become the first RAF officer to escape from a POW camp, but certainly not the last. Many benefited from Harry Burton's escape as he gave lectures to aircrew of his experiences. Harry Burton stayed in the RAF after the war had ended and retired as Air Chief Marshal Sir Harry Burton, KCB, CBE, DSO, in 1973.

2.   Sixth Time Lucky

On 29 June 1941 an Australian from New South Wales climbed into the cockpit of his Wellington bomber of 115 Squadron for an attack on Bremen, his 14th operation. Pilot Officer Allan

McSweyn, later flight lieutenant, took off at 11 p.m. for a journey that by the time he returned was to have taken two and a half years. About ten minutes from Bremen his aircraft was hit by flak having at first been coned by searchlights. He had taken the usual evasive action but as he seemed to be getting clear his starboard engine was hit and started to overheat. He throttled back but did not shut down the engine altogether. Carrying on in the best traditions of Bomber Command he bombed his target from 10,000 feet and then turned for home. As he did so he was once again coned by searchlights, but no flak followed which usually meant a night fighter in the area. Their fears were right as one suddenly opened up from 600 yards and then the searchlights went out. As the night fighter closed in he fired again and smashed the W/T set and put the intercom partly out out of action. The glass in the cockpit was smashed and the already damaged starboard engine set alight. The rear gunner, Sergeant Gill, returned the fire and reported a He113* falling in flames, but after this both turrets were unserviceable.

Then from the astro dome the second pilot, Pilot Officer Wild, reported a Me110 about to attack. It came up from below, and during this attack Gill was wounded in the shoulder and Wild in the right hip. By now, the engine was well alight, the flames going back so far they set the tailplane on fire. It was impossible to try and control it so McSweyn gave the order to bale out. All the crew got out as McSweyn held the aircraft straight. He then made his way towards the escape hatch. As he did so, he noticed that there was no fabric on the starboard wing and the metal had begun to melt. At that moment there was a terrific explosion and the whole wing came off and the Wellington turned over on its starboard side and went straight down.

He remembered nothing more until making a soft landing in the paddock of a farmhouse at Bremervorde in Germany.

The rear gunner Sergeant Gill had landed in a tree and in the daze of being wounded and having to bale out he pressed his release parachute harness, dropped forty feet and broke his back in the fall. The rest of the crew remained with him until a

* Without doubt a Me109 – the He113 did not see combat contrary to the popular belief by the RAF in WW2.

German doctor arrived, but he died the next day. McSweyn remembers:

'In baling out I had lost my flying boots and while waiting in the farmyard a German came in on a bike and went inside. I waited for about 45 minutes and then got on his bike and cycled for the rest of the night in a southerly direction, and during the day I hid up and then began again as soon as it was dark.

'As I passed Bremen I saw a German fighter station seeing on the field many Me110s. I spent the rest of the day in hiding watching the aircraft, having noticed one isolated aircraft near the boundary perimeter. Near it was a mechanics' hut with a sentry on guard. When it was dark I made my way towards this lone aircraft and climbed in but despite doing all what I thought were the right things, I could not get the engines to start. The continual trying, of course, brought one of the mechanics out from the hut. He walked under the aircraft and towards the port engine and then called out something to me, so I tried again and in doing so I nearly knocked his head off with the prop. To say the least he wasn't very pleased and came around to find out what I was playing at. As soon as he saw me, of course, the game was up and he called the sentry over, and so my first escape attempt of many was over.

'I was allowed a bath and shave and given a very comfortable pair of boots plus of course food and drink. I was then asked if I would like to meet the German pilots, I was not too keen as it was likely that one of them had shot me down, but they insisted so I was taken to the officers' mess. I found it very similar to an RAF mess, the same age of men, all keen on flying. They asked why I had left Australia to fight for the British. The unanimous opinion was that Germany with Britain should be fighting the Russians, and not each other.'

He was sent to Dulag Luft at Frankfurt where 'I was put in a cold cell, first having been stripped while my clothes were searched. They did not exactly interrogate me but more had a chat in which they hoped you would reveal details of your Squadron and operation etc. There were stool pigeons in the camp dressed as sergeants who tended to be there one day and then gone the next.

'In a compound later I saw three of my crew. The usual thing was to ignore each other but they were so pleased and surprised to see me that they shouted, "Hello, skipper, thought you had bought it." Of course, the Germans then knew when I had been shot down etc as the three had been picked up in the area of the crash.

'On 9 July I was sent to Oflag IX at Spangenberg by bus. This was an old castle built in 1315 near Kassel. It was surrounded by a dry moat, in which the Germans had put wild boar as a deterrent to attempting to escape.

'While I was here I did make one attempt to escape, with a Squadron Leader Svendson, a New Zealander. We ran a rope from a gate on the castle wall that we climbed over, to the side of the drawbridge. This we crawled along, crossing over the moat. Although we had chosen a rainy night, a German sentry came out of his box for one reason or another and saw Svendson. I was also caught but managed to break away and get back to my bed without being identified. Svendson was given seven days in the cells, and so escape number two had also failed.'

At the beginning of October McSweyn was sent to Dossel-Warburg, Oflag VIB, which was situated in the small town of Dossel, three miles from the railway station at Warburg, where conditions were bad. The camp contained many Army officers, and it was from them that an escape attempt stemmed in April 1942. 'The idea was headed by a Major Stallard of the Durham Light Infantry,' McSweyn explains, 'and success depended upon being able to put out the perimeter lights and the sentry searchlights. Most of this work on the electricity side was taken on by Lieutenant Searle RE and Lieutenants Frank Weldon and Lister of the RA. The lights would have to be out of action for thirty minutes to enable it to work and men to get away.

'To get over the wire, ladders of eleven feet long were made, under the wing of Captain Steve Russell of the Black Watch, Lieutenant Cruickshank Gord, Gordon Highlanders, and Majors Parker and Wylie RE. These would be placed against the wire, while attached to the top was a duckboard which was to be launched across the space between the two fences by means of two three-foot handles; the duckboard itself was eight feet long.

'Three teams of ten and one of eleven were organised. Diversions were to be set up by Major Cousins of the DLI. The date of the "go" was given as 30 August at 10.30 p.m. when the lights in the camp would be shut off. All the teams were blacked up and carried rations.

'All went reasonably well – three teams managed to get their ladders up okay but one failed. I was one of the back-up teams but not one of the first teams over and so I was picked up after two hours. Some were away for two or three days, and three army officers, Major Arkwright and Captains Coombe-Tennant and Fuller made it back to the UK, where they arrived on 7 November 1942.'

They had made their way to Holland where they had contacted the Comète line.

'In all, at this camp, I was involved in five tunnel schemes. One, started in winter, we did not bother to shore up as the ground was so hard but when the spring came it began to cave in, including some under the huts which took the foundations with them.'

In September 1942, with 800 others, McSweyn was sent to Oflag XXIB at Schubin (Polish Szubin), near a small market town in German-occupied Poland. The camp was situated in the grounds of a girls' school.

'Here we began a tunnel,' he remembers, 'which was completed in five months but the Germans became suspicious, set up extra floodlights and doubled the guards, besides adding mines between the wire and the huts. In the end the Senior British Officer, Wing Commander Harry "Wings" Day, forbade the scheme to use the tunnel because of the possible loss of life it would involve.'

Another attempt involving the use of ladders over the wire was planned. The same method as before was employed to fuse the lights etc. A party of 20 was involved, who managed to get in the hut closest to the wire on a windy stormy night. 'We were all set to go,' he remembers 'and at the given time the people with the ladders rushed the wire and began to throw lines over the wires to fuse them. All went well but one major factor had not been considered – the searchlights in the towers were on a different circuit to the wires around the camp, so when the lights went out the searchlights stayed on and they could see exactly what we were doing. A mad scramble was then on to get back to the barrack block. This was managed but when the Germans came searching they made us stand outside from 10 p.m. until 8 a.m. in the morning while they searched every room and block in the camp.

'Another tunnel I was involved in, was with Oliver Hedley and Christopher Cheshire, the brother of Leonard Cheshire VC, but this was discovered when there were only 12 feet to go.

'In April 1943 the camp broke up but before it had, I changed identity with a Private John McDiarmaid of the Seaforth Highlanders. We managed to get false ID cards and put our fingerprints on them and swopped with each other. This we did while on the train to Sagan, Stalag Luft III. For three months I worked as an orderly doing every job one could imagine. Then I would throw down my tools and refuse to work. In this way I built up a reputation as a troublemaker, a pain in the neck for the Germans. The Senior British Officer, Group Captain Kellett, knew my plan and suggested to the Germans I be transferred to another camp. This took three months in all.

'And so, in July 1943, I was posted to Stalag VIIIB at Lamsdorf, which was mainly an army camp, with, on average, about 10,000 men. The rule was that if you were a private soldier you could be made to work, if you were an NCO you could volunteer to work, and select where. If you were an RAF NCO you were not even allowed out of the camp let alone work outside. This went back to the fact the German Luftwaffe was the cream of the German forces. All the educated men were in the Luftwaffe and the Germans thought in England it worked the same way, and so the RAF POWs were thought to be more valuable than the army. It was thought, too, that they could, certainly later in the war when the writing was on the wall, be used as valuable hostages.

'So with all this in mind, I promoted myself to Corporal before

I reached the camp and told them my papers for this promotion had not, as yet, come through. For the first week I volunteered to go out with a party digging potatoes on a farm, 30 to 40 miles north of Breslau. There were very few guards and one day I just walked away from the farm.

'The next day I contacted some Polish workers who gave me a bike and I rode nearly all the way to Danzig but, the latter part I walked. It took me five days sleeping during the day and riding at night.

'At Danzig I made my way to the quay and got on a small Swedish boat, hiding in the coal bunker. Having got in with a French party of workers on the quay they also got me some papers. The ship moved off and I thought I was safe but after ten minutes at sea a launch came alongside and three or four Germans with dogs came aboard. They started to search the ship calling out in English for me to come out, but I stayed where I was thinking they were just making a random search and would soon go away but they didn't. Instead they threw tear gas bombs into the bunker, and I had no option but to come out as my eyes by now were streaming with the gas. They manhandled me in rather a rough manner and when I arrived back at Lamsdorf I was given ten days' solitary confinement and a bread and water diet.

'At Lamsdorf there were two Canadian soldiers, who had been captured at Dieppe, Sergeant Major McLean and Sergeant Larry Pals. I contacted them and we started an escape committee and I told them of my identity change and the reason. We were joined by a Czech Jew, Private Lowenstein. The two Canadians had completed a tunnel which was already twenty to thirty feet outside the camp; it just needed someone to use it.

'I decided to give it a go travelling as a Frenchman unfit for further work in Germany, but I needed someone who spoke German, and so chose a driver, Geoff Williamson, who spoke fluent German and knew the railway system in Germany having been in Germany pre-war. He was, in fact, from England but had lived in New Zealand for about ten years and had been captured in Crete. With the help of Lowenstein I forged a medical certificate which said I was suffering from TB of the larynx, and was being sent back to France to recover.

'We entered the tunnel on 19 September, a Sunday, at 1 p.m. The Canadians organised a football match inside the camp, which turned out to be a free for all which amused the guards so much they completely devoted their attention what was happening in the camp and not what was happening beyond the wire.

'I was wearing a pair of brown slacks, brown double-breasted coat and carried a small attaché case, while Williamson had a pair of plusfours, a black coat and also had a small case. We each had 400 Reich Marks and chocolate etc for the journey.

'When we were walking outside the wire a sentry shouted to get a move on, for as "civilians" we were in a restricted area. We were heading for the station at Lamsdorf but to get there we had to walk through the guards' living area. But we were not stopped. At the station we bought our tickets, and eventually we were on the express train to Berlin. On route there were several Gestapo checks but we got through.

'When we reached Berlin we found there were no more trains until the morning, so we booked into a small hotel where each day the register was checked at 8 a.m., so we left at 6 a.m. to avoid this.'

At 10 a.m. they caught a train to Mannheim, via Frankfurt, arriving in Mannheim at 10 p.m. They found the station badly damaged and the town was even worse. No trams were running and the debris was piled high, from a raid two weeks before.

From Mannheim they went to Saarbrucken, where they stayed for four days. They were told of a French work camp which was pro-British and were welcomed there. Their leader, Pierre, took them, on one occasion, to a café or bar. When they arrived, there were as many Germans in there as French. One man, after a few drinks, began to tell the Germans that they were hiding two British POWs, but thankfully they took little notice of him. After four days, Pierre introduced them to a French worker called Georges who was due to go home on leave but was fed up with waiting for the necessary papers. So on the 24th they were taken by Georges, to Auboue, on the frontier. The last six kilometres they did on foot. The frontier consisted of three barbed wire fences a few feet high, and there were sentry boxes at intervals. 'We decided to walk in a line,' recalls McSweyn. 'I walked behind Georges who suddenly almost walked into a sentry, whom he had not seen since he was standing behind a tree. He shouted, "Halt", so I sneaked up behind him and hit him with a rabbit punch on the neck and then grabbed him around the throat until he passed out.'

That night they stayed in a small hotel, but were woken early the next day by Georges, to say the Germans were searching, obviously because of the tangle with the Germans the night before.

'We caught a bus to Longwy but got off earlier. In error, Georges had taken us back into Germany, but he rose to the occasion and took us to the railway station and hid us. He then went off and later took us to the marshalling end of the station and said he had made arrangements with his contacts for a train to be shunted down to us, that was going back into France. It arrived and we scrambled on board. We were welcomed by the train driver who then drove the train up alongside a carriage and we were put aboard having missed all the checks that were going on by the German Field Police outside. The train went straight down to Lunnerville. Here we left the station and George went off to make his contact and then came back with a Pierre Bonsay, who had been a colonel in the French army in WW1.

'He took us to his home and gave us a bed and a meal. The next day a lady arrived and took us into the town and the police station. The gendarme was the local Resistance leader and he took all our papers and gave us new authentic ones. He then called up two gendarmes and they promptly handcuffed us and took us to the local railway station, and under escort we were taken to Lyon.

'Here our contact was one of Pierre's relations. We were given a wonderful meal. At 9 p.m. a young man of about 19 turned up.' He was Maurice de Milleville, who with his mother Comtesse de Milleville had helped other RAF evaders, including the 'Cockle shell-heroes'. She was Mary Lindell of the Marie-Claire line and known as Marie. 'The following day we set off with Maurice and a young helper named Ginette on a train to Ruffec, where we stayed in the Hôtel de France, where Mary Lindell kept her organisation's HQ.

'We stayed here for three or four days and were joined by two Polish sergeants in the RAF, Bakalarski and Raginis, who had escaped from Lamsdorf some six months before and got into Poland where they worked with the Resistance. After another three or four days, during which time Maurice and Ginette had been down south arranging for us to get across the Pyrenees, we were then taken by truck to Limoges where we boarded a train to Toulouse, and then on to the Spanish border. The idea was to get into Andorra, so we travelled down to Foix.

'In Foix we were to make our final contact who would get us across, a man named José. He met us at the station with the news there was a flap on and Germans were looking for escapers, so we returned to Ruffec. Three or four days later an attempt was to be made with Geoff and the two Polish sergeants going ahead as their knowledge of German was so good, they had a good chance. After they had gone, another group turned up. Captain Bat Palm, a South African, Len Martin and Harry Smith, both Canadians, and another South African, Mike Cooper, serving in the RAF on Spitfires.

'We again set out for Limoges by truck but on the way the axle broke. Marie [Mary Lindell] spoke to a farmer and persuaded him to lend us his truck in return for a few extra gallons of petrol. But when we arrived we had missed the train we had intended to get so we spent the night in a hotel. While here we went down to dinner with Marie in her British Red Cross uniform with full British decorations and speaking madly in English only yards from five German officers who were also dining there. She had no regard at all for the Germans and thought they were idiots.

'The next day we caught the train and met up with our contact José. He had arranged for two Basque guides to get us across the Pyrenees. We later met them and said goodbye to Marie who had done a marvellous job to get us this far.

'That night we left for what was supposed to be a six hour

crossing of the Pyrenees. After about four hours it began to snow and was bitterly cold. Our clothes were not really suitable for this sort of weather, and we had to halt for the night as Harry Smith had chest pains. We stayed until morning in a cowshed. It had a roof but no sides. At 8 a.m. we set out again and walked all that day through very heavy snow and a blizzard. That night we found a small hut and decided to lie up for the night as Mike Cooper was very, very tired and cold, as was one of the guides. We set off the next day and had to cross and crawl across a small gap of about 18 inches on hands and knees with a drop of about 300 feet on each side.

'Both Mike and the guide were becoming ill again and whereas we kept Mike going, the guide suddenly became unconscious and seemed to be frozen stiff. We tried to warm him and revive him but it was hopeless and he seemed dead. We wrapped him up as best we could and placed him in some form of shelter and with great reluctance decided to leave him. From here Martin and Palm went on to find shelter and we came behind helping Mike. They had found a hut and broke in and started a fire which meant we could get our wet clothes off and warm up.

'About 8 p.m. we set off again. By following a stream we came to a road and a sentry post with five Spanish soldiers. We were so weak we had no option other than to surrender. They gave us a hot drink and bread and then escorted us to Utaroz, a village some three miles away and handed us over to the local police who stuck us in a filthy cell, but let the guide, who was known to them, go to a local inn. After a little bribery we were allowed to join the guide in the inn, but still under guard. The guide told us he had posted a letter to the British Consul for us.

'The next day a Mr Frost arrived in a station waggon from San Sebastian. He was able to bail us out, and after six days we were taken on a two-day drive to Madrid. We stayed with the Australian First Secretary at the Embassy and then after three days we were taken to Gibraltar. It was here that I met Airey Neave, who told me the two Poles had made it but that Geoff had died in a blizzard.

'From the reports that Bakalarski and Raginis made on their

return, the fate of Geoff Williamson was confirmed. They had hit a blizzard and heavy snow and Geoff ended up by being carried, but at 1 p.m. on 26 October he got so tired he could not even walk down hill on his own. Between 6 and 7 p.m. he died and they left him in the mountains somewhere near Pic de Rudlo in the shelter of some rocks. He had come from his adopted New Zealand, to Crete, then Germany only to die in the French Pyrenees.

'The two Poles on their return to the UK were awarded DCMs. I was flown home from Gib in a Dakota to Whitchurch, Bristol and on landing we ground-looped, and the aircraft was written off, but with no injury to the 20 passengers and crew I am glad to say.'

McSweyn eventually returned to Australia and arrived on New Year's Day 1946. In March 1944 Flight Lieutenant Allan Frank McSweyn was recommended for the Military Cross which was approved. Few awards have more justly been given than this one. Determination not to be confined, being prepared to go to extreme lengths, incredible hardships: they are all there in this story of a man from 'Down Under'.

3.   Berlin Bale-Out

Sergeant Harry Simister of 158 Squadron was just short of his 20th birthday when he joined the RAF in April 1940. By 1943 he had completed 20 operations with No.158 Squadron as a flight engineer when his tour suddenly came to an abrupt halt.

'I was a member of a Halifax crew which was attacked by an enemy night fighter, immediately after we had bombed Berlin on 31 August 1943,' ran his evasion report. 'The two port engines were set on fire and the controls were shot away. After a few minutes I received the order to bale out. I landed in a field about five miles south of Berlin, just before midnight.'

He quickly hid his parachute and remained in a wood for the

night and at dawn he removed his badges of rank and flying badge and also cut the tops off his flying boots, making them into shoes. Then for some three days it was a case of walking at night and hiding in woods during the day. On 3 September, Harry saw a bike leaning up against a house which he stole and peddled his way towards Brandenburg but turned off before reaching there and set off in a north-westerly direction. Once again spending the night in the woods, he set off the next day passing through Schwerin and then took the main road for the port of Lübeck, which he reached that night.

When morning came he made for the docks and began looking for neutral ships and found a Swedish vessel guarded by a sentry but walked straight past him, up the gangplank, without pausing. He went into the galley where he met six Swedes; showing them his cigarette case with RAF embossed on it, he was able to make them understand who he was. He was given a meal and discovering that one of the sailors could speak English, asked him if he could hide. Harry was told that the ship was not sailing till the next day and to come back then and take his chance. However when he returned the next day the ship had gone! Harry wandered about for the rest of the day looking for a likely ship but with no other ships available he left the docks and that night slept in the wood.

On 7 September he decided to make for Rostock but there were no neutral ships there either so on the 9th he returned to Lübeck. He tried to buy some cigarettes but was told he needed coupons so he went into a public house and asked for a beer, handing over a 100 Franc note to cover the cost, and telling them he was Swedish. After some hesitation he got his beer! Seeing the proprietress sitting in a corner, Harry approached her and asked for food – up to this time he had been living on food tablets from his escape kit and stolen apples. She gave him some black bread to eat.

Returning to the docks he saw a Swedish schooner. Once again he walked past the guard without any problems and boarded the ship. However, finding all the doors locked, as the crew were ashore, he made his way to the wheelhouse and promptly fell asleep. He was later awakened by one of the returning crew; again he showed the cigarette case and was given a meal. He found out from one of the crew who spoke English, that they were not sailing for eight days, and that there was nowhere to hide on the ship. That night he slept in a bus shelter, and the following day, 10 September, decided to make for Holland on his bike. His route took him through Hamburg, Bremen and Osnabrück to Rheine, where he reached the river.

'On the way I had a puncture,' read his report, 'so I exchanged it with another one which was leaning against a wall of a café in a small village. On arrival at Rheine I went to the railway station hoping to find a wagon bound for Holland. There were many people about and I had to be most careful not to be seen loitering around. As I was unable to find a wagon labelled for Holland, I went to the outskirts and spent the night there.'

On the 13th he cycled towards the Dutch/German border where he saw passes etc being checked so he had to make a detour through a wood. By going over two fields, he finally got over the border into Holland. On the 16th just before reaching the Belgian border he stopped at a café in the village of Borkel Schaft, asked for something to drink and told them who he was. Louise, the girl in the café, went and told her mother, Madame Steenbergen, who supplied him with a civilian suit and put him in touch with the Resistance movement.

The next day a Dutchman named Frank Spee came and accompanied him on a bicycle across the border, where his brother who was a guard ensured that they wouldn't be stopped, to Exel. Here he stayed for three days, and then went onto Neerfelt where he stayed with the Spooren family for about a week. It was here that he met Sergeant Wallace and was given a false ID card.

Towards the end of September, Harry, together with Sergeant Wallace, travelled by train with a woman guide to Brussels via Antwerp and then to Virton where they stayed for two weeks. On 13 October they entered France with a guide, walking over the border to Ecouvier. From there they travelled by train to Nancy via Montmédy where they stayed the night, then journeyed on the next day to Belfort and on to Mont

Belliard. The next day they walked to Audincourt and stayed the night; the next morning they went into the woods with a party of woodcutters and waited until evening. The two flyers were then taken to a guide who was waiting to take them over the border into Switzerland. Reaching Faly they were immediately arrested by Swiss guards and spent two days in prison before being sent to Bern and the British Embassy.

Harry Simister recalls: 'We spent the time there living in a hotel. Then we were taken to a ski resort at Arosa, where the embassy had two chalets for escapers and evaders; almost all RAF aircrew. Here we spent most of the time skiing. In the summer season we went to Montreux in the Vevey region. Finally, in August 1944, we left Switzerland by climbing over the mountains to France. Once in France we stayed and fought with the Free French Forces and with their help we made contact with the Americans at Sisteron and hitch-hiked a lift to St Raphael on the Riviera. From there we had a 'busman's holiday', flying to Naples, where we met the British Army, then to Tunis, Algiers, Oran and Casablanca. From here Coastal Command flew us to St Eval in Cornwall, landing one year and ten days after baling out over Berlin. (10th September 1944).'

In November 1944, Harry Simister was recommended for the Military Medal. He later continued flying with Transport Command, collecting POWs from all parts of the world and then dropping food supplies to the people in former occupied countries, who had so gallantly opposed the Nazis and helped others like him to make their way home. Later when he went on to civilian flying at Majorca in Spain he had his leg pulled and was called 'Ace Evader of the RAF'.

4.   'You are Tommy pilot?'

In October 1944 a force which gets very little acclaim today in the history of the RAF in WWII was operating, and operating with all the high traditions of the RAF. This was the Light

Night Striking Force part of the Pathfinder Force. They operated with Mosquitos, acting as night bombers and as diversion raiders for the main force squadrons. On 14 October 1944 one of the units operating on a diversion raid to Berlin, for the main force going to Duisberg, was 692 Squadron, based at Graveley, alongside 35 Squadron with their Lancasters.

One of the crews detailed that night was Flying Officer Frank Dell and his navigator, Flying Officer Ronald Naiff. They took off at 1.30 a.m. in Mosquito, MM 184. In the area of Münster the fighters managed to get in amongst the Mossie Force and mark the route the Mossies were taking. As Frank Dell relates;

'As we came over Münster, up came the searchlights when suddenly we got hit from behind. In any event I lost control. I think the elevators were shot off and we stood up on our nose and fell away into a spiral dive. We were both forced down in our seats with little hope of getting out. My navigator had less chance, as his chute was still on the shelf. In a short while the aircraft broke up and I found myself out in the fresh air. I had my seat pack on and pulled the ripcord and the chute opened successfully, but at a height of 24,000 feet it was going to take an age for me to get down. In fact it took about twenty minutes before I saw a dark shape. I thought it was a wood but in fact it was a newly ploughed field. I hid my chute in a ditch and made for a cart track which I started to walk along, when suddenly I heard an engine sound and looking back I saw torchlights and heard voices. I assumed they were looking for me so I got off the track, and around the back of them, then followed their progress up the road.

'I then turned off the track into a wood and spent the night there until daybreak. I was only wearing my battledress jacket under which was my polo-neck sweater. The sleeve of my jacket was torn, and my face was cut and grazed and I was feeling very sore just as you do after a hard game of rugby.

'I opened my escape pack to see what it contained. The first thing I saw was a cellophane packet which contained tablets. Two were missing, the two I had taken when I first landed on the ground. I thought they were Benzedrine tablets to keep me alert, but as I now found out they were water-purifying tablets, so it just shows you that in the main taking tablets is all in the mind. In the pack was a needle and thread which enabled me to repair the sleeve of my jacket. One might as well be a tidy evader.

'I had a compass but no silk map. (This was because when Brussels had been liberated in September crews were landing there on the way back from ops for a bit of a binge and the escape packs were coming back without the foreign money and the silk maps.) So with no map I decided to make tracks in a westerly direction towards Holland, a 100-mile journey I estimated. In the wood I became very lonely and sad at losing my navigator, Ron Naiff, but in a way it helped me as I became determined to get back to visit his parents.

'In the middle of the day, quite suddenly, there was a horrendous noise. It was ear-splitting. The trees shook and dead leaves came down all around me. What the devil could it have been – I had not heard anything in the war as yet like it. Then suddenly I realised that a vehicle I had just followed was not looking for me but was a V-2 rocket carrier. At that time, we in the UK had only heard rumours of rockets and explosions in the East End of London.'

After hiding during the day he walked a further 20 miles. 'Just before daybreak I came upon a farmhouse and another shelter and spent the whole day there, while outside the usual activities of a farm were going on. They had no idea I was there but in this situation animals are a problem with their sense of smell. Each time the horse and cart came by the horse would look around at the shelter. Small children and dogs were also a problem, but no one came too near and I was okay in that respect but I was getting very cold and started to shake badly. I decided to get out and walk about to get my circulation going.

'I set off down the road. It was pitch black and I bumped into a man repairing his bike. He grabbed my arm and spoke in German. My reply also in German, was that he should strike a match to see what he was doing. Then, making suitable grunting noises I carried on my way. Suddenly ahead I saw a small hut, like a sentry box, which could be the frontier or border between Germany and Holland. It was raining now and

I made a detour around the post, then I saw another little farm with a chicken house at the back, but thankfully for me there were no chickens, so this became my lair for a while, but I was unsure if I was in Holland or still in Germany. I looked for the tell-tale signs like windmills. By now I was getting a little low and needed some help.

'I moved on and found another farm. This one had a welcome straw-covered loft in a barn so I took off my wet uniform and hung it up to dry and lay down and fell into a deep sleep.

'I awoke to the sound of aircraft overhead and then machine gun fire. I heard footsteps on the stairs of the loft, then excited voices. It was two 16-year old boys, they both saw my uniform. One, in broken English asked, "You are Tommy Pilot?" I said, "Yes." The boy replied, "Be still. We have German soldiers in the farmhouse".'

It turned out that a German truck had been strafed, hence the machine gun fire. They had jumped out of their truck to seek shelter in the farmhouse. The two boys themselves were on the run, in a sense, as all men between 16 and 60 had to register for forced labour. The only alternative, if you did not register, was to go into hiding, which they had done. One of the boys was the farmer's son and the other, who spoke a little English, was the son of the local schoolmaster. He said he would speak to his father that night, for he might well know someone who could help. The farmer's name was M. Breukelaar and the farm was near Aalten.

'The farmer's wife gave me a cup of milk,' remembers Frank. 'She told me wisely to drink it slowly having not eaten or drunk anything for some time. When I looked in a mirror for the first time I had two black eyes and a five day growth of beard. I stayed for 24 hours at this farm and then another man came for me on a bike. He told me to sit on the front of the bike and off we went. We arrived at another farm which had a beehive at the back, under which was a trap door which led to an old disused bread oven about 8 feet by 4 feet and 6 feet high in one part. I could sit up but not in the main part of the oven. The ventilation came from the chimney, so I would not suffocate. I was given a blanket, milk and bread and then the trap door was closed again.

'At meal-times it was the farmer's wife who brought me food. On one occasion she put her hand on my head in a motherly way, and this did it for me. Up till then I had put on a proud front and had not dropped my guard but when she did this I burst into tears. It was a sort of anti-climax, having bottled the whole thing up. A candle was left for me and matches so I could, if I needed to, have a light. In all I spent about two days and nights in the oven.

'After two days they came and took me out and gave me a pair of gym shoes so we would not be heard walking along the road. I still, however, kept my flying boots which I had cut off at the ankle to make them look like shoes. The pieces I had cut off were lined with sheepskin and so I put one piece up the front of my battle dress and the other up the back for extra warmth.

'They took me to yet another farm and this time my home was to be an attic. All the time I had been holed up they were checking with London that I was who I said I was. The farmer here was Henrick and the name of the farm was Klein Entink. During the day I helped with the many chores there are on a farm.

'Then one day we heard an aircraft flying very low and obviously in trouble, as it had smoke trailing from it. It was an American P51. All of a sudden, up came the nose and out came the pilot. This soon brought a lot of Germans into the area, while the Resistance men went out to look for him. When I saw them coming back I foolishly went out to greet them and as we walked back to the farmhouse along came two German soldiers on bikes. I saw them but I don't think they saw me. Just beside me was a haystack and it was this that I was shunted into by one of the Resistance men. The Germans stopped and asked the Resistance men questions but soon went on their way unaware I was around the other side listening.

'When night came the American pilot had still not been found, so I was asked by the Resistance to teach them a phrase in English which the American would know if they called it out in the woods. So I got them to repeat over and over, "Come out, you silly bugger. We are your friends". When they had got it off fairly well they left once again to look for him, but as before they returned without him.

'After about three days he was eventually found and brought in. His name was Joe Davies. I asked him where he had been hiding and he replied, "Well, all night the Germans were walking up and down shouting, Come out, you silly bugger so I stayed hidden. I had also hurt my knee in baling out so I could not walk far." '

'It was then decided to move both of us on as the area was too dangerous, so we were moved to a farm owned by the marvellous Bernhardt Prinzen. He had ten children and his farm was at Ijzerlo. In the area, because of his name, he was known as "Prince Bernhardt". I was told that Jan Kett was controlling the Resistance movements in this area.

'At first the children were a little nervous of us and on one occasion when we were washing as best we could everything went quiet. When we looked up there were ten pairs of eyes looking at us through a window. They were anxious to know if we were white all over?'

It was at that time that the former Humphrey Dell became Frank. Jan Kett found Humphrey unpronounceable, and his second name Francis became abbreviated to Frank. This name stuck in RAF circles and in Frank's post-war service in the civilian airlines when it became known that he was called Frank by the Dutch. His family, however, called him Humph.

'When liberation came, things were a little tricky as a party of German parachutists were billeted in the farmhouse, but, during the night they left and Bernhardt came to say to me that he thought a Tommy tank was at the bottom of the road. Being the only Englishman there, I was elected to go and speak to them. It proved to be an advance armoured car of the 2nd Canadian Army and as I walked towards it, its gun followed me. I banged on the side and said I was an English airman, a pilot. With that the turret lid opened and what I first saw was a handlebar moustache, complete with steel helmet. He gave me a broad grin and in a deep voice said, "Jolly good show, old boy." We were soon away, hardly having time to say our goodbyes. On our way to Tilburg we saw the largest traffic jam we had ever seen or are likely to see. It stretched for 80 miles, bumper to bumper.

'I will always remember, while on the run, the sound of singing voices coming from a train. A solo tenor voice would then be taken up by hundreds of voices, to the tune of the "Hebrew Slave" chorus. It gave me a most uneasy feeling. Many years later, when driving along in my car, I heard this tune and suddenly realised what they were singing. The line the train was on led to Belsen.

'My navigator Ron Naiff was never found but his name along with 20,000 other airmen and airwomen who have no known graves is recorded on panel 208 on the Runnymede Memorial.'

The operation on 14 October 1944 had been a great success; out of 1,448 aircraft sent out only 9 were lost, and only one Mosquito. This was Frank Dell's of course. The loss rate of 6% was quite remarkable, but undoubtedly Frank would have preferred it to be just that little less!

V

Norway and Denmark

In Scandinavia, the hope of most evaders and escapers was to reach neutral Sweden, and there are many heroic tales of evasion after the Norwegian campaign. There were few during the rest of the war, and those making their way to Sweden often had perilous and dangerous journeys across the mountains. Once there, though, the difficulties put in their way before they were returned to the UK were not so great as in Spain, and their treatment much better. Nevertheless, as will be seen, it was not all that easy a matter. As Air Vice Marshal Bennett found, it was better to be an escaper, than an evader.

*

1.   Two Tickets to Paris

On 13 August 1940 the Battle of Britain was at its height, but operations were continued elsewhere as well. Sergeant Bill Magrath of 82 Squadron, No. 2 Group, was an observer in a Blenheim Mark IV which took off from Waton at 0900 hours to attack Aalborg airfield in north-east Jutland. Twelve aircraft took off in a formation four waves of three, A Flight leading, and Sergeant Magrath flying No.3 in the second Vic of B Flight following 100 feet lower.

The operational plan was to fly round the north of Denmark, turn south and approach the airfield from the east, making full use of any cloud cover. All went well, until about two miles from the coast the clouds suddenly disappeared. The plan had miscarried and they were much further south. Now it meant flying over most of Denmark to the target. Surely they would turn back and abort the mission, Bill thought, but no, they kept on going.

'Suddenly I got for the first time, and the last I am happy to say, an absolute feeling which was just like an electric light being switched on: I was not going to return from this one! I had in the past been able to look at a new member coming to the squadron and know he was going to go missing. Now I was doing it to myself. Strangely it did not worry me.'

They were about 20 to 30 miles from Aalborg when a swarm of 48 Me109's found them. They were outnumbered four to one. The Germans were refuelling at Aalborg en route for Norway – 'Our engines were still warm,' said one German pilot afterwards, 'and we were all in the air inside two minutes. We attacked them from behind as one man. One or two bursts was enough; it was like being on a gunnery range. Within ten minutes it was all over and the sky was clean.'

One Blenheim was hit straight away and blew up. By now Magrath was down in the nose on his belly looking through the bomb sight ready for the bombing run. More fighters attacked. They lost an engine just before they dropped their bombs and then were attacked again. Sergeant Greenwood, the rear gunner, had been wounded and lost consciousness and Magrath took over the gun, though as he says, 'with little hope of hitting anything.' Then the aircraft caught fire and it was getting uncomfortably hot. They were now over the fjord. The pilot, Sergeant Blair, had tried to ditch the aircraft, but when about 40 feet from the ground, the port fuel tank exploded causing the aircraft to crash.

Bill continues: 'I got to my feet and, I saw the sea coming up to meet us. The time was about 2 p.m. Then I blacked out. When I came to I saw the aircraft all around me. The pilot had blood over his face and I was lying with my inflated Mae West in shallow water. I felt like I was floating, but in fact I had been quite badly injured. We had come down near a little island called Egholm. The local farmer and his son had waded out and pulled us ashore (many years later I gave them a bottle of whisky for what they had done) and a Danish doctor gave me first aid but I needed hospital treatment, and so out came a motor boat named the *Mira*. At the helm was Gauleiter Karl Bruns, who was in charge of construction at Aalborg airfield. While in the boat I did notice a nice-looking girl with very nice legs, so I thought, "Well you may be badly hurt but there is nothing wrong with your senses". I did in fact have a broken shoulder and was blind in one eye.'

The whole squadron had been shot down, save for one aircraft that returned with engine trouble: 11 aircraft, 22 men were killed, 9 prisoners of war. The rear gunner in Magrath's crew, Sergeant Greenwood, had three bullet wounds in his leg.

At the beginning of October 1941, Bill was sent by train to Rouen and from there on to a prison camp on a nearby racecourse, housed in British Nissen huts and surrounded by British barbed wire! The RAF other ranks were given a hut to themselves. It was here that Magrath met Sergeant O.B. James, who had crashed near Morlaix in France and due to the injuries from the crash had given himself up. It soon became apparent that repatriation had fallen through, and a plan to escape was discussed. The party who were going to escape were Sergeant Oliver James of 83 Squadron, who had had his left arm amputated, Sergeant Patterson, Sergeant Maderson and Magrath. They were given 750 francs each by Pilot Officer Coleson, which came from the RAF officers in the camp who were paid in French currency.

Magrath and James studied several means of getting out and decided that the only way was to cut the wire. They managed to get wirecutters from the toolbag of a French worker and made a hole in the wire. They left the compound along with Patterson and Maderson about 2045 hours on 21 November 1941. Cover was provided by the noise from groups of army other ranks, some of whom were bartering clothing for cigarettes over the wire to the Germans. They crept through the hole in the wire, covered by Nissen huts in the next compound. They got through two more fences by gates which were not properly guarded, climbed a grandstand and got into a drive, and then a country lane. They reached a copse, where about 2225 hours Magrath and James separated from the other two, as they had previously planned.

They made their way to Les Essarts, six miles south of Rouen. On the way they crossed a small aerodrome which seemed to be in process of construction, and made a considerable noise climbing some corrugated iron to get onto the aerodrome. They saw a light, probably from a bicycle, flashing along the outside, so they lay in the centre of the aerodrome for about 25 minutes and then got on to the main road to Les Essarts, where they went to an inn and got some bread from a servant girl. From there they went on to a small village, where a girl took them to the Mayor, who advised them to go to Oiselle-sur-Seine and to get themselves civilian clothes. At that time they were nattily dressed in blue pyjamas over khaki trousers!

On 23 November they tried to reach Oiselle, but mis-navigation brought them straight back to Les Essarts. It was a Sunday, so they went to the church where they found the curé conducting a children's service. They had to ask his advice in the presence of some of the children and he sent a boy of nine to the boy's uncle and Magrath and James were instructed to go there. The man, however, was out and they were told to return in the evening. They did so and were given complete sets of civilian clothes and a lot of food. By that time rumours of their escape had reached the village and they were advised to go on sleeping in the woods.

On 24 November they woke early and went to Oiselle, arriving about 1000 hours. They went to the station and asked for two tickets to Paris and were told there was no train till 1700. They returned then and got the tickets without difficulty, although they put down a great deal more money than they actually cost. The train was crowded and they had to stand in the corridor all the way, but at the barrier at Paris, no questions were asked.

They walked the streets all that night, then finally went up to an old lady and told her who they were. She took them to her home, where her son and his wife gave up their bed for them. They slept there that night and were given food; next morning they went to the curé of a neighbouring church, but he was in bed. They went to another church, but the curé there was frightened and talked volubly and very fast. A guide to Paris bought at the Underground gave the address of the Anglican Church near the Etoile. At the church however, they found a notice from the US Embassy saying that the church was shut and under the protection of the Embassy, so they set out for the Embassy, on the way passing the French Red Cross Office. There they spoke to a lady, who took them inside, gave them a British Red Cross parcel, fifty francs, and two oranges each. She then led them to the Irish Catholic church near the Etoile. The senior clergyman interrogated them, as he thought they might be German, but it turned out that Magrath came from the same town as the priest so he was able to satisfy him that the two were genuine. They kept them for one night and next day a French doctor called and told them that on the following day they would be sent to Nevers to a doctor friend of his. One of the Irish priests, who had been a padre with the BEF, bought the tickets, gave them 250 francs each, and escorted them to the station. They remained in Nevers for over three weeks while arrangements were made for the next stage of their journey. They crossed the Line of Demarcation between Nevers and Clermont Ferrand by ferrying the Loire in a small boat on the night of 19 December and were taken by car to Chemin-Sur-La-Fosse, where they got a train for Marseille, arriving at 6 a.m. on 22 December. On Christmas Eve they travelled to Toulouse and on the 27th to Port Vendres, whence they crossed the Pyrenees on foot to Vilajuiga, with two guides and four Belgians and reached there at 0500 hours on 29 December. They were then taken by train to Barcelona and handed over to the British Consulate-General.

Then it was just a case of them waiting for a ship back to the UK. This took until 4 March 1942. It seemed that officers who evaded or escaped, were given preference as they were flown home!

Once back in the UK, Bill Magrath was recommended for the DCM, but was later awarded the Military Medal, as was Sergeant James. James went on to operations with a night fighter squadron based in the UK and was killed in 1943, as was his brother who was a wing commander.

Owing to his injuries Bill was judged unfit for further operational flying, and so went on to become a navigational instructor and was given a commission. Recently he was the Mayor of Salisbury.

2.   Attack on the Tirpitz

On 11 April 1942, No 4 Group Bomber Command reported the German battleship *Tirpitz* to be in the Aas Fjord, near Trondheim, Norway, and the intention was to attack this capital ship in this fjord, with heavy bomber aircraft of Nos.4 and 5 Groups, during the next moon period. The target date was set for 25 April, or the first suitable night thereafter. The plan was to attack the ship with 4,000 lb bombs carried by 76, 44 and 97 Squadrons, followed up by a low attack on the battleship by 10 and 35 Squadrons, each carrying $4 \times 1,000$ lb mines. The mining attack was to be carried out from 150 feet, and the mines were to be dropped close to the stern and between the ship and the shore.

For the CO of 10 Squadron based at Leeming it was to be his first operation since taking over the Squadron. Wing Commander Don Bennett, a famous Australian pre-war airman who was to have an equally distinguished future as the CO of the Pathfinders, had been posted to 10 from 77 Squadron on 14 April. With 77 he had flown on 13 bombing raids since joining them on 2 December 1941. The attack on the *Tirpitz* was his 14th mission. The operation in fact took place on the night of 27 April and he took off in Halifax W 1041-'B' at 8.40 p.m.

'The operation was a special one on behalf of the Royal Navy; to roll a mine under the soft belly of the *Tirpitz*. I led the squadron in at low level in bright moonlight,' he reported, 'along the worst route you could possibly have, over defended islands, and heavy coastal defences and close to support ships.

On nearing the target we were fired at by flak, and the rear gunner, Flight Lieutenant Howe, was wounded in the face, but he reported that he was all right. On this night visibility was good but on approaching the ship we ran into an unexpected whitish smoke screen, at about 400 feet. As this happened, up came the flak from below and the aircraft received further hits. We could see the flashes from the guns and assumed that we were directly over the *Tirpitz*, in which case it was too late to release the bombs.' However as he made a second bomb run the plane was hit by flak and a fire started behind the starboard inner engine.

The second pilot, Sergeant Harry Walmsley, flying his tenth mission, recalls: 'The captain coaxed the aircraft in a shallow climb to about 1,000 feet on the altimeter. The aircraft flaps caught fire and the undercarriage started to lower. The decision to bale out was made when the ground was probably less than 700 feet beneath the aircraft. I left the Halifax by the front hatch pulling the ripcord almost immediately. The harness tightened and the 'chute opened. Within seconds I was falling onto a thick carpet of snow.'

Bennett recalls: 'I found myself in a doomed aircraft and no parachute, but Flight Sergeant J. Colgan, my flight engineer, came forward with my 'chute and clipped it on to my chest, and in doing so risked his life and saved mine.'

One wonders today what course the war would have taken, and if the Pathfinders would have been formed if this action had not been taken by Flight Sergeant Colgan.

'As I got out of my seat,' Bennett continued, 'the starboard wing folded up and as I left the aircraft I pulled my ripcord. There was no time for counting to ten or even one. I hit the snow just as the 'chute opened and promptly fell on my head. The trip to Sweden took me three days and three nights, during this time I lost about three stone in weight and suffered from frost bite.

'The moment we had landed the German soldiers were out in hundreds with dogs looking for us. The dogs were my main worry, so to get away from the dogs I had to cross a stream; the temperature at the time must have been minus 15. The water in the stream was flowing but the banks were about ten feet wide and covered in ice so you had to slide across the ice and into the water to get to the other side and so shake off the scent to the dogs. By this time I had joined up with one of my crew, Sergeant C.R.S. Forbes, the wireless operator, who came from Newfoundland. It was a case of wading across the stream and pulling yourself out holding on to a tree branch that was hanging over the bank.

'On the last night I received help from the Norwegians. It was a little farmhouse up in the mountains, and the door was opened by a man. I said to Forbes to get ready to run if need be but then the man said, "No, don't do that, come in." He had in fact lived in Australia and spoke good English. Here we fed with whatever they had, our clothes were dried on a stove and he let us lie in front of the fire for two hours sleep; the only sleep we got in three days.

'We were then handed over to a chap whom we followed, with a careful plan. If the Germans were coming he would light a match and we would jump into a ditch at the side of the road, but we didn't see any Germans and he got us right up to the frontier. The last few miles was clear snow all the way; you could see the frontier for miles. There were two cairns of rock, one with the colours of Norway and the other Sweden.

'When we got into Sweden, as they were neutral, they strictly and properly put us into an internment camp. The weight I had lost soon came back within a week. There was no meat to eat so for the first time I ate Silver Fox.

'Then one day, in drove a car with a Swede at the wheel and two ladies, all of whom spoke English. They went and saw the Commandant, a colonel in the Swedish Army, and they said they wanted to see me. I had previously had a bad confrontation with the British Legation who had sent up a junior official to see what I wanted in the way of help. The Swede, however, was a friend of Count Bernadotte and he arranged to get me released to go down to Stockholm for an interview.' As an evader, Bennett would have been interned. He was determined to avoid this at all costs. If he could claim capture by the Germans, he would be repatriated. He therefore invented a story which then had to appear in his eventual debriefing, that after landing he had been captured by a lone German skier. He surrendered and the skier went off to find the other members of his crew – whereupon Bennett promptly escaped. A tall story, but it worked! 'I saw the Count,' Bennett continued, 'who at first was not at all helpful so I told him I am going to sue him in their own courts for wrongful imprisonment and that it would be public knowledge. He said he did not want this, so I asked to be freed and this he agreed to. An aircraft was sent over from Leuchars, which pleased the British Ambassador in Stockholm, as he had been trying to get a 'plane over for months. The Pathfinder idea, of course, was being born in England and I was needed there urgently. The plane was a Lockheed mail plane, and I arrived 30 days after taking off to attack the *Tirpitz*.'

In the meantime Harry Walmsley had met Colgan and they crossed the Norwegian countryside in four days, trudging through thick snow in their flying boots, crossing streams and even going over a mountain range on the last day. Walmsley continues: 'On 28 April we called at an isolated house. The man was not friendly but a meal was prepared by women members of the household. He could not speak English and being suspicious of him we left after eating and headed northwards in case he contacted the occupying forces. With the necessary cover in the pine forest some 300 yards from the house, we resumed an easterly direction.' Later that day a man in uniform clothes found them in the forest, and told them the man had indeed reported them – though he had been more frightened at their appearance than hostile. However the Germans were now searching the area. He gave them bread and a kind of sausage meat and wished them well.

Continuing their journey eastwards they came to a detached house with an outhouse into which they staggered and fell into an exhausted sleep. They were discovered the next morning by the owner who gave them a hot meal and dried out their flying boots before they moved on, being told Sweden was just three miles away. Unfortunately, 'we later learned that a Norwegian mile is equal to six English miles!'

'It was getting dark as we came out of the pine woods on a plateau at the top of a mountain range. Two men and two women on skis approached us. They spoke English and seemed to know of our earlier presence in the lower foothills and took us to their wooden cabin by the side of a frozen lake on the plateau. We were treated like royalty. A huge meal, facilities for washing ourselves, a bunk each for the night, a stove for warmth and for drying out our uniforms. We gave them 120 Kroner from the escape kit for their kindness and help.' (They only had one between them as Walmsley had lost his in baling out.) 'We declined the offer of skis, before walking the next morning across the frozen lake which straddled the border. We crossed the border and were immediately picked up by a Swedish patrol .... We were interrogated before being taken to an internment camp at Falun some 150 miles north of Stockholm. There we were delighted to meet Wing Commander Bennett and Sergeant Forbes.' By courtesy of the British Legation in Stockholm they were allowed to buy civilian clothes, and also allowed to visit the local baths for a steam bath, swim and shower. After three weeks Walmsley was taken to a hotel in Stockholm, while Colgan remained at Falun. This was because the pilots were thought to be more important to get back as it cost ten thousand pounds to train a pilot. In fact Colgan did not get back until September 1942. On 26 May Walmsley came back with Bennett, 'an absence of just 30 days from our country,' Walmsley says.

On 10 May Wing Commander Bennett was recommended for the DSO and Sergeant Harry Walmsley the DFM. These were approved by Air Marshal Harris on 27 May.

3.   First Out of Denmark

Donald Smith, a Canadian, joined the RCAF in 1940 at the age of nineteen. In 1941 he volunteered for active service and was posted to a fighter squadron in England where he serviced Hurricanes and Spitfires. In late 1942 he remustered to aircrew and after completing a flight engineer's course was posted to No.75 Squadron RNZAF at Newmarket where he joined the crew of Flight Lieutenant Charles Woodbine Parish. Parish had already had a near brush with death when his aircraft crashed into the Channel in 1940. Parish, the only survivor, swam seven miles in the dark to the English coast.

On the night of 20/21 April 1943 they were leading a group from 7 Squadron PFF in Stirling 'M-Mother' which left Oakington at about 2000 hours to bomb Stettin. They had been chosen to lead the formation as Parish and their navigator, Pilot Officer Bob Vance RCAF, were the most experienced in the Pathfinders at that time.

They were approaching the coast just north of Korsor on the return trip when they were attacked by an Me110 night fighter. Although evasive action was taken the attack resulted in the fuel tanks in both wings being set on fire. At 2 a.m. Parish gave the order: 'Sorry, boys, you are going to have to jump, best of luck.'

The aircraft was hit again near the mid-upper turret and cannon fire came through the floor. Donald had been instructed to use the rear escape hatch as they had extra crewmen on board and he used the damaged floor as a ladder to reach this destination. On reaching it he found the wireless operator, Sergeant Louis Krulicki, crumpled up near the hatch which he had partially opened. On fully opening the hatch Donald was pulled out by the slipstream and he managed to open his parachute just before the aircraft crashed anhd exploded, killing all the other members of the crew. He was the only survivor.

In the report he made to MI9, Donald states that after walking for some hours and then resting 'I then went to a farm nearby and asked the way to Copenhagen. I was in battledress, but had cut off my badges and the pockets of my blouse. The woman at the farm pointed out the town of Slagelse, about two and a half miles to the south-east.'

Donald continued walking in an easterly direction crossing

two main roads until about 2100 hours when, at a loss as to which way to go, he saw a solitary farm worker and asked again the way to Copenhagen. The man could not understand him but took him to his home where he was given food and the man's wife indicated the way to Soro.

On leaving the farm he kept walking until he reached a large wood beside a railway line, it was now just after midnight on 22 April, and feeling too tired to go any further he hid in the wood and slept until about 0430 hours. He had used the outer flying suit he was carrying as bedding but his sleep was disturbed by the field mice that were running over him. By now his feet had started to blister from wearing the loose-fitting, fleece-lined, flying boots and he wondered if it was worthwhile to keep going or give himself up. However he received help from a farmer and continued: 'I approached a white farm and went into the yard where I saw a pump. A man came out of the barn and took me to a tap inside. After using some sign language, I think he realised that I was an Allied airman. He went into the house and brought out a bottle of beer and some carrots.'

By now he was feeling more confident that he could make it to Sweden and started walking down some secondary roads and soon passed through the small village of Hom. Shortly after this he sat down to rest his feet but it started to rain and he decided to get into some thicker bushes for protection. He was, however, close to a small white farmhouse and he chose the latter as a point for further rest. His knock was answered by a middle-aged woman who could not speak English and called her husband, who realised Donald's predicament and hurried him inside. The woman noticed the difficulty that Donald was having with his feet and immediately fetched water and towels in order to tend to them much to Donald's relief, as there was one large blister stretching from toes to heel on each foot. Food was then placed on the table and he was invited to eat with the elderly couple. Before he left the woman gave him some more sandwiches and a bottle of beer to take with him.

He recalls: 'When I started off again I found it almost impossible to walk, so I decided to look for a place to sleep that was dry. Around 1900 hours I noticed a small horse stable all by itself beside a peat bog. After looking over my hotel for the night, I went down to the pond for a wash and shave. I decided to cut the uppers of my flying boots to make a pair of shoes out of them. As I was doing this a man, two women and two children came walking up the path beside the peat bog. The man noticed me and immediately sent the women and children away. I could plainly see that he (George Rasmussen) recognized me as an Allied airman. After trying to make him understand where I wanted to go, he shook his head, pointing at my clothes. He then made the sign of the swastika on his arm and indicated to me that there were a lot of Gestapo in the area. He led me into the stable and with some sign language made it clear that I was to stay there until 2100 hours.'

George Rasmussen returned at the stated time, bringing with him civilian clothing and other useful articles. He took away Donald's flying suit and heavy white sweater. These Donald later learned were used to provide clothing for George's family. Having made the exchange of clothing George pointed to his watch and indicated that Donald should not leave until after 0500 hours. There was a curfew on around Borup and anyone out during the curfew period would be shot on sight. When George left Donald climbed into the horse's feed trough and fell asleep.

From his debriefing report: 'At about 0530 hours the next day (23 April) my helper took me to his home in the village of Dalby for breakfast. He gave me a Shell road map marked with the route for Copenhagen, 20 Kroner, a clasp knife and a shaving mirror. (I had a safety razor with me.) In return for this help I gave the Dane, who was obviously very poor, the 1500 French francs contained in the purse issued before leaving my station. He then took me to the main Ringsted-Kode road and left me. I walked along this road, and just short of Kode took a by-pass road which runs north-east to the coast road. On this by-pass road I went into a farm and was given coffee and bread and cheese. After reaching the coast road I took a branch road which runs inland to Taastrup.'

He had now travelled over 100 kilometres in the two days since being shot down. Nearing Taastrup he went into a farmyard in the hope of getting some food and knocked at the kitchen door of the farmhouse. This was on Good Friday, 23 April. The door was opened by a Mr Thorvald Sorensen and he saw a large family gathered for an Easter dinner. He was invited to join them although he felt uncomfortable about his appearance. After a hearty meal Mr Sorensen explained that with the number of people already at the farm they could not risk him staying there overnight but wished him luck on his journey.

At about 8.30 p.m. he reached a farm near Glostrup where the farmer, Mr L.C. Pedersen, told Donald that if he had picked the next farm he would have probably been arrested as the owners were Nazi sympathisers. As it happens he had made the right choice, for the local schoolteacher, Mr Marborg, spoke English and was an active member of the local Resistance. Next morning as he entered Glostrup, Donald passed several members of the Gestapo but was not stopped for identification. Mr Marborg had already bought railway tickets for them both to go to Helsingor and within a few minutes after boarding the train they were entering the main station of Copenhagen. German troops were everywhere so they went outside the station until the train to Helsingor was due to leave. Donald was stared at but nothing was said to either the Germans or Hipos (Danes in the German forces). Donald noticed that every bridge along the way was well guarded against the predations of the very active Resistance. On arrival at Helsingor they headed for the docks but found that the ferries to Sweden were heavily guarded and their attempts to find a rowing boat were unsuccessful as the Germans had either removed the oars from the boats or they were under the view of machine gun posts. At this point Sweden was only two miles away but as Donald had lost weight on the meagre diet he had existed on he was in no physical condition to attempt to swim the very rough and cold waters of the sound.

Donald told MI9: 'The schoolmaster left me about noon without having put me in touch with anyone who could help me. After he had left I walked north along the coast looking for a boat, but could not find one. At night I went to a house on the main road north of Helsingor where the people spoke English. They gave me supper, and I stayed until we had listened to the BBC nine o'clock news. I went back along the main road towards Helsingor and spent the night in a small furnished summer house on the beach. This house was empty. During the night a Danish policeman looked in, but did not say anything.'

By the morning of 26 April he was beginning to feel the effects of losing so much weight and became very frustrated. In despair he walked up to a house having decided to give himself up if help was not forthcoming. When he knocked at the door it was opened by a middle-aged lady who spoke fluent English. He told her of his predicament and she called her husband, Folmer Dalsborg. Mrs Dalsborg explained that as they had three small children in the house it would be very risky for them to have him stay for any length of time. Nonetheless she immediately prepared a cooked meal and coffee and after dinner offered him the use of their bath, a gesture that Donald appreciated. He was then shown into a bedroom and told to rest.

Donald recalls: 'As I lay in bed, the door suddenly opened and the very excited Mr Dalsborg came in shouting, "You will go to Sweden." He disappeared just as fast without telling me how I was to get there. I lay in bed and thanked God for the help. A while later a very distinguished gentleman came into the room. He spoke fluent English and I learned that he was married to the daughter of a Major Barson who lived near London. He asked me for some identification. I had lost my identification book when I was shot down. It was later found and handed over to the Resistance movement. I did carry some of the things I had cut off my uniform and was still wearing the long winter underwear which we used when flying. It had a "Made in England" label on it. I was sure that I had convinced him that I really was an Allied airman. He told me to stay where I was and he would be back later. Around 1800 hours he came back into the room and told me to get dressed, after which he went to a house down the street. Later that evening another gentleman came to interrogate me. He informed me that he would try to get in touch with Intelligence in London, by radio, to confirm my story. At this point he pulled a snub-nosed revolver out of his side pocket and said, "You know what we will have to do if we are unable to raise London? There are a lot of lives at stake." The remainder of the evening was spent very quietly listening to the radio and I prayed they would be successful.'

The second visitor was Major Fleming, chief of sabotage and the underground, and his visit resulted in a sleepless night for Donald. Donald's fears were unfounded and the next day a Mr Barson came for him and took him to his home where he was introduced to several members of the Resistance. During the few days that Donald stayed with the Barsons, Mrs Barson taught him a few words of Danish and took him to the local shops.

On the evening of 29 April Mr Barson told Donald that he would be leaving for Sweden that night, but did not mention how. He was taken by taxi and train to a large white house at Skodsborg, about eight miles from the Swedish coast. Here he met more members of the Resistance movement and was requested to empty his pockets of all unnecessary articles and a couple of the girls asked if they could have his silk escape maps. A boat could not be found that day and he was taken to the home of one of the girls, code-named 'Gretha', who had asked for the maps.

'Gretha', Mrs Silivia Tjorn, recalls: 'Sergeant Smith was interrogated thoroughly, London Intelligence were contacted by radio to confirm his story. There were too many lives at stake to take any chances. His story was confirmed however – although reported "killed". The escape was planned to take place within the next few days, in the meanwhile shifting from one safe house to another. I and another friend took Donald Smith into Copenhagen to see the sights, had lunch at a first-class restaurant, showed him the Royal Palace, Houses of Parliament, Tivoli etc, conversing in English not withstanding German soldiers and tanks parading the streets; *all* Germans were given the "cold shoulder" by the Danes and ignored everywhere. We seemed quite without fear in those days and made a joke out of everything not withstanding the fact that we risked being caught tortured and shot, as were many of our members. The only times I was really worried were when a wireless operator came to the house to send messages to London as the Germans were able to plot a house in a very short time. We had our look-outs placed at the end of the street who were sometimes able to warn of an approaching car. It also meant having to get the maid and children out of the house on some pretext or other. My husband was at his office every day, so I would have been faced with the music if caught. Today I often shiver at the thought of risks taken in the name of patriotism, and the danger to my family – but it was worth it in spite of the fact of being parted from our children for nearly two years.'

Donald returned to the house at Skodsborg where members of the Resistance were assembling a two seat Kayak, which was to be used for his escape. He was then taken to the Police Head-quarters and introduced to Lars Troen, a Danish officer cadet, who was to be his fellow paddler. He was also introduced to Captain Basse and Sergeant Malling of the Copenhagen Police who gave them instructions on what to do if seen by a patrol boat. Donald was given photographs of Copenhagen which showed the Shellhuset building which was being used as Gestapo Head-quarters and asked to tell the Intelligence people that it should be bombed.* Leaving the Police Headquarters Donald and Lars passed their time sightseeing in the company of Chris Hansen, who was a full time Resistance worker in the guise of a Danish policeman.

Returning to Skodsborg, Donald was asked if he had ever paddled a kayak. When he replied with a negative answer Lars said, 'Don't worry, I know how.' At 2300 hours the attention of the Danish beach guards was distracted by Mrs L Duss Hansen while her husband pushed the kayak with Donald and Lars aboard, out into the sound. The water was very cold with a fast running current and Donald had difficulty in maintaining a rhythm with Lars. At one point a patrol boat with a searchlight approached them, but the kayak dropped between two waves

---

* The raid on the Gestapo Headquarters took place on 21 March 1945, with the aircraft coming in at roof top level. The Resistance workers on the top floor managed to escape with very few casualties.

and by lying flat the beam missed them and they were able to continue their journey. They paddled for about three hours before they found a stretch of beach without barbed wire. Donald landed in Sweden around 0300 hours, 1 May 1943.

They made their way to the British Legation at Helsingborg where they were met by a Mr Crew, who had been told by the Resistance that they were coming. He took them to his home in his charcoal-burning car which had a top speed of 10 mph! Mrs Crew prepared a breakfast for them and Donald was given a dry pair of shoes and socks to replace those he was wearing which were soaking. As Donald was in civilian clothes he was declared to have entered Sweden illegally and was put in jail; had he been in uniform he would have been interned for the remainder of the war. The police treated him exceptionally well; after two days he was given an identity card and allowed to leave the jail, although he had to report every day. After being kitted out with new clothes by Mr Crew Donald was registered as a guest at the Savoy Hotel in Helsingborg.

Unbeknown to Donald his escapade had attracted attention, as he recalls: 'In the afternoon I was told that the Crown Prince and Princess of Sweden were staying at the Grand Hotel. (Crown Prince Gustav Adolf – later King of Sweden.) He had been informed of our escape from Denmark and he requested that I come up to their suite and have a talk. I entered the room to see two gracious people sitting in chairs side by side, just like the pictures of our King and Queen. I proceeded to within a few feet of them, bowed and waited for him to speak first. Both the Prince and Princess put out their hands for me to shake. He welcomed me to Sweden and hoped my stay would be a happy one. He asked me to sit down and we talked for about half an hour. He was very interested in how we had managed to escape out of Denmark, as I was the first airman to have ever escaped from there.'

He was sent home to Canada on survivors' leave, sailing on the *Empress of Scotland* from Liverpool, a journey of seven days to Halifax. Having attempted to telephone his family in advance of his arrival, but without success as his mother was out, he travelled by train to Toronto. His mother was overcome at his homecoming, but all his father said was, 'I told you he would be all right.'

In 1977 Donald returned to Denmark and met some of the people that helped him during his enforced stay there. Silvia Tjorn, who was awarded a Certificate of Merit for her Resistance work, recognised him immediately although they had not met for 34 years, and pointed out his escape map decorating the wall of her living room.

4.   A Couple of Burglars

Königsberg, East Prussia! From the moment that Harry Wilson, navigator of Lancaster 'QR-D' of No. 61 Squadron based at Skellingthorpe, heard of the target for the night of 29 August 1944, he knew he was in for a long trip. Only a few days earlier he had taken part in an unsuccessful operation on the same target, and had logged a flight time of 10 hrs 50 mins. Little did he realise just how long a round trip he would have on this later occasion. Harry, his skipper (Flight Sergeant Bruce Loneon,) and the rest of the crew had only made five previous trips together and were still settling down and as 'QR-D' had been given to them brand new, considered that they were operationally still 'running in'.

As they flew back over Denmark they were feeling confident about another trip successfully completed. Their composure was shattered when without warning, the starboard inner engine was hit by flak. It was such a perfect shot they thought they had been tracked by radar. Within seconds the flames from the engine were threatening to burn away the tail plane, although the engine was feathered and the fire extinguishers operated, 'It was,' in Harry's own words, 'like trying to put out the Fire of London with a water pistol.' The result was inevitable and Bruce Loneon gave the order to 'bale-out'. The members of the crew left the doomed aircraft with Bruce Loneon being the last to jump.

Harry Wilson recalls: 'At 4.15 a.m. on 30 August 1944, I, who had never baled out before, was swinging on the end of a parachute. It was just getting light, a nice morning really, and I was still in the air when the Lancaster I had just vacated crashed on to Danish soil. I landed quite safely in a field, no bones broken, so I pulled in my parachute and stuffed it under some cabbages. It would obviously be found, but I had no time to dig a hole. I started running – any direction just to get away from my landing position. I stumbled into a ditch and realised that it would be a great place to hide my Mae West. Quickly I undid the tapes, pushed it down into the mud and ran on. A few shots rang out but there was no sign of anybody, so I presumed that some other members of the crew were in trouble. Finally I could run no further. I climbed over a fence and lay still in the undergrowth; all was now quiet. I had achieved the first object, stressed in all escape lectures, I was away from the aircraft and had hidden my parachute and Mae West. All I had to do now was to contact the Resistance.'

He remained in hiding for the rest of the day and took stock of his position. He had maps of the area, but no Danish money. The authorities had issued other currencies but in their wisdom had not considered Danish necessary! During the day he had maintained a watch on a nearby farm and outbuildings, and managed to attract the elderly farmer's attention. The farm was at Valgaard, near Farso, and the family who owned it – Mr and Mrs Kjor – looked after Harry for a week.

Harry takes up the story: 'The days I spent lying in the straw above the cattle, whilst at nights I came into the house, heard the 6 o'clock news in English, had a wash and a meal then returned to the barn. I was always uneasy in the house, because if I had been caught, the Danes could not plead that they did not know I was there. On the second day of my enforced sojourn, a Mr and Miss Sonne and later a Mr Hald, who could all speak English, came to interrogate me. They knew all about the crash and actually had pieces of the wircless set that had been taken from the wreckage. They were willing to help me and fitted me out with civilian clothes. Whilst I stayed at Valgaard, plans were being laid to get me to Sweden. I learnt that my pilot, Bruce Loneon had also contacted the Underground movement, but that the rest of the crew were prisoners.'

Shortly after this Harry cycled to a house in Farso where he met up with his pilot, the two of them were then taken by car to a lonely road and transferred to a police car. From that point onwards they were 'prisoners' of the Danish police and whilst in the custody of the two officers, Nielsen and Pietersen, were taken by train to Copenhagen. On the train they had a compartment to themselves whilst people stood in the corridors. It was a huge joke to Nielsen who on being asked if the prisoners were dangerous, had replied that they were only 'a couple of burglars'.

Harry recalls: 'By now I was "Jens Kristian Hansen", and I still have my Danish identity card with my photograph (taken in Britain and carried on all operations) overstamped by the police. We had an uneventful journey to Copenhagen where everybody was overjoyed to see us. Although it meant death, they actually vied with each other as to where we would stay. By day we walked about and took a chance on a sudden police check, but we were always escorted and obviously the Danes knew what they were doing. At night we stopped indoors, staying a few nights with a Kis and Antonius, presumably underground names, who never opened the door without a gun in their hands. Everybody treated us so well; they let us use their homes, and their wardrobes, as though we were members of their family. I remember that everybody in Copenhagen seemed to ride a bicycle. Germans were everywhere. The diesel works in Copenhagen had been recently raided by Mosquitos and everybody had their little story to tell.'

One dark night in September they were collected by a swarthy character who took them to the docks. The black car was driven at speed through the town with lights flashing and sirens wailing. The driver nonchalantly commented that it wasn't his car but that he had stolen it from the Gestapo. Nobody would dream of stopping a Gestapo car! On arrival at the docks they were taken aboard a Swedish ship. After a few drinks the driver left and the Captain took them below to join others already in the hold. During the night the ship sailed and the next day they were told that they could come up on deck. In the straits near Malmo the ship stopped and they were taken off, by motor boat, and landed on Swedish soil. They were immediately taken to the British Consul in Malmo who gave them ten pounds each, which was eventually stopped from their pay! They managed to convince the Swedish Consul that they were escaped aircrew and should therefore be repatriated to England.

As Harry relates: 'Two days later we caught the train to Stockholm, where we were treated extremely well by the Consulate. We were completely kitted out at the town's largest departmental store and we stopped in a hotel where we ate everything in sight. About a week later we flew back to Leuchars in Scotland; I was in the bomb bay of one Mosquito, my pilot in another. The German fighters often lay in wait for the Mosquitos doing these trips from Sweden, but we got away with it.

'The next day we travelled down to London to be interrogated and then given survivors' leave, during which time I celebrated my 21st birthday. Our adventure was over; my pilot returned to Australia whilst I returned to operations.'

As a sequel to these events, about three months after his return, Harry was forwarded a letter by the Air Ministry in London. The letter was from his friends in Denmark giving an address in Sweden to which he could write. He sent a carefully worded reply, giving no mention of his escapade or their assistance. As a result of this, some two months later he was under court-martial for 'attempting to communicate with countries under enemy control'. The case was a sensation in Bardney, with the Judge Advocate being brought up from London. He was taken off operational duties, presumably to prevent him from baling out and joining his German friends! He won his case as common sense prevailed and Harry was able to continue operations with 9 Squadron until the end of the war.

On 29 August 1986, exactly 42 years after hiding there, Harry returned to the farm where it had all started. Vagn Kjor handed him pieces of his Lancaster, a couple of escape maps and his escape money. He spent a night at the bungalow now the residence of Mr Sonne's son, and met Mr Hald again which brought memories flooding back.

In spite of extensive enquiries in Copenhagen, Harry has been unable to trace either Nielsen and Pietersen or Kis and Antonius but the friendship with two of his other helpers, Else Badgaard and her husband continues.

5.   Six Sacks of Potatoes

It was shortly after midnight on Tuesday, 26 September 1944. Despite the wild and stormy weather, an all Canadian crew of 407 Squadron under Flying Officer G.A. Biddle, were on a routine anti-submarine patrol off the coast of Norway. 407 Royal Canadian Air Force Squadron was one of the few all Canadian squadrons serving with Coastal Command, and known as the 'Demon Squadron', in 1944 it was based at Wick on the east coast of the northern tip of Scotland. One of the wireless operator air gunners, was Flight Sergeant E.H. Firestone, who shared the watch on the radar set with another wireless operator/air gunner, Pilot Officer Kenneth W. Graham. They were about 30 miles off the Norwegian coast when Harvey Firestone changed watch and returned to the rear turret of the Wellington. He recalls: 'I had no sooner settled into the turret, and completed my checks on the equipment, when the aircraft shook slightly and a large fireball gushed out of the exhaust of our starboard engine. Much to my dismay, I realised that the engine was on fire.'

Having reduced the weight of the aircraft they were able to maintain an altitude of about 800 feet and at about 6 a.m. they sited the mountainous coast of Norway. Biddle spotted the entrance to a fjord and headed towards it but as they approached they saw some ships escorting a submarine. They had little option but to fly over the small convoy as they had no fuel left for evasive flying.

The ships opened fire on them, and Harvey, in an attempt to confuse the gunners, fired off some Very lights hoping that they would think that they were a friendly aircraft. This worked for a moment but they were soon under fire again. By now the remaining engine had been hit and a final message was sent by the wireless operator, Warrant Officer George Grandy, and everybody got ready for a forced landing in their crash positions.

The pilot was now attempting to make a wheels-up landing in what appeared to be the only spot possible. The Wellington hit some trees with its port wing and then Biddle brought the tail down first, to slow them up and then jammed the nose in. It slewed around then came to a very sudden stop; they had landed in a mere 65 feet! Grandy and the radio fell on top of George Death, Neil was thrown from his table and had a gash on his head, but Biddle was OK, having been strapped in. Harvey Firestone hit his head on the main spar.

Harvey Firestone recalls: 'Graham and I from our position had no way of knowing that we had made it to land. We fully expected to see water come pouring into the aircraft. Ken was anxious to exit the 'plane; he helped me to my feet, and literally threw me through the hatch. As I was on my way out, I saw Biddle coming out of the front hatch. I, for the first time, realised that we would not have to contend with water, we had made it safely to land.'

They had come down at Haegland, six miles south-west of Os, Norway. By this time a small crowd of people had arrived, and after attending to Neil's injuries and setting fire to the aircraft, the crowd had grown to some thirty strong. They were informed by them that there was a German Garrison at Os and another at Bergen, and told by a man that a group of Germans would soon be there and that they should take a route through the mountains to the east. Harvey turned to leave with the others and, as a gesture of gratitude, thrust the Very pistol that he was still holding, after setting the aircraft on fire, into his hands.

'After the war,' he says, 'I learned that the man's name was Magnus Astvik and he was one of the leaders of the community and the principal of the local school.'

The crew headed in a south-easterly direction, getting as far from the aircraft as possible. The terrain was rugged and heavily wooded, making progress slow. They buried their Irvin jackets and flying boots and turned their battledress jackets inside out, in order to look like civilians of the area. They crossed small mountain streams, even walking up one for some distance, in the hope of throwing off any dogs which might be used to track them. Later they heard the Germans had indeed used dogs. They continued on for about three hours; finally at the crest of a hill they came across what looked like a hydro installation but on checking their maps were unable to pinpoint their exact location. Climbing another hill they discovered that they were not too far from the shore of a fjord.

Nestled in a small cove at the foot of the mountain were four or five cottages scattered amongst the trees. It was agreed that Neil should go and see if he could get help. Meantime they concealed themselves among the brush and watched him picking his way cautiously down the steep slope. Finally to their immense relief, he appeared in a clearing at the side of the house and waved. He was accompanied by a woman, Ingeborge Bjornen.

She recalls: 'I spoke a little English and I explained to the Canadians their whereabouts. Marta Brueroy led them up into the woods and hid them in a slope of large boulders.'

In the meantime Ingeborge had gone to try and make contact with Herald Lunde, but he was not at home, so she went home to confer with her father, Hans. They agreed that they should contact Einar Evenson, also their neighbour Johannes Ferstadvoll. He and her father then went to see Einar and arranged to bring the airmen to Bjornetrynet at nightfall, and they were guided to him and his men and left in their care.

During the early hours of the morning of 26 September, Einar, a group leader of the 2nd Company of the Milorg Norwegian Resistance in Lepsoy, was having his breakfast when he heard the aircraft approaching, and knew it was in trouble and looking for a landing place. When making enquiries he found the crew had survived and were in the area of Bjornen. When he arrived he found Hans and Johannes were waiting for him. Hans asked Einar's father, Kristian, if he would allow him to use his 30-foot motor boat in order to try to cross the North Sea to the Shetland Islands. He said he could, but it was not wise to make the trip in such bad conditions. They all agreed that the crew had to be taken off the peninsula that night or they would surely be captured. The only way this could possibly be done was by row boat and that would mean enlisting the help of others. Einar accepted the responsibility of doing this, while Hans and Johannes agreed to see to it that the airmen would be brought over to Trynevika, a small cove on Bjornetrynet, that evening. Einar would arrange for the manpower for the boats to be at the rendezvous point. The men Einar enlisted in the dangerous job of manning the two row boats were Thorvald Jacobson, Magnus K. Rottingen, and Hans Holmefjord, who were all strong oarsmen and knew the waters well. Also Nils Rottingen who had lived in the US for some time and spoke English was asked to help.

Pieces of cloth were to be wrapped around the oars at the rowlocks. The Germans were on their guard and had placed seven sentry boxes over an area of some three-quarters of a mile, where the possibility of escape might occur. Einar arranged a meeting with Magnus Hauge, leader of the second company of the Milog in Os, for the following day in Lepsoy on Strono, a large island some five kilometres from the rendezvous point. The Milog had been using a boat house as a meeting place.

Harvey Firestone recalls: 'It had been occupied earlier in the summer by the Germans but was considered to be a relatively safe place to hide us for a short period, even though the German garrison at Rottingen was just across the water, less than a mile away, and the trip to Strono would be very hazardous. The thought was that we were to stay in the boathouse during the hours of darkness, leave before daylight, climb up into the thickly wooded hills nearby, and to remain there during daylight hours, returning to the boathouse under cover of darkness in the late evening. This was to be our routine until 1 October.'

Early in the evening of the 26th the five oarsmen assembled and prepared for their journey to pick them up, and at 8 p.m. under cover of heavy clouds and heavy drizzling rain, but with calm water they set off hugging the shoreline. The Canadians were told of the plan and shortly before 7 o'clock Ingeborge and Johannes left Bjornen and started working through the woods towards them. When she arrived she signalled that they were to hurry and follow them down through the trees and underbrush. They descended down to a small clearing which was covered with rocks and here had to wait for the row boats.

'We had been waiting for about an hour,' recalls Harvey Firestone, 'when suddenly a row boat materialised out of the misty darkness. We all seemed to spot it simultaneously. There were two men in a large row boat drifting in towards the rocky shore. The man in the front was frantically waving for us to join them. We thanked Ingeborge for all she had done, waved our thanks to Johannes and hurried to scramble on board the row boat.'

The boat was tossing and pitching and the six of them presented quite a sight in their attempts to get aboard. The boat was quickly guided out from among the rocks and into the fjord, the oarsmen rapidly settling down to a strong rhythmic stroke. George Death and Harvey were sitting beside each other when George remarked that he hoped he would not be seasick; Harvey's only worry was the rain running down his neck.

The Norwegian sitting behind them in the boat took off his raincoat and threw it over their heads. He leaned over and asked in a form of Brooklyn accented English, 'How's that, Bud? Feeling better now?' This was their introduction to Nils Rottingen who had lived in America and was to be the interpreter. Some years later Harvey found out that the other oarsman was Thorvald Jacobson.

They travelled on for about 500 metres and then noticed another boat hidden against the shore. There were three men in the boat and it was obvious that they were waiting nervously for them to appear. The two boats drifted together and they were told three had to get into the other boat. The other three Norwegians were Einar Evenson, Magnus Rottingen and Hans Holmefjord. The visibility improved. On one occasion they spotted a German patrol boat crossing their path, but it did not spot them. If they had been in some sort of motor boat, they would have been heard and seen.

They were in open water for about fifteen to twenty minutes then once again moving between islands. The lead boat pulled over close to shore and one of the Norwegians clambered ashore. He had gone to see if it was safe to proceed. As they proceeded they saw, looming out of the darkness, a bridge across their path. This was the bridge between Brueroy and Rottingen and was about three metres wide and less than three metres high. Standing in the middle of the bridge was a German sentry.

As they approached the bridge the German seemed to be looking straight at them, but he suddenly turned and walked off. They had been on the water for well over two hours when finally they made it to the small island of Strono and into the boathouse. A coal oil lantern was lit, and they were left in comfortable beds, but before daylight were to leave the boathouse and climb into the mountains.

By now the German search for the crew was fanatical and many raids and interrogations were taking place. So far the Germans had scanned all the areas except the area of their hiding place. The main problem now, for the Norwegians was food, and a plan was afoot by the Milog organisation to move them on.

The next few days were the same. Up before dawn, into the woods, and back as darkness fell to the boathouse. In the meantime Magnus Hauge cycled off for his meeting with Einar. They met in a sawmill shed not far from Einar's home in Lepsoy. They discussed events of the previous day and how things would be organised in the future.

Magnus returned home and called Johan Viken on the telephone, telling him that he had 'six sacks of potatoes' and asked him what arrangements could be made for their pickup. As the hunt grew closer, Jacob Hjelle decided the airmen should pass along to a small cabin at Botnane, this would involve a 30-kilometre trip along the fjord followed by about five kilometres of land travel. This transfer was arranged for Sunday, 1 October, the choice of Sunday was dictated by the reduction in activity at the U-Boat training centre at nearby Hatvik. They were to be taken in a 21-foot motor boat, the type used by people in the area when they were out fishing. Five of them were put in the hold of the boat where the fish were normally kept, and a tarpaulin thrown over them. On one occasion a sentry boat came speeding towards them and when the distance was less than 200 metres it suddenly turned to port and went off. The Canadians, of course, under the tarpaulin, had very little idea of what was going on. At one point they were put ashore and later returned for, and re-boarding the boat continued in a northerly direction. They imagined that the Norwegians had gone to make sure everything was all right ahead.

They finally got ashore again when the word 'Tyske', meaning German, was shouted and they hurried on through the trees until they came upon three boathouses. They noticed a ladder leading up to a trap door in one of them, and crawled up into a small storage area where they stayed for about half an hour. They heard the boathouse door open and a head and shoulders came up to the top of the ladder. This was their first introduction to Mowinkel-Nilsen, otherwise known to British Intelligence, SOE, Norwegian Section as R-15. Mowinkel-Nilsen had escaped from Norway in February 1942 and was wanted by the Germans. He had been trained in Scotland by Special Forces and had then parachuted back into Norway with a radio operator. After asking them if they required a doctor he went off and came back after about half an hour with two men.

They were taken to the farmhouse of Martha and Valentine Valentinesen, where they were given a massive bowl of porridge. Nilsen wanted details to enable him to identify them with the Intelligence people in England. But the wireless operator, in trying to word the message to England had heard a rumour, put about by the Milog to confuse the Germans, that the plane had crashed with eight armed Commandos, and had radioed that it was a crew of eight and not six. However by answering various questions and giving details of their nicknames etc, they eventually overcame the confusion.

The Norwegians supplied them with fresh clothing and footwear that would be more suitable for the next stage of their journey, this would involve walking for some distance and a boat trip of about a mile. They left before dawn the next day and disembarked from the boat onto a small beach and began walking through the brush again until they reached a small cabin. On entering the cabin they were introduced to Hans, a nom de guerre for Ivar Dyngeland, who was also being sought by the Germans, for his work with the Resistance. Following a meal made up from the food they had been carrying – thin slices of bread spread with condensed milk – they had their first cigarettes since the crash, the uncured tobacco which they were not used to causing them some discomfort. They were then told that they were to remain with Ivar and that Nilsen had men posted around to watch for German patrols.

Although the cabin was only about 12 foot by 12 foot, and somewhat cramped they rolled out their sleeping bags to catch up on some well needed rest after Nilsen had left. It was the first time they had slept in Norway without having to have a watch posted. When they awoke the following morning they discovered that Ivar was not only their guard, but also their cook as well. When they looked outside, they could not help but be reminded of Canada, and one of the crew suggested that as the Norwegian Air Force, composed of Norwegians in exile, had set up a training centre in Toronto called 'Little Norway', they in turn should call the cabin and the area surrounding it 'Little Canada'.

On 6 October the first All-Canadian daylight bomber raid in history took place over the Bergen area, where the targets were the U-Boat bases. As they were ten to fifteen kilometres away from the targets they were able to watch the proceedings from a point of vantage. Seeing the flak that was being sent up their sympathies were with the crews in the aircraft. Hoping that they would all get safely back they wished that they could be with them. The raid was successful and some shipping was hit; unfortunately some of the bombs had gone astray and some children were killed and others hurt in a nearby school.

On 8 October they were told that they were leaving 'Little Canada' and were taken to a farmhouse and given a meal and then once again were on their way to another boat house where Jacob was waiting for them. Haldor and Laura Orrebakkem, neither of whom spoke English, were to take them by boat on the next leg of their voyage. They were put ashore after a little while, on a small island where a man, whom they did not know, and with whom they could not communicate, indicated that they should stay with him. After a short while another boat appeared, and they were beckoned by the man to get aboard. This was a much larger boat than they had been on before, belonging to Sverre Ostervoll. He headed it to a very small rocky island on which there was a fisherman's cabin, with a radio, and told to wait for a certain message. They were left, and told they would be picked up again that night, and taken by boat back to the Shetlands.

Night slowly turned to day and still no one came. They remained in the hut the following day and all through the night once again, when a message came via the BBC. 'It rains in the mountains', which was repeated the following day. Next evening the message was heard a third time which meant that the boat would be at the rendezvous point the following night, at the arranged time.

Finally on 11 October, Sverre turned up in his boat and took them out to a large ship. They had expected a British ship, but it was Norwegian. The sailors explained that other members of the crew were off-loading ammunitions and supplies for the Resistance movement. The ship was 110 foot long and was an American-built sub-chaser, captained by Leif Larsen and was called *Vigra*. After midnight on 12 October they crossed the North Sea in a raging gale and reached Scalloway in the Shetland Islands. They had finally returned from their last patrol.

Their Norwegian friends received the message on the BBC

the following night, 'Coconuts on Holiday'. For the gallant
Norwegians who had helped them there were to be
repercussions. Hanna, Ingeborge's sister, who had in fact not
been at home during the time that they had been helped was
arrested by the Germans, as they thought she must have helped
in their escape. She was tortured and spent the rest of the war
in prison, as did Pernille Evensen, Einar's mother. Magnus
Hauge was also arrested and tortured, and also spent the rest of
the war in prison.

Harvey recalls: 'In 1979 on the day I was to leave Canada to
revisit Norway, I was approached by a stranger while working
out in a gymnasium, who had overheard me talking to a friend
about my trip to Norway and why I was going there, he told me
that he had been there at the same time. In all innocence I
asked him what he was doing in Norway at that time, and
looking me straight in the eye and pointed a finger in my face
and said, "Looking for you!" He had been in the German Army
and had spent what he described as a miserable four days
searching the area; he told me that there were over 4,000
troops in the area looking for us. But in the words of Magnus
Hauge, we were just "Six sacks of potatoes" that had to be
delivered.'

VI

Italy

Escapes from Italy were most numerous at the time of the Armistice. When it was clear that the Armistice was imminent orders were issued to the SBO's in the POW camps in Italy that at the Armistice everybody was to stay put, and not to wander round the countryside in search of the advancing British, since it was feared harm could be done to the advance by well meaning attempts to help with sabotage behind the lines. Unfortunately, the British miscalculated. Instead of leaving Italy undefended, the Germans rushed troops in to occupy the country and over half the POWs were simply herded into trains and taken to POW camps in Germany or Poland. Those that did attempt to escape were often quickly recaptured. However, some did, despite their orders which indeed some SBO's had almost invited them to ignore, evade successfully, and there were many both successful and unsuccessful break-outs from the trains transporting POWs out of Italy.

One such escaper played a major role in the most famous escape organisation in Italy, Major Sam Derry. He managed to reach Rome where the British Legation cooped up in the Vatican throughout the war had managed a fruitful relationship with Monsignor Hugh O'Flaherty and in the end helped to organise the shelter of a vast number of evaders and escapers in the villages around Rome.

One story included in this section, however, did not take place on Italian soil. Indeed in this remarkable escape story, the participants decided to take the law into their own hands before they reached Italy and a POW camp.

*

1. A Visit to the Vatican

On 15 July 1940, Pilot Officer Eric Garrad-Cole took off from El Daba. After attacking enemy concentration at El Gazala his Blenheim L1491 was shot down near Tobruk and hit the sand in a cloud of dust. He shouted to his navigator, LAC Smith, to get out, but when he realised that Smith had been hit and could not move, he undid his straps, clambered out through the roof hatch and pulled him out after him. The air gunner, Aircraftman Dollin, was clambering out of the rear hatch, and they were quickly surrounded by screaming, black-shirted Italians. Smith had been wounded in the back by a cannon shell and as Garrad-Cole was examining him an Italian kicked sand into the wound. Garrad-Cole turned and hit him as hard as he could and immediately a rifle was stuck into his chest. For a moment things looked dangerous. At that moment an Italian officer arrived, knocked the rifle aside and asked in perfect English what the problem was. When he heard he sent for an ambulance and Smith was taken away.

Dollin and Garrad-Cole were removed to a barracks overlooking Tobruk and were interrogated. They gave nothing except complaints about the treatment of Smith, a British POW, and demanded to see the commanding officer. Next day an Italian general in full dress uniform arrived, apologised again for the incident and gave Dollin and Garrad-Cole permission to exercise in the prison yard as well as to visit Smith in hospital, where they found him fairly comfortable and being looked after by an elderly nun.

The next day Dollin and Garrad-Cole were moved to a camp near Giovanni Berta where they found three officers – two of them RAF – and 14 other ranks. Conditions were appalling, the OR living in buildings which had previously housed cattle, and every man covered in flea bites.

Work soon began on making a hole in the latrine wall with a view to scaling the outside wall at an unguarded point. However, the efforts were soon discovered and the commandant threatened reprisals unless the perpetrator owned up. Garrad-Cole and Peter Mead, a Naval officer, decided to own up and were given 30 days' solitary confinement, later reduced to 20 days through the efforts of the Senior British Officer, Bruno Brown.

By the time the sentence had been completed the camp complement had risen to 20 officers and 60 men. Dollin and Garrad-Cole were taken to Tripoli – a two-day journey – and embarked on the Italian liner *Marco Polo*. On arrival at Naples, the prisoners were herded aboard a train and transported to the prison camp at Fonte d'Amore outside Sulmona d'Abruzzi. Garrad-Cole was searched and released into a compound which was to be his home for the next 12 months.

His first escape attempt went quite smoothly to begin with; Garrad-Cole, along with David Pike RAF and Lieutenant Pope, a Naval officer, donned bogus Italian uniforms, collected blankets, ladders and ropes and scaled the wall at a blind spot. The plan was to steal an aircraft from Foggia and fly to Malta. Raging blizzards, however, put paid to this and the trio decided to steal a boat instead and sail to Yugoslavia or Greece. But an encounter with a suspicious Italian landed them in his headquarters where they remained for two days.

Back in Sulmona they were again sentenced to 30 days' solitary, but after two days, on orders from Rome, they were moved to Aquila to serve the remainder of their sentence. On returning yet again to Sulmona they found chaos; the commandant, not knowing how the escape had been effected, was having the entire compound dug up in search of a completed tunnel which he was convinced existed! When things were back to normal another tunnel was started but was slow work due to the rocky terrain. Garrad-Cole discovered later that this tunnel was exposed when a donkey wandered over the exit, causing it to collapse.

The SBO had succeeded in gaining permission for parties to leave the camp on organised walks. On one of these Garrad-Cole instigated a mass-escape but the element of surprise was too short for success and another term of solitary confinement followed for Garrad-Cole and George Patterson, although one man, Dan Reagan, managed to stay free for nine days before being recaptured.

On 24 December 1941, Garrad-Cole arrived at San Romano, having been transferred along with six other officers, all deemed to be a bad influence on other prisoners. The chance of escape from this camp appeared to be possible only through the church so Flight Lieutenant Lucky, who spoke fluent Italian, pretended to be a Roman Catholic. He was then able on his weekly visits to build up an accurate picture of the church's interior. Unfortunately, on the day Commander Brown and Tony Dean-Drummond started knocking a hole in the wall, a monk had decided to sweep out the church, so that attempt came to nothing.

As the summer of 1943 wore on the main topic of conversation was whether the Italians would hand the POWs over to the Germans. Plans were therefore made to take over the camp from the Italians at the first sign of this happening and Garrad-Cole found himself in an assault squad under Major Dermont Daly who had served in the Commandos. The group went into training, and when on 8 September 1943 the Italian government signed an armistice and a column of German vehicles was seen moving towards the camp, they were able to burst out of the camp.

They reached an isolated farmhouse where the owner, who had lived in America and spoke good English, persuaded them to stay for ten days. Then, however, they became restless and decided to move on. Garrad-Cole and Branny-Richards headed south, finding shelter on one occasion with a cockney woman who had married an Italian. In her house they enjoyed the luxury of a real bed, the first for a long time and, for Branny-Richards, the last. In November, while they sat in a woodcutter's hut, two Germans walked in and took them prisoner. At daybreak they were marched along a path by Mt Meta. Garrad-Cole asked for a cigarette, which he received. While the guard's attention was distracted Branny made a dash for freedom and got away. Garrad-Cole had a machine gun pressed into his gut and his nose bloodied. The sight of blood, however, seemed to satisfy the Germans and the moment of danger passed. Branny-Richards, sadly, was blown up in a minefield on the day after his escape.

Garrad-Cole was taken to a German POW camp at Frosinone and from there by train to Germany. During the journey, however, 23 officers escaped through a hole in the side of the boxcar, Garrad-Cole among them. With Fane Harvey, Garrad-Cole spent two days in the Gallese district before deciding to travel to Rome. There they thought the best person to approach would be a priest so Harvey went up to one in St Peter's Square and explained in his best Italian that they were escaped British POWs. The priest looked startled and said he was unable to help them but if they would wait there he would send someone who spoke English. After about forty minutes a young priest arrived and told them – in perfect English – that he knew of someone who might be prepared to hide them. This turned out to be Signor Secundo Constantini who, before the war, had been caretaker at the British Embassy. He and his family still lived at the Embassy which, locked and deserted, was under the protection of the Swiss and it was to this building that he led the fugitives. Civilian clothing was produced but no suit could be found to fit Garrad-Cole. The young priest, Father Robert, was able to provide one the following day and the two evaders were able to enjoy nocturnal walks in the Embassy gardens. Signora Constantini supplied wonderfully satisfying meals and real beds to sleep in.

After about two days Brother Robert came to tell them that he had persuaded the Father of a nearby Lithuanian Seminary to take Harvey and Garrad-Cole in so they left to take up residence in two rooms on the first floor of the seminary, where they remained for over a week. On the tenth day they were told by a Russian priest that a search of all seminaries was to be undertaken by the Germans so once again Brother Robert spirited them away to yet another family, Renzo and Adrienne Luccidi, on the via Flaminia. Here they found three other POWs already established, Jock Simpson, John Firman and Pat Wilson.

Garrad-Cole then stayed at another seminary, this one French, and then at the home of a retired Italian colonel and his wife and it was here that he heard on the wireless of the Allied landings at Anzio. During the first week in February

1944 Garrad-Cole went to the Vatican for the first time to have tea with the remarkable Monsignor O'Flaherty, with whom he had first come in contact while in POW camp at Sulmona and to whom he had got a message through Brother Robert. Things had become rather tense at the colonel's house due to the presence of a Fascist in the downstairs flat and Monsignor O'Flaherty was able to arrange for Garrad-Cole to move to the home of the Marchesa Christina, a staunch anti-Fascist. During his time with her he had a very close encounter with some Gestapo men who took away his identity cards, complete with photograph, which necessitated his having a new set. Christina was able to arrange these for him after he had hidden with friends of hers for as long as it took for his moustache to grow! Then, armed with the new ID cards, he was moved to the home of yet another friend of Christina's.

Arrests in Rome were now commonplace, as were reprisals, so Garrad-Cole thought of escaping by small boat to the Anzio beachhead, but gave this idea up in favour of an overland journey. This plan he also gave up, however, and returned to Rome. Here he was hidden by a sympathetic officer in the Italian Cavalry, who had himself gone into hiding rather than support the Germans, and remained until the first Allied troops arrived in June 1944. He was then transported to Anzio by jeep, flown to Caserta then Casablanca and finally England where he landed at St Mawgan, Cornwall. He had been away from England for 6¼ years.

In recognition of his services to Allied forces in Italy, Monsignor O'Flaherty was presented by the British Ambassador in Rome with the Order of the CBE on 12 June 1947, although it had been gazetted on 24 April 1945. He died on 30 October 1963.

The Rome Organisation up to the time of being liberated had assisted some 3,928 escapers and evaders of whom 1,695 were British. The story of Monsignor O'Flaherty was recounted in the book called *The Scarlet Pimpernel of the Vatican*, on which was based the CBS TV special in early 1963 called *The Scarlet and the Black*, which starred Gregory Peck in the role of the indomitable Irish priest.

Eric Garrad-Cole, or 'Gary' as he was known, was recommended for the MC by the Commander-in-Chief of the Allied Central Mediterranean Force, General Alexander, on 10 October 1944. A full account of his escape attempts was related with his recommendation.

2. Escape by Hi-jack

In May 1942, Lieutenant Edward Strever, a South African pilot, and his crew, which comprised two New Zealanders, Sergeants John Wilkinson from Auckland and Ray Brown from Timaru, and Pilot Officer William Dunsmore RAF from Liverpool, were posted to 217 Squadron on Malta. Wilkinson and Brown were newcomers to Strever's crew. They had been shot down ten days previously; their pilot and navigator were wounded, which led to their joining Strever and Dunsmore. On 29 July 1942 just before 9 a.m. they were detailed, with eight other Beaufort crews, to attack three Axis ships off Sapienza. At 11.15 a.m., Bill Dunsmore began to pick up a couple of blips on his search radar screen. Then ahead, about eight miles or so, they saw the convoy of merchant ships together with five destroyers plus fighter cover. Strever turned the aircraft for the attack. Amid flak they roared low towards the ships and at about 800 yards Strever shouted to Dunsmore, 'Now!' and he replied, 'Torp gone.' Then the starboard engine was hit.

At the radio Brown sent out an SOS as it was obvious they were not going to make it. The sea was rough at the time and the eventual ditching heavy. In the nose, and up the front Strever and Dunsmore went under. As soon as the aircraft came to a halt Wilkinson jumped on to the wing and tugged at the dinghy release. The whole tail unit had snapped off just aft of the mid upper turret, and was floating on its own about 100 yards away. Brown stepped off the aircraft and joined Wilkinson in the dinghy. The Beaufort was now half submerged but still no sign of Strever or Dunsmore. Suddenly Dunsmore appeared holding the navigation bag, followed by Strever. They too clambered into the dinghy with the other two. Dunsmore, in getting clear of the aircraft, had gashed his arm rather badly, but Wilkinson, with the first aid kit, managed to fix it for him. Shortly afterwards an RAF Baltimore aircraft circled them but then flew off. Suddenly they saw another plane coming in the distance. It turned out to be an Italian seaplane, a Cant Z506B. It circled the dinghy and then came in and landed some fifty yards away.

The downed crew then began to paddle towards it, but Strever, probably thinking this was taking too long, dived into the sea and swam to the plane. He then swam back with a rope, the other end being tied to the Cant. Meanwhile, all the guns, maps and codes were dumped over the side.

When they arrived on the Cant they met the pilot, Alessandro Chifari and his crew of three. Finally, in the rough sea, they got off for a two-hour flight. The landing place, Strever guessed to be one of the Greek islands. Here they were put through a rigorous interrogation, then given a change of clothes and a meal, and found out that the next day they were to be taken to Taranto in Italy. They discussed the possibility of capturing the aircraft, and flying it to Malta.

The aircraft, another Cant, had a pilot, second pilot, engineer and wireless operator/observer, also a corporal acting as their escort, armed with a .45 revolver. The crew were going home on leave and so in good spirits. The pilot was Captain Gaetano Mastrodrasa, who told them he was going home to see his baby for the first time – or was he? The corporal soon began feeling airsick, and in front of him there was a 90-minute trip. Seeing his stricken face Wilkinson, who was sitting across the table from the observer, decided to take his chance and yelled, 'Look!'

When the observer turned his head to look, Wilkinson promptly hit him on the jaw, then jumped over him and grabbed the corporal's revolver. He handed the weapon to Strever and then advanced towards the pilot, using the corporal's body as a shield. Strever followed him. The pilot was trying to get his Luger pistol out, but decided not to seeing Strever already with a gun in his hand. The second pilot however had got his Luger out and was aiming it at Strever. Luckily Brown had seen him and threw a seat cover at him, knocking the gun from his hand. There was a scrimmage while everyone tried to grab the gun; Dunsmore won it. The pilot had put the Cant into a dive, hoping possibly to land it on the sea but a threatening gesture with the gun from Strever made him think again, and he brought the aircraft up and level. They then tied up the Italian crew.

Strever took over the controls and made a rough course for Malta. They decided to untie the second pilot and get him up in the cockpit to help with the navigation and check out the flying instruments as the petrol, for instance, was in litres and not gallons. They had no idea whether it would last long enough for them to reach Malta.

When the word 'Malta' was mentioned, the Italian cried, 'Spitfires!' The great awe and fear of this aircraft was clearly shown on his face. It posed another problem for the hi-jack crew. But the amount of petrol they had was now the most urgent problem. They had been flying for about an hour and fifty minutes, and the look on the engineer's face indicated there was something wrong so they untied him and he changed over the petrol tanks. They now had an hour's flying time left. When they sighted Malta the tanks were almost dry. They were coming in, as they say, on a wing and a prayer. As they came in to land they were attacked by Spitfires and suffered some minor hits. The landing went quite well, apart from the fact that the engines stopped as soon as they touched down, having finally run out of petrol. The Cant was towed away to the RAF seaplane base at Malta and found to be not too badly damaged.

On 23 August 1942 Lieutenant Edward Theodore Strever and Pilot Officer Dunsmore were given immediate awards of the DFC, and Sergeants John Aston Wilkinson and Alexander Raymond Brown the DFM.

The pilot of the Baltimore which had circled the dinghy, but of course did not know who the crew were, was a friend of Ray Brown. When they failed to return from the strike he sent a telegram to Ray's next of kin, but Ray got back just in time to stop it. The pilot was later to be Ray's best man at his wedding in New Zealand.

3.   Foggia to Munich

'We did risk life many times for the great cause of Freedom,' recalls Michelo dal Borgo who lived in the Belluno Province of Italy, and helped an airman in 1944 who had been shot down and baled out.

'It was one hour after midnight on 14 June 1944, and I was returning home after having delivered mail to the Pisacane Brigade who were operating on the Visentin Hill. Suddenly a plane came out from the mountains over us with one engine not working too well. After a large circle supposedly to look for a suitable landing spot, the plane directed itself towards Vittorio Veneto town. But the engines took fire and the plane crashed in flames at a place called Cadola di Ponte nelle Alpi. From my point of observation I saw the fire of the burning plane and thereafter a white parachute descending over the woods. I directed myself immediately towards that point hoping to bring help to the pilot, but I did not succeed in locating him owing to the great darkness. About five o'clock I went back to the same spot but I didn't see anything because the pilot had sheltered himself in a factory of a neighbouring village. Together with another partisan we finally succeeded in finding him, and took him to my home, where he stayed for two weeks.'

Another Italian helper, who saw the crash, Martino Barattin remembered, 'I saw the plane drop in the Cadola zone on the left bank of the Piave river in the commune of Ponte nelle Alpi. The parachuted men were contacted and our friend dal Borgo took them to the village of Quers in the commune of Piave D'Alpago.'

The aircraft they saw was Wellington V-Victor of 37 Squadron based at Tortarella near Foggia. Their target had been the main railway station in Munich. The pilots were Lieutenant Tom Megaw of the South African Air Force and Pilot Officer T.W. Reynolds. It was Reynolds' first operation. They took off at 8.40 p.m. on 13 June to attack Munich but were hit by flak after bombing successfully.

'I had baled out about 5,000 feet and landed safely in bushes and rocks on the side of the Dolada mountains,' recalls Watson Reynolds. 'I hid my chute in the soil and rocks and moved away from the area until I came to a track which led me to the village of Arsie. Here I climbed a ladder into a hayloft and stayed there through the rest of 14 June while I examined my emergency rations and silk map of Italy.

'When dusk came an old villager came up into the loft for hay, and I attracted his attention. He appeared to be very scared and soon made off, but was soon back with others, one a lady teacher who spoke French. I explained I was from the crashed aircraft and a look of relief came on their faces. I was taken from the loft into the house and given coffee and roasted barley. Two tough-looking men then turned up and took me away and hid me in a barn, then went back and found my chute, donating the scarce silk to the villagers. I stayed in the barn for two days, food being brought each day at dusk.

'The Germans were making an intense search for us in the area. The locals had, however, informed the Germans that all the crew from the crashed aircraft had been killed and to strengthen this they had even had a mock funeral.

'The area had become too hot for me to stay there so with two partisans, and Michelo dal Borgo, we went to the dal Borgo home at Quers. I lived in the upstairs room for about seven to ten days, then moved on to Casa di Bruno – Bruno was the alias of another partisan. It was here that I met the navigator, Gordon Mansbridge and wireless operator, Chick Anderson.

'We then travelled on to Montanes and the first meeting with Martino di Carlo Barattin, who was the chief of Resistance in the area. We were taken to a stable and met one English and three New Zealand soldiers, who had been there for months.

They had been captured in the Western Desert in 1942 and been POWs up to the time of the Italian Armistice.'

After a while at Montanes, he and the bomb aimer, Harry Crowther,who was also at Casa di Bruno, started to think about moving. The helpers asked them to stay, but as Reynolds puts it 'we felt we should be doing something more positive.'

'Our soldier companions said the best way out was to head for Yugoslavia,' he recalls. 'The only other alternative was south to Florence where the Allies were, or west to Switzerland, or to make for the coast. We decided to make for Yugoslavia.

'We made our departure amongst tears and farewells and so with our guides set off along the mountain track. Descending was more difficult than ascending. We reached Claut and a long descent to Forno di Sopra, and then to Ampezzo and to Tramanti di Sopra where we met a British officer and corporal wireless operator in the Special Services. They were there to co-ordinate partisan activity and receive supply drops. They sent messages ahead of our arrival and we were given clothing and supplies then carried on with the help of Mosca – "The Fly" – a partisan. We gathered there was an airstrip, code named "Piccadilly", used by the RAF. Mosca was to take us over the most dangerous part of the journey eastwards across the Tagliamento river and the coastal flat plain north of Udine. The river we crossed at night, amidst searchlights probing the night air. We hid in a vineyard to dry out, for the whole of the next day, then we crossed the plain at a good pace with a new guide. It was to our advantage that the area was covered with vineyards in full bloom so we were able to crouch behind the vines for cover, but at roads and railways we had to wait for them to clear.

'We then went east to the Yugoslav border, where a couple of young Yugoslav guides came across to meet us. When we reached the landing strip at Piccadilly in November 1944 there were about 100 ex-POWs and evaders there, but we were the only RAF personnel. On 8 November two RAF Dakotas had come in having dropped supplies to the partisans, and were due to take back a load of wounded partisans for treatment, one a high-ranking officer in the partisans, and if room, us.

There was room so we set off back to Allied lines. We landed at Bari, were debriefed, and were then sent to the officers' mess.'

Watson Reynolds arrived back in the UK on 27 November 1944 and was eventually posted to No 7 Pathfinder Squadron at Oakington.

'In 1949 I went back to Italy,' he told me, 'this time with my wife who had served in the WAAFS. We met Martino di Carlo Barattin, and had a re-union at the village of Montanes where I again met Antonio Polenta. It had been his stable I had lived in some five years before. I was able to take them all manner of foods which of course were very welcome. I also met the priest who had been at the Casa di Bruno when I met the other members of my crew again.

'In 1955 I again re-visitied Italy, this time by car so I was able to get around even more and visit everyone once again. In 1965 Martino and Michelo paid me a visit staying with me for three days at Waterbeach; my home.'

It is sad to have to record that Lieutenant Tom Megaw, having successfully baled out, was later found dead, with his chute unopened.

4. Thirty Days on the Run

During World War II there were a number of South African Air Force Squadrons operating in North Africa and later in Italy. Lieutenant Hinton Brown was serving with Number 1 Squadron SAAF, based in Italy. On 3 July 1944 he was part of a team led by Colonel A.C. Bosman DSO, DFC, which took off just before lunch on a fighter sweep over the airfields north-east of Florence.

Brown recalls: 'This was the day when all my trouble started.' He was not down for any team that day but as some of Colonel Bosman's team had already flown, there were a few vacancies, and he flew as the colonel's number two. Two flights of six took off, but before long Ben Odendaal's number two turned back so Brown took his place. On their way home they ran into fierce 88mm anti-aircraft fire.

Brown continues: 'Most of it was behind the colonel and I heard him say, "What have I done to those chaps, that they are shooting at me?" I was having a quiet chuckle to myself thinking, "Rather him than me" when I smelt cordite. Next thing my oil pressure dropped to zero and my revs went up. I called up and told the colonel I had been hit and was intending to bale out.'

He then jettisoned his hood and took off his helmet. Heading for the hills he was fired at again and rolled onto his back. As he attempted to bale out, his parachute stuck behind the fixed perspex hood, and he found himself suspended upside down, his head out of the cockpit and his body pinned to the fuselage by the air flow. He had heard that a Spitfire pilot in a similar predicament had got out of it by kicking the control column with his feet. As his feet were about level with the spade grip of the control column he gave it a big kick, which forced the nose of the aircraft up, and he popped out like a cork. He pulled his ripcord and floated gently down to earth. As he looked down he saw a Spitfire with red wing tips and the markings of No.1 Squadron flash underneath him and fly straight into the side of the mountains – it was his Spitfire.

He recalls: 'In my right hand I still had the ripcord, as I remembered being told that in the event of a bale-out, and the ripcord was not brought back, I would be charged 2/6d so thought I had better take it back with me.'

He landed fairly heavily on his right leg, spraining his foot as a consequence. He released his parachute and staggered up the hillside, meeting an elderly Italian on the way down who told him that the Germans were in the town in the valley. Brown returned to his parachute, discarded his Mae West and collected his escape kit.

'The elderly gent then took me up the hill to a house where they gave me a glass of vino and a couple of eggs, which I was expected to suck raw. After they told me to "via" quickly, so I followed my new found friend up the hill, finding it difficult to walk with my injured foot. I came to a path which I had only been on for a few minutes when two armed men sprang out of the bushes. They were dressed in civilian clothes with red scarves around their necks – the Partisans had found me and was I glad to see them.'

His foot became much more painful and when he was given the choice he decided to stay in a nearby village rather than remain with the Partisans. A doctor came to look at his foot, who turned out to be just a third year medical student, but as there were no hospitals or nursing homes in the mountains, he was an important man to have around. The student said he had not broken anything, but weeks later when he got back to Allied lines an x-ray showed that he had in fact cracked a bone in his foot.

The next day he was taken on a three-hour donkey ride to a group of houses where he spent the day. While here he heard about another pilot who had baled out the same afternoon as he had, but who had been shot by Fascists while coming down in his parachute. When Brown returned to the squadron he learnt that it had been Doug Judd, with whom he shared a tent, who had baled out on the same day and had been killed.

On 5 July the 'doctor' told him he was taking him to stay with a civilian family. They were very friendly and had seen him coming down. The toilet arrangements were a little primitive to say the least; all it entailed was looking for the nearest bush outside and squatting down! Sometimes he would have to change direction because someone was already occupying the bush he was heading for. 'I had a bed and sheets again,' he continues, 'or rather shared them with the doctor and fleas! The food took some getting used to: flour and water minestrone, pastacuitta, bread and cheese, and coffee made from ground burnt wheat. One thing I couldn't get used to was sucking a raw egg – I got them to boil them for me.'

The next day two Englishmen arrived whom Brown had heard about: Captain George Rex-Day and Lieutenant Bob Wilders, both of whom had been taken in the desert, but had escaped when the Italian Armistice came. They said they would return the following day and bring a donkey for Brown to ride back on. Eventually Bob Wilders arrived with a donkey and as soon as darkness fell they went on their way arriving later at Donacele, where he met Padre Don Francesco, whose house Brown was to stay in. He only had a pair of sand-shoes, so Bob contacted the doctor and got a pair of German boots for him.

The next few days were spent quietly in the village, occasionally listening to the radio. Then on Friday the 14th: 'I awoke at the crack of dawn and next thing, heard hasty footsteps so I leapt out of bed and started gathering my clothes. The next thing, the Padre ran into the room and told me that the Germans were practically on the front doorstep. I didn't worry about putting any clothes on as I thought that I would be hiding in the hole underneath the building. On getting outside the house, I heard a voice calling me to hurry, so I climbed over the fence and followed an old man. It was about 4.30-5.00 then, and dawn was just breaking. I went through the village just in my shirt – I had my pants, coat, etc. in my hand. Still, I didn't worry about modesty at a time like that. I hadn't had time to collect my shoes so was running barefoot as fast as my sore leg would let me. I eventually branched off into the woods and got about 20 yards into them when I stopped. I wanted to go in deeper, but was frightened of making a noise, thus attracting attention. Then followed a miserable morning – just crouching down in the bush. I had one scare when I heard footsteps coming towards me in the bush. I really thought that I had had it then, but fortunately it wasn't the Germans, but only an Italian escaping. A little later a bantam rooster and a couple of hens wandered down my way, and every time I moved the rooster would start squawking. I had visions of a hungry German after a meal – and so coming into the bush to capture the fowls – but fortunately nothing happened.'

He waited until 2 p.m., then carefully made his way back to the village to find the Germans had been looking for him. They had given his description, 'as a blonde who limped!' He later learned that a woman spy had given him away, and the Padre and three other men of the village had been taken away for questioning. The Germans also looted the village, taking away the only alarm clock, all the medicine they could find, the

Padre's wireless set and many other things including the sheep. It was now time to move on. Bob decided to leave early the next morning so Brown said he would leave in the afternoon. However Bob didn't get away as planned so at about 3 o'clock they left the village together.

They were now walking each day, being helped and fed along the way, and only having one brush with Germans. On 19 July they met another Englishman, a private soldier named Charlie Keville who told them it was getting dangerous in this area, and it was decided that the next day, 20 July, they would move on.

On that day they walked past a number of Germans who were digging trenches and generally preparing for the expected Allied offensive. They later came across a farmhouse and made themselves known to the farmer, who offered to put them up for a week or so. The routine for the next few days was to sleep until about 9 a.m., a hot bowl of cow's milk for breakfast, and then a walk up the mountain, from the top of which they could observe a battle taking place in the valley. They bumped into some people from the village of Montagna, who told them that a South American pilot had baled out and was now hiding in a village near home. They decided that the next day they would cross over the mountains in search of this pilot. Brown felt this pilot may be a South African, and not a South American as had been described.

When they arrived at the village, they were made very welcome. Charlie Keville went off to contact the pilot who was staying with the Partisans. The pilot arrived back with a partisan escort; he turned out to be a friend of Brown's from number 4 Squadron SAAF, Lieutenant Tony Bristol who had been hit by ack-ack, but had managed to get as far as Sansepolcro, before baling out, and from there on he had been looked after by the partisans. Because of the interest that pilots seemed to attract from the locals, it had been decided that Brown would be a soldier, consequently when Tony arrived on the scene his cover was about to be blown. Fortunately no one in the house could speak English and they were able to concoct a story about knowing each other in South Africa. 'The partisans asked us to go back with them, promising they would have us across the line in no time – so we said good-bye to our friends and moved on to the next village. That night the partisans dressed up to kill, bands of ammunition strung across their shoulders, pistols stuck into their belts and red scarves around their necks. They paraded around the village kissing the girls good-bye and announcing that they intended raiding the 8 gun emplacement just below us. We decided that if this was to happen we would beat it for the mountains as we did not want to be around when the German reprisal would undoubtedly take place. Needless to say nothing happened. Later we were to learn that the partisans were not as brave as they made out – when four Germans walked into the village one day – 30 partisans headed for the bush, discarding arms as they ran.'

Bob and Charlie had risen in rank by this time; everybody was calling them 'Capitano', while Tony Bristol and Hinton Brown were merely *Tenante* and hardly counted!

Next day a few of them had lunch with Luigi Batti and his wife. Luigi came from the village of Sansepolcro where he owned a cafe but decided to hide out in this mountain village until the war passed by. That evening they had a special dinner with the Partisans, and a duck was killed and prepared in their honour. Suddenly the news came that the British were three miles from Sansepolcro, and they were treated as heroes, being plied with wine. It was also Charlie's mother's birthday.

On 29 July, Bob and Charlie had still not turned up from the day before, when they had gone to visit another village. Then they had a message from Bob telling them a farmer whose house was actually on the front line was taking them through the lines and if they were successful, the farmer would come back for them. While they were waiting, there was a knock at the door and: 'The next thing we were meeting Cliff Andrews who had been taken prisoner in Tunisia. Cliff turned out to be Charlie's friend who should have met up with Charlie shortly before we decided to move on. Anyway he had received Charlie's note requesting him to follow us – and here he was. Cliff's feet were in a bad way as he had been walking in boots with wooden soles and heels. Luckily Luigi Batti managed to find a pair of shoes which fitted Cliff perfectly. The news seemed pretty bad, we heard that the Germans had moved into the partisan village and intended setting up a hospital there. We were also told that small pockets of Germans were dispersed at vantage points on the mountain and they were all around us.'

On the evening of the 31st, they heard that the farmer had returned and that Bob and Charlie had crossed the lines safely. Later he told them that the English had sent a message telling them to stay where they were as the army would be up in a day or so. However, the farmer said he would return the day after next, and they could go across if they liked.

On 2 August, to make himself look more Italian, Brown rubbed soot into his hair, his week's growth of beard, eyebrows and moustache. It was now time to say goodbye to Luigi and his wonderful family who had been so good to them during their short stay in the village. They set off with three Italians in the lead, who were also keen to cross the lines, the farmer following and Cliff Andrews, Tony Bristol and Hinton Brown bringing up the rear. Every Italian they passed warned them that the Germans constantly used the same path. The farmer guide went ahead occasionally to see if the coast was clear. They eventually arrived at the German side of the line and rested behind a hedge. The farmer told them to stay there while he scouted the area but when he finally returned he said that his house had been occupied by 15 Germans, and a machine gun post had been set up in his front yard. He explained that they would have to walk right through the farmyard. As walking through the yard at the same time would cause alarm, they would be taken in batches.

'When our turn came,' Brown recalled, 'we followed the farmer's son. We walked right through the middle of the farm buildings and on rounding the corner of a barn, we came across three Germans sitting on a bank at the side of the path and behind them a machine gun mounted on a tripod. We shuffled past them trying not to look suspicious, and made it successfully behind a haystack and out of sight of the soldiers. The Italians said ahead lay the British.

'It wasn't long before we came to a wide river bed – the Tiber we believed. On the far bank we caught sight of a man in uniform looking through field glasses. We were not sure who he was so decided to walk upstream a bit before crossing, so as to give him a wide berth. On crossing the river, which was not very big, we climbed up the bank and shortly afterwards came across a soldier sitting in a Jeep. We rushed up to him and asked how close the British were – he thought we were Italians and took some time convincing that we were South Africans. We were taken back to Advanced Headquarters, where we were interrogated after which we were given a fine meal consisting of bully beef.'

They were then taken on to Arezzo, where they were given three blankets and a ground sheet and spent their first night back in a haystack. After debriefing next day Brown persuaded the officer to send them back to their squadrons and not to Naples. He then got through to his squadron on a field telephone and told them he would be reporting back as soon as he could.

'We then said good-bye to the brave Italians who had taken their lives in their hands to get us safely through the lines.'

5.   A Temporary Stay in Italy

Another of the South African Squadrons in Italy was number 2 (Cheetah) Squadron SAAF, based in 1944, at Forli. In this squadron was a Lieutenant Robert Bell who, on the night of 31 December 1944, was a member of a flight of four Spitfires that took off on a mission to dive bomb and strafe motor transport at a position north-west of Imola.

During the raid his aircraft was hit by 40 mm anti-aircraft fire. The throttle control was put out of action together with his radio. The main damage however was to the propeller, the aircraft started to vibrate violently and he lost height. He immediately headed south in an attempt to reach Allied lines but it was obvious he wasn't going to get very far. As baling out was out of the question due to his height, he was forced to land in German-held territory in the Ferrara district of north-east Italy.

The belly landing went quite well, but after a short slither along the ground his aircraft turned over and he found himself hanging upside down from his straps. 'In the urgent struggle to get out,' he recalls, 'I somehow set the aircraft's cannons off, and started up a hell of a racket.'

Once out of the aircraft he took off his Mae West, removing his escape kit, cigarettes and matches and then set light to his parachute and maps underneath the plane. There was much shouting from people near some houses about half a mile away and they started shooting. Apparently they were Germans. 'I now made off hot-foot in the opposite direction,' he says, 'towards some farm buildings in the distance.' To his surprise he was not pursued although he was shot at. He found an empty stable, crawled into some straw and tried to recover himself. Some time later he heard a lot of shouting around the stable, but inexplicably his pile of straw was never searched. The Germans did, however, set light to the building next door.

When it was dark he set off in what was a roughly southerly direction. He came to a low fence over which he stepped. As he did so he saw a large notice on the fence on which was written, 'Achtung-Minen'! ('Beware Mines') – it was a minefield! This explained why he had not been directly pursued after landing. His salvation was the time of year and the frozen ground.

He continued walking, keeping clear of any houses. From time to time dogs barked as he passed and at one stage he heard a party of Germans singing, it was New Year's Eve! Allied bombers were dropping bombs a few miles away and he had to lie flat on the ground when any flares were dropped. The moon was bright and he realised he must find shelter. Eventually he saw a haystack and settled down to try to get some sleep. He was very tired and extremely cold; one foot was icy wet where he had earlier slipped through the ice when crossing some water furrows. Next day he found a stable, and hid in a manger. He was discovered by two Italians, who promised to return with help. None came, however.

As soon as it was dark he set out away from the road, quenching his thirst with ice dug from a frozen canal. He knocked at the first house he could find and was given some food, wine and some old clothes to replace his flying clothes, but could not stay as there were Germans in the next room.

It was by now 2 January and Robert had been on his own and without water for three days. The next house he came to he knocked several times, but they did not seem to hear. Finally it opened. The house was full of Italian women and children and only one or two men. The lady of the house lost no time in closing and bolting the door tight. Realising he was no friend of the Germans someone muttered 'refugee', Robert nodded and said, '*si, si*, refugee'; they were all excited but very frightened yet there seemed to be some relief.

They took him into the next room which was a stable with cows and pigs, and asked if he wanted water and food; they were all waiting to know who and what he was. He opened his tattered Italian jacket exposing his battledress and pilot's wings and said, '*Inglese*!' the word was magic to them. The mother gripped his arm, he thought she was going to cry. They rattled off dozens of questions at him, but he could not understand them. He told them he was a South African and explained what had happened. A son came forward holding out a piece of broken flying equipment from the aircraft that had come down three days previously. He had seen the whole thing happen, so at least they knew now where he came from.

When the father came in he was introduced to Robert and on his insistence *vino* was liberally dispensed. The question of help was then discussed which took a long time due to the language barrier. It was agreed that he would stay the night and a start would be made the next day. Would he mind sleeping in the stable? The very fact that he was sleeping under the roof of somebody who was going to help was enough. A large bed of hay was made up and a blanket and two or three coats brought. Robert's new friends were Giuseppe and Ida Zamboni, their daughters Celide and Iside and their son Alfonso. Each one bade goodnight, and before leaving Giuseppe Zamboni banked up hay against every crack and cranny he could find to make sure Robert did not get too cold.

He was at the farm for a day and then Robert returned to the kitchen-cum-living room and was told to shave off his moustache and the few days' growth of beard. Robert remembers: 'I was given an old razor which I optimistically tried to sharpen on the palm of my hand. With the aid of a thin piece of mirror and some very rough soap I completed a shave which I am sure still remains as the most uncomfortable one I ever had and I hope am ever likely to have.'

Suddenly Mrs Zamboni came rushing in in a great panic and said that the Germans were approaching the house. Robert was hidden near to an irrigation furrow in a bed of hay. In order to get low down in the hay he had nearly to submerge himself in ice cold water, which he imagined had percolated through from the furrow. In fact it was a false alarm as the Germans were only there to bring some washing to be done.

It was now time for him to move. He was given an ice sledge, and lying on this, on his tummy, went along with Alfonso, who was also on a sledge. A half a mile or so along the frozen furrow Alfonso left him and said to wait where he was, and he would come back for him. After a time Alfonso returned and excitedly told him they could return as the Partisans were coming to the house. Mrs Zamboni told Bell to get undressed so she could dry his clothes by the small kitchen stove. The fact that he should get undressed with most of the family around did not strike him as being out of place.

During the early afternoon two Italian men arrived and he was told to get ready to leave. As he was in civilian clothes he decided to put his ID disc in his shoe, as German soldiers would shoot any enemy persons masquerading as civilians.

'I was now', Bell continues, 'given instructions what to do but it was difficult to understand. It seemed I was to follow someone on a bicycle and to go *piano, piano* (in English, very gently).'

At one point they were stopped and he was asked by a German for directions, which he evaded by feigning a sore throat. They ended their ride at a small house occupied by Italians. It was also used by a recuperating German officer as his office, and when he went off duty Bell assisted him getting his arm, which was in plaster, into a sling.

After this Bell moved to another house where he stayed with a party of partisans and lived there for the next three weeks. Among the people living there were Marsini Rugero, and his younger brother Guiseppe, three Russians, and other Italians. They had to live in the upper storey of the house, as it was in an area flooded to a depth of about six foot by the Germans. During the day the party spent their time playing cards, chatting and breaking up the ice around the house to form a moat making it more difficult for anyone to gain entry. One night they tried to escape across the water to the Allied lines but encountered a storm and one of the three long canoe-like boats was lost with all aboard. The Germans then started to check up on those odd hide-outs in the marsh area.

Bell continues: 'On 20 January, about midday, an armed party consisting of a German captain and two men came to investigate. During the short encounter the captain was shot but the two men with him escaped. The captain was brought into the house and some of his equipment removed. I could have had his Luger, a fine weapon, but felt it safer to remain unarmed for the time being.

'Our position was obviously now very precarious and I, with some others felt we should leave immediately. Some felt we should wait until nightfall – this would have been suicide. However early in the afternoon the whole party set off across the ice. Care had to be taken as the ice in some places was thin – in fact my friend Julio was lost through the ice.'

They kept going and reached a low embankment about a mile from the house where they took shelter until dark. Continuing south they reached a house occupied by friends and after a brief stop continued until they reached the edge of a canal. They started to climb down the bank when a flash and an explosion took place in their midst. A young Italian lad of sixteen or seventeen (the youngest in the party) had trodden on a shoe-mine and was fatally wounded. Robert recalls: 'As I had been standing next to him, I caught some of the blast. My thighs felt numb and dully painful but I did not appear, at first, to have caught any of the shrapnel. Later I realised that there was some blood on the inner part of my thighs.

'We were told to get across the canal and on to the bank on the other side, moving a short distance along it. It was now freezing cold and raining heavily. I had on a thin coat and a pair of rubber gumboots. Both coat and boots were sodden. From time to time very loud cracks rent the air as either shells or bombs fell a short distance away. Now followed a grim and bitter night. We huddled together, some standing and stamping their feet. I could not stand for long so most of the time sat dropped next to one of the others. As the night dragged on my feet became more and more painful – no doubt they were freezing up. My thighs were also paining. It was a nightmare night. It was impossible to get warm or dry. We were totally exposed – continuous freezing rain or sleet, the ground was frozen but wet from the rain. The party dislocated by the mine explosion, and divided into smaller groups, seemed unable to move on. We were now near the front line and there appeared to be no direct way through for the time being.'

Their positions appeared to be in the direct view of a German post about a mile to the south on the Reno River, at San Alberto. During the day Bell inspected his thighs; he appeared to have been lucky as the flesh wounds, although somewhat painful, did not seem to be too serious and had stopped bleeding. They lay where they were all day, all that night and the next day. Beginning to get frustrated he felt an attempt had to be made to get through. Help might never come. Furthermore the Russians had gone off on their own.

On the night of the 22nd he set off across the ice in the direction of San Alberto. All went well for about half the distance until he found water on the ice and the further he went the deeper the water became. Having no inclination to fall through the ice he turned back. Near the water's edge he found a boat, but it was half full of ice and could not be moved. For the rest of the night and the next day he was forced to lie low hiding from the Germans. Returning to where he had left the others, to tell them about the boat, he found they had gone. He was alone again.

He continues: 'I believe it was the early hours of the 25th that I realised that I must make a final attempt to get through, as soon I might be too weak to make the effort. I got myself up and stomped off along the ice towards San Alberto, I say stomped because my feet had now been frozen for some while.'

He continued to cross the ice when it suddenly became thinner and he fell through, fortunately only up to his waist. He waded on until he reached an embankment. Shortly after he came upon a house which seemed deserted. Entering the house he lay down in a state of exhaustion and with some difficulty pulled off his gum boots to try and relieve the discomfort. Early the next morning, he saw another house near by and shortly after heard great consternation; realising he had been discovered he decided to give himself up and walked out at the back to meet a very aggressive body of men with sten guns. They appeared to be partisans and after he produced his ID disc they became friendly.

He was at least now with friends as this was an outpost. That night he was carried to the river and was taken across in a boat. Reaching the other side he was again carried on somebody's back to a British post and taken to an Advanced Field Hospital at Ravenna, apparently run by both Italians and British. His feet were packed in ice to keep them frozen and he was then taken to No 66 British General Hospital at Rimini, arriving about 2 a.m. The first two days there were the worst, when his feet were unfrozen and the circulation allowed to return. There was a serious danger of losing part of both his feet through frostbite and they became very discoloured and the toes black, but he was fortunate in losing only a few toes on the left foot and none on the right. In all he had to spend nine months in hospital.

Robert Bell recalls: 'I subsequently discovered that most of my companions had been shot by the Germans during their attempted crossing through the lines. The abiding memory of this experience is the wonderful courage of the Italians. After many years I was able to contact the Zambonis. We have become great friends and have visited each other on several occasions.'

VII

Greece

After the fall of Greece, some evaders found their way to Crete only to be caught up in the fall of that island a month later. The majority of troops on the island surrendered, but nearly a thousand managed to evade successfully, with the help of caique routes established by Dudley Clarke's team across the Aegean, or in the submarines *Thrasher*, *Torbay*, or *Triumph*, detailed to pick up evaders.

*

1. Invasion Imminent

When Wing Commander Edward Howell took over 33 Squadron on 5 May 1941, he had been in the RAF for seven years. In 1939 he was involved in training in the UK and in 1940 he was posted to Turkey, but en route became part of ACM Longmore's staff in Egypt. Eventually, in October, he did reach Turkey where he set about training the Turkish Air Force. In April 1941 he was recalled. He reported: 'I took over command of No 33 Squadron on 5 May 1941. At that time the squadron had just been evacuated from Greece and was in a state of considerable disorder. Slightly more than half the personnel had reached Egypt and the remainder were at Maleme in Crete.'

Enemy activity increased steadily and rapidly right up to the invasion. On 14 May Me109s made their first appearance over the island. To meet a wave of about 30 of them Wing Commander Howell had exactly three serviceable Hurricanes available.

In the two battles of 14 and 16 May the squadron succeeded in bringing down 14 enemy aircraft, mostly Me109s, but it was clear that no useful purpose could be served by maintaining such a tiny force of Hurricanes in Crete, and on 19 May orders arrived from Middle East recalling all serviceable aircraft to Egypt. 'Back went my one Hurricane,' reported Howell.

'As soon as I saw the first parachute troops arrving [on 20th May] I gave orders for the assembly of the squadron to be carried out. I myself proceeded with a number of men to assembly point.' Events then moved at such a pace that it was impossible for the squadron to assemble and Howell went back to Battalion HQ.On his way he was hit by tommy-gun fire; his left shoulder was smashed and an artery cut in his right arm. His coinpanions, ran an MI9 report, applied a tourniquet and he made a dash for safety. He managed to cover 100 yards and then fainted. In spite of his wound Commander Beale, accompanied by the two airmen, crawled to where Wing Commander Howell lay. The spot was very exposed and close to the enemy, who flung a grenade (that missed) just as Beale and the airmen reached Wing Commander Howell; but they persevered and succeeded in dragging the helpless man into cover. Beale then departed to secure help. He got back without further injury and organised a rescue party.

It never reached him. Howell described what happened: 'I lay where I was, intermittently conscious, for two days and nights. On the third day I was found by German parachute troops who covered me with a blanket and gave me water. Later that day I was carried to the nearby village where I found a Flying Officer Cullen (Medical Officer No 33 Squadron) attending the wounded of both sides.'

During the four days prior to the invasion of Crete, Cullen had been confined to bed, suffering from dysentery. In spite of this severe disability, he immediately went about his duties attending the wounded from the moment the attack began on 20 May.

He continued to tend to the wounded until he was also captured, whereupon he evacuated his wounded to a nearby village and established another aid post. Here he worked unceasingly among both British and enemy wounded, being joined on 23 May by Captain Longmore, NZAMC, and later by Captain Stewart, also of NZAMC. The three of them treated over 1,000 cases before these were transferred to hospitals in Greece.

On 24 May Howell was flown by Ju52 to Athens where he was placed in a British POW hospital, largely staffed by personnel of the 5th Australian General Hospital. He had bullet wounds in the left shoulder and right fore-arm and both arms were broken. By the time he reached Athens, his wounds were in an advanced state of sepsis. He suffered from osteomylitis for ten months, and for eight of these was unable to use either arm. It was during this time that he met a nurse, Sandra Poumpoura, working for the Hellenic Red Cross under Madame Zanas, both of whose work Howell praised highly. She was later to become a 'helper' to many evading airmen.

During the autumn they were informed that the hospital was to be taken over by the Luftwaffe. Howell guessed that they would be air-lifted to Germany and accordingly got together six of the RAF men and concocted a plan to seize the aircraft during the flight. Their destination was to be Egypt or Turkey, depending on how much petrol was in the tanks. First, however, the proposed flight was postponed and then it was cancelled. It was generally assumed that one of the German 'stooges' had overheard discussions of the plan and had alerted his superiors.

In December, when he had recovered sufficiently, Howell was moved to Dulag 183 in Salonika, along with the remaining hospital staff and patients. In October, three MOs, including Cullen, and about 40 staff and 200 wounded had already left the hospital and been taken on an Italian Hospital Ship to Salonika. The idea was to transfer the POWs to Germany, but the wintry weather made it impossible for a train to get through and Howell was moved to a German hospital. There conditions were, naturally, much better and he remained there for six weeks.

Three NCOs in the camp, Sergeant Pilot Derek Scott, 3 Squadron RAAF, Staff Sergeant William Gamble and Staff

Sergeant Ted Bryant, both of No 5 Australian General Hospital, were planning to escape. They had found a key which fitted a door in the main administration block, through which it was possible to get out of the camp. Howell said he would accompany Scott – the only fit RAF man in the camp, having recovered from burns received while baling out over Libya – provided he was fit enough. He hoped to reach Mondania and from there arrange a passage to Turkey with smugglers. Unfortunately he suffered a relapse and was sent to Kriegslazarett 3/602, where, after six weeks, he found he could get out more or less as he pleased. On 27 March, a hospital train arrived at Salonika and he was told to be ready to leave the next day. He escaped that evening, and two days later his wound healed.

Getting out of the camp proved surprisingly easy and by dawn Howell was well on his way. Keeping to high land he reached Zagliveri then on 30 March he headed for the Athos peninsula where he hoped to shelter in one of the monasteries. All the time he was receiving food and shelter from peasants who had themselves barely enough to live on. In Riza he was advised to go to Mondania and a guide, an old man, took him as far as Vavthos, where, after checking that the place was safe, he spent the next two nights in a hotel.

When he was within an hour's distance of Mondania he was told that he would be better to make for Nikolaos as Mondania was full of Germans. On the way he went to a farmhouse and found a group of British soldiers being sheltered by a Greek cavalry officer and he was allowed to join them while they all waited for the Greeks to procure a boat. When no boat had appeared at the end of three weeks the men started going off in pairs until only Howell and Watson were left. On 28 April he joined 20 Greek officers who had paid 1,000,000 drachma for a boat and they all set off for Kouphos. There they hid in the bush for two days, when a caique arrived to take them on to Ibros. By mistake they landed at Lemnos, but were able to pick up the boat again after realising their error and finally arrived at Imbros. Here they handed themselves over to the Turkish authorities who sent them on to Canakkale where Howell spent two weeks in quarantine. The British Consul arranged for him to go to Izmir and from there he went to Ankara. On 31 May he left Ankara for Cairo, the end of the line.

While in Ankara Howell dined with the British Ambassador, Sir Hugh Knatchbull-Hugesson and told him his story. He also visited the Greek Ambassador to tell him about the friends he had had to leave behind, and the Ambassador promised to do all he could to assist them.

Alex Zanas and his wife became leading figures in the assistance of British evaders in Greece, and arranged for their escape via Turkey to the Middle East. In September 1941 Alex Zanas went to Salonika and there formed an organisation similar to the one in Athens. At the beginning of 1942, no less than 11 of his family were arrested by the Germans for aiding British personnel. Finally, in February 1942, he was arrested and sentenced to 18 years' imprisonment. He was tortured and interrogated and ended the war a cripple. In 1945 he was awarded the CBE. Sandra Poumpoura was awarded the MBE in 1945, as was her brother, Taki a surgeon. In September 1941 she and her brother organised an evacuation to the Middle East of a party of British officers; two months later one returned to assist, and they became his closest collaborators. They were all arrested when the Italians caught three men. As they were trying to escape the officer, called Atkinson, was wounded. Sandra and her brother, tried to save Atkinson by saying he could not be moved knowing the law was they could not shoot a wounded man, but they did. He was put up against the wall, despite his two broken legs and shot. Sandra and Taki were taken away and tortured by being tied down and having their backs and feet burnt in an attempt to make them give the names of the people they worked with.

Her brother was sent south to a camp and was later released by the Americans, Sandra going to Italy where she stayed until liberated by the Canadians in 1944. Today she is the Greek representative for the RAFES and visits all the known Greek 'helpers'.

In January 1943 Tom Cullen was begining to think up a plan to escape and finally teamed up with a quarter master, Sergeant

John Greig RAMC, but it was not until 29 February 1944 that the plan was carried out when the Guard Commander had gone on leave for 22 days. The second-in-command was very slack, and they noticed that the guards were leaving some areas unattended.

On the 29th they changed into civilian clothes and with a ladder got over the moat (very much in the way that McSweyn had made his first escape). The ladder would be pulled back over by another prisoner later. Then they went around the side of the guard room and out by the main exit. There was only one guard and he was being occupied by another sergeant discussing some reports.

Once outside they were picked up by a Pole in a lorry and taken to Bydgoszoz, then after a day or two by van to Gdynia, and thence by bus to the docks area. They were given shovels and followed a guide on to a Swedish coal boat, and went into the hold to help trim the coal and stayed there until it was full. They sailed some hours later and after 24 hours hammered on the hold and the engine room to attract attention. The crew did not know they were there but treated them very kindly. They landed at a small port near Malmo, and were handed over to the police, who sent them to Stockholm via the British Consul. Cullen arrived home on 19 March 1944.

On 19 December 1941 Wing Commander Howell had written a report concerning the work done by Tom Cullen, and suggesting this should be recognised in some way. On 28 July 1942 he was recommended by HQ Middle East for the MC, based on this report, but in 1944 when he returned he was awarded the MBE.

Wing Commander Howell himself was awarded the OBE. While a POW he was awarded the DFC for the period of 14 to 19 of May 1941 when he was recorded having shot down one Me109, and damaging another; he was also credited with a Ju52 Transport aircraft. He later wrote a book on his experience entitled *Escape to Live* published in 1945. As well as the awards already mentioned, 23 Greek nurses from the Hellenic Red Cross were awarded the King's Medal for Courage for their services to British wounded at Athens during the period of the enemy occupation.

2.   A Million To One Chance

On 6 April 1941 Flight Lieutenant Dudley Honor arrived on a posting to 274 Squadron based at Sidi Barrani in the Western Desert. He had previously been with 145 Squadron at Tangmere England, taking part in the latter part of the Battle of Britain. At the beginning of the war he had been with 88 Squadron having served with them in the Battle of France, and then when France fell he returned with the squadron to operate from Driffield, and then Belfast. In action in the Western Desert, Dudley Honor destroyed two Me109s in early May and damaged two more, while on 20 May he destroyed a Macchi on the ground.

When the Battle of Crete began, the squadron operated long range Hurricanes over the island. Honor shot down a Me110 and shot up a Ju52 on the ground on 19 May. The next day he destroyed another Ju52 and a Me109. On the 26th he and another pilot, Flight Lieutenant Down took on another long-range sortie to ground strafe Maleme airfield, on Crete. He recalls: 'As we approached the airfield we saw two transport aircraft circling ready to land. On the ground there were aircraft everywhere and in all there must have been around 150 of them so it was difficult to decide on a target. Finally I decided to attack two waiting to land, but they came in too fast for us to get a good shot at them so I sprayed everything in sight with machine gun fire. I then saw a formation of troop-carrying aircraft coming in at about a 1,000 feet and prepared to attack them. The leading machine was an Italian S.79, I gave it a short burst from close range and it burst into flames and went into the sea. I then attacked a Ju52 loaded with troops, which turned on to its back and hit the sea.

Suddenly there was a series of explosions around me. Two cannon shells hit the Hurricane and the elavator and aileron controls went but I continued to take what evasive action I could. The first attack was from an Me110 and the next from an Me109. This continued for about 15 minutes, and I was hit in the engine. There was an awful smell of cordite and my speed was up to about 220 miles but I got it down to 120 and hit the water. The Hurricane sank in fifteen seconds. I had gone down to 40 feet with the hood still closed and my safety harness still fastened, but by the time I got the hood open the cockpit was full of water.

'I undid the safety harness and turned the knob on my Mae West, which, luckily for me, was a German one which had belonged to an air gunner of a Ju87 which had been shot down by my squadron. The German ones inflated automatically whereas the British ones had to be inflated by mouth. In my case there would have not been the time to do this. (Later British ones were modified to inflate immediately.)

'The sea was very rough and I was battered about by the waves. After a couple of minutes I realised I still had my parachute strapped on which I quickly discarded, and then my trousers which were hampering my attempts to swim against the rough sea and cross-currents. I tried to swim on the crest of the wave and rest in the trough and carried on like this for three hours until I was within twenty yards of the shore. To my despair it was not a beach but cliffs, and it took me another hour finally to float into a cave, and sit astride a stalagmite, which I sat on like a hobby horse.

'I tried to wring out my wet clothes but waves kept washing over me and having no trousers I tried to keep my legs warm by wrapping my clammy shorts around me. I spent nine hours that night in this freezing cave which was the worst and longest time of my life.

'In the morning after two attempts to climb the cliffs I swam to a little headland and dried my clothes in the sun. I later found a herdsman's hut and there pondered upon my next move. A whirring noise above made me look up to see two eagles looking down at me.

'That night I found a disused church and in it German matches, an incense burner, and a stagnant well from which I had a long drink, then I spent the night on a bed of twigs. The next day I found another hut in which I found dry lentils and beans. With some paraffin and my German matches I lit a fire and cooked myself the first meal I had had so far.

'The following day I climbed an ascending valley and came

upon a sight for sore eyes. A little patchwork of green and golden fields, set around a cluster of white houses. It took me four hours to reach the village and when I did boys came running out and took me to the church, where the priest gave me water, goats' milk, cheese and rye bread. They told me there was another RAF pilot at the village. He turned out to be Sergeant Kerr of my squadron who had been shot down the day before after shooting down a Ju52, which I had witnessed, and then he'd been shot down by a Me109. We spent three days at the village but on the third day decided to move on, and so started out with four guides climbing the mountains over to the other side. I was however, still walking in my shirt tails having been unable to get another pair of trousers.

'We arrived at another village after about four to five hours' walk. At this village six people had been shot by the Germans for withholding information so they were naturally a little frightened and advised us to give ourselves up. In a house nearby were some Greek soldiers who had been captured previously by German paratroopers at Maleme. Some were wounded but they were very friendly and dressed my sores with a first aid kit they had. They also gave us boiled eggs and a bottle of water each. I was given a pair of Greek sailor's trousers, which I still have to this day.

'A Greek sailor wanted to go with us and two other Greeks in civilian clothes. One whose name was Evzone, made his allegiance clear that he was pro-British, and he explained through an English-speaking Greek officer, that he had helped a British senior officer to escape, and had shot four Germans, while he himself had been shot in the chest. He said he would take us to Heraklion which would take about four days.

'We christened Evzone "George" and we set off through an orchard but after two hours the soles came off our boots, but he said he would repair them knowing a place where he could get twine and some wire. Meanwhile we sat by the roadside and waited for him. He returned about half an hour later and made an excellent job of repairing our boots.

'That day we walked for seventeen hours. The names we called George are unprintable, but he did not understand and kept going. This was the pattern for the next few days but when we got to the Plain of Omalos we were told by a man not to go to Heraklion as the Germans were already there, but to make for Sphakia where the British were being evacuated.

'When we got to the village of Livaniania, about five miles from Sphakia we heard an aircraft approaching. Kerr said, "It's a Sunderland." We heard it land on the water nearby but by this time Kerr's feet had been cut to ribbons on rocks, so he insisted we go and leave him. We climbed over cliffs for about a quarter of an hour when we came upon 30-odd Greeks. They were signalling with a torch to the Sunderland which had caused it to land, I took the flashlamp from them and signalled in morse, "RAF here". A voice called, "Swim for it." I replied, "I can't, I am too exhausted and my arms are raw." Eventually a one-man dinghy turned up at the foot of the cliff, manned by one of the Sunderland's pilots. He took me aboard and although it was a little crowded it was very comforting.

'I had promised to take George to Alexandria but we were unable to go back for him, or Kerr, as the sea was rough, and getting rougher. He was later taken POW and spent the rest of the war in Germany.

'When I got on board I realised how lucky I had been. It had been a million to one chance; the Sunderland had come out of Egypt to pick up General Weston and his staff from Sphakia and the crew were watching for signals along the coast, but seeing the SOS from the Greeks had in fact landed at the wrong place. I navigated them down the coast to Sphakia taxying along the water all the way, so the Sunderland became a boat for this part of the journey.

'There we took aboard General Weston and his staff. They were all in. The wireless operator gave me a packet of Woodbines and very welcome they were. I gave one to the General and it's amazing how the difference in rank floats away in such circumstances. I also drank no less than six cups of tea. We arrived at Alexandria and in the mess in Aboukir I was given cigarettes, beer and a huge meal. After breakfast the next day I borrowed a plane and flew back to the desert and 274, I had not even had a shave.'

When he arrived back Dudley Honor went straight back on duty and declined any sick leave, to which of course he was entitled. In August he became commanding officer of the squadron. Meanwhile, on 3 of June 1941 a signal was sent from HQ RAF Middle East that Flight Lieutenant Dudley Sandry Garton Honor had been awarded a bar to his DFC. The recommendation mentioned his evasion and also the fact he had up to that time shot down 9 enemy aircraft. He continued to fly operationally in the Mediterranean until after the Invasion of Italy in 1943. Thanks to his evasion, Dudley Honor became the first man to be awarded the badge and certificate for a very special club.

The Late Arrivals Club
Squadron Leader George Houghton, a Public Relations Officer in Cairo in June 1941, when the tide of the desert war was turning against the Allies, recalls, 'The idea of the "Late Arrivals Club" came while I was having a meal in a French restaurant in Cairo with a friend.' The friend was Le Capitaine Pompei, who at the time was flying with 274 Squadron under Peter Wykeham-Barnes. At that time it just took the form of a newspaper story that Houghton put out, but C.P. Robertson, the Press Officer at the Air Ministry, gave the story wide circulation and the idea took off.

'Soon pilots were applying from all over the place,' he recalls. 'Some had been in Abyssinia, Syria, Greece, and the Western Desert. So we then had to form a club, I designed the badge and got a metal beater who had a little shop off the Boulevard Suleiman Pasha in Cairo to manufacture them. I concocted a bit of copy, and this was printed in the form of the "Late Arrivals Club Certificate" by a printer called Schindler.' The badge showed a winged flying boot, and could be worn on their uniform. The initial order was for 50 badges. When the fighting in North Africa finished, however, some 492 had joined the club. Hobson's the clothiers in London later made the badge and in 1968 one could still be bought for £1.

During his time as Press Officer George Houghton had some 100 certificates made up, before he moved to Algiers with Lord

Tedder who had joined Eisenhower as AOC in Chief Mediterranean. He was later appointed to the staff of ACM Sir Trafford Leigh-Mallory at AEAF HQ. When Sir Trafford left for the Far East he stayed in Europe operating in the battle area until the end of hostilities, and covered the Belsen Trials at Lüneburg. His wife had also been on Sir Trafford's staff, and on his departure became Houghton's Personal Assistant. He was now a Group Captain Commanding Air Information, SHAEF and Deputy Director of Public Relations, Control Commission for Germany. For this work he was awarded the OBE in 1945.

3.   Bale-Out Over Crete

In September 1942 10 Squadron was based in Fayid. Normally based in England, 16 Halifaxes and their crews were sent to the Middle East in mid-1942 to carry out attacks on such targets as Tobruk. It was a composite squadron with some aircraft and crews from 227 Squadron. On 5 September 1942 eight aircraft of 10 and 76 Squadrons were detailed for an operation to attack dispersed aircraft at Heraklion aerodrome on the island of Crete. Flight Lieutenant Hacking was assigned to lead a group of three in the attack, in aircraft 'C'. His flight engineer was John W. Macfarlane.

They took off at 4 p.m. and arrived over the target at 7.15 p.m. The flak was intense as the bomb load of 11 × 500lbs was dropped in one stick and bursts were seen across the main runway. Soon after this the mid-upper gunner, Sergeant Carson, reported smoke coming from the starboard outer engine. This was feathered and the fire extinguished, but as they swung round to port they were hit again, starting a fire in No.5 starboard petrol tank at the same time as another burst hit the port wing. Macfarlane told the pilot that he thought the situation was hopeless and the order was given to bale out.

Macfarlane recollects: 'On landing I recovered consciousness (as I had apparently been knocked out by either a blow from the parachute opening or striking the exit coaming) to find a Cretan couple looking most concerned.'

Joe Bradley, the wireless operator, joined them and, having ascertained that the two men were British, the Cretans kissed them on both cheeks and assured them they would be safe. Then another Cretan man turned up and some sort of argument took place. The original man, Grigoris, (known as Georgie) prevailed, helped by the showing of a knife; it transpired that the second man had wanted to hand the airmen over to the Germans.

Georgie then led them to a vineyard and told them to wait there with a young boy until he returned, which he did an hour and a half later. With him he brought a man named Christos and some traditional Cretan clothes for the pair to change into. In a short time they all set off walking across country, making only brief stops at a church and a farmhouse, where they were given food. They were then taken by Georgie to a cave on a hillside where they remained until 9 September, during which time they were fed by shepherds. On 9 September Georgie and Christos returned and took them once again on their way until they reached the house of a priest, Anthimos Vasilakis, where they were given food, wine and cigarettes.

On the 10th they spent the day on a hill above a farm and then, at dusk, continued on their way, passing along roads frequented by Germans. Both guides were armed. That night was spent in another village. On the 12th they arrived at the foot of Mount Kedros, having failed to contact the British Agent at Paraskevi, and were led into the hideout of a band of partisans where they remained for the next two days and were treated like heroes. Further, successful, attempts were made to contact the agent and they moved to another place in the mountains, about an hour's distance.

On 30 September the party broke up for the winter and Macfarlane and Bradley were brought down to Paraskevi where they remained for five days, living in a lean-to while the villagers built a house for them. They moved into it on 6

October and Macfarlane stayed there until 28 October, Bradley leaving on the 14th.

Macfarlane says of this time: 'We were six months in the hills and never had anything but the most marvellous treatment from the Cretan people, whose endurance and fortitude and humour under such difficulties is beyond praise.'

During their time on Crete, Joe Bradley operated a hitherto disused W/T set, establishing contact with HQ, Middle East, and passing on much valuable information. John Macfarlane assisted in this work, and both helped English Special Operations agents to good effect.

They finally escaped to Egypt in a Royal Navy Motor Launch. In this launch they brought off all the Cretans the boat would carry, and on reaching Cairo, were treated splendidly by the Greek community. During their stay in Crete they had had a few narrow squeaks. On one occasion they were having a meal when a scrounging German soldier, begging for eggs, came in, but all was well and he did not discover who they were. During one mountain journey Macfarlane fell and hurt his leg, and broke some bones in his ankle. A Cretan doctor had him brought down on a donkey to be treated, but all he could do in the circumstances was to strap up the ankle and make Macfarlane comfortable.

Three of the crew were killed and buried with full military honours at Kastelli Pediada village cemetery. Three Greek priests and hundreds of local peasants attended the funeral. Pilot Officer Turner, the navigator, was picked up by the Cretans, but did not feel safe in the house they had taken him to, and ran off. He was later arrested by the Italians. The Germans wanted to take him but instead the Italians shipped him to Rhodes by Cretan fishing boat. Fortunately this was stopped by a British submarine and he was taken off.

There were 150 casualties in the raid of 5 September and 18 aircraft were written off, while two Halifaxes were shot down. Within 10 minutes of aircraft 'C' being shot down, a crash tender had arrived. Inhabitants of Kastelli Pediada were taken hostage and sent to prison in an attempt to force the local inhabitants to hand over the surviving members of the crews who had baled out, but later the hostages were released.

On 22 May 1943, Sergeant Joseph Bradley and Sergeant John Macfarlane were both recommended for the BEM. In the recommendation it mentioned how they had both evaded and helped with wireless operators' work. On 2 July 1943, the award was changed to the Military Medal.

On 26 October 1986, a plaque was unveiled, dedicated to Cretans who had sheltered wartime RAF evaders. This was presented by the Bomber Command Association, and unveiled by Group Captain Ken Batchelor CBE DFC, chairman of the Bomber Command Association, a wartime commander of RAF Mildenhall and a squadron commander at Tempsford.

VIII

Poland and Hungary

'One of the joys of escaping in Poland was that the population was so strongly anti-German,' point out Foot and Langley in *MI9: Escape and Evasion*. Yet Poland was a long way from home, and the Germans were not the only enemy. Those trying to make their way east often met a far from friendly reception from the Russians, and those remaining in hiding in Poland could find themselves in equal danger, as Thomas Blatch's story shows.

Hungary too had many pro-British sympathisers among the aristocracy, and as the country was not occupied by the Germans till 1944 evaders and escapers were interned if discovered. But it was a hostile internment, and the authorities subjected many to rough treatment.

*

1. Under Sentence of Death

On the same date and operation as Macfarlane of 10 Squadron (5 September 42 to Heraklion), but flying with 76 Squadron, Wireless Operator Thomas Blatch – always known as Terry – was also shot down by a fighter and by anti-aircraft fire. In the attack he suffered shrapnel wounds in the head and left foot.

When fire broke out the order was given to jump but when Blatch landed safely he found he was unable to walk and twenty-four hours later he was captured. He was taken by a Ju52 transport aircraft, along with Afrika Korps wounded, to a hospital in Athens. There was little chance of escape there as his leg was in plaster following surgery. He was then taken by train through the Balkans via Sofia, Belgrade, Vienna, finally ending up at Dulag Luft at Obsel Frankfurt, where he spent 10 days being interrogated. From there he was taken to Stalag VIIIB at Lamsdorf.

It was at Lamsdorf that he made his first attempt to escape. The idea came when he was in the camp hospital and met up with an old friend, Lieutenant Chris McRae of the RAMC; before the war he had played fullback for London-Scottish and Blatch had been on the wing for London-Irish. The plan was to change places with Private Cheeseman of the East Surrey Regiment. In this guise he was sent on a working party to a coal mine near Dabrowa, which was near the Polish border. Blatch takes up the story: 'I was on the night shift and I managed to effect my escape through a disused air shaft to the surface and thence by climbing over the surrounding wall. I had obtained civilian clothes from Polish workmen and I had a map and a compass which I had brought from the main camp. I also had a fair amount of chocolate and biscuits etc saved up from Red Cross parcels.

'I headed east and next day when I was going through a small village I made contact with a Pole who was engaged in smuggling activities over the border. Next day he took me over the border and on to the town of Skawina where he introduced me to a member of the Armja Krowa Movement (Home Army).

'I told him who I was and satisfied him as to credentials [established from London by an ex-Army Captain with the code-name Zenka, the leader of a group operating between Skowa HQ-Leg-Proszowici]. I told him that I intended to make my way back to the UK eventually and while he said this would be most difficult to accomplish he promised to pass me on to people who could help me further.'

After staying with the Pole for two nights, Blatch was taken to a nearby village called Minoga, where he met a Polish student, a relative of the first Pole. This student was an active member of the AK Movement and was known as Drem. Blatch quickly struck up a friendship with him and discussed with him the possibility of escape. His suggestion was via Libau, Estonia.

Through him Blatch was furnished with Polish papers, clothing and money and, during the seven weeks of freedom enjoyed by Blatch, Drem made himself completely responsible for his welfare. Blatch spoke quite good German so could pass himself off as Polish and made a decision to stay with Drem and assist in every way possible, whilst always seeking the means of return to England. He swore allegiance to the AK, mandatory for anyone joining the Home Army and carrying the death penalty for informing or betrayal.

Blatch was not idle, as he explains: 'Among the major sabotage carried out and in which I took part were destruction of German road convoys by force of arms, the destruction of the local SS headquarters Prezensyl, and the destruction of an ammunition-carrying train south of Warsaw by delayed action charges.

'After the train-wrecking job a very thorough check was instituted the same night in Warsaw and I together with many others was taken to Gestapo HQ for questioning. Unfortunately although I managed to satisfy the German speaking questioners, I did not pass muster with the Poles' interpreter who suspected me because of my language difficulties.

'I finally told them who I was and said that I was simply an escaper. However, they were not satisfied and I was taken to Monte Lubitsch prison where I was detained for three weeks under sentence of death. Apparently, however, steps had been taken to check up on my identity and on 23 April 43 I was taken back to Lamsdorf.'

On 20 March 1944 Blatch made his second escape attempt from Lamsdorf this time accompanied by Private Parker, a Commando. They got through the wire, which had been cut, and made their way to the railway station at Annadorf. They had civilian clothes, a compass, a map, food, money and ID papers, supplied by a camp interpreter. They boarded a train for Stettin and arrived there about 30 hours later. There they made friends with some Polish dock workers in the hope of getting on board a Swedish vessel. Where the Swedish ships were berthed, the workers were French and a contact was made, but instead of hiding them, he informed on them and they were arrested. Blatch's identity had been discovered after his previous escape and so he was now back to being Warrant Officer Blatch and as a result was transferred to Stalag IIIA at Luckenwalde.

He was not to remain there for long. He reports: 'About 12 July 1944 I managed to escape by walking out of the camp with a party of Yugo Slavs in civilian clothes, having persuaded one of them to stay behind in order to keep the numbers of their party unchanged. I had got into the main (international) compound from the small British camp by feigning toothache and getting a chit to go to the hospital which was situated in the main compound. Once there I had little difficulty in obtaining civilian clothes and I then just waited until the party of Yugo Slavs was due to leave.'

He got on a goods train bound for the east, and arrived in Posen the next morning then hid up there until dark. He made his way to the outskirts of the town where he entered a café. Through the proprietor and a married couple who lived in the café he was put in touch with the AK Movement again. Word was sent to his Polish student friend and in about five days he arrived. Two days later the two of them moved down to the Przensyl area again.

By this time, General Bor-Komarowsky had declared his intention of reclaiming Warsaw from the Germans and went into action on 1 August 1944 at 5 p.m. During the 'Warsaw Uprising' Blatch was attached to a unit which was defending the west wall of the Protestant Cemetery in Wola, a district of Warsaw. Intense fighting began on the third day with tanks of the Panzer Division. It was a bitter struggle with many atrocities and house-to-house fighting for five days. On the sixth day the company commander, Tryw, was severely wounded and Blatch replaced him, with Drem as his second in command. Both were wounded attacking German mortar positions and required surgery. There were few drugs available and their wounds became infected. While in hospital they were visited by General Bor-Komarowsky, Commander-in-Chief of the Home Army and General Chrusiel, Comandant of the Warsaw district.

They were evacuated to the south of the city and got out

through the southern perimeter at Czerwakow, then went on to Czestochowa for recovery. Blatch then began operating again in the Krakow district with the same group. He writes: 'About 26 August 1944 an attack on a German ammunition dump in the Lodz area was planned by the Resistance movement. It was on a large scale and the strength to be employed was in the region of one complete division. However, the attack was badly planned and when the party of which I was a member went in to attack we were immediately surrounded and forced to surrender. Of the twelve in my particular section five were killed and the remainder captured.'

Blatch was identified as having been in Monte Lubitsch in 1943 and was classified in a special category. But the end was now in sight. In Blatch's own words: 'Towards the end of April 1945 when the camp at Altengrabow was evacuated, Warrant Officer Bird (RAF) and I got away and after five days' travel contacted forward elements of the Russian Army in the Brandenburg area about 5 May 45.'

In 1946 Thomas Blatch was awarded the MBE.

2.   The Mother Who Waited

In 1943, a cockney lad named Arthur Newman found himself serving in No 37 Squadron as an air-gunner. His first experience at hitting the silk was in 1943 while attacking Milan from his squadron's base in Tunisia. He says:

'Our port engine blew up and then the starboard engine caught fire, which means on a Wellington, with only two engines, you have to get out quick. The pilot shouted he was losing control and we were in a dive and, so on the given order, I baled out. The next thing I knew I was on my back in some prickly bushes, with a bump on my head and an aching leg. I headed for a house, a small farm dwelling, and in my best French asked if they could help me. Although they were Arabs from Morocco, they were of the Jewish faith as, of course, was I.'

From here he was picked up by the Americans and taken back to his squadron. By the time of his second jump by parachute they were based in Italy. This trip was to, of all places, Hungary. The target, the Manfred Weiss Armament Works located on the Csepel Island in the Danube, at Budapest. Newman remembers clearly:

'Suddenly a flash and a smell of cordite. We had been attacked by a Me110 firing a cannon from below, and we were strafed from nose to tail. Most of the crew were killed in this attack. The ailerons and rudder controls were shot away and the starboard wing set on fire, and the pilot gave the order to bale out. I thought, "Here we go again Arthur." As I was about to leave the aircraft I looked back and saw the other gunner who had been shot through the chest and stomach by the cannon fire. He was dragging himself along as his legs were useless, and his hands charred stumps. Smoke was coming from his burning body.

'I hit the ground hard, so hard that it knocked me out for a little while and I came to with the parachute wrapped around me. My idea was to try to swim across the Danube but I soon decided the water was far too cold to attempt this. The next thing I knew was the Hungarian police picking me up. When they searched me they found my fountain pen, and thought it was a bomb. To prove it wasn't I took the cap off and wrote "Winston Churchill."

'They seemed to think I was a spy and said they were going to shoot me. So I took the bull by the horns and said, "Okay then, shoot me, let's get on with it." This seemed to do the trick as the policemen said, "Oh you are not a spy, you goddam brave, I like you." '

Newman was taken from Budapest to Vienna, then to Frankfurt, to the Dulag Luft interrogation centre. From here he was sent to Stalag VI at Heydekrugge in East Prussia. When the Russians began to advance the camp was evacuated and they were on the march, along icy, snow-bound roads living in barns at night. No one seemed to know where they were going or why. To the east of them were the Russians, to the west the British. But Newman was not about to vanish without trace, and attempted to escape. He recalls:

'In a snow storm I dropped out of the column and hid behind a tree, and I then joined three Americans who had done the same thing. I saw a man in uniform and on his cap was not the German insignia but the Red Star of Russia. I shouted, "Ruski! Russian!" With this he came towards me with his bayonet thrust in front of him which he had just used to kill a pig. I said. "RAF, Boom, Boom," pointing to my air gunner's brevet. At this he put out his arms and greeted me, saying, "Churchill. Very good." He then gave me the pig's head and told me the way to go, but as soon as I was out of sight, I threw the head away. I was not that hungry!'

A little later Newman saw a jeep with soldiers from a Canadian division in the First Army. He told them his story and from there it was a flight home and off to the POW Reception Centre at Cosford. He went to a hospital in Middlesex where his mother was very ill. When the doctor saw Newman he said, 'I don't know how she is still alive.' Newman replied, swallowing hard, 'I think I do.' He remembers poignantly:

'I held her hand and she opened her eyes and said, "Hello Arthur, I knew you would make it back." She never spoke another word and 48 hours later she was dead.

'Some six weeks later, as I sat on a train in my demob suit on the way home, two ladies in the carriage whispered to each other, "He is so young, he must have just been called up." The other replied, "Yes, but at least he will have missed the war!" '

IX

Yugoslavia

Evasion and escape in Yugoslavia were complicated by the deep and bitter political divisions in the resistance to the Germans, and often by the fact that the partisans were often reluctant to part with what they saw as more fighting men for their cause. The American OSS shouldered the responsibility of repatriating evaders that came their way, in co-operation with the two Resistance movements: Mihailovich and his Chetniks, and Tito and the partisans.

*

1.   The Chetniks

Bill Goodbrand evaded in Yugoslavia. He relates: 'The date was 1st July 1944, the place Foggia, Italy, and I was the navigator of a Wellington bomber crew of No.40 Squadron. We were listed on the battle order for that night's operation. This was to be an anti-shipping mining strike on the River Danube, east of Belgrade. Our aircraft was a new Wellington MkX Number LN744 delivered from the replacement pool and this was to be our first operation in her ....

'We took off from Foggia Main and crossed the Yugoslav coast at 10,000 feet. The group (205) Halifax had dropped a sky marker and we were dead on track. Another marker was to be dropped 10 nautical miles north-west of Belgrade and at this point we started losing height to be at 200 feet when commencing our run from a small island in the Danube. We were due at 0003 hours but someone got out of place and went

in at our time and was hit and exploded. (Returning crews gave
our aircraft as it was our time.) We followed, and, as the banks
of the Danube at that point were higher than our 200 feet, the
flak and machineguns were actually firing down at us. Just
after dropping our mines we were hit badly and although Wally
Booth, our skipper, managed to get back up to 800 feet it was
obvious we were not going any further. We headed south and
then baled out. I was second last out and was, I think, still in the
air when I heard our aircraft crash, I landed in the middle of a
field of wheat or corn or possibly just long grass. I bundled up
my parachute and tried to hide it and my harness in bushes at
the edge of the field. While still doing this I heard the engine
noise of what appeared to be a heavy truck and realised I must
be fairly near a road. Then while I retreated into a small wood
at the edge of the field I saw a searchlight beam mounted on
the truck traversing the open country and realised the
Germans must be out looking for us. They did not leave the
road however and soon the night was quiet and still again. I
climbed a tree, wedged myself into a fork and waited for
morning.

'When it was light I found there was a farm about quarter of
a mile away and it seemed to be the only habitation in sight.
Eventually I saw people moving about at the farm and, while
not approaching it, I stood on a small hummock behind a
hedge and let myself be seen. Judging by the activity I had
succeeded but nothing happened for some time. Then I saw
three men crossing the field obviously coming towards me, I
rose from where I had been sitting and as they approached I
wondered who on earth they could be. They were armed to the
teeth, cross belts of ammo over shoulders and knives and guns
in waist belts. In addition they were carrying rifles. They were
bearded and wore forage caps with a skull and crossbones
emblem at the front. At least they looked friendly, as, with huge
grins, they pointed to themselves and said "Chetnik" and made
gestures to come with them. This I did with some misgivings
because at briefing our rear gunner, André de Schrynmakers,
had specifically asked about the position of the Chetniks as the
area we were operating over was believed their territory. The

information officer had said that all Allied aid to the Chetniks had stopped early in May and the attitude of the Chetniks was not at all predictable.

'We walked for quite a long way down dusty lanes across fields through woods and the further we went the more I realised that fleece-lined flying boots are not meant for walking. My three escorts chatted away, but since they had no English and I certainly had no Serbian, communication was limited to smiles and back-slapping. Eventually we reached an isolated farmhouse and on being ushered in I was delighted to see our pilot, Wally. We were given large mugs of hot milk into which had been put bread and sugar and left to sit on a bed at the end of the room while all the Chetniks present, about a dozen, held a heated discussion round a long table. An elderly man came over and it transpired he had worked in America for many years coming home to Yugoslavia to retire. His English or American, was fair and we pressed him about getting to the coast with a view to getting back to Italy. After some time his reply effectively shut us up. He pointed at the Chetniks, touched the knife he wore in his belt and making a horribly significant gesture of throat cutting he said, "You feel nothing, all over very quick". Not exactly comforting but as we later found out the German authorities had been dropping men dressed in RAF uniforms and speaking English into the area with a view to finding out who would help Allied airmen. It is no wonder the Chetniks were taking every care.'

Goodbrand and Booth, however, apparently satisfied them and soon all were enjoying a glass of slivovic, a tipple which Goodbrand was to find as enjoyable as the wine of his own country – whisky. Soon they were on their way again and their next stop was at a small village where they were taken to a hall for a meal. There they found André, their air-gunner, and Mason, the wireless operator already present. The meal was a most satisfactory one – roast suckling pig plus the inevitable slivovic – which was just as well, as it was to be their last decent meal for some time. Eventually, after much speech-making (none of it understood by the RAF quartet) they were led off to bed. As most of the men, and certainly all the women, crowded into the bedroom with the crew, Bill Goodbrand kept his trousers on – 'for obvious reasons and to the general amusement.'

The following morning the Chetniks took them to an isolated farmhouse where they found their bomb-aimer, Les Wetherall, who had landed on a roof and then damaged his ankle dropping to the ground. With Les in a horse-drawn cart the party set off next morning, riding until they met a group of Chetniks on horseback. These turned out to be their next escorts and one man in particular impressed Bill Goodbrand, who recalls:

'He was about 45 years old, medium height, full black beard and long hair of the Chetnik. (When Belgrade fell to the Germans the Chetniks took an oath not to shave or cut their hair until Belgrade was liberated.) We were to be with him and his party for only 3 weeks, but in that time I learned to love that man like a second father. He had some German, I had school-boy German and was amazed at the forgotten words that suddenly popped into my head. Our communication was such that eventually in our fractured German we were sharing rude jokes.'

Horses were provided and Bill was grateful for the riding lessons he had taken in South Africa while doing his aircrew training. A slow trek began into the mountains, moving mostly at night and lying up in farmhouses during the day. Sudden departures became commonplace and phrases signifying the imminence of Germans were soon familiar to the fugitives.

Food was taken at isolated farmhouses and although it was obviously scarce, the lion's share was always given to the evaders, usually bean soup, cheese and coarse bread, washed down with slivovic.

The Germans were everywhere, often too close for comfort. On one occasion the crew members decided to buy drinks for their Chetnik friends, using some of the dinars they had obtained for the American dollars in their escape kit. As they sat on wooden benches outside a country 'pub' a party of German soldiers arrived. They had come, however, only for a drink and were soon on their way.

The refugees were by this time a mixed bunch as they had been joined by a blond Russian named George, who had been captured at Leningrad and deserted from a work battalion in Yugoslavia; Nino, a captain in the Italian Army and an Austrian Doctor of Music. The party continued travelling for about three weeks, always higher into the mountains. Finally they arrived at a farmhouse where they discovered a large group of American airmen and four other members of their own squadron who had been posted missing prior to the operation of 1 July.

It was now time for the Chetniks to leave them, but their journey was by no means over. Bill Goodbrand writes:

'Although there were in excess of two hundred Americans, we did not travel together but in smaller groups linked by the Chetniks. Again the pattern was lie up during the day and move out in the late evening.'

The group continued to move around but now came the breakthrough. One of the American officers had somehow acquired a radio and the signal 'Yanks in Yugo' was transmitted at intervals. It was later discovered that an RAF wireless operator in Bari had picked up the message but had at first, perhaps understandably, treated it with scepticism. However, by dint of asking various personal questions concerning the members of the group, he was able to establish the validity of the contact and things began to move. First came a message to stand by at a certain time at a designated position. The first night, nothing happened, but the following night a Dakota flew over and three 'chutes were seen descending, bringing with them two American Army officers and a sergeant with full radio equipment, codes etc. The next night came supply 'chutes with K-ration packs, cigarettes etc, in large quantities. These were distributed throughout the group, a gesture greatly appreciated by the RAF and RCAF contingents.

There was then a lull of several days before the message came to climb to the plateau where a reasonably flat area could be used for landing and take-off. When the group arrived there they were treated to the sight of several P40 aircraft (Lightnings) wheeling over the German aerodrome, ensuring that they could not become airborne. Then came the six Dakotas, landing one after the other on the makeshift airfield, taxiing to the far end – engines still ticking over – the loading and finally the take-off. The whole operation took no more than six to eight minutes from start to finish.

Bill Goodbrand remembers the final stage of his journey: 'The flight was happily uneventful and we landed at Bari. We split with the Americans then, with grateful thanks to the Dakota crews, we were taken by a WAAF officer to an army camp. She had appeared confused as to who or what we were and the personnel at the army camp were even more confused. However, after our clothing had been burned, ourselves deloused and thoroughly washed, I managed to phone 40 squadron at Foggia, and the following day a squadron gharry picked us up and took us home to 40 Squadron. We arrived back on 13 August – lucky for some.'

'Much has been said about the Chetniks collaborating with the Germans, and indeed Tito had General Mihailovic executed after the war. I can only say, and I am sure the sentiment would be endorsed by in excess of two hundred Allied airmen, that at no time was there any sign of collaboration, and indeed the very opposite seemed to be the case. The Chetniks and the people of the areas we were in could not have treated us better nor looked after our safety more carefully, and I for one will always be grateful to the very fine gentlemen who wore the Skull and Crossbones cap badge.'

2.   With Tito's Partisans

Flying Officer Alan Day joined 253 Squadron in June 1944, flying Spitfires, when the RAF's Balkan Air Force was formed. He was to spend the next eight months in attacks on German convoys and the escorting of Dakotas in supply dropping in Albania and Yugoslavia. It is interesting to note that while

Flying on these operations he and most of the other pilots wore, not flying boots, but army style boots and gaiters which in the circumstances of having to bale out in a rocky terrain would prove more suitable than the flying boot. There was always the likelihood of losing the flying boot in baling out or while parachuting down to earth. Gaiters made the going easier and defended the lower part of the leg from laceration. Of course, no Spitfire pilot would claim that he flew well in boots, but like all things they got used to it.

Each aircraft was unusually equipped with a Sten gun which was clipped to the armour plate on the left side of the cockpit. It was there as a means of defending oneself or of evading capture on the ground. Each pilot also carried a Commando-type knife in his right gaiter, intended not for defence but to puncture the dinghy on which the pilot sat, which, if damaged, could inflate in flight.

On 26 February 1945 Day set out to attack a motor transport convoy in the area of Bos-Novi in Yugoslavia. His Spitfire was hit in the glycol tank by small-arms fire. At the time he was flying virtually at ground level and in a valley. He pulled hard on the control column to climb as quickly as possible, knowing he must try to obtain a height of at least 500 feet above the surrounding mountain peaks. The radiator temperature was now going off the clock, so his only course of action was to bale out. Some three months before he had witnessed a colleague failing to drop out of his inverted aircraft, so he was going to try a different method. He called up his No.2, disconnected his radio plug, jettisioned the cockpit hood, selected full forward on the aircraft trim and, holding back the control column against the force exerted by the trim tab, undid his cockpit straps. 'As I did this,' he recalls, 'I shot out of the cockpit. One leg did get fouled up but I managed to kick myself free of the aircraft, and was soon landing amongst the snow-covered mountains. I used my Commando knife to cut the shrouds from the canopy and during the daylight hours, hid between the rocks, wrapped in the canopy with snow for a front door.' He trudged westward, hoping to reach a friendly Partisan group in Yugoslavia. He knew there were three active Groups:

the Tito group, who were considered to be safe and helpful; the Chetnik group led by General Mihailovic whose attitude was uncertain though possibly helpful with regard to the provision of food and in other ways; the third group were German-trained and called Ustachi, and were to be avoided at all costs.

In his escape kit Day had the usual Horlicks tablets and chocolate, but for water he had to resort to melting snow. He navigated by the stars and kept to the mountain area, avoiding the valleys. After four days he suddenly awoke to find himself looking into the barrel of a tommy-gun held by a 'Red Star' soldier, who was one of Tito's group. He joined their small party which numbered five, none of whom spoke any English. In his escape kit he had a Croat phrase book, but as they did not understand anything in this it was of no use, but one word, 'Raff', (RAF) seemed to mean something to them.

They were, at first, a little cautious of him, which was not surprising as his uniform was non-standard. He was wearing a khaki battledress, khaki shirt, a white sweater, a pair of US Army officer's trousers and black army boots and gaiters. With a four-day growth of beard he hardly looked like a RAF officer.

He travelled with them along the mountain tracks, and they slept around a control fire in deserted stone shelters which were possibly shepherds' summertime huts. They soon joined a larger group, numbering fifteen in all. In the party there were two female soldiers who seemed to enjoy equal status with the men. All carried revolvers or machine guns, and most had Mills bombs suspended from their waist belts. The food consisted in the main of meat balls with garlic, rough bread and some thin soup with dumplings. After three days' trekking, sometimes on foot and sometimes on horseback, Day was delivered to number 37 Military Mission. Here there were two British soldiers, one officer and one NCO. They had a radio set and made a daily call to Bari at 6 p.m., from their office overlooking a disused airstrip. While Day was with them they had a Christmas air supply drop which included a flagon of genuine Nelson's Blood, and each enjoyed a tot as a nightcap.

Breakfast was prepared in the Mission house on a woodchip fire in a tin which resembled a small kiln with a 3-inch wide chimney. On it they cooked real spam and eggs. These were traded for with the locals for English or American cigarettes. Day tried one of the local cigarettes but there was no similarity to the Balkan Sobrani cigarettes, which he remembered his father once smoked. After waiting four or five days a radio message was received that a Dakota was on its way to pick Day up, and when it arrived the engines were kept turning whilst he and two or three soldiers clambered aboard. In two or three minutes they were away and Day had the great satisfaction of seeing Spitfires of his own squadron, 253, escort the Dakota back to base. A week or so later, after interrogation and delousing, Day was back on operational flying. (Ironically, Day's first operation, on 2 April, was to escort Dakotas in supply dropping to Piccadilly Hope, Yugoslavia, as the airstrip was named).

Altogether Alan Day completed 98 operational sorties, involving 180 flying hours, for which he was later awarded the DFC.

X

The Middle East

MI9's activities in the Middle East took a slightly different form. Run from Cairo, it was under the direct auspices of Colonel Dudley Clarke, accountable to and hand-picked by Wavell, C-in-C Middle East, when it was clear that hostilities were about to begin with Italy, to organise deception in the Middle East. Dudley Clarke himself, a former Hussar, was an eccentric and brilliant man who gathered round him a first class team both to deceive the enemy on general war plans and to organise deception in the battlefield, with dummy tanks, imaginary divisional signs etc. On his team was Jasper Maskelyne of the famous magician's family. From September 1941 Clarke also took over evasion and escape; it was run by Lt Colonel Tony Simonds, who inherited and built up a chain of escape routes by caique across the Aegean, with their own naval base in Turkey and another base at Antiparos. The numbers of evaders were high, especially after the fall of Crete, when by the autumn of 1941 nearly 1,000 had successfully evaded.

Airmen who were shot down in the desert, despite the 'goolie chits' supplied to them explaining to the Arabs in Arabic they would be rewarded if they returned the airman to his own lines, met a varied fate. Some Arabs were pro-British – or at least anti-Italian – and were happy to oblige; others were only too eager to betray them and take them straight to the Germans. Clarke had agents in the desert and the Long Range Desert Force was also invaluable in tracking and helping evaders, but in such hostile terrain, survival was difficult, and many perished.

*

1.   Evading On A Camel

In May 1942, 148 Squadron were based in Egypt, and with it was Sergeant Michael Mackintosh. On 31 May 1942 he was detailed as second pilot for an operation against Derna aerodrome.

'It was a beautiful night for operations with a full moon and excellent visibility,' he recalls. The crew was Flying Officer Bill Astell*, pilot, pilot officer 'Bish' Dodds navigator, Sergeant 'Tiger' Philby, wireless/operator, Sergeant Fred Hooper and Flight Sergeant Ian Robinson were the gunners.

The trip to the target was uneventful and the ground defences poor. The first stick of bombs was dropped from 5,000 feet, but as they dropped flares prior to the next bombing run they were attacked by a Me109 night fighter. The starboard engine was put out of action, and the wing set on fire. The hydraulics were also damaged and the undercarriage fell down. The rest of the bombs were jettisoned when once again the fighter came in and attacked. Mackintosh was trying to pump the undercarriage back up by hand and in this attack he was hit in the elbow. The force spun him around and into the bomb aimer's panel. 'Bill asked me if I had been hit,' says Mackintosh, 'and in a very disgusted tone I replied that my arm had been shot off, as at that moment I only had feeling up to my elbow. When I looked at my arm it was in fact still there but appeared to be only just hanging on and was twisting and swinging in all directions, with blood pouring from the wound. It was not a very pleasant sensation.'

Besides the damage already mentioned, a fire started in the fuselage and the instrument panel had been shattered, while Tiger, operating his guns, had been hit in the right thigh.

'The order came to bale out, but as my right arm was useless I had to get Bish to fasten on my chute. He picked up my dangling right arm and put my fingers around the rip cord handle, but it fell away. I again replaced it but again it fell away as I opened the trap door. The only way was to put my left

* Later F/Lt DFC. Flew on the famous Dams Raid with 617 Sqdn but failed to return.

hand over my right to stop it falling away, and I was able to pull the handle.

'When I went out into space we were at a height of 2,000 feet, and the early part of my descent was a blank but soon I saw the ground coming up towards me so I slightly bent my legs to prepare for the landing. It came with a terrific thud and I found myself on the ground in a curled-up position. For a few seconds I was unable to move. To listen to oneself groaning, and being unable to stop was a most unpleasant sensation, I finally stood up. My helmet was missing and bombs were falling all around me. My field service cap was in the shoulder strap of my battledress, so I removed it and tucked it under my right armpit, hoping to bring some force to bear on the pressure point and so check the flow of blood from my injured arm.'

Mackintosh soon picked up the North Star and set out in a south-east direction with his arms folded across his body. His right desert boot was damaged and the heel was out and the sole flapped about.

After 15 minutes he met Fred Hooper who had been heading north. His first task was to fix up Mackintosh's arm. Luckily he had had some hospital training so he knew what he was doing. He cut the sleeve out, and with handkerchief and gun-cleaning material (known as four by two), he bandaged the arm.

'My left arm was also hurting,' recalls Mackintosh. 'Fred set to work and exposed my left arm. This had been hurt in the upper part, so once again he bandaged me up. We then set off on a desert track but soon I had to stop as I was not feeling very well, to the extent that I told Fred to go it alone and leave me. He was very reluctant to leave me but I finally persuaded him to go on, so once again I was alone.

'After a while I set off but only very slowly. I soon came upon my aircraft, Wellington AD653-R for Robert. It was just about burnt out, and I walked around it calling out to see if anyone was still trapped inside, not that I could have done very much if they were. The engines had turned over and were facing the other way, but the distinct tail of the Wellington was still standing up proudly.'

From the official records it transpires that Flying Officer Astell and Pilot Officer Dodds had no time to bale out and crash-landed R for Robert about one or two miles south of Martuba. They had extricated themselves from the wreckage and after destroying all the important equipment set out themselves on the desert track. Michael Mackintosh continues:

'After making certain there was no one in the aircraft, I set out, still on the desert track, walking for about two to three hours. All seemed to be going quite well. My brain was quite clear and I was taking stock of all around me but I could not keep up the pace I had set myself and just as dawn broke I had to stop for a rest and so I sat down and then lay down on the sand. In retrospect, very foolishly.

'I became very cold and decided I must move on but this was easier said than done as I seemed to be glued to the ground and it took several attempts before I finally got to my feet. From a nearby wadi I could hear the sound of sheep and goats and the voice of an Arab. I knew Senussi Arabs had helped other airmen to evade being captured from behind enemy lines so I decided to go to them and hope they were friendly. At this stage I was leaving a trail of blood behind me and flies were beginning to attack my wounded arm so it was now time to try and find help.

'The wadi was very deep but there was no sign of the enemy. At the bottom were three tents. Outside one an Arab was tending to the sheep and goats. By this time my legs were very unsteady and I was staggering about, and the Arab, when he saw me, looked alarmed so I greeted him in Arabic telling him I was English and I needed food and water, and asked if he was a friend of the English. He replied the English were good and the Italians bad. He then led me down to the farm and into a tent where I was greeted by all present including the Sheik, Braiham Haarak, an old man with a grey beard.

'A young girl gave me a glass of goat's milk, then another Arab entered the tent. He was Yadem Abdual Mustaffa Said and he spoke some English. He removed the bandages from my arm, washed the wound, applied some form of powder and then freshly bandaged my arm. I was offered food but declined as I had no appetite but did accept another welcome glass of goat's milk. The Arabs put their heads together discussing my case. Yadem then said he was taking me somewhere I could hide in the day so I left the tent accompanied by Yadem and Braiham who rode a horse. By now I could hear aircraft engines being tested on the ground and I then saw several German fighters in the air. The two Arabs took me to a cave at the side of the Wadi where they placed a blanket on the floor for me to lie on; in the circumstances it seemed very comfortable. Then a boulder was rolled into the entrance and I was again alone.

'It was not long before the flies started to disturb me and I noticed several bug-like insects being attracted to the exposed parts of my body, particularly my injured arm. They seemed to gloat on my blood. Every time I killed one it was like a blood blister bursting. About midday, Yadem returned with milk and water, but the food he brought I refused.

'All day I could hear aircraft overhead, and in the evening Yadem came again to take me to the farm. I managed to crawl out of the cave and stand up but only with the help of Yadem. However, when he left me to go back into the cave to fetch the blanket, I fell down and all went blank. I think he thought I was going to die, and wanted to take me to the nearest German hospital, but this gave me the incentive I needed to get up once again and once up, I stayed up but only with the help of the rocks nearby. We later reached the farm and all was well.

'The next day we again set out but not to the same cave. As before Yadem returned during the day with milk and water but as he was about to leave, motor vehicles were heard coming down the wadi. They stopped in front of the cave and I could hear car doors slam, and voices raised. Yadem told me to say that he had just found me and was about to hand me over. When we finally looked out we saw four armoured cars about twenty yards away, stuck in the sand but finally they made off towards the farm. In the evening when Yadem returned he said they had been to the farm looking for me, looking for an "English major" who had been shot down at Derna, my name being clearly marked on my abandoned parachute.

'Braiham said he had not seen me but would keep his eyes open as he wanted the reward he would get if he found me. I reminded Yadem that he would be rewarded if he got me back to the British lines and he replied, "I want no reward, my reward is getting you back to your English comrades, no more." They hated the Italians because of the way they treated the Arabs, and disliked the Germans because they were friends of the Italians.

'The cave we were heading for was 10 kms away but I said I was going to try as soon as dusk fell to make the British lines at Gazala but he said I was not well enough and if I waited a few days he would arrange something, so I agreed. We set off, having had a make-do sling made for my arm and it was a little easier but I still had to hang on to Yadem.

'To urge me on, Yadem kept telling how the cave was just in front or just around the next bend in the wadi. I was all in and realised I would have to rest for a few days so they left me a good supply of water and then set off back to the farm. By following the shadow in the cave entrance around, as the day went on, I tried to estimate the time. I examined my tunic and found all four pockets had been holed and my pocket torch which was inside my breast pocket was shattered. The globe itself had vanished. I noticed maggots, not only on the blanket, but my elbow as well. There were too many to brush off. In actual fact as I found out later they were saving my arm by eating away the infection.

'Later Yadem came and made me up some lemonade and said they had a plan for my escape. They were going to take me to a British patrol but to do this they would have to borrow a camel and I would have to sign a chit to enable them to borrow one. We set off and all the village came out to see us off. They told me the next time I flew over to drop them tea and sugar. After one day's travel we came to another Arab encampment where I was made welcome, and in the roofs of the tents were letters from RAF and Army personnel who had passed through.

'By now I was getting very tired of riding on a camel. I was sitting at its back and my legs were getting rubbed raw by the

LATE ARRIVALS CLUB
(Founded Western Desert, June 1941)

THIS IS TO CERTIFY, that

Sgt. Mackintosh . T .

of *148* Squadron   *Western Desert*

is hereby nominated a member of the

Late Arrivals Club

IN AS MUCH AS HE, in *the region of Derna*

on *night of 31ˢᵗ may 1942*

when obliged to abandon his Aircraft, on the
ground or in the Air, as a result of unfriendly
action by the enemy.

SUCCEEDED in returning to his Squadron, on foot
or by other means, long after his Estimated Time
of Arrival.

IT IS NEVER TOO LATE TO COME BACK.

———

*This member is permitted to wear the Emblem of the Winged
Boot on the left breast of his Flying Suit.*

continual back and fore motion of the animal but we finally reached a wadi where we met a British officer and two signal-men. They were members of the Long Range Desert Group observing German troop movements on the Benghazi/Derna road.

'By now I was all in. One of the soldiers gave me a drink and when I asked what it was he said it was issue rum. A signal was sent to Cairo for a patrol to meet up with us and while waiting for them I met the famous Popski and his Private Army. He told me of some of his experiences and I realised what wonderful men they were. I travelled on his horse to meet the patrol of the LRDG, and so well were the patrol camouflaged that we were on top of them before we saw them.

'It was a New Zealand patrol, in three vehicles, accompanied by a British doctor, Captain Chapman of the RAMC. The journey to an oasis took three days, and here a DH89 Red Cross plane had been sent to pick me up but owing to an air raid it had been wrecked and another had to be sent. When it arrived I was flown to Cairo and into a RAF hospital.

'They wanted to take me on a stretcher but having got this far on my own two feet I declined. It was now 26 June. I later learned that Bill Astell had reached Cairo. Dodds was a POW in Italy but later escaped. Tiger grounded by the 109 had broken the other leg in his parachute landing and the remainder were also captured and were POWs for the rest of the war.

'Although my arm was locked and at right angles I managed to get back on flying but on a very restricted category. In 1956 while still in the RAF, at Dyce, I once again met Yadem. He was now a Corporal in the Libyan Army and on a course in Birmingham. He had traced me, via my mother.'

Today Michael is a head of department in a school in Scotland and teaches among other things cricket and this despite his arm being two inches shorter than the other one. The surgeon had made a new elbow joint out of the bone that was left, and he still has a lot of pain. His elbow grinds like a coffee machine, when he moves it, but he still has his own arm. If he had been picked up quickly by the Germans or British they would probably have amputated it.

2.   Two Weeks Underground

In the desert war the Wellington squadrons were the mainstay of the bombing operations. In one such squadron, No.148, a navigator in one of the crews was Sergeant Ken de Souza, the pilot was Sergeant Hal Curtois. On 19 September 1942 Wellington HF840 took off from Kilo 40 at 8.31 p.m. and reached the Sollum area at about midnight. The port engine suddenly caught fire. At the time the second pilot, Sergeant Prosser, was at the controls but as soon as the fire started, Curtois took over again. He at once turned for home and jettisoned the bombs. Meanwhile the aircraft was losing height rapidly and the captain ordered guns, flares and movable equipment to be jettisoned. At this time they were flying at 2,000ft and about 35 miles south-west of Mersa Matruh. The fire was extinguished, using the extinguisher, which stopped the engine. The starboard engine was by now also misfiring so at 12.45 the order was given to bale out.

De Souza landed on a shingle bank, breaking his watch on impact. His water-bottle strap had burst as his 'chute opened so he was now without water and the means of telling the time. His watch had stopped at 01.05. He buried the watch along with his parachute, and started walking in an ENE direction towards El Alamein, 140 miles distant. Ken de Souza recalls subsequent events in diary form:

Night 1: 20/21 Sept 1942: Started walking about 01.30 hours and continued until a couple of hours after sunrise. Checked RAF Escape tin contents. 1. Horlicks tablets – thirst-provoking, therefore no help. 2. Water-purifying tablets (– would be helpful if there were any water to purify!) 3. Small rubber bag. 4. Tiny escape-saw – might be helpful. 5. 'Goolie-chit' – indispensable if I met any Arabs. 6. Chalk and opium tablets. Flying boots painful to walk in. Walked barefoot across dusty plain interspersed with gravel. Found scrap of Afrika Korps newspaper: *Der Kampf*, blackened, almost-dry tin of pineapple (English label).
Became aware – as I have been ever since – of my unseen

Companion. At 'his' instigation I turned north and almost immediately found place where nomads had stopped. Miraculous find of a pair of discarded plimsolls. Torn across instep but they fitted me! Buried flying boots. Also found blanket. Rolled up in it against a boulder and slept the day.

Night 2: 21/22 Sept 1942: Walked east again starting before sunset. Found camel skeleton near dried-up water-hole. Tormented by thirst. Heard and then caught glimpse of Wellington flying westerly course. After about 6 hours, sank down to sleep the sleep of exhaustion. Woke to find stones glistening with dew – not enough to satisfy, but enough to give me strength to continue. Found wrecked British gharry among rocks to the south. Found nest of oil-drums covered with tarpaulin. Rested there. Awakened midday by Fieseler-Storch spotter plane which used my 'hide' for target practice. Bullet-holes all around but none in me! ...

Night 4: 23/24 Sept 1942: Staggered up one hill after another always expecting to glimpse the sea ... Found dew in the nick of time. I was nearly all in. Reached Fuga airfield, 4 Ju52 at dispersal. Walked through southern part of airfield, between enemy tents, undetected! At dawn heard clatter from coastal railway near El Daba. Lay up all day watching the goods trucks shunting etc.

Night 5: 24/25 Sept 1942: Decided to hitch a lift on train. Before sundown crawled to about 300 yards from line. Alas! All railway activity ceased at sunset!! Walked along railway track then in ditch at north side. Circumvented a pill-box (Unmanned?). Sounds of battle to my south – starshells and tracer lines. Giddy and de-hydrated. Bolt-less rifles and chianti bottles lying about. Also clothing, books, papers etc. Trod carefully in my plimsolls (minefields?). When battle a long way behind me I saw a cluster of tented dug-outs. Joyfully went to this camp. At first I mistook *'Chi va là?'* challenge for French – but it was Italian – the wrong army!

De Souza was taken in a German truck to Mersa Matruh transit interrogation camp. There he was re-united with Hal Curtois, who, after a nine-day trek, was also brought in. He had managed to crash-land the aircraft when the crew baled out. De Souza and Curtois had been together throughout their time in the RAF, apart from specialist training. As they each had qualities the other lacked, they made an ideal escape team.

They were moved to the POW transit camp at Benghazi, where they swapped places with two other prisoners to get on a party about to be moved to Italy. They had hopes of being transported by Ju52, and perhaps of emulating another POW aircrew who had taken over a Ju52 and had made good their escape. Instead, Curtois and de Souza found themselves in 'the hell hole hold of a ship', destined for Brindisi.

In PG75 Bari, their time was made more miserable by a total lack of Red Cross parcels, appalling food and swarms of fleas. Another move, this time by railway cattle trucks, brought them to PG70 Monte Urano on the Adriatic coast. Here, for the first time, they met kindness among the local population who served them wine on the railway platform. This gave them the hope that they might find help amongst the inhabitants of the area if they could escape from the camp.

De Souza's digest continues:

November/early December: Some didn't survive the malnutrition/starvation. Too weak from hunger to escape – difficult to walk! Just before Christmas Red Cross found us. Parcels, bulk and individual, began to dribble through. 'Personal parcels' pilfered and mostly didn't arrive at all.

Late spring and summer: Thanks to Red Cross food, various activities started up. I was reporter on Camp Wall Newspaper. (I have photos of *The 70 Times*.) PG70 a flax factory/storage depot before the war. Editorial office = the weighing scales room, weighbridge a few feet away outside (central position in camp). PG70 staff put 2 beds under weighbridge platform. Entry by taking up (and replacing?) a couple of floorboards. Italian armistice and Germans took over PG70. Moved compound 1 (2,000) men to Austria. We stowed under weighbridge 2 cookhouse tureens from No 1 compound, one we filled with water and kept one for a toilet

– both with lids! Also first aid equipment and 2 Red Cross parcels. Prepared to live there for 2 or 3 weeks. Hal and I took up residence under platform just before our compound (No 2) was due to be moved. After camp emptied of POWs, Fascists guards lunched regularly at 1 p.m. at front of camp. German trucks often came in by night. After 2 weeks, *contadini* [peasants] allowed in to collect straw for their animals. Contacted two peasant women. Walked out with group of *contadini*, our belongings carried on their heads!

The only name Ken managed to get from these very brave people, who really started their escape off, was Maria. She had been the one he had first spoken to in the camp. Their first contact outside was Marcelli Primo, who was a fruit seller and local factotum. He took them to a deserted cottage on a slope overlooking PG70. Here they lived for three weeks until they found a family who would take them in. The figure on the head of escaping POWs at that time was 1,800 Lire, and the risk to the local people was death if they were caught helping.

On the morning of 2 November 1943 Primo took them to the Brugnoni family who lived about six kilometres away; they treated them like sons. Ken de Souza had never known such kindness. Their shirts and pullovers were dyed by the family's daughters, Stella and Ines, from their khaki colour to a chocolate brown. They were fed very well and regained their strength and fitness. Ken helped with the farm work, although not too successfully with the oxen. He also taught the children from time to time as all the schools were closed. It was due to this that he decided, after the war, to become a teacher.

He worked hard at becoming a *contadino* in his mannerisms, and speech, and he was loaned a bicycle by Pacifico Brugnoni which enabled him to get around the area and find out the strength of the local Germans. On one occasion he was cycling along the autostrada when a German sergeant in a truck threw him three packets of cigarettes. He jumped off the bike and just managed to snatch them from the path of an oncoming German tank. Both Hal and Pacifico were smokers so were delighted with the cigarettes.

Ken also met Father Dom Mario at his flat opposite the railway station, at Porto San Giorgio, as well as an Italian Communist named Etteri who met the RAF men in the fields, to say that a group of Inglesi *paracadutisti* were stranded in the local town of Fermo. The local Italians were terrified as one of the men had been arrested and they might soon come looking for the rest. Ken arranged with Pacifico to have the group, which turned out to be of the SAS, accommodated in the local farms with friends and relatives of the Brugnonis. The group consisted of Captain Cameron, Lieutenant Darwall and Corporal Drake, the wireless man. They had been landed by sea to blow a bridge before the front line was stabilized. They wanted information about the German activity at the railway station which Ken acquired by having tea with Dom Mario. Ken and Hal were also required to gather a party of 22 escapers who would all escape together, so Ken cycled around trying to locate them. They were finally assembled at a place near the coast – close to the mouth of the River Tenna.

Finally on 21 January, 1944 the group made it. Darwall cut the barbed wire at the autostrada and the party went down to the beach at 10 p.m. They were taken off in a wooden dinghy towing other rubber dinghies but they had to swim the last few yards when the wooden dinghy sank. They were picked out of the water by an Italian MTB being used by the Royal Navy and five hours later were landed at SAS HQ, Termoli, and returned to England on HMT *Ranci* from Taranto.

Sergeant Frampton, in the Wellington's crew, had reached an Allied base at Kilo 40 on 30 September, 1942 only 11 days after being shot down. An MI9 report on his escape commented:

'The Arabs Sgt. Frampton met were all extremely courteous and friendly, and very helpful. They looked after the two sergeants extremely well, and gave them, among other things, some tea made of herbs, possibly mint, which was found to be very good. They were extremely anti-German, and their attitude was vividly expressed by the old Arab who illustrated his opinion of the Germans by throwing his hat on the ground and spitting.'

3.   Crash-Landing in the Desert

On 29 September 1942, Flying Officer Raymond Sherk, a Canadian from Ontario, who was serving with 601 Squadron in North Africa, took off in company with two other Spitfires for a long strafe on an ammunition train in the vicinity of 'Charing Cross' near Mersa Matruh. They failed to locate the train but on their way back at about 14.30 they shot down a Ju52, for which they were later each credited with one third. At 1531, when they were about 30-40 miles behind the lines in the Qattara Depression, Sherk switched over from his long-range petrol tanks to his main tank. The engine, however, cut out, due to an air lock. At the time, Sherk was flying at about 200 feet and was able to crash-land successfully, indeed, had no time to do otherwise. He called up his flight leader on the W/T, got his acknowledgement and, after blowing up his IFF, left his plane and started walking due east. He walked and slept during the next 24 hours and at one point his hopes were raised when two Spitfires flew over. They, however, failed to spot him.

He continued walking until he got within a mile of his own lines, where he was surrounded by an Italian patrol and captured. He was searched and his watch and trinkets were removed. He was then taken to the officer in charge who interrogated him in good English. When Sherk refused to answer questions the officer retrieved his belongings and parcelled them up. Sherk soon discovered why, for at noon the next day (1 October) he was taken by field ambulance to Army Headquarters, 'pretty exhausted'. There his watch and rings were returned to him.

Sherk made an attempt to escape at this stage. His report reads: 'I had to sleep with my guards in the sand. During the night I attempted to slip away quietly, but was discovered when I had got only about 100 yards away. I therefore proceeded to fulfil the functions of nature and rejoined my guards without arousing suspicion.'

He was next taken to El Daba, where the Germans were in charge, and interrogated by a German claiming to be a 'Corporal Barnes' who produced a bogus Red Cross form on which were about thirty questions. Sherk filled in only his name, rank and number, whereupon the officer became 'quite furious', and showed him forms which he claimed had been completed by other officers. Sherk recognised none of the names and remained adamant about name, rank and number. His flying suit was removed and he was thoroughly searched. The belt containing his maps and a compass was discovered but a compass in a packet of cigarettes was overlooked. The 'corporal' then discovered that Sherk's flying suit was German and threatened to have him shot as a spy but still Sherk refused to answer his questions. He was put into a tent along with a man who claimed to be a South African lieutenant and who said he was an air observer. Sherk, however, suspected him of being a stool pigeon and resisted his efforts to pump him.

On 4 October Sherk and the South African left El Daba for Mersa Matruh. The lieutenant said he was going by Ju52 to Italy and that Sherk 'was a fool to suffer discomfort when he could easily tell them at least something'. He was then handed back to the Italians. After interrogation he was put into a tent with a pilot officer who said he came from Southend and that the Wellington he had been flying had been shot down. Sherk had no reason to suspect him of being a stool pigeon, especially as he was able to refer to Sherk's wing commander by name. In conversation it came out that Sherk's squadron was 601 and that he had walked for a day before being captured. The pilot officer also caught a glimpse of the compass in Sherk's cigarette packet. Later that day Sherk was transferred to Fuka where a guard insisted on him producing cigarettes, and, on finding the compass, was highly delighted and thereafter kept his revolver cocked.

From Fuka Sherk was sent back to El Daba, where the German 'corporal' was very surprised to see him, and on 6 October he was moved to Mersa Matruh. In company with a number of other prisoners of war he was transferred to Derna. While there he met up with two RAF officers, Flying Officer McLarty and Pilot Officer Trevor Hardie, and on comparing notes they discovered that the pilot officer from Southend had also been bogus.

On 15 October the POWs took train for Bari where Sherk was quarantined for three weeks before being allowed into the compound. Of this camp his report states: 'Conditions in this camp were extremely bad. There were no Red Cross parcels. Complaints were put up and the Commandant said he wrote to Rome but received no reply. Many ORs died through sheer starvation. Medical supplies were poor. Cats were eaten by many. Complaints did not receive any attention by the Commandant and his assistant. They were entirely responsible for a considerable amount of the privations of this camp.'

Sherk remained at Bari until March 1943, when he was moved to Sulmona, arriving there on the 4th. Conditions at this camp were much better and he became a member of the Escaping Committee.

On 12 September, following the surrender of Italy, the camp was evacuated and Sherk and McLarty made for the foothills, only to be captured by the Germans on 16 September. Later on the same day, the party halted by the side of a mountain, and Sherk again decided to make a break for freedom. 'There were five ORs besides ourselves in the party. McLarty and I asked the German guard if we could get into the shade of a nearby rock about 25 yards away. We were granted permission, and at a favourable opportunity, after leaving a cap on the rock as a decoy, we rolled down the mountain and hid in some scrub. The search passed completely over us.'

Sherk and McLarty evaded capture and on 19 September they met up with another group of escaped prisoners who had been advised by some Italians to head for the village of Roccacasale. This they all did and remained there, cared for by the villagers until the beginning of October, when the village was surrounded by the Germans. Once again Sherk and McLarty escaped and this time were led to safety by a shepherd, up a mountain track, where they met a South African War Correspondent, Vys Kriege, and Lieutenant Rochberg, an Austrian Jew. This group stayed together until they reached Campo di Giove where they remained until 18 October. The Germans had machine-gunned the village on the 17th and there were rumours that they were combing the woods so

Sherk, McLarty, Rochberg and Kriege set out on foot, walking south-east. They arrived, on 23 October, at Cupello – minus Rochberg, who had gone off on his own, feeling that the party was too large. A guide took the three, plus five ORs and twenty Italians, through the lines on 25 October and on the 26th they fell in with 1st Canadian Division. The division took them to Campobassa and then by truck to Foggia, where Sherk saw his old squadron. Then they went by aircraft to Bari, where Sherk left McLarty, who was sick, and proceeded to Taranto by train. From there he was flown to Algiers, where he, too, fell sick and spent a week in No.2 Hospital. On his recovery he left Algiers and was flown to Rabat, then Gibraltar and finally London, where he arrived on 13 November.

On 15 March 1944, now with 401 Squadron, Sherk took off from Biggin Hill to escort Marauders over the Pas de Calais. On the way out, as before, his engine failed. He bailed out and came down near a wood three kilometres north-west of Beaumont. He rolled up his parachute and ran for cover. Sherk's report reads: 'Some Frenchmen had seen me coming down and by the time I reached the wood one of them had caught up with me. He thought at first that I was a German but when I told him that I was in the RAF he helped me over a fence surrounding the wood and buried all my flying kit under a tree. He then whistled to his companions and about six other Frenchmen came up to me. We started running and as I went along I took off my RAF battledress jacket and the first farmer gave me his jacket to put on. When we had gone about a mile we stopped. I took off my flying boots and RAF trousers and my companions gave me civilian ones in exchange. One of the men also gave me a beret.'

They then left him and he made his way northwards. He stopped at a house and was given a drink, then hid in the nearby fields until two men came to collect him. They took him to a house in Hebuterne where the woman spoke a little English. He learned that her husband and son were both POWs in Germany. After staying there for three days he met Roy Carpenter of the USAAF who was sheltering in a neighbouring village, and on 27 March they were both guided to Bordeaux then on 4 April on to Dax by train.

They decided it was too dangerous to continue by rail and their guide, a young French boy, left them. They set out alone and walked to Bidarray where they approached a farmer and told him they were parachutists. In his own words Sherk described the incident at his debriefing: 'I do not speak good French and at first the farmer did not seem willing to believe us. However, when I showed him a piece of parachute cord which Carpenter had tied round his greatcoat he said at once that he would do what he could for us. He took us to his house and his son then took us on to a friend of his. We stayed with him for the night and the following day he introduced us to a man who said he would guide us across the mountains.'

On 5 April they crossed the frontier into Spain. On the 6th their guide left them and an old lady took over. She took them to Errazu where she handed them over to the authorities. They were not interrogated beyond giving details of their names and ranks, and as they had managed to change 1,000 francs for 60 pesetas, they were able to spend that night in a hotel. The next day they were escorted to Pamplona where they again filled in forms giving their personal details.

Sherk finally reached Gibraltar and from there returned to the UK, arriving on 2 May 1944. On 30 May 1944 he was recommended for the Military Cross but somehow this was not approved or was overlooked, despite an Air Ministry memo stating his award would be in the *London Gazette* of 22nd October 1944. In January and June 1945 Sherk was awarded a Mention in Despatches.

4.   Desert Helpers

It was 6 December 1942 when Beaufighter TS045, letter 'G', of 252 Squadron became airborne from Berca airfield in Benghazi, its mission an armed reconnaissance.

The pilot was Squadron Leader Derek Frecker, DFC, and his

navigator, whose story this is, was Pilot Officer Tom Armstrong. Although the Beaufighter only had two in its crew, on this occasion they had a third member, Sergeant 'Paddy' Clarke, who came from Northern Ireland. On the ground he helped look after T5045 and talked the CO into letting him fly on this mission. He wanted to see a few Germans blown up on the ground.

Near the airfield at Wadi Tamet they saw six lorries parked together on the road and attacked. One was seen to go up in flames and hits were seen on the others, but at the same time they themselves were hit by flak from a gun post in the north-west corner of the airfield.

There were two direct hits on the nose, one of which pierced the armour plating and smashed the instruments; it also shattered the windscreen. There were also two direct hits on the starboard engine. Frecker turned inland with oil pouring from the oil cooler which had been smashed, and when the engine had just about had it and started to smoke, he crash-landed at 13.20. This was successful, without any injuries being sustained. Tom Armstrong wrote an account in diary form of what then happened:

> 1st Day: 1640: Started walking with tank of water and remains of kit in nav. bag slung between the three of us – rather heavy on shoulders. We look like tinkers' convention without donkey carts. Sgt Clarke's heels (or lack of same in stockings) giving trouble. Many rests.
>
> 1815: Decided to have dinner and sleep (?) Dined off one tin of bully and biscuits. Wrapped the 'chute silk around our bodies and lay on maps and charts – but were frozen.
>
> 2nd Day: Monday, 7 December: 0100: Decided it was too cold to stay still so draped ourselves with water bottles, ration bags, etc. and set off. Found it easier to stay on course by stars, than in daytime. Everybody pretty tired – many stops until we got cold and then walked on until we warmed up again.
>
> 0600: Expecting dawn.
>
> 0700: Dawn – a beautiful sight.

0740: Shoulders and ankles aching so decided to park for day.

0800: Sun up – very welcome. Found we had drunk one water bottle full each and decided to go easier in future. Inventory of stores:- 5 tins bully and biscuits, 5 emergency rations, Mr. Frecker's bag – 2 tins salmon, two tins sardines, two tins pears, tin of milk, 50 cigarettes, 1 box of matches. Sgt. Clarke and I both have lighters and extra petrol.

0815: Have just finished writing this – waiting for it to warm up when we will eat.

1000: Still quite cold with wind blowing – unable to sleep.

1100: Breakfast off half tin of salmon. A little warmer now, made wind breaker from odds and ends. Quite good – but not much sleep.

1545: A swarm of locusts pass over.

1715: Dined off remains of salmon, bandaged feet and packed up.

1805: On way. All pretty tired, not making very much headway.

3rd Day: Tuesday, 8 December: 0200: Too tired to carry on so huddled together and tried to get some sleep – freezing cold.

0700: Set off again, still not making very good time, feet giving trouble.

0800: Breakfast – half tin of bully.

1200: Stopped – sky very cloudy – no sun getting through. Pretty cold wind blowing – dozed but not much sleep. Decided we will make for road and hang on until our forces come (we hope) or prang a gharry. Saw an aircraft this afternoon. On, on – All pretty fagged out.

1700: Dined from rest of bully – pretty hard to get down.

2000: Sky still overcast – no stars to steer by so decided to stay night. Put up our windshield and lay down. We did get some sleep huddled up together. There was some rain making us pretty damp. Mr Frecker's heel rather bad ....

5th Day: Thursday, 10 December: 0700: On, on again – Mr Frecker's heel rather bad.

0830: Breakfast – half tin of bully. Filled up bottles – not much left in tank now.

0930: On on once more and sighted the sea. Glorious sight.

1200: Too hot to go any further so rested in the shade of large bush. We have passed over many wadis this morning. Everywhere very green but no signs of water. Reckon we will make road before nightfall. Quite a number of 'planes have been flying down road.

1600: Decided to move on again as not much headway has been made today.

1630: Stopped. Still too hot. Had dinner – rest of bully – water going very quickly.

1730: On on – saw two natives and a camel but no sign of a camp.

1930: Can see lights on road. All traffic moving west. Quite a lot until late on. Dossed down and did our best to get some sleep. Celebrated reaching sight of road with tin of asparagus tips – delicious.

6th Day: Friday, 11 December: 0800: Traffic started moving west again well before dawn. Found ourselves a good hiding place and had breakfast. All our water bottles were empty. All that remains in tank is one cigarette tinful each, duly put into our bottles. Observed a few more natives.

0910: 24 single-engined fighters moving east.

1100: Decided to move further up to the road. This we did hiding behind a hillock about a mile from road. Some soldiers dead ahead on road. They do not appear to have any tents and we cannot understand what they are doing. Not much traffic at first, but later quite a number of lorries moving west packed with troops, to us a goodly sign, our one worry now is water. Sky has been clouded over all day and it has been none too warm. A recce party (Mr Frecker and 'Paddy' Clarke) discover that there are about 80 Italian soldiers on the road in front of us – we still don't know what they are doing, but they are making a lot of noise doing it. Decide it will be best to retire to a safer position at night. We have dinner (rest of salmon) and then retire. All our water except the emergency cans is gone. We have seen quite a lot of Arabs knocking about the place and decide we must contact them in the morning and risk if they are friendly or not. We make ourselves as comfortable as we can for the night and our troubles start – rain – lashings of it – water in the wrong form.

We put maps over us but they soon get wet through, then we get wet through. It goes off after about two hours, leaving us wet, cold and very miserable, dreaming of hot chai and similar nectars. We dry ourselves as best we can and then try and get more sleep but the rains come once more. We spend the rest of the night trying to get warm and decided we will seek the Bedouins as soon as light comes.

7th Day: Saturday, 12 December: We are very miserable at daybreak. See Bedouin boy and have words with him but he does not seem to understand and is rather frightened – he runs away. Two men next come near with two children. They are quite friendly when we explain who we are and what we want, and promise to look after us. They take us over the escarpment, light a fire, dry our clothes, get us as much moya as we want – our dreams start coming true – and make us some wizard coffee and produce dates to eat. We spend some uncomfortable moments when some neighbouring Arabs visit the gathering, but have to suffer the indignity of pretending we are Germans until they leave. Cigarettes (Italian) complete *petit dejeuner*. We move on to new place where they light another fire and dress us as Arabs in blanketlike affairs – must be about four times the size of an Army blanket. Next, food is produced. German herrings in tomato sauce (delicious) and they make us hot macaroni (Italian) and tomatoes (English) while we doze for a while. We finish off with tea and coffee. We are still wondering when we shall wake up. It is five minutes off five now, the sun is shining and everything is really pleasant. We don't know what they are going to do with us for the night yet. We saw six Stukas going west this morning, one towing a glider. Two Macchis seem to be patrolling the road. One of the Bedouins has produced some soap, scented too, so we are looking forward to having a wash later. They even produced china saucers with floral design and spoons and forks. After dark they took us very cautiously to an Arab tent. Here we got more coffee, goat's milk, eggs and more macaroni, etc.

Feeling very full and contented we went to sleep on a straw mat with a carpet over us and slept the sleep of the gods. We seem to have struck lucky meeting this Arab – he is the Sheik of a Senussi village – about twenty tents. His name is Ali Ben Athman, and his two right-hand men are called Mahommed and Msud. The village is about ten miles inland from Bir-en-Maim.

8th Day: Sunday, 13 December: We had eggs (boiled in teapot) for breakfast, coffee and dates, and had to hide under our blankets all morning – very uncomfortable. Boiled rice and tomato for tiffin with coffee. Had wash and shampoo in afternoon. (wizard). Rice again for dinner with goat's milk and coffee and so to bed. Our rears and hip bones are quite sore with all this sitting and lying about. The only time we can obey the calls of nature is during the hours of darkness. Very awkward.

Rained most of day and night ….

12th Day: Thursday 17 December: Had a bad night last night. Many bites and much scratching. Woke up at 0550 to find it teeming with rain and the tent full of goats.

1000: Two German armoured cars came to the village. Great panic – hid us under boxes and huge piles of rugs – very uncomfortable – nearly smothered us. They took three of Ali's sheep. As soon as the armoured cars had gone they took us about three miles outside the village and hid us behind some bushes and left us with instructions to keep low. We heard the armoured cars patrolling around us all day. One came very close, about 200 yards, we could hear them talking. The weather was glorious.

1850: Msud came to take us back to the village. He told us the Germans had taken another nine sheep. On nearing the village we saw they were driving all the sheep and goats out and also evacuating the women and children. Armoured cars were still patrolling about the place and so we assumed the role of shepherds and got well away from the village driving the sheep and goats until midnight, when we were absolutely exhausted. We have only had dates to eat today, but there was plenty of water ....

14th Day: Saturday, 19 December: Mahommed and Msud went away at dawn and we lay low again. Our only food was dates and German bread. We heard armoured cars again, one came within 400 yards. We afterwards discovered it was probably British. The weather still kept fine. Kittys still bombing but further west.

1100: Ali returned with some more dates, German bread and water, and went away almost immediately on recce.

1430: Ali, Mahommed and Msud returned with glad tidings for us. They had sighted eight British armoured cars about fifteen kilos south of us, but they had gone off before they could reach them. Ali had an Army greatcoat that had been left behind. The Germans were still in the coastal region north of us. Ali lit a fire, made us some tea and then they all went off promising to return at night. They had not turned up by 10 p.m. so we lay down and tried to get some sleep.

15th Day: Sunday, 20 December: 0280: Ali, Mahommed and Msud returned with all our kit. They made a fire, brewed some chai and produced some very nice boiled mutton for us. (Presumably the remains of the sheep the Germans had stolen.)

0300: Suitably refreshed we set off with very light hearts and walked until six when they found another river bed for us to hide in. They went off at 7 o'clock to find the British and returned at 11 with an armoured car belonging to H.Q. Troop 'B' Squadron, 1st King's Dragoon Guards. They took us to their Field H.Q. and gave us a hot meal – words can't describe it. They sent us on by lorry to a New Zealand Brigade H.Q. where we had a nip of whisky – our first drink since crashing and gave us a wizard meal. We still had the Arabs with us and they were fixed up pretty well. We slept at the ADS that night. They treated us extremely well, provided hot water for us to have a good tub down, clean pyjamas and stretchers to sleep on with lots of blankets. We were in heaven.

16th Day: Monday 21 December: We had breakfast in bed and then set out by car for Division HQ at Nofilia, still taking the Arabs with us. We arrived in time for lunch and afterwards were interrogated. They also interrogated the Arabs and got information about water wells and the terrain, etc. The Arabs were given 2000 lire and promises of tea, sugar, biscuits, etc. which the A.L.O. (S/Ldr. O'Day) was to bring back with him from Marble Arch the following day. He took us to 211 Wing at Marble Arch that afternoon in his car. They treated us very well and put us up for the night, and arranged that we should go back the following morning by Hudson.

17th Day: Tuesday, 22 December: Had breakfast and were interviewed by Press correspondents. Had photographs taken and made record for radio. Then back by Hudson to Berca via Agedabia arriving just in time for a beer and tiffin.

In Cairo they were made members of the 'Late Arrivals Club' and were presented with certificates and a silver winged badge, known as the Flying Boot to wear on their battle dress blouse. When Armstrong arrived back in England he had six months off operations when he joined 235 Squadron, flying Beaufighters, then Mosquitos on anti-shipping sorties, completing tour of operations and ending his flying with 99 operations in his log book.

On 26 November 1944 Tom Armstrong, now a flight lieutenant, was recommended for an immediate DFC by the officer commanding RAF Banff, Group Captain Max Aitken, former Battle of Britain pilot and later Sir Max Aitken, head of the Beaverbrook newspaper organisation. In his recommendation his tour of the Western Desert was mentioned, also his being wounded on 28 July 1941 when attacked by three enemy fighters and his aircraft damaged. It also mentioned his evasion in December 1942.

One must give the Arabs the greatest credit for their bravery in helping Allied servicemen as they did in World War II, particularly the Senussi tribes, who risked a great deal in this work and asked little in return.

XI

The Far East and the Pacific

The war with the Japanese was entirely different in tenor to that in the West, since the Japanese did not observe the Geneva Convention regarding the treatment of POWs. Moreover, it being the ultimate crime in the Japanese book to surrender and the greatest dishonour a man could undergo, it followed that prisoners were held beneath contempt and treated accordingly. There was little incentive to escape, however. Not only was the terrain the other side of the world from home, but the natives were unlikely to be friendly, and, worst of all, death was the probable penalty after recapture, and a similar fate was meted out to all helpers or even non-helpers in the camp. After the re-entry in Burma, the native populaces became more friendly to the British and evasion there became more possible. Nevertheless certain limited help was given to those who had the will and the luck to escape or evade. At the fall of Hong Kong Lt Colonel Sir Leslie Ride set up a British Army Aid Group in Hong-Kong with the help of the anti-Japanese Chinese Communist party, and achieved not only aid to a limited number of escapers from POW camp in Hong Kong, but also a great deal of useful intelligence. In New Delhi MI9 had an advance base, working with Clarke in Cairo, which in 1943 became known as E Group. It supplied escape aids to aircrew on a much grander scale than in the West, organised search and rescue parties, and passed on information about the whereabouts of POW camps so that later in the war bombing raids could be avoided in those areas.

The fall of Singapore in February 1942 raised an enormous

problem. In 1941 a lieutenant-colonel of Marines, Alan Warren, in Singapore to organise guerilla activity behind the Japanese lines, realised that should Singapore fall there might be thousands of army personnel needing an escape route and he set one up across Sumatra to the port of Padang. In the event it was used by civilians and service personnel, but sadly in many cases either the ships were sunk en route or the evaders were recaptured.

*

1.   Cat and Mouse on New Britain

On 3 November 1943, 11 Beaufighters from 30 Squadron, five Bostons of 22 Squadron and fighter cover of Kittyhawks of 77 Squadron, led by Wing Commander W.S. Arthur, were ordered to make a combined attack on a plantation at Palmalmal, on the south-east coast of New Britain Island at Jacquinot Bay. This all-Australian group, which left Goodenough Island at dawn arrived over the target at 7.20 a.m. The Bostons were carrying 500 lb bombs and were led by Wing Commander Bill Townsend, a 27-year old regular airman from Hawthorn, Victoria. His wireless operator was Flying Officer David McClymont from Sydney.

Their target was a bridge west of the house on the plantation. They went towards the house then swung toward the bridge and levelled over it, hoping to confuse the enemy into thinking they were attacking the house.

As Townsend, flying at a speed of 260 mph in Boston A28/29, pressed the bomb quadrant release switch, his aircraft was hit by ground fire which passed through the open bomb bay doors and exploded in the fuselage. A twin barrel type 96 25mm machine cannon probably scored the mortal blow. The explosion set the bomb bay tank alight, destroying the hydraulic system and the wireless electrical system and all the fuel cocks and controls simply disappeared. Their air speed carried them a few miles and Townsend held the aircraft off the water until it completely stalled. He saw a submerged reef and put the aircraft down on it so that they would be in shallow

water rather than deep. The aircraft was put down as it was –
without flaps and with the bomb doors open. The pilot pulled
the tail down, causing the aircraft to aquaplane along the surface
of the water for 150 yards before plunging and coming to a halt.
The coral reef on which they settled was six to eight feet below
the surface, about 200 yards offshore, near the village of Mollo-
kut, and the crew found themselves up to their necks in water.

Townsend was worried that the escape hatch might have
buckled in the crash. He reported: 'It must have taken us 15
minutes to paddle ashore as we lost one of the paddles about half
way in. These paddles were a glove type which are pulled onto
the hand. The water was much deeper between the plane and
the beach, and had we crashed 10 yards to the west, the plane
would probably have submerged immediately.'

David McClymont had been wounded in the left arm which
did not help their progress in paddling. One escorting Kitty-
hawk was also hit and later crashed into the sea, with the loss of
its pilot. Townsend continued:

'There was no beach at the place where we landed but a low
bank about three feet high. The trees grew to the water's edge.
We removed from the dinghy the ground sheet, rations, cord,
fishing lines, and emergency tins of water. We then deflated the
dinghy by cutting it, and hid it as well as we could. Later, we
learned that a friendly native who arrived before the Japs, rehid
it more thoroughly. The Japs did not find it as the natives later
reported that it was still hidden.

'This native also covered up all our tracks as the Japs, after
searching the area, suggested to the natives that we must have
perished, being eaten by the sharks. The Japs believed that there
were four men in the plane rather than two. The native had not
actually seen us and he could not understand how we vanished
so quickly. The Japs came only a few minutes after we started
inland and we could hear them shouting in the bush behind us.
The same native tried to overtake us in order to guide us to his
Luluai, but he was unable to follow our tracks when we reached
ground that was covered with a thick layer of leaves. The Japs
questioned him, but he truthfully had not seen us.'

They headed west for several days, over the mountains. He

reported, 'During this trip, as most of the streams were dry, we drank water from bamboo and pools in the dry creek beds. We rationed our supplies to make them last as long as possible, as we couldn't find anything in the jungle to eat, even though we had the booklet, *Friendly Fruits and Vegetables*. During that time, we managed to light only two fires as the wood was very wet.

'We took quinine each day, and found the iodine very essential for cuts. I had a blister on my left toe the first day, but taped it up immediately and had no more trouble with it. We also used the mosquito repellant, but we were not bothered with mosquitoes after the second day because we were getting up into the mountains.'

After three days' travelling the airmen were in the clouds and could see for no distance at all and so were unable to take bearings. On the sixth day they came to a dried-up river bed and decided to follow its southward course; this they did for 2½ days before reaching a junction. They then proceeded westwards for about 1½ miles until they reached a waterfall, where they camped for the night.

Rations were by now very low but the pool at the base of the falls provided their first bath. The pool also contained small fish but they had no luck in catching these. Driftwood was used for fires to boil the billy.

Then it was on the march again, led by the headman. Townsend reported:

'On the tenth day, we explored up and down the stream. At a point about ½ a mile below the falls, we spent the afternoon climbing to the ridge where we stayed the night in an old native lean-to. The next morning, we travelled on a path about seven miles southward. At this southern point we thought we must be getting close to the coast, so we retraced our steps almost to the camp site of the previous night. On 12 November, we went north-westward along the trail and found an old overgrown garden in which we found paw paws and green bananas. The trail improved nearer the village. We arrived at a native village. It was raining hard that day, and was very cold at that elevation. We were rather well received, although the natives were a bit amazed. We read our Pidgin phrases which they understood, but they laughed at us a lot while we were talking. Then we suggested some Kai Kai. The natives cooked some bananas, taro, and brought drinking water. They agreed to take us to a friendly chief, who turned out to be an old boss boy.

'On Sunday, 14th November, we left for another village, led by the head man, a former Mission boy. Here we had a very good feed. We were given "Tabiac belong Masta", a very good food, similar to the custard apple, about 4″ in diameter, with a dark green skin. The white flesh is in globules with large black seeds. It tastes like fruit salad and ice cream. A similar fruit is "Tabiac belong boy" which is not so good or as large. Most of the boys spoke good Pidgin. There was a Jap sign on one of the huts which had been posted by a patrol some weeks before.

'The Tul Tul told us that night, about a chief being "No.1 belong Australia", and told us where he was located. The next day he implied that "No.1", had issued instructions that any airmen found should be brought to him, and that he would take us there the next day.'

So, on 15 November the group left early in the morning and followed a good trail to the south-east. In the afternoon gunfire was heard and Townsend's group became nervous that they were being led into a trap. The Luluai, however, reassured them and that evening they reached a coastal village where they again met sympathetic natives who provided food and drink. Razor blades were bartered for these, much to the natives' delight! A general meeting was held at which the natives decided on the best way to conduct the group to their next destination. On 16 November a boy took them to another village where they remained until the 18th, by which time 'No.1' had heard where they were and had sent a message to say he would meet them at the mouth of a stream on the coast.

At this time, 'No.1' or Golpak, to give him his proper name, was about 60 years old. He spoke Pidgin but no English. He had been in Rabaul as a boy of fourteen, as a plantation labourer under the Germans, and later a boss-boy on an Australian plantation. When he retired from work he became 'Luluai' (chief or headman) of his village and several years before the war had been appointed paramount Luluai of the

Mengen group of villages.

The evening of 18 November found the group in yet another village. Townsend takes up the story:

'The Luluai took us about a mile into the bush, where his people built us a home complete with dishes and silverware. It was then that he told us about the guns and white soldiers, and also about a party. I sent a note on 20 November to this party, saying where we were and that we were making no attempt to join the party as it might jeopardize their position. At this time, the Japs were putting pressure onto this Luluai and his men, to try and find out where the white men were located. There was to be a big jap "Talk-Talk", but this Luluai and one other didn't go, claiming they were sick ....

'The Japs jailed all the people of two villages, but a picinini escaped from them and ran to our hut to tell us what had happened. The Luluai used his strategy and moved us all south-eastward to the end of a peninsula instead of going deeper into the bush. He insisted that we walk barefooted in order to disguise our tracks. This was very unpleasant and our feet were cut rather badly by the coral in the peninsula.

'We climbed the first range of hills and established a rough camp, remaining here until about 0530 hours on 8th December. We were awakened that morning by rifle fire from the Jap police boys. The enemy had been led into the camp by some of the native boys who had been beaten by police boys and Japs until they revealed our position.'

One of the police boys came rushing into the camp, shooting, and Townsend and his group escaped in the uproar, running down toward the sea. From there they were led to a small cave where they remained until 17 December. The Luluai's daughter cooked the food at night so that the smoke would not reveal the hiding place.

On 17 December, by which time it was obvious that the Japanese were not going to release the villagers and that the Luluai was considered a fugitive, the evaders were once more on the move, this time further inland and to the north to a new village, built by the natives in order to escape from the Japanese. A reply from Major Fred Hargesheimer of the party at the coastwatching station was awaiting them there, saying it would be best for Townsend's group to join up with them. On 19 December Townsend's group headed towards the main party's camp, using a very old track, and arrived on the 20th. The next day they left and, accompanied by Hargesheimer, walked for 5½ hours to reach his camp, where they stayed until 1 February.

Then came a messsage to the effect that, if the airmen could be at a certain position on 5 February, they would be evacuated. After walking for four days without sleep, Townsend, McClymount and Hargesheimer were stumbling up a beach when they suddenly spotted a submarine about 1,000 yards offshore. With the aid of another group of coastwatchers, torch signals were flashed and USS *Gato*, under the command of Captain R.J. Foley, acknowledged. Small boats were despatched to effect a transfer and following a rough boat ride, the evaders climbed aboard the submarine. They remained submerged until dusk as the sub continued its patrol, Captain Foley wanting to show the airmen some action. They, however, had had enough!

After the Australian Force arrived in 1945 and occupied the area of Townsend's crash, parts of his aircraft were returned and a small stud box was made up. Bill Townsend, who rose to the rank of Air Vice Marshal, kept that box until his death. In 1982 the wreckage of his aircraft was revisited. It was lying in about 22 feet of water on the lagoon side of the reef. It was facing east and still had two unexploded 500lb bombs lying only yards from the wreck. At high tide the aircraft was lifted right out of the water. On examination it was found that 2-25mm shells had passed through one wing without exploding; some forty odd years later. Bill Townsend was surprised to learn he had crash-landed with two bombs still in the bomb bay.

Golpak continued his work throughout the war and afterwards became a successful businessman and was awarded the MBE. In 1959, he died, age 70 and with numerous contributions, including one from the RAF Escaping Society, a small memorial to him was erected at Jacquinot Bay on 6 May

1961. In 1961 an idea came to Fred Hargesheimer for a school which was badly needed by the villagers. To build one would cost about 15,000 dollars. It took two and half years to raise, but in 1964 the Airmen's Memorial School was unveiled at Ewasse, the village where he and Townsend first met. Today they are both trustees of the school and its first teacher was none other than Golpak's son Koulia who 18 years earlier, had sounded the alarm of the Japs entering the village.

The Australian Branch of the RAF Escaping Society of which Bill Townsend was for some time President, assisted with the donations for a dormitory to accommodate the children who could get home only at weekends. In addition to setting up the fund to build the school, Fred and his wife, Dorothy, spent four years teaching at the school.

Bill Townsend went on to become Deputy Chief of the Air Staff in Australia and served in Vietnam. Sadly, in April 1987, Bill after a long illness, fought with the same tenacity as his evasion in the jungle, died. The appointment of a new acting President of the Australian Branch of the RAF Escaping Society has been made. He is Philip Laughton-Bramley, now 87 years old, who was taught to fly by Blériot, and a man who knows more about the Escaping Society and organisation than anyone else. I am sure that Bill Townsend could not wish for anyone better to follow him.

2.   Evasion from New Britain

On 7 February 1944 Squadron Leader J.E. Todd took off from Darwin in Catalina A2434 of 11 RAAF Squadron on a night bombing mission to Kavieng, New Ireland, with Flying Officer Ian Ralfe as second pilot. Ian Ralfe recorded in the interrogation report of 15 April 1944:

'We were the sole aircraft on this mission, a nuisance raid just to keep the Japs awake, and to do as much damage as we could to airdromes and shore installations.

'At approximately 2300 hours we approached the target in bright moonlight. Before we made our first run over the panapai strip, we were flying at an altitude of 9,000 feet. No bombs were dropped on the first run and the A/A fire was light. On the second run over panapai, the two 250lb bombs and numerous incendiaries were tossed out and photographs were taken.'

However, they had been hit in the tail plane and fin by the ack-ack fire. As they were flying over New Britain, Todd instructed Sergeant Harry Jones, the armourer, to bring the three reconnaissance flares from the blister to the bunk compartment. They had been set to go off at 5,000 feet but Todd told Jones to change the setting to 4,000 feet. As he turned the setting ring, a stream of sparks flowed out from the flare similar to a Roman candle. There was a lull then the flare, full of magnesium, exploded. Flying Officer Liedl, who was in the blister at the time, saw a thin trickle of smoke coming out and then sparks and jumped into the bunk room to try to throw the flare out of the aircraft. Sergeant Howards had seen this, too, and opened the blister to make it possible for Liedl to throw it out, but just as he picked it up, it exploded, burning his face, eyes and hands. The force from the heat and the explosion forced Liedl and Jones out of the bunk compartment and into the blister. Flight Lieutenant B.P. Stacy, who was extra second pilot, was also forced back which meant that all four were trapped. Everything in the bunk caught fire including the two remaining flares. The other members of the crew tried to extinguish the blaze, as did Jones in the blister, but the fire seemed to increase rather than diminish. To add to this, they were almost suffocated by black smoke from the burning rubber of the dinghy which was kept in the bunk compartment and which had also caught fire.

An SOS was sent out on the radio, telling of their predicament, as the fire had now spread to the engineer's compartment, and the first engineer, Sergeant Woolley, advised Todd that the aircraft was in danger of breaking in two in the air. Todd then made a rapid crash landing about 50 yards from the shore. As it hit the water, the aircraft swung to the right and rose 50 feet in the air. The fire by this time was raging intensely and ammunition and sea markers were exploding. Todd instructed everyone to abandon the aircraft, and they waded ashore at Malakua, hiding behind rocks to avoid the exploding ammunition.

Once they had sorted themselves out, Todd and Ralfe set out to find a place to spend the night and Jones and Woolley went back to the burning aircraft to destroy classified equipment, code books etc. They brought back small water tanks and a thermos of cold tea and also a pair of binoculars. The cold tea was used as a burn application for some of the crew. They kept a careful guard and next day saw three natives. Two ran away on seeing them; the third a boy, came up to them. The flight report continues:

'He told us that the Japs had seen the aircraft crash in flames and had sent him to look for us. He advised us to get away from the beach back to an abandoned plantation and there hide. This native spoke quite good English, and among the things he said to us was: "Why the hell didn't you get out of here last night". He seemed very frightened of the Japs and appeared anxious to leave us. He told us that had there been four instead of ten of us, he might have been able to hide us himself. He told us that the Japs had made slaves of the kanakas in this area and had them working on a big road a few miles east.'

They decided to retreat into the interior but suddenly 'we heard sound of Jap commands from the direction of the beach. Some of us were certain that the commands were in English and were "Halt ... one ... two". From this we gathered that our two guards had been jumped by the Japs and taken prisoners. We heard no shots fired. The remaining members of the crew immediately gathered the equipment which was lying on the ground and dashed into the bush in approximately a northwesterly direction, with the exception of F/Lt. Stacy who ran approximately north-east. He was entirely without equipment and was never seen or heard by any of us thereafter, nor was any news ever learned from the natives concerning his fate.'

The remaining seven members of the crew came together about 100 yards further into the bush and then split up into two parties: Todd led one off to the west and Ralfe took the other in a north-westerly direction. Ralfe reported: 'We proceeded for 2½ days into the mountains living the entire time on palm trees and one paw paw from a deserted and overgrown garden. The first day we travelled away from the beach we were for the most part in swamps. We then came through some low mountainous country where sufficient palms and water vines to sustain us could be found. But, after proceeding past this narrow stretch, we reached extremely rocky country, full of dry gullies and lacking both in food and water. It was apparent that we could not exist on the land in such a region. As we were making our way into the interior, we had found it necessary to cross a fairly wide crocodile-infested river. This we did by tying several logs together with the shroud lines of our parachute.'

They decided to turn back and make for the coast, continuing from there in a south-westerly direction toward the Allied beachhead. Soon after turning back they came upon a native trail leading in a south-easterly direction and, despite having decided to travel south-west, they followed it. In 3½ hours they arrived back at the clearing where they had seen a Japanese rice tin earlier!! They elected then to make camp on one side of the bay and build a fire on the other.

During their stay in the clearing, Jones shot a pig and Liedl a bush fowl. The former was eaten with relish and the latter kept in reserve. Ralfe made several attempts to increase the food supply by shooting fish, with no success. Even baited safety pins proved no attraction and a spear was no more effective. On the third day, a Jap river patrol in two canoes came up the river. 'The Japs jumped out as did one of the natives and the other native remained in the canoe and paddled swiftly downstream,' reported Ralfe. 'Within five or six minutes a large canoe with eight Nips and two natives came around the bend into the bay followed by the other native in the small canoe. They had obviously seen our fire, and, as we saw them approach, we dived into the swamp in back of the clearing without attempting to recover our equipment (a parachute, the medical kit, one knife, and much of our clothing), which was back in the main camp.

'We made our way through the sac sac swamps, and then, to throw the Japs off our trail, we forded the river. We struck a southwesterly course toward the coast and kept to it for approximately four days. We had to travel through unbelievably rough country: mountains, swamps, swollen rivers and creeks. During this time we had no food other than the palms and one malted milk tablet every other day for each of us. We were able to save our atabrine and took one tablet every other day. After four days we reached a Jap road near the coast. We spent the night in a deserted village.'

They decided to risk staying there and 'the next morning, we found a large native canoe on the beach. The canoe was in a dilapidated state, the outrigger having rotted through, and the canoe itself having been holed through by borers. We decided to repair this canoe and fill it full of coconuts. Then we would sneak down the coast by night and hide along the beach during the day with the intention of making our way down to our lines.'

Attempts were made to plug the holes in the canoe, which, however, proved too heavy for the quartet to paddle, and was abandoned. By this time insect bites and scratches were becoming infected and large sores appeared on their bodies.

Natives came down to the deserted village and bartered food for safety pins. They had evacuated the village and moved to another, new one further back in the mountains, coming back only to collect food from the gardens in the old village. The first group left and at about 8 p.m. two others arrived who were able to communicate to the airmen that the Japanese were only four miles distant and were on their way back to the village the following day. The next day the crew moved to the new village which they reached after four hours' walking. The natives told them of the presence of a white party on the north side of the island and agreed to take the RAF men there, a seven day journey. At the natives' suggestion the four stayed on at the village for three days to give them a chance to recover their strength, which they did to a certain degree, although the sores on their bodies became considerably worse. After the respite, the natives decided to send ahead to the white party for assistance. Then: 'We continued on, and, by easy stages but through extremely difficult country, we made our way to the north side of the mountain ranges. The natives dispatched by the white party reached us after about four days bringing with them European food, clothing, medical supplies and all the equipment we needed, as well as a cook boy and doctor boy. By this time, our number of natives had grown from 18 to 85 because all the natives seemed to know of the presence of the white party and were anxious to join us in our efforts to reach them. After six days one of the members of the white party came out and met us. We were forced to remain with him at the spot where we met for some time due to F/O Liedl's condition, and a fever which a member of the white party had contracted; but eventually on or about 4 or 5 March, the three of us excepting F/O Liedl, joined up with the white party. F/O Liedl and the white man who came out to meet us reached us approximately a week later, having been delayed by their illnesses.'

This white party turned out to be three Australian officers and one sergeant, plus three native police boys who had been dropped many months before for intelligence work, by submarine. Their camp was in the mountains and overlooked the main Jap base. The Japs knew they were there but had failed on several occasions to capture them. Malcolm Wright and Lou Searle had lived in the area pre-war and knew the natives of the Nakanai tribe. Over a hundred of this tribe were armed with .303 rifles, shot guns and hand grenades, which had been dropped weekly by Flying Fortresses. They regularly ambushed the Japs. The jungle and mountains terrain of the area was very rugged and with his native force Wright was able to keep the Japs at bay. Any Jap patrols who came looking for them were mostly ambushed and wiped out.

During the many weeks they stayed with them Ralfe and his party did their share of intelligence work and trained the natives to shoot. Eventually they were taken to New Britain by two US patrol boats, which stole in one night by prior arrangement, to a deserted beach.

To get to this beach they had to get through Jap lines but this, with the help of the natives, went without a hitch. It was a case of being with the right people. The Coast Watchers Force, as their party were called, survived the war and later Wright wrote a book about his experiences.

Ralfe returned to Australia and completed another tour of operations, for a year, with No.2 RAAF Squadron. Of the six members of the crew who were captured only Flight Lieutenant Stacy survived, he had been sent to a POW camp in Japan. The others were kept in a camp at Rabaul, where they were either executed or died of disease or ill treatment. Squadron Leader Todd and his party, were also captured after separating from Ralfe's group. Todd died of illness while a POW on 22 July 1944. The other four, according to the Japanese, were killed by Allied bombing while imprisoned at Talili.

3.   In the Bay of Bengal

On 27 August 1944 Pilot Officer Rupert Horwood, an Australian, and his navigator, Wireless Operator Charles Bateman, of 177 Squadron, were detailed to take part in strafing operations along the Burma-Siam railway in the area of Moulmein to Anankwin. They took off at 11 a.m. along with three other Beaufighters and on reaching the target were soon in action, attacking a train at Thanbyuzayat. Then their aircraft was hit in the starboard engine by Japanese light anti-aircraft fire. It was now 2 p.m. and they were at a height of 50 feet. The aircraft in front was also hit in the port engine and the pilot called up to say he was returning to base. Both aircraft turned back together. Horwood's Beau had been hit in the starboard oil tank, which was holed and oil was pouring from the engine. Finally, at 2.30 p.m. it cut out altogether. Horwood set a course for Rangoon Bay and managed on one engine to climb to 1,500 feet.

Horwood reported: 'We flew on one motor some 530 miles and were forced to ditch in the sea approximately 10 miles off the Arakan coast in Burma, not far from the then border of India (Bengal).'

The starboard engine generator had stopped and as a result there was no VHF or wireless; the accumulators were nearly flat. The aircraft was ditched at about 1800 hours, when it broke up in the swell, but remained afloat for about 1½ minutes. The dinghy inflated and both officers swam to it and climbed aboard, Bateman wearing his Beadon suit and Horwood slacks and a long-sleeved shirt. He had, however, managed to grab his parachute bag which contained his Beadon suit and Bateman had a compass and a silk map. Horwood had struck his head on the reflector sight and Bateman was slightly wounded in the face and shoulder.

During the night they drifted in the general direction of the island of Akyab and by morning, considered they were about two miles off the north-west coast. They paddled for a time, making little progress, until a storm blew up and carried them seaward to the south-east, when they lost sight of land. When the wind changed direction they were blown past the south of Oyster Island, which they tried, without success, to reach. Rain now added to the general discomfort of their condition and the protection provided by the dinghy was useless. At one point an aircraft passed overhead and they fired their Very pistol, without being spotted. By nightfall they were somewhere south-east of Oyster Island.

The next day they again saw land but were unsure as to whether it was the Mayu Peninsula or the Boronga Islands, and another day was passed in great discomfort, due to storms. About mid-morning, two aircraft passed overhead but again the firing of the pistol brought no response. On trying for a third time to fire the pistol, this time at a Beaufighter passing overhead late in the afternoon, they discovered that the wet had penetrated the cartridges, causing them to swell, so that they would not fit the breech. They were now powerless to attract attention by signalling.

By now, exhaustion and pain from sores caused by the

seawater were adding to their discomfort, and they could do little except drift, this time in a north-westerly direction. At about 2100 hours they recognised the point of Kyaukpandu and paddled towards it. The surf around the island was very heavy and swamped the dinghy which, however, stayed afloat and was washed ashore after about 20 minutes. On staggering on to land both Horwood and Bateman found great difficulty in standing up, eventually succeeded in moving the contents of the dinghy and then the dinghy itself up on to a ledge. Their feeling was that they were probably behind Japanese lines.

As they were concealing the dinghy, a patrol of five men walked down the beach, about 50 yards away, so the two airmen stayed in hiding until they had passed, when they made themselves as comfortable as possible and fell asleep.

The following morning they approached some natives who were in a field behind the beach. They made the airmen conceal themselves during the day, covering them with brushwood and bushes and explaining that the Japanese were in Alethangyaw, not too far distant. This meant that Horwood and Bateman were about 10 to 12 miles from the British positions. After a most uncomfortable day, during which they received food and cigarettes from the native sympathisers, they were led to the British lines, where transport was arranged for them. They arrived at Cox's Bazaar at the beginning of September.

Rupert Horwood later received the DFC.

4. Jungle Evasion

In 1945, 47 Squadron were operating DH Mosquito fighter-bombers from Khumbirgram in Assam. Flying Officer Eric Fisher was one of those who found himself having to bale out over the Arakan jungle.

On 14 April he was flying as navigator to Flight Lieutenant

A.E. Scott, a Canadian. Leading another Mosquito they took off at 8.30 a.m. to attack a suspected petrol/bomb dump at Toungoo, 200 miles north of Rangoon. They arrived in the target area about two hours later and although they were unable to identify the target, they made four low-level runs. As they climbed away on the fifth a 20mm cannon shell came through the port side of the aircraft and burst on Flight Lieutenant Scott's side. Fisher recollects:

'He ordered a bale out but as we were climbing to the north and he was obviously badly injured, I delayed, knowing that his only chance lay in getting back over the bomb-line to Mandalay. Almost immediately the port engine caught fire and I baled out at around 4,000 feet. Flight Lieutenant Scott got out at about 800 feet.'

Fisher landed safely in a clearing but Scott was not so fortunate and was observed suspended from a tree. Fisher, after getting rid of his parachute, headed north, hoping to link up with Scott, unaware of the pilot's plight. Suddenly Fisher heard whistle blasts ahead, which he assumed came from Japanese soldiers maintaining contact, so he turned about and picked up a trail heading south.

He recalls: 'After a short while I entered a clearing where an elderly gentleman was gathering wood. With sign language, and what appeared obvious, I asked for assistance and he led me on down the path. We eventually came to a small village where by good fortune the headman spoke English having received an education at Rangoon University.'

Fisher stayed in that village for nearly a week, hiding during the day in the jungle and returning at dusk to sleep. By now the Japanese were retreating in fair numbers and it was decided for the safety of the villagers that Fisher should leave. On the fifth night he left the village in a donkey cart, accompanied by a guide from the Burmese 'Freedom Fighters' operating in the area.

Fisher's memory is still fresh: 'We travelled all night and eventually arrived at an informal camp occupied by men, women and children who had been forced to leave their villages. We moved around during the day and at night the men appeared to go off harassing the enemy – I was not allowed to join in!'

After another week had passed news came that the British Army were moving south on the road to Rangoon so the party marched east and eventually arrived – a motley crew! – on the road. General Messervy* happened to be going down in his jeep and he was somewhat surprised to find an airman so far from home. He arranged for the sick and wounded Burmese to be transported to the local hospital while Eric Fisher was taken to the nearest airstrip and flown out. He arrived back with the squadron on 27 April.

From the official records, Scott and Fisher were flying a Mosquito, letter 'K' and were hit by flak over the target area. A black object was seen to fall from the aircraft and was thought at the time to be a bird. The aircraft then became unstable and liquid was seen pouring from the port engine, which was observed to be on fire. The aircraft began to climb as the pilot obviously tried to put the fire out, then the navigator was seen to bale out, followed by the pilot. The pilot landed in a tree and the navigator in a clearing.

When Eric Fisher arrived back after evading capture with the help of natives he said a shell had hit the aircraft and nearly blown Scott's arm off. Sadly he did not survive and later died from loss of blood when found by a friendly native. The area they had baled out in was eight miles west-south-west of Yedashe, and the aircraft had crashed about 200 yards away from where he had landed.

---

* Lieutenant General Sir Frank Messervy KBE CB DSO, Commander of 4 Corps, British Army, knighted for his command of the 7th Indian Division in the Arakan, 1943-44.

5.   Twenty-Three Days in the Jungle

In January 1945, 28 Tactical Reconnaissance Squadron was based at Kaleymo in the Kaban Valley, Burma. Flight Lieutenant R.G. Johnson was commanding 'A' Flight. He had previously been in the Fort Garry Horse, Canadian Army, having enlisted in September 1939. In 1940 he applied for re-enlistment in the RCAF; this became effective on 1st January 1941.

After qualifying as a pilot Bob was given a commission as a pilot officer in October 1941 and from January 1942 to April 1943 he served with 123 RCAF Squadron in Nova Scotia. He was then sent to England and then India where, in November 1943, he arrived at 28 Squadron where he stayed until March 1945.

Johnson took off from Kaleymo on the morning of 14 January to carry out a reconnaissance flight of roads, bridges and waterways in the Pokakku-Pagan area along the Irrawaddy river. The object was to determine the Japanese lines of communication over which troop and supplies were being transported. His No.2 was Flight Lieutenant Gavin Douglas, an experienced pilot but on his first operational mission. The low-level flight was uneventful until Johnson saw movement a short distance south of Pagan. While checking it out, he felt two impacts on his aircraft and knew he had been hit by fairly heavy flak. Glycol was spraying through a hole in the aircraft between his feet; a quick check of the instrument panel showed a height of about 1,500 feet, temperature rising and oil pressure almost zero. Smoke was also coming from the engine. Johnson told Douglas he had been hit and headed north-west. Ground conditions looked too rough for a crash landing so he decided to bale out. In his own words:

'I told Douglas by radio of my intention and just before I pulled the wireless plug I heard him say, "Good luck, old chap". I was losing height but stayed with it until I was passing over a village on the west bank of the Yaw C. At that point I was very low so jettisoned the canopy and tried to climb out. I had difficulty standing up so jettisoned the escape panel on the starboard side and rolled out. I saw the tailplane pass in front of my face then pulled the ripcord. It seemed only a second or so until I landed with a jar and tumbled sideways. I was on top of a ridge with a deep gully to the north. My pistol was missing, probably caught on the aircraft as I rolled out. I snapped off my escape kit from under the parachute seat cushion and ran to the west along the ridge. Within a few minutes I heard voices so I went into the gully. The wireless cord was a bother so I yanked the earphones from my helmet and stuffed mask, cord and phones into a hole in the ground. I ran west along the gully. About five minutes later I heard a lot of yelling then saw people about 500 yards away running toward me along the ridge on the north side of the gully. There were others on the south ridge ahead of me. I climbed the north ridge and slid down a steep slope, the only cover was low scrub bush. By chance I slid into a shallow depression in the hillside, eighteen inches or so deep and the bush was more dense at this location. I burrowed in, pulling the foliage over me, then remained motionless. The voices were suddenly loud and very close. I carefully slid my knife out but otherwise did not move. People came so close I thought they would hear my heart pounding but I was not discovered. At one point I looked up the hill and saw a Japanese soldier with rifle on top of the ridge. The talking and shouting would sometimes be close to me and sometimes at a distance and there was also the barking of dogs. I decided to stay under cover until dark and during the long wait I debated with myself the pro and con of surrendering or fighting if I should be discovered. I decided that if there was only one I would try to silence him quickly but otherwise I'd surrender and hope for the best. It was an immense relief when darkness came and all was quiet.'

Johnson waited another hour or so then climbed a ridge and followed it west, moving cautiously and stopping at frequent intervals to listen. He came to a village, gave it a wide berth and continued on rough terrain until the glimmer of first light in the sky made him seek a hiding place. This was a cave-like space in the roots of a dead tree which he checked out for snakes and then crawled into.

He dozed off and on, hearing occasionally the sounds of

aircraft in the near distance, probably Hurricanes from 28 Squadron. He then turned his mind to his escape kit which he had actually devised and equipped himself, and which contained Horlicks tablets, Benzedrine tablets, chewing gum, salt tablets, fish line and hooks, needle and thread, mepacrine tablets, water sterilising crystals, bandages and sulpha powder. He also had a bar of hard chocolate, a canvas water chargal, a flashlight and batteries, a money belt containing Indian rupees, a magnifying glass, a metal mirror, maps and compasses. His leather boots, thick woollen socks and tropical weight battle dress would stand him in good stead. He calculated he would have to cover 100 miles and had supplies for 31 days.

His first task was to find water as he found it hard to swallow his mepacrine tablet 'dry'. Chewing grass and roots did little to alleviate his discomfort and Horlicks tablets did not satisfy his hunger. Having studied his map he waited until it was truly dark before starting out. The first stream bed he came to was dry and digging to a depth of 2-3 feet produced no moisture. This situation was repeated at two further stream beds during the night and by morning, Johnson was tired and discouraged. He found a fairly dense clump of bush and settled down for the day.

Johnson recollects:

'It was now the 4th day and it was obvious I had not travelled the number of miles as planned. Digging for water took a lot of time and by this time my fingers were raw and sore. I was afraid of infection. As well, it had been necessary to stop to rest frequently the previous night. I decided not to dig for water as it seemed of no avail and I would then be able to cover more ground. I set off again after dark and had walked only an hour or so when I had to stop for a rest. I do not remember starting up again but suddenly found myself stumbling along and shortly came to the terrifying realization the kit was not on my back. I was in a state of panic and alternately cursed and cried as I searched for it. I eventually calmed down and started a systematic search trying to retrace my steps in a series of square search patterns. It must have been about 3 hours later that I found some of my tracks in sand and there was the kit in the place I had stopped to rest. At this point my curses changed to prayers and I was so exhausted I fell asleep and did not awaken till daylight.

'I had been keeping track of the days by making marks on the map and continued to do so although I don't remember much of the next 3 days and nights. My tongue was swollen, my throat parched and I seemed to have a continuous high temperature. It was after midnight on the 7th night when I came upon a bullock cart track which ran north and south. I followed it north and soon realized I was walking in soft mud. I hurried along and soon found myself in water a few inches deep. I gulped and gulped until I regurgitated. I had been gulping half mud and half water. Realizing the water was used as a watering place for water buffalo I looked for the deepest part and drank some clearer water.'

Having heard voices in the distance, Bob Johnson decided to move cautiously and found a hiding place before daylight. On the ninth morning, having lost the track, he decided to continue walking for a few hours after daylight in order to make up time. This resulted in an unfortunate meeting, as Johnson describes:

'After a short time I suddenly found I was close to the edge of what appeared to be a clearing. On moving cautiously forward I saw a native woman with a basket on her head walking along a path toward me. Thinking she had not seen me I dropped to my knees. She came slowly toward me, peering into the bush, with a wide grin on her face and it was obvious she was aware of something. I tried to pretend I was a dog by making barking noises but she was not fooled. She parted the bushes so I stood up and stepped forward. Her expression changed abruptly. I pointed to her basket and by signs indicated I wanted something to eat. She shook her head and at once hurried off in a northerly direction along a cart track. I crossed the track and open area then crouched in the bush. The woman did not look back but I could then see she was going directly to some huts. Almost at once a number of native men, brandishing bamboo staves and shouting, ran out from among the huts in my direction.

'I ran away from the track and was making a lot of noise in my haste. The shouting was getting louder so I scrambled into a very dense clump of bush, pulled twigs and leaves over myself, then remained still. The shouting came closer then started to fade and I realized the natives were following the track thinking I had gone in that direction. I moved off to the west, stopping frequently to listen, and after a few miles found a good hiding place.'

For the next three days Bob kept to his original policy of moving by night but ran out of water and did not find another buffalo water-hold until the third night. During these three days he was unable to get a pinpoint and was consequently unsure of his accurate position. He headed to the west and north on a zig-zag course hoping to find Yaw Chuang, his original objective. There were unpleasant aspects of nature in addition to the rigours of travelling; spiders and their webs caused great discomfort and, on one occasion, a cobra crawling over his legs while he slept made Johnson grateful for his flying boots and gaiters.

With water in his chargal, Bob was in good spirits, convinced that he was approaching the Yaw Chuang and that night he set off on a westerly course. Before long, he found the elusive stream. He stripped off and bathed, refilled his chargal then set off on the south side of the Yaw Chuang. Just before daybreak he heard the sound of buffalo and natives. He stopped immediately and a voice hailed him, but he scrambled into hiding among some bushes. When the natives had moved on he proceeded into the hills and found a hiding place for the day.

His high spirits prevailed, so convinced was he that he had arrived at the junction he had been heading for. The country was hilly but walking was not too difficult. The next day brought the realisation that he was, in fact, lost. He climbed a high peak to find a landmark and deduced that he was about four miles north of where he thought he should be. He decided to rest during the day and retrace his path to the Yaw Chuang at night.

By daybreak he was near the village of Kyankleit and once again found bush in which to hide for the day. This happened to be near a village shrine and the noise of visiting natives made sleep difficult. However, darkness brought quiet and Johnson set off again in a westerly direction. On his trek he came upon sleeping men, whom he took to be Japanese. Fortunately he did not waken them and continued on his way, this time in a northerly direction. He skirted one village then came to another, Pasok, where he hid in the hills and fell asleep. He awoke to the sound of chanting and covered himself with twigs and leaves while about 20 men chopped bamboo trees on the hillside below him.

With the coming of darkness he again followed a cart track northwards. During the night he heard bullock carts approaching and hid in the undergrowth, assuming the carts were carrying Japanese soldiers. He detoured, then went back across country to the Yaw Chuang, when he followed the stream until it was time to take cover for the day.

By this time he had lost a considerable amount of weight and frequent rests were necessary. Food, in the form of berries or other edible growths, was non-existent and the Horlicks tablets, while providing a certain amount of energy, were not hunger-satisfying. Nevertheless, he pressed on until he found himself in an area of sparse vegetation. Suddenly he heard the sound of a low-flying twin-engine aircraft. With his flashlight he flashed the first letter of his name repeatedly in morse code. The aircraft did not circle but flew off in an northerly direction. RAF or Japanese? He had no way of knowing, although he was certain he had seen the navigation lights flash in recognition.

By daylight he was hiding in an open area on the side of a hill. From out of the blue came a DC3, flying low along the valley. Johnson hurriedly got his metal mirror out and tried to attract attention by reflection of the sun. There was no response and the DC3 did not return. However, Johnson took the fact the aircraft was flying low with open doors to mean that it was searching for a drop area and that he would be well-advised to head for Gangaw – a greater distance that he had at first contemplated.

He takes up the story:

'All at once I was aware of voices in the bush on the east side of the track. I crept closer and concluded the language was not like any I had heard used by natives. Keeping close to the bush I crept along the track and saw the glow of some fires through the bush. Very shortly I came to a stream and was looking for a shallow place to cross when I heard a rattle of stones on the other side of the stream. I ran behind a clump of thorn bushes and crouched on one knee with my knife in my hand. I remained motionless for quite a time when suddenly there was a splash and clatter of stones. A figure, with rifle and bayonet extended, rounded the thorn bush. I dived at him and we both sprawled on the ground. I lunged with my knife hitting him on the back but there was no penetration. He started to roll over. My right hand, which had been my support as I lunged, happened to be on a fair sized rock. I swung the rock in an overhead motion and hit him in the face just as he rolled. There was no sound from him and he did not move.

'I got to my feet, splashed across the stream, and went as fast I could along the track. After about two hundred yards the track went across some open ground. I hurried on and was on the upgrade of a slight rise when a Japanese soldier appeared walking toward me. He was very close when I saw him and I instinctively felt that to run would be fatal. I slouched by him and as soon as I reached some bush I took cover. Almost immediately about 20 or more Japanese came along, all carrying packs and rifles. There was also a couple of bullock carts. I remained in the bush at the side of the track and very shortly a large number of Japanese passed by, perhaps a hundred or more. I moved away from the track into the hills and pondered as to what my next move should be. Just at daylight I crept back down to the track and saw another small group of Japanese pass by. I went back into the hills and found cover for the day.'

It seemed likely to Bob Johnson that the Japanese might be retreating and that friendly forces might be somewhere in the general area, so he gave thought to how he might make contact. He decided to avoid the cart track and head across country to the north towards the village of Lessaw. At dusk he started to move. Soon he saw camp fires ahead and took the decision not to risk trying to pass them. On returning to the track he heard voices so retreated to the hills – a bad decision at this time could be fatal. Throughout the night he heard the sound of fighting in the distance to the north – mortars and the rattle of automatic weapons. During the day, however, all was quiet.

When night came, things were still quiet so Johnson returned to the track again and proceeded until he came to a village. Removing his footwear, he walked straight through and continued to walk until daybreak by which time he reckoned he was near Lessaw. On moving off the track to seek cover, he heard the creak of leather and the jingle of chains. He had no idea whether these heralded friend or foe, so remained in hiding. During the day he saw DC3s drop supplies at the east end of the long valley in the vicinity of a couple of knolls. At dark he set off again and walked throughout the night, hearing sporadic gunfire as he did so. By daylight he was within sight of the two knolls and decided to climb one in search of a vantage point from which to spot the drop zone, if the DCs came back. As he stopped to drink from his chargal he heard movement and looked up to see three Indian soldiers coming over the crest of the hill. His spirits rose, as he details:

'It flashed through my mind that I was safe at last and started to raise my hands. The soldier nearest to me had an automatic weapon at about his hip level and just as I raised my hands he pulled the trigger. There was the swish of bullets around me before I dived behind the tree. I yelled in English, "Do not fire, I'm a British officer". There were another couple of bursts which thudded into the tree and threw up dirt from the ground. I yelled again, this time in Urdu. No answer and no sound. I pulled out my handkerchief, waved it around the tree and shouted again. Still no sound. I thought they might be circling around the knoll so I jumped up, scrambled down the hill and across the valley to the closest hill and bush. I ran along a ridge for a short distance then hid under some dead, fallen trees. All was quiet the remainder of the day .... I walked down into the valley and after a mile or so I heard voices through the bush ahead. I crawled forward and saw a group of natives in a dried up gully. There was about a dozen men and also women and children. There were cooking pots over fires. I watched them for a short time then decided to risk making contact. As I scrambled down into the gully the women and children ran off but the men remained. By sign language I indicated I wanted some food. Their expressions were neither friendly nor antagonistic but they were obviously apprehensive. I guessed they may have been obliged to leave their village because of the recent fighting. I sat down with legs crossed and the men crouched in a semicircle in front of me. I desperately wanted to show them I was friendly so got out my last small piece of chewing gun, broke it in two and handed a piece to an older native who seemed to be in authority. I chewed my piece and he did likewise. He broke into a grin and chattered to the other men. Suddenly they were all smiles, the women and children came back, and as a result of signs and gestures I was given a bowl of rice. I ate more than I should have under the circumstances. The old man handed me some sort of a cigar which I think was rolled up bamboo leaves. It was not pleasant but I had a puff or two just to please him. I had a card in my kit with several native dialects in phonetic phrases and I tried to converse with them. The only words which triggered a response were *Ungli* and *Japoni*. When I repeated *Ungli* over and over the old man pointed to the south-west. Again by sign language I indicated I wanted him to take me to the *Ungli*. He nodded but indicated that first we would sleep and when the sun came up we would go.'

Johnson was very aware of the unhappy experience of Ken MacVicar, Officer Commanding 'B' Flight who had crashed behind Japanese lines and made his way back just two weeks prior to Johnson's bale-out. He had crashed near a village and, on making contact, found the natives to be friendly. However, within half an hour, the Japanese had arrived and MacVicar had been extremely fortunate to avoid capture. Johnson, therefore, slowly rose and indicated that the party should leave then. The native did not seem to be too pleased but nevertheless nodded agreement.

The party set off, Johnson very much on the 'qui vive' as he recalls: 'I indicated he should walk ahead of me and I took a boy of slight stature with me. A couple of other men trailed behind. For what it was worth I made sure the old man saw my hand on my knife. We walked down the valley through sparse bush for several miles and suddenly came to a stream. About 100 feet ahead of me a group of Indian soldiers were washing themselves in the stream and a soldier with a rifle was standing guard on the bank. We walked up to him and I said, "Commanding Officer *kidhur hai*?" He looked at me and casually said "*Udhur hai Sahib*" and nodded to his left. He sloped arms and off we went, natives included. Within half a minute we walked into a shallow ravine where the officers of the 4th/14th Punjabi Regiment were having their evening meal.'

The commanding officer, Lieutenant Colonel Steele, was very interested to know where Johnson had encountered the Japanese and, having been shown the location on the map Johnson carried, said they would break camp the next day and head for that area. Johnson was taken by jeep, along with a wounded Chin hillman, to Tilin, a distance of about 20 miles. But the journey was not without incident.

Johnson again: 'The track was extremely rough and we had about 20 miles to cover. We had gone about 4 or 5 miles when I saw a lot of brown skinned men on the track ahead and they quickly disappeared in the bush. The jeep came to an abrupt halt and I scrambled behind a large rock. When I found courage to peek around the boulder I saw a British officer, nattily dressed in bush hat, shorts, socks complete with tabs and he was walking toward us. I stood up and he said, "It's OK, chaps, we are a Chin patrol". We chatted for 5 minutes or so. He was part of V force and had been operating alone in the Chin Mountains for more than a year organizing native resistance ....

'We pressed on and arrived at Tilin where the medical officer dropped me off at a landing strip. When I approached the pilot of the first DC3 to come in and explained my position he merely said he was very sorry but he had strict orders not to take any passengers. I was utterly astounded that he wouldn't take me as by this time I was a sad-looking sight with scruffy beard, thin as a bean pole, tattered battle dress but still with wings and rank stripes on my tunic. It was just as well as it turned out because at that time I had need to find a latrine which I did with some haste. I practically exploded and it occurred to me this was the first bowel movement I'd had since the third day after I had baled out. Feeling considerably better I went back to the strip to try the next aircraft. This time the pilot, an Australian, was very sympathetic and agreed to take me to his destination at Imphal main strip. After we were airborne I talked him into dropping me off at Kalemyo. He told me 28 Squadron was no longer there but 221 Group HQ was nearby. On landing I went up to the tower and called Group HQ by land line asking for Air Commodore Vincent. The AOC was a fine person and knew every pilot in his group. His aide-de-camp answered the phone and I heard him say to another person, "He says he is Flt/Lt Johnson of 28 Sqdn." I could hear the AOC say in a loud voice, "Johnson, Johnson, where in the hell *is* he?" He then came on the line and after a few words, said his staff car would be there in a few minutes to pick me up.'

On 6 February at Group HQ Johnson was greeted by Air Commodore Vincent and General Stratomyer, who was visiting at the time. He remained there until the arrival of Squadron Leader Huxtable, and intelligence officer. He then returned to 28 Squadron at Yeu in Central Burma.

A few month later he was awarded the MC, gazetted on 5 June 1945.

6.   Hide and Seek on Puket Island

In 1945 Rangoon fell, not to the British divisions pushing down from the north, but to 15th Corps from the sea. The war in Burma was now virtually over, and scouting for the coastal forces meant undertaking masses of urgent missions which the army had given them. Despite the tremendous risks their casualties were very few. Now South-East Asia Command planners were looking forward to the push down the Malay Peninsula to Singapore itself, but for this they would need airfields, advanced bases, harbours and landing beaches. In the early stages of this planning it was vital to get a closer look at Puket Island so a scouting group went in and with it were two RAF officers whose job it was to look for likely airstrip sites. The party was under the charge of Major Ian MacKenzie who had landed in a tank on the Normandy beaches on D-Day. The party also had a detachment from the Royal Marines. They were to be taken on the journey of 1,200 miles by two submarines from Ceylon and across the Indian Ocean to Puket Island. The two submarines were HMSs *Torbay* and *Thrasher*.

Torbay landed her party with Flight Lieutenant Guthrie detailed to look for suitable airfields but they were soon located by the Japanese accompanied by Thai police and only Guthrie survived, as a POW. *Thrasher* landed three canoes at Bangtau Bay, their mission to look for suitable airfield sites which were deep inland. Major MacKenzie was in charge of this party and had Flight Lieutenant Bertie Brown from the RAF with him. He was a former Hurricane pilot but had adapted to his new role of seeking sites for landing strips that RAF aircraft could use in the future. They landed safely and hid the canoes in the cover of nearby trees although the beach seemed deserted. By the time dawn came up they had reached the first proposed airfield and Bertie Brown climbed a tree to take a few photographs. While he was doing this MacKenzie decided to take a closer look, which was when things started to go wrong. A Japanese patrol came marching down the other side of the embankment that they themselves were on, and then along the road came a Thai police patrol. Although the patrol nearly stepped on the party's heads they were, for some reason, not seen. When they had nearly reached the bush near the proposed airstrip and were counting how many coconut trees would have to be knocked down by the bulldozers, they decided to have a look round the other side. They picked their way around but while they were filtering past a field a native saw them and yelled and pointed. They shot off into the jungle as fast as they could run.

On the beach side of the forest they spotted Japanese bunker positions facing the sea, which they managed to photograph, and on the edge of the airstrip dug up soil samples. Things then started to hot up when, with dogs barking, Japanese troops seemed to be all around them. It was obviously time to head back to the beach where the rest of the party were guarding the canoes. They hid in the bushes and tried to sleep, but Major Maxwell, the Marine officer, was suddenly awoken by a posted sentry who told him that a motor launch was coming up river, full of Thai police. At this point MacKenzie and Brown saw that the Japanese had made camp where the canoes had been hidden and realised that way out was blocked. Both sides opened fire as an immediate reaction but Major Maxwell then stood up and waved a Union Jack, basing this gesture on what he had been told – that the Siamese were friendly – then walked into the river.

The Thai officer ordered Maxwell to strip and indicated that he wanted the whole party to surrender but suddenly one of the Thais opened fire and all hope of negotiation with the Thais was over. Maxwell gave the order to open fire and dashed back across the beach, stark naked, amid a hail of bullets. Sergeant Smith's tommy gun jammed and 'Mac' MacKenzie had the end of his toe removed by a bullet. The party fled, making a wide, straggling detour of the beach until they reached the next bay. Here they slept behind the jungle-fringed beach until first light when they set off south to a spot overlooking their emergency rendezvous. Here they were again attacked, this time by troops from a launch. Smith was hit in the head but managed to struggle to his feet and keep going. Sporadic attacks continued throughout the day but at night the fighting died down and the party was able once again to head for their rendezvous rock. A sentry was posted to look out for the submarine but nothing arrived that night. The next day Brown swam out to the rock, where he remained all night and the next day. At one point a Japanese search party landed but he was able to avoid them.

The next day, 14 March, they had to face up to the fact that the only alternative open to them was to tramp ten miles across the jungle-infested island to reach the rendezvous spot for *Torbay*. This took ten days, during which time they had to dodge parties of Japanese who were scouring the island for them. Bertie Brown remembers that they were very hungry during this time, as food was extremely scarce. They drank rainwater trapped in plantains or chewed the centre sections of the plantains. All the time they were taking it in turns to carry Smith whose head wound was giving them grave cause for concern as there was nothing they could do for him.

Eventually they reached the rendezvous beach but there was no sign of *Torbay*. Dawn came and MacKenzie and Brown set out to look for a canoe they could steal, but without success. Two of the Marines, Brownlie and Atkinson, decided to search along the coast in the other direction with a view to procuring some of the rations which had been buried during the flight from the Japanese, a desperate hope, given the numbers of the enemy known to be in the area.

Brown and MacKenzie were left with by now dangerously ill Smith,and took it in turns to sample berries, all of which proved inedible. In the afternoon a Japanese patrol appeared but they remained undetected. Another time they were not so lucky, for as they returned from foraging for food, they spotted a lone Japanese running away from their hideout. MacKenzie, finding that Smith was conscious enough to understand what was being said, impressed upon him the fact that they had been discovered and that he must on no account fire if the Japanese returned. They did and Smith was taken prisoner. Again there was nothing the other two could do.

For four days they played hide-and-seek with Japanese patrols then on 25 March – emergency escape day – they arrived at the beach to await once more the appearance of *Torbay*. Suddenly, a lone figure was seen amongst the trees. This was Atkinson who told them that Brownlie was dead and that he thought that Major Maxwell had been captured. Their party had succeeded in getting back to the far side of the original rendezvous point, but had been unable to proceed any further, due to the heavy Japanese presence. They had turned back to join up again with MacKenzie's group and on the way Brownlie had been shot by a Japanese patrol and Maxwell had gone missing.

That night the three survivors watched again for *Torbay* and again were disappointed. They knew that by this time *Thrasher* would have left on another operation but hoped desperately that *Torbay* would still be waiting around. In fact *Thrasher* had returned to the pre-arranged rendezvous for five nights after landing the parties and then rendezvoused with *Torbay*, when Alec Hughes swam across to *Thrasher* for a conference. It was decided that nothing further could be done and *Thrasher* proceeded on another operation. As both *Thrasher* and MacKenzie's group swear that they were at the designated rendezvous point on 13th March it seems likely that signals went unseen and that the two parties were in hiding, a matter of a hundred yards or so from each other. Then before the final emergency rendezvous night, *Torbay* was told that no further attempts were to be made to pick up the shore party, due to the danger of further compromise. Thus the party were left in an area crawling with Japanese.

From his previous involvement with OSS Brown knew there was a unit on Orial Island and the three waded and swam their way to a small island about half a mile offshore from where they planned to steal a barge then make their way to the larger island. But the barge sailed at dusk so that scheme foundered, leaving the trio no option but to try to make for a Thai village. For once luck was with them and they reached a clearing dotted with huts, where they were immediately surrounded by Thai villagers. These were clearly terrified of the Japanese and refused to give the evaders any food so they eventually broke into a shop, where they found a Thai family in the upstairs room. Although they had no ammunition left, they still had their revolvers and the appearance of these was sufficient to persuade the family to give them some food.

The next day a note was delivered from the District Officer, stating he was friendly to the British and was willing to help them. It was decided to take a chance and MacKenzie followed a boy to a clearing in the jungle where he met the friendly officer who gradually convinced him that his best chance lay in surrendering to the Thai Navy. He accordingly scribbled a note to the other two and they were led to the clearing. A lorry arrived to take them to the Siamese seaplane base, where they were handed over.

Bertie Brown still has personal thoughts: 'At no time had I any intention of being taken by the Japanese. I knew they had promised to execute all survivors of this kind of mission – "war canoes" they called them. I kept one little hand grenade handy as a last resort. The Thais allowed the Japanese access to us and I was interrogated by the Kampui Tai. I avoided much of this by using my dysentery to good effect, and spoke in a broad Geordie accent most of the time! I felt sorry for the face my interpreter was losing in front of his superior officers. I talked a load of rubbish most of the time ... The Thais put me in hospital in Bangkok and fed me up between these sessions. They were very kind and not at all friendly with the Japs.'

Bertie Brown visited Bangkok in 1983 and found the jail he was locked up in. It is now a school. For his efforts Bertie Brown was awarded the MBE, which was gazetted on 9 April. 1946.

Epilogue

We have not Forgotten

The Formation of the Royal Air Forces Escaping Society

On 29 December 1944 an RAF exhibition was opened in Paris, where Donald Darling had set up an MI9 Awards Bureau after the liberation of the city. At the opening, the Chief of Air Staff Air Chief Marshal Sir Charles Portal's message said: 'Our airmen are proud once again to be on French soil and to continue there in co-operation with French air crews to fight against the common enemy. The Royal Air Force will ever be mindful of the debt it owes to the people of France, men and women, for their courageous help given to air crews forced down in French territory. The record of this help over the last four years will provide a tale of which you can always be proud and for which the British people will always be grateful.'

After the war in Europe was over, the idea of cementing the bond in tangible form took hold on both sides of the Channel, and thus was the Royal Air Forces Escaping Society born. On 11th June, when the war had been over for a month, the Foreign Office approached Sir Charles Portal suggesting the presentation of a Lysander to the French Resistance might be a much appreciated gesture. Six weeks later this request was granted and the gift made. Meanwhile an association had been formed in Paris called L'Oiseau Blessé (wounded bird) to bring together all persons who helped save British and Americans who were stranded on French soil during the German occupation. The aim of the association was to preserve the

380

bonds of friendship created and to help when necessary the families of those who died under the most tragic conditions as a result of their aid to escapers and evaders. ACM Sir Charles Portal was asked whether he would accept the chairmanship of this association and if he would send a representative from the RAF to Paris to discuss the matter.

The letter was from the President of the new association, Georges Broussine, MC, code-named Burgundy and leader of the Brandy escape organisation. When he joined, the head of the organisation had been Maurice Montet, pseudonym Simon Martel, a French fighter pilot. He was arrested, but escaped to Britain via the Pat O'Leary line and was trained by MI9 for operations in France. The Halifax from which he was to be parachuted was shot down by flak, but he survived. (The pilot, Pilot Officer Kingston Smith also evaded capture, reached the UK safely.) Broussine managed to help 255 men to safety, many over the Pyrenees via Andorra. After the Normandy invasion he was arrested, but once again escaped and survived the war.

Portal, decided not to accept the offer of the chairmanship of L'Oiseau Blessé since he was actively considering setting up an association along similar lines in Britain; the membership should consist of RAF escapers and evaders and their helpers, 'the main purpose being to have some sort of annual reunion if possible and to assist any of the French members who through the loss of a breadwinner or for any other reason connected with an activity on our behalf are in need of financial assistance.' Since he would assume the chairmanship of this new association, he explained to L'Oiseau Blessé, he unfortunately could not accept their offer for a similar position in their organisation.

Lord Tedder, too, was concerned that due recognition should be given and wrote in July to the Secretary for Air, Harold Macmillan, suggesting that some sort of recognition in the form of a letter and memento should be given to the people of France, Belgium, Holland and Denmark who had helped bomber crews who had baled out during the bombing of Germany. Arrangements were made for letters of thanks to all foreign helpers to be signed by Lord Tedder for western Europe, Field Marshal Alexander in the Mediterranean and Lord Mountbatten for the Far East. The Awards Bureau at the War Office were to attend to compensation and awards.

Meanwhile Air Commodore Sir Ronald Ivelaw-Chapman*, who had been chosen by Portal as the RAF representative to be sent to Paris, had been meeting Donald Darling in Paris and gaining the experience of his five years' experience in the evasion field. As a result, Commandant Martel was asked to be the chairman of the French section of the new proposed RAF organisation. From the French point of view he was ideally suitable.

Now the task began to compiling lists of all the RAF members who had escaped through France – a formidable job as 125,000 records had to be checked. Ten WAAF Intelligence Officers were attached to MI9 for three weeks for this purpose.

What to call the new organisation? For the time being it was referred to as The Dodgers' Club, and a draft letter was drawn up to all prospective members on 30 August. 'When you escaped or evaded capture, you probably received assistance from a French man or woman who showed in this way their courage, their belief in our victory and their high regard for the Royal Air Force. Most of you will remember the names of those person who gave you this help and you will probably like to be able to renew the friendships made then under the stress of circumstances I know that for their part many of them would welcome the opportunity to keep in touch with you.' The letter went on to say that Lord Portal was to be the President, Air Vice Marshal Sir Basil Embry the chairman and the chairman of the French section Commandant Martel.

Sadly the day after this letter was drafted, Martel was killed in an aircrash.

On 18th September a meeting was held in Paris formally to

---

* He had come to fame during the Kabul airlift and had caused a furore when he was shot down in Brittany, with complete knowledge of the D Day invasion plans in his head. He had been rescued by Burgundy and kept in a safe house. Not safe enough! He was captured by the Germans – fortunately not till after D Day.

set up the new association, at which among others Air Vice Marshal Embry, Donald Darling, and Georges Broussine, were present.

The following points were agreed upon. The organisation would hence forth be known as The Royal Air Forces Escaping Society, and for the present it would be under the guidance and direction of the Air Ministry until established on a firm basis; ultimately it was hoped that the RAFES would become international, though non-political. Although starting with France, it would include all other countries where escapers and evaders were helped. It was agreed that a comprehensive card index of all officers and airmen serving with the RAF or Dominion Air Forces who escaped or evaded from countries under German occupation, together with the names of those who helped them,would have to be kept. To enable the secretary of the Society to compile this it was agreed that five clerks, plus five typewritters would be necessary. They would work in close co-operation with the Awards Bureaus who had all the information.

The rules of the Society were also set up in September 1945 at the British Embassy in Paris. They ran as follows:

Rule 1: The name of the Society shall be the RAF Escaping Society.

Rule 2: The Society shall be non-sectarian and non-political.

Rule 3: The objects of the Society are:

To give financial assistance to surviving helpers and dependants of those who lost their lives through assisting members of the Royal Air Force, Dominions Air Forces, and those Allied Air Forces who served within the framework of the RAF, to evade and escape.

To make donations to worthy charitable institutions situated in the countries concerned, as an expression of thanks from evaders and escapers generally for the assistance given to them.

To encourage reciprocal visits and re-unions between members of the Society and their helpers, both in the United Kingdom and on the continent, and to contribute towards the travelling accommodation and other expenses of those helpers who in the sole opinion of the Executive Committee should have such aid for the purpose of visiting members in the United Kingdom.

To assist helpers in any matters affecting their good relations with the British Commonwealth, to facilitate service by members one to another and to their respective helpers, and generally to foster the friendship formed between evaders and escapers and the people living in the former enemy-occupied countries who helped them in all theatres of war.

Rule 4: Membership of the RAF Escaping Society shall be open to members, past and present, of the Royal Air Force and Dominions Air Forces, and all those Allied Air Forces who served within the frame work of the RAF, who successfully escaped from captivity or evaded capture between 3 September 1939, and 9 May 1945, in the European and Middle East theatres of war, and between 8 December 1941 and 14 August 1945, in the Far East Theatre of war, as the result of a forced descent whilst on an operational mission, and who reached Allied or Neutral territory. 'Allied' does not include 'Enemy-Occupied'. Proof of ability to comply with these conditions must be produced by applicants when requested by the Executive Committee.

Rule 8: All those helpers who assisted members and whose claims to have helped have been substantiated by the respective Awards Bureaux set up for the purpose, or by prima facie evidence submitted by the member concerned, shall be deemed Honorary members of the Society, and no subscription shall be levied.

The Outcome

On 27 May 1946 a committee was suggested for the RAF Escaping Society consisting of; one serving RAF Officer, one RCAF officer, and two ex RAF Aircrew. The committee was formed 19 June 1946. The chairman was Sir Basil Embry, and members Air Commodore Whitney-Straight, Flight Lieutenant Don Southwell, the secretary F/Lt Dales, Air Commodore Burns as Treasurer and two aircrew escapers.

On 24 July 1946 at the Palais des Sports, Brussels, some 14,000 citizens in Brussels were presented with the Tedder and

Eisenhower Certificates for helping British and United States escapers and evaders.

The first certificates were presented to Mlle Andrée de Jongh and Baron Jean François Nothomb, leaders of the *Ligne Comète* escape route.

On 17 September 1946 the French Awards Bureau of MI9 held a ceremony at one of the largest cinemas in Paris, the Gaumont Palace, at which 2,000 Parisians were present who, during the German occupation, assisted members of the Allied forces to escape from French territory. This ceremony marked the virtual conclusion of the work of the Bureau, which in the last two years of its existence had investigated between 25,000 and 30,000 claims.

The first meeting of the RAFES was held on 3 May 1947, at the Bush House Restaurant, Strand, London. At the meeting a report showed that 732 members had joined the Society in 1946, consisting of 606 in the UK and still serving overseas, 87 from Canada and 39 from Australia. On 28 May it was announced that the design for the Society emblem or badge had been chosen out of 50 designs submitted: the designer was Keith Nolan. It took the form of a torch rising out of the sea to the sky symbolic of always accepting the challenge and finishing the race and even passing the torch to the next.

On 3 January 1948 Sir Basil Embry wrote to Sir John Slessor, to ask if a sum of £20,000 could be nominated to the RAFES. This money was allotted and it was the foundation of the Society as it is today.

In 1948, also, a new medal was approved, the King's Medal for Service in the Cause of Freedom. It was awarded to many 'Helpers' who had assisted airmen to evade or escape capture.

In 1949 in Brussels a Mass was held in honour of eight Belgian members of the Comète Underground Organisation who had been arrested and shot by the Gestapo for helping Allied airmen. In the same year it was decided to widen the scope of the Society from Western Europe to the Middle and Far East.

In 1954 75 children were entertained by the Society; 31 came from France, 23 from Belgium and 21 from Holland. They were taken around London and treated as VIPs; all were children of 'Helpers'. A stained glass window was dedicated in Brussels to the 216 men and women of the Comète line who died in helping more than 800 men escape from Belgium during WWII. Over 5,000 Christmas cards were sent in 1953 in seven languages to 'Helpers'! Today, in 1988 some 3,000 are still being sent.

In 1954 a four-year-old child Francine Schmit lay dying in France, of a rare disease. Her Grandfather wrote to the only man he knew in England, Albert De Bruin, whom he had helped escape in WWII. The letter was promptly acted upon. 'The men who never forget' contacted the Great Ormond Street Hospital for sick children. They in turn said 'Yes', there was a known treatment. A professor in Paris knew the technique. One of the 'Men who never forget' was Wing Commander Yeo-Thomas GC a wartime agent and Resistance leader who lived in Paris. The professor was quickly found and within three days Francine was in hospital. Today she is alive thanks to the Society.

In 1957 the Australian branch of the RAFES was formed, with its president Sir Thomas White DFC, a veteran of WWI. It now has 135 members.

In 1958 to perpetuate the memory of the outstanding risks and sacrifices made on behalf of the RAF, and Allied aircrew, also to foster the spirit engendered by these events, a trophy was presented to the RAF by the RAFES. It is donated annually for the best individual feat of combat survival or comparable feat of challenge and achievement carried out by a member of the RAF during operations or recognised training. It is open to all members of the RAF/WRAF. The member of the RAF who was awarded it in 1983 was Squadron Leader Bob Iveson, who was shot down in the Falklands War and evaded capture for some sixty hours, and did it in the fine traditions of the WWII Evaders. His father was a group captain in WWII and a bomber pilot, with the DSO and DFC.

In 1964 the US Air Forces Escape and Evasion Society was formed with 34 men who had escaped from occupied France in 1944 via Operation Bonaparte. Their rules are very similar to the RAFES.

In 1965 the Canadian branch of the RAFES was formed with its first president, the Hon Angus MacLean. It started with 33 members.

In 1968 a pub at Mabledon Place London WCI was opened as 'The Escapers'; it had previously been the 'The Kentish Arms'. The pub was 'unveiled' by AVM Harry Burton CBE DSO and Oliver Philpot MC DFC of 'Wooden Horse' fame. The pub had much memorabilia connected with escaping. The pub has now been renamed but all the memorabilia can be seen at the Torbay Air Museum, Devon.

In the late 1970's the BBC put on an excellent series *The Secret Army* which dealt with Resistance and escape stories. One of the actors who played a leading part was Bernard Hepton. On one of the Sunday appeal programmes, Bernard spoke on behalf of the RAFES,which raised some £12,000. Never before or since has such an appeal for the Society raised so much money.

The chairman each year puts on an appeal to all RAF stations which never fails to raise less than £3,000. Other ways funds are raised are by donations and fund-raising made anonymously. Group Captain Bill Randle raised £78,321,80 through air shows and other enterprises, such as a first day cover series.

In 1982 came the RAFES Marathon. A relay of twelve runners ran over one of the famous escape lines starting in Brussels on 14 May 1982,and ran via Lille, Beauvais, Paris, Vendôme, Ruffec, Castillon la Bataille, Mont de Marsan, and Biarritz to arrive in St Jean de Luz on Saturday, 22 May. The runners were made up of British, US, Belgian, Canadian and French airmen or ex airmen. For the RAFES there were two, Brin Weare, and Ian Croad. The run was to celebrate the 40th anniversary of the Comète Line.

An RAF Escaping Society plaque has now been unveiled in Ottawa, Canada, and Canberra, Australia, as well as in the Bomber Command Museum in London. A memorial plaque has been dedicated in Gibraltar Cathedral by the RAFES, and was unveiled in May 1988.

The RAFES is unique amongst charities with its aim of maintaining contact with thousands of patriots throughout the world who helped members of the RAF and Allied Air Forces to evade capture and so return to their units. Two taken at random are: Madame Jeanne Wolf, who arranged that the man with whom she worked was to give three rings on the bell. He came one day and gave one long ring on the bell. She thought it was the Gestapo and as a result of the shock, became partially blind, but still she was able to shelter one evader in 1943, and six in 1944. She was awarded the King's Medal for Courage at the end of the war.

And Mrs Hollingdale who was awarded the BEM at the end of the war, after assisting some 210 British personnel to escape until she was arrested in 1943. Her husband was tortured by the Gestapo and died on 12 March 1944. He was English and had served in WWI; he was working with the War Graves Commission in France. She ended up in no less than fourteen concentration camps, including Belsen, and Buchenwald. During this time she was tortured, but did not disclose her contacts. She died in 1984, aged 88, and in her will she left the BEM and her other medals to the RAFES. When a 'Helper' dies a brass plaque engraved 'IN MEMORIAM. The RAF Escaping Society', is sent to the relatives for the grave.

Perhaps the final word should rest with Ernest Bevin who told ACM Sir Basil Embry, 'Your Society does a damned sight more good in Europe than all my Ambassadors rolled together.'

Alan W. Cooper
London
June, 1988

Sources and Acknowledgments

Books
Airborne Invasion, John Hetherington
Beyond The Wire, Roy Marlow
Desert Squadron, George Netherwood
Down in the Drink, Ralph Barker
Escape from Singapore, Richard Gough
Escape to Live, Edward Howell
Evader, Dennis Teare
Evasions, Ed Cosgrove
Little Cyclone, Airey Neave
MI9 Escape and Evasion, 1939-45, M.R.D. Foot and J.M. Langley
Safe Houses Are Dangerous, Helen Long
Saturday At MI9, Airey Neave
Secret Sunday, Donald Darling
7XXX90, Charlie Potten
Single to Rome, E. Garrad-Cole
They Flew Through Sand, George Houghton
They Have Their Exits, Airey Neave
Wait for the Dawn, D. Nabarro
Winged Hours, Frank Griffiths
Wingless Victory, Anthony Richardson

PRO References
Air 14, Air 24, Air 27, Air 20, WO 208, Air 40, Air 2, FO 371.

My acknowledgement and thanks to the following:
Public Records Office, Kew, Air Historical Branch, MOD, Flypast, Airmail, Ministry of Defence Gloucester (Mrs O'Rourke), Foreign Office, Air Gunners Association, Bomber Command Association, RAF Museum Hendon, Ralph Barker, C.H. Thomas, F/Lt A.J. Shaw, 450 Sqdn, Group Captain Ken

Batchelor CBE DFC, Group Captain W. Randle, CBE,AFC,DFM, Major D. Henderson GM, R.A. Scott, R.C.B. Garrity, Mrs M. Sheridan. Mrs E. Baveystock, Roy Vigars, Philip Laughton-Bramley, A.E. Spencer, Ralph Patton, John Millar, Ed Patrick, Carst Peterson, Ole Ronnest, Karlheinz Franz, Countess Andrée De Jongh GM, Anne Brusselmans GM, Madame Elvire De Greef GM, Janine De Greef, Andrée Antoine-Dumont, Squadron Leader Eddie Hearn DFC*, J.J. Piot, Sandra Poumpoura MBE, Sylvi Tyern, Dr. G. Ferrari, Walter Zambelli, Paul Veerman, Daniel Basteyns, Mrs W. Allitson and the late W. Alliston, DFC, T. Armstrong DFC, L. Barnes MBE, L. Baveystock DSO,DFC,DFM, R.F. Bell, Air Vice Marshal D.C.T. Bennett CB,CBE,DSO, T. Blatch MBE, J. Brough, B. Brown MBE, L.H. Brown, Air Marshal Sir Harry Burton, KCB,CBE,DSO, A. De Bruin, Art De Breyn, R. Cant, G. Carter DFC*, W/Cdr E. Garrad-Cole MC, Air Marshal Sir Denis Crowley-Milling KCB,CBE,DSO,DFC, T.H. Cullen MBE, A. Day DFC, Captain F.H. Dell, H.F. Firestone, E.G. Fisher, F.E. Fuller, H.S. Furniss-Roe, W. Goodbrand, Gp Captain F.C. Griffiths DFC AFC, R. Gradwell, G. Hand, E. Harrop, Wing Commander F.W. Higginson OBE,DFC,AFC,DFM, Air Chief Marshal Sir Lewis Hodges KCB,CBE,DSO,DFC, Group Captain D. Honor DFC*, Wing Commander R. Howell OBE,DFC, Wing Commander R.M. Horsley, DFC,AFC, R.S. Horwood DFC, Squadron Leader T.H. Hutton,R.G. Johnson MC, R.W. Lewis DFC, S.M. Leslie, R.W. Lonsdale DFC,MM, Hon Angus MacLean PC,DFC, J.W. MacFarlane MM, Major M. MacKintosh, W/Cdr G. McMahon, W.J. Magrath MM, H.R. Merlin, R.A.E. Milton MC, H.E. De Mone DFM, B. Morgan, S/Ldr A.J. Mott MBE, A.F. MacSweyn MC, D. Nabarro DCM, J.L. Newton MM, A.K. Newman, R. Parkinson, D.L. Phillips MM, Ian Ralphe, T.W. Reynolds, W.T. Simpson MM, H. Simister MM, R.J.F. Sherk, D.V. Smith DFM, K. De Souza, E.T. Strever DFC, Denis Teare, Air Vice Marshal W.E. Townsend CB,CBE, P. Wasik, W.T.B. Weare, C.F. Weir, Squadron Leader R.C. Wilkinson OBE,DFM, H.W.D. Wilson, Rev G. Wood, W. Wynn, T.D. Young.

Index